GIOACHINO ROSSINI

ROUTLEDGE MUSIC BIBLIOGRAPHIES
Series Ed: Brad Eden

COMPOSERS

Isaac Albéniz (1998)
Walter A. Clark

C.P.E. Bach (2002)
Doris Powers

Samuel Barber (2001)
Wayne C. Wentzel

Béla Bartók (1997)
Second Edition
Elliott Antokoletz

Vincenzo Bellini (2002)
Stephen A. Willier

Alban Berg (1996)
Bryan R. Simms

Leonard Bernstein (2001)
Paul F. Laird

Benjamin Britten (1996)
Peter J. Hodgson

Elliott Carter (2000)
John L. Link

Carlos Chávez (1998)
Robert Parker

Frédéric Chopin (1999)
William Smialek

Aaron Copland (2001)
Marta Robertson and Robin Armstrong

Gaetano Donizetti (2000)
James P. Cassaro

Edward Elgar (1993)
Christopher Kent

Gabriel Fauré (1999)
Edward R. Phillips

Charles Ives (2002)
Gayle Sherwood

Scott Joplin (1998)
Nancy R. Ping-Robbins

Zoltán Kodály (1998)
Mícheál Houlahan and Philip Tacka

Guillaume de Machaut (1995)
Lawrence Earp

Felix Mendelssohn Bartholdy (2001)
John Michael Cooper

Giovanni Pierluigi da Palestrina (2001)
Clara Marvin

Giacomo Puccini (1999)
Linda B. Fairtile

Gioachino Rossini (2002)
Denise P. Gallo

Alessandro and Domenico Scarlatti (1993)
Carole F. Vidali

Jean Sibelius (1998)
Glenda D. Goss

Giuseppe Verdi (1998)
Gregory Harwood

Tomás Luis de Victoria (1998)
Eugene Casjen Cramer

Richard Wagner (2002)
Michael Saffle

GENRES

Central European Folk Music (1996)
Philip V. Bohlman

Chamber Music
Second, Revised Edition (2002)
John H. Baron

Choral Music (2001)
Avery T. Sharp and James Michael Floyd

Jazz Research and Performance Materials
Second Edition (1995)
Eddie S. Meadows

Music in Canada (1997)
Carl Morey

North American Indian Music (1997)
Richard Keeling

Opera, *Second Edition* (2001)
Guy Marco

Serial Music and Serialism (2001)
John D. Vander Weg

GIOACHINO ROSSINI
A GUIDE TO RESEARCH

DENISE P. GALLO

ROUTLEDGE MUSIC BIBLIOGRAPHIES
ROUTLEDGE
NEW YORK AND LONDON

Published in 2002 by
Routledge
29 West 35th Street
New York, NY 10001
www.routledge-ny.com

Published in Great Britain by
Routledge
11 New Fetter Lane
London EC4P 4EE
www.routledge.co.uk

Copyright © 2002 by Denise P. Gallo

Routledge is an imprint of the Taylor & Francis Group.
Printed in the United States of America on acid-free paper.

10 9 8 7 6 5 4 3 2 1

Cataloging-in-Publication Data is available from the Library of Congress.
ISBN 0-8153-3474-5

This book is respectfully dedicated
to Ruth Steiner
For Research Methodology,
Fall Semester 1992

Contents

Preface

A BRIEF OVERVIEW OF ROSSINI STUDIES

In the early decades of a new century, Gioachino Rossini arrived like a "colpo di cannone" (to borrow Don Basilio's phrase) into a world that judged its music against standards set by the *Settecento* titans Cimarosa and Paisiello. His compositions quickly attracted both detractors and supporters, and the fruits of their energetic aesthetic debates form the first corpus of Rossini literature. Henri Montan Berton, for example, condemned music like Rossini's as unnatural and "mechanical"; without even stooping to use Rossini's name, Andrea Majer attacked his music as the product of the unnecessary "liveliness of his imagination." A growing band of champions responded, among them Giuseppe Carpani in his *Le Rossiniane* and the newly converted Stendhal, whose *Vie de Rossini* helped to spread the composer's reputation. It is ironic, then, that, just a decade later, Rossini, the upstart, had become synonymous with tradition. Pitted against Vincenzo Bellini in a spate of comparisons referred to as "parallelomania," Rossini's complexity and "noisiness" suddenly epitomized grace and elegance while the younger composer was perceived as "sentimental." Exiled patriot Giuseppe Mazzini lauded Rossini for "reconsecrating the Italian school," an opinion shared by many of the composer's contemporaries. As Giovanni Pacini would later note in his autobiography, he and his colleagues had striven to imitate Rossini's style simply to survive in the *primo Ottocento* theatrical areana.[1]

---

[1]See item 129.

Rossini retired from the Italian stage in 1823 with *Semiramide* and, just six years later, from the French stage with *Guillaume Tell*. Although recent research demonstrates that it was never his intention to withdraw completely, the physical and psychological turmoil accompanying his next twenty-six years precipitated his doing so. Although he had been traveling between Paris and Bologna, by the late 1840s, his health forced him to remain in Italy where he was subjected to a series of futile "cures" for his debilitating maladies. Moreover, his emotional distress increased with the perception that he had been rejected by his homeland and was in personal danger during its political unrest. The composer's "silence" during these difficult years was misinterpreted by contemporary critics as laziness. Rossini characterized himself quite differently—he suffered from cowardice, as he wrote to Ferdinando Giorgetti, for he lacked the courage to take his own life.[2]

In 1855, Rossini's second wife, Olympe Pélissier, insisted that they return to Paris, where the composer eventually rallied and recovered. His final thirteen years, popularized by his famous Saturday *soirées*, brought him to the status of living legend. By the time of his death in 1868, Rossini's biographical legacy was set. Stendhal's *Vie*, more fictional than factual, had inspired a host of imitations and adaptations, thus creating and perpetuating the earliest Rossinian mythology. Critics of the composer's "silence"—and those who carried tales of his sharp wit and excellent table—molded the image that dominated the next hundred years: Rossini, the comic master who pillaged his own scores to turn out others, had eventually abandoned his career to live life out with a fork rather than a pen. Coupled with the critical dismissal of most of his works, this misunderstanding resulted in biographies and commentaries that considered his career through *Tell* and concluded with a sole chapter dedicated to his remaining thirty-nine years. While the Stabat Mater and the Petite Messe solennelle merited discussion (probably because they were performed publicly and reviewed), the pieces of the *Péchés de vieillesse* barely received a mention.

After his meeting with the composer in 1860, Richard Wagner called for a "competent historian" to undertake a study of Rossini's music.[3] The first such research, compiled by Giuseppe Radiciotti, was published in his *Vita documentata* (1927–1929)[4], a three-volume work based on archival study that provided a foundation for serious scholarship. Yet, as Bruno Cagli has noted, what could have been a point of departure became the standard reference work upon which later Rossini studies were based.[5] Thus, because of its seeming completeness,

---

[2]See item 64.
[3]See item 136.
[4]See item 164.
[5]Cagli discusses Rossini research in "Momento di Rossini," item 609.

Radiciotti in many ways stalled Rossini research. Cagli suggests that the "Rossini Renaissance" of the 1950s was responsible not only for reintroducing the composer's works to the stage repertory but also for piquing renewed interest in study. In 1955, for example, the Conservatorio G. Rossini in Pesaro offered a voice in the *Bollettino del Centro Rossiniano di Studi* to those associated with the institution as well as to guest writers.[6] Over the next twenty years, interest in Rossini developed into serious scholarship, primed by works such as Luigi Rognoni's *Gioacchino Rossini*, which not only reprinted significant commentaries by the composer's friends and contemporaries, including Geltrude Righetti-Giorgi's *Cenni di una Donna cantante*, Antonio Zanolino's "Una passeggiata in compagnia di Rossini," and Edmond Michotte's account of the visit between Wagner and Rossini,[7] but also introduced the catalogue of Rossini compositions compiled by Philip Gossett upon which subsequent works lists have been based.[8] In the early 1970s, Cagli, Gossett, and Alberto Zedda led a major initiative: the publication of the Fondazione Rossini's *Opera Omnia di Gioachino Rossini*, with Zedda's critical edition of *La gazza ladra* beginning the series in 1979.[9] The Rossini bicentennial in 1992 saw the publication of new biographies, musical studies, and analyses, which gave recognition to the *seria* works as well as to the discovery that the so-called "years of silence" were instead filled with music. In addition, several conferences demonstrated vigorous scholarly activity. Under the direction of Cagli and Sergio Ragni, the Fondazione Rossini published the first of the multivolume series *Gioachino Rossini: Lettere e documenti*, a significant source of documents that provides the evidence needed to destroy the misconceptions that have distorted Rossini's image for more than 150 years.[10] Finally, new editions of the works that had lain dormant in archives and libraries have provided performance materials for revivals, and recordings of these works ensure that they will never again be forgotten.

In a brief overview of Rossini studies, it is impossible to name all of the scholars—past and present—and their contributions. A glance, however, at the author's index of this volume demonstrates the activity of scholars such Cagli, Gossett, and Zedda, as well as (in alphabetical order) Scott Balthazar, Marco Beghelli, Annalisa Bini, Alfredo Bonnaccorsi, Patricia Brauner, Mauro Bucarelli,

[6]For a history of the *Bollettino*, see Sergio Monaldini's index, item 22.

[7]See Rognoni, item 476; Righetti-Giorgi, item 131; Zanolino, item 138; and Michotte, item 160.

[8]Gossett's role in Rossini research—and indeed in the study of nineteenth-century opera—cannot be overestimated. As Cagli notes, Gossett's "patient and tenacious work" has identified the sources of Rossini works, thus providing the basis for "every aspect of future critical work on Rossini." See item 609, page 6.

[9]See the appendix on editions and facsimiles for a list of volumes in the Critical Edition; items 857, 858, and 859 explain the edition's criticia and methodology.

[10]See item 29.

Alberto Cametti, Giovanni Carli Ballola, Stefano Castelvecchi, Rodolfo Celletti, Marcello Conati, Paolo Fabbri, Sabine Henze-Döhring, Paolo Isotta, Guido Johannes Joerg, Leopold Kantner, Bernd-Rüdiger Kern, Friedrich Lippmann, Massimo Mila, Reto Müller, Pierluigi Petrobelli, Sergio Ragni, Franco Schlizter, Marco Spada, and Marvin Tartak. In the first decade of another new century, Rossini scholarship is thriving. It is hoped that this *Guide to Research* will assist and encourage others to join in the crescendo.

A Word about the Fondazione Rossini

In his last will and testament, Rossini left a portion of his estate to Pesaro, the city of his birth. This inheritance was used to begin a *liceo musicale*; when the school became the Conservatorio "G. Rossini" in 1940, the state conferred its management to the Fondazione Rossini. Serving as far more than just a legal entity, the Fondazione has become the source and inspiration for the advancement of Rossini scholarship. Its earliest score publications were the *Quaderni Rossiniani*. Among its current initatives are critical editions of the composer's works, the libretti and their sources, and his correspondence and documents. Continued scholarship is encouraged and presented annually in the *Bollettino del Centro Rossiniano di Studi*. The Fondazione also inspires conference activity and oversees the museum housed in Rossini's birth house in Pesaro. The American arm of the Fondazione's activity is The Center for Italian Opera Studies (CIAO) at the University of Chicago.[11]

PURPOSE AND SCOPE OF THIS VOLUME

This volume has been designed as a tool for those beginning to study the life and works of Gioachino Rossini as well as for those who wish to explore beyond the established biographies and commentaries. To that end, items run the gamut from general music history reference works to specific studies, including Rossini staples, such as Stendhal, Radiciotti, and Weinstock, and the most recent investigations that seek to reevaluate the composer and his contributions. Whenever they have been deemed accessible, contemporary nineteenth-century sources have been cited along with their modern editions and commentaries. General subject areas include: Rossini's biography and iconography, historical and analytical studies of his operatic and nonoperatic compositions, his personal and professional associations, the artistic milieu and venues in which he worked, and the reassessment of his role in the development of nineteenth-century music.

---

[11]Current information on the activities of the Fondazione Rossini and CIAO are available on their websites. See items 875 and 873, respectively.

This volume's contents range from sources published in the early decades of the nineteenth century to works currently in progress. The first step in collecting materials for inclusion was an examination of major Rossini bibliographies, beginning with the one compiled by Philip Gossett for *The Revised New Grove Dictionary of Music and Musicians* (2000). Also, whenever possible, works cited in other annotated items were located. Searches for relevant books and articles were conducted regularly over a three-year period on databases including the Online Computer Library Center (OCLC) WorldCat, RILM Abstracts of Music Literature, Dissertation Abstracts, and Doctoral Dissertations in Musicology. Online and in-house library catalogues provided sources for the volume. These institutions included the Library of Congress, the New York Public Library, the British Library, the Bibliothèque National, and music libraries at The Catholic University of America, The University of Maryland-College Park, The University of Chicago, Peabody Conservatory of The Johns Hopkins University, Loyola University-New Orleans, Tulane University, and UCLA. Most of the sources were examined and annotated by the author. In some cases, when books or journals could not be accessed, their published abstracts were utilized, as is noted in their entries. Unexamined sources are also included and are marked as such.

Works selected for this volume include:

- Books and articles in English, Italian, German, French, and Spanish. Rossini research exists in other languages; readers may access these sources easily by using the databases and library catalogues listed above.
- Ph.D. and some D.M.A. dissertations. Master's theses were not included.
- Books, relevant chapters, and articles from journals, Festschriften, and conference reports. In general, program booklets, liner notes, and performance reviews (even those published during Rossini's lifetime) have not been annotated. Also excluded were textbooks, musical scores, and recordings.
- Major websites that reflect scholarly activity as well as performance and research activities of major Rossini music festivals.

Readers will note that, in some cases, annotated items only contain a mention of Rossini. These works were included because their general subject areas hold promise for future investigations. For example, some of the locative studies suggest new research in reception history; studies of certain twentieth-century composers could lead to further recognition of Rossini's late compositions and of his influence beyond the nineteenth century. As is commonly the case, more recent studies often present radically different views on Rossini's works and career; therefore, readers are encouraged to examine the items indicated with cross-references. These and other cross-referenced items are denoted by an asterisk (*) followed by the title of the work and the main item number. Items under each chapter subheading have been alphabetized by author's last name.

The 878 items in this volume represent the rich past and healthy present of Rossini studies; it is my hope that they will encourage an equally vigorous future.

Gioa*chino* or Gioa*cchino*? A Note on Rossini's Name

Although Rossini's first name appears with one "c" or two, the spelling considered more accurate is the former.[12] In annotations, I have chosen this spelling; the bibliographical citations maintain the spelling as it appears in the published titles.

All attempts have been made to standardize capitalization of titles. In citations, however, titles have not been altered.

ACKNOWLEDGMENTS

Compiling an extensive annotated bibliography requires persistence, patience, and a lot of help. Thus, I offer my thanks to the following people who offered their support, encouragement, and counsel over the past three years:

To Michael Collins and James Parsons, who suggested this project to me over tea at the annual meeting of the American Musicological Society in Boston in 1998. In particular, I am grateful to James Parsons who remains a generous colleague, ever ready to read drafts and offer perceptive comments. He is a valued friend.

To Gregory Harwood (*The Verdi Guide to Research*), Philip Tacka (*The Kodaly Guide to Research*) and Linda Fairtile (*The Puccini Guide to Research*) for sharing their experiences and insights.

To all of the librarians who assisted me, including Laura Dankner and the staff at the Music Library at Loyola University-New Orleans, where this project was begun; Henry Grossi (now of The Library of Congress), Maurice Saylor, and the staff at the Music Library of The Benjamin T. Rome School of Music at The Catholic University of America, my home institution; Linda Fairtile and the staff at the Music Division of the New York Public Library; Ned Quist (now of Brown University) and Betsy Clark and the staff at the library of The Peabody Conservatory of Music; Bonnie Jo Dopp and the staff at the Music Library of The University of Maryland at College Park; Bridget Risemberg and the staff at the Music Library of UCLA. Warm thanks to my new colleagues at The Library of Congress, Ruth Foss, Henry Grossi, Wayne Shirley, Charles Sens, Deta Davis, Patricia Baughman, Susan Clermont, Sam Perryman, and Kevin LaVine, all of whom cheered me on at Seat C26 and eventually entrusted me with my own set of keys.

---

[12]See item 43.

To scholars and colleagues who generously shared their time and work with me, including Hilary Poriss, Jon Cheskin, Renee Norris, Karen Ahlquist, Roberta Marvin, and Mark Katz; special thanks to Emanuele Senici who allowed me to use his proposal for the significant work-in-progress he is editing: the *Cambridge Guide to Rossini*.

To Patricia Brauner, director of CIAO at The University of Chicago, who *very* patiently answered all e-mails about the Rossini Critical Edition and the *Bollettino del Centro Rossiniano di Studi* and who helped me through a last-minute moment of panic.

To Reto Müller of the Deutsche Rossini Gesellschaft, who so generously sent me Rossini sources, including copies of the complete run of that society's publication, *La Gazzetta*, and who graciously permitted me to use a Rossini photograph from his personal collection for the cover of this volume. He promptly answered all of my numerous e-mail queries, offering information and constant encouragement during the final months of this project. I could not have completed the project without his aid.

My deep appreciation to Philip Gossett for his generous assistance and for sharing information about his work, both published and in progress. If one person is responsible for inspiring and stimulating the study of Rossini, it is he. I thank him for his time and wisdom.

To Routledge Music Editor Richard Carlin, who was patient during aborted library visits, computer disasters, a tornado, and an anthrax scare. Thanks, too, to Sara Brady, Robert Byrne, and Lisa Vecchione, who took me through the final stages of this project; and former series editor Guy Marco, who helped me begin it.

To my colleague at Catholic University, Grayson Wagstaff, who understood the time needed to complete a book and often took on more than his share of our Division duties.

To my doctoral advisee Stephanie Poxon, who took time away from Barber's *Vanessa* to check and recheck the data in these entries. Her energy, precision, and, above all, her generous spirit and good humor helped me through the tedious parts of this task.

And finally, to the people who helped me stay sane: Kim Steele, Ann Cincotta, Aryeh Hecht, and Cara Baruth. The greatest thanks of all goes to my husband, Al Gallo, who, as always, solved my computer woes, provided encouragement, and reminded me constantly of this project by creating Rossini screensavers for every computer I use. And to my sons, Carmelo and Brian: Thanks, Carmelo, for allowing me to transform your bedroom into "Rossini Central" while you were away at college, and Brian, for your renditions of "Largo al factotum." You'll make a wonderful Figaro!

Chronology of Rossini's Life

1792 Born in Pesaro on February 29 to Giuseppe Antonio Rossini (known as "Vivazza") and Anna Guidarini. At the time of his son's birth, Giuseppe, a horn player, was the town's public *trombetta*. He also could claim experience in theater orchestras and church ensembles. Anna, a soprano, would perform both *prima* and *seconda donna* roles during Rossini's youth.

1798 Anna Rossini begins a career that, over the next ten years, would gain her contracts with theaters in cities such as Ancona, Jesi, Ferrara, Bologna, Imola, Fano, and Lugo. In Pesaro, Giuseppe Rossini tries unsuccessfully to become an impresario. Through his parents' activities, young Gioachino receives tutelage in theatrical professions.

1799 Arrested for his liberal political views, Giuseppe Rossini is imprisoned until the following year.

1801 Gioachino plays viola in the theater orchestra in Fano during the *carnevale* season. His father is granted membership in the Accademia Filarmonica of Bologna as "professor of horn."

1802 Having lost his post in Pesaro, Giuseppe Rossini moves his family to Lugo, the town of his birth. There, Gioachino begins studies with Giuseppe Malerbi in voice, cembalo, and composition; these latter lessons inspire Rossini's earliest sacred pieces. The boy also studies horn with his father and probably performs along with his mother in theatrical engagements in Imola.

1804 Gioachino is listed as *maestro al cembalo* during the *carnevale* season in Ravenna. In April, he arranges and performs a concert at Imola's Teatro Comunale, singing a duet with his mother and a cavatina of his own composition. He also may have been involved with Anna Rossini in the autumnal opera season in Reggio Emilia; meanwhile, Giuseppe Rossini undertakes impresarial duties in Lugo. The three are summer guests of wealthy merchant Agostino Triossi at his villa at Conventello, where Gioachino composes the six *Sonate a quattro*.

1805   Gioachino performs the role of Adolfo in Paër's *Camilla ossia Il sotteraneo* at Bologna's Teatro del Corso.

1806   Like his father before him, Gioachino is admitted into the Accademia Filarmonica. After private lessons with Angelo Tesei, he enters Bologna's Liceo Musicale, studying voice, cello, piano, and counterpoint. The latter subject is taken with Stanislao Mattei, in whose *La passione di Cristo* Rossini sings the role of Maria Magdelena. Gioachino makes his last vocal appearance at the Liceo's end-of-year student recital. Father and son play the autumn season in Forlì, Giuseppe as first-chair horn and Gioachino as *maestro al cembalo*. There, Gioachino composes a substitute tenor aria for Weigl's *L'amor marinaro*.

1807   Documented absences from coursework at the Liceo over the next few years suggest Gioachino's continued theatrical activities. Father and son again work together as musicians in Faenza. Perhaps this engagement is Giuseppe Rossini's last.

1808   One of Rossini's student compositions, the prize-winning cantata *Il pianto d'armonia sulla morte d'Orfeo*, is performed at the Liceo's convocation. He continues as *maestro al cembalo* at various theaters, a function he fulfills until 1811.

1809   During the *carnevale* season in Ferrara, Rossini composes a substitute aria for another Weigl opera, *Il podestà di Chioggia*.

1810   In spring, Rossini plays keyboard for programs at Bologna's Accademia dei Concordi. Abandoning his studies in counterpoint with Mattei, he soon becomes actively involved in opera composition when tenor Domenico Mombelli offers him a libretto entitled *Demetrio e Polibio* (not performed until 1812). He also fulfills a commission for a one-act *farsa* at Venice's Teatro San Moisè, *La cambiale di matrimonio*, which premieres on 3 November. Other compositions from this year include the tenor cavatina "Dolci aurette che spirate" and a set of variations for clarinet and orchestra.

1811   Rossini directs Haydn's *Creation* at the Accademia dei Concordi and composes the cantata *La Morte di Didone* for Ester Mombelli (not performed until 1818). By early autumn, he is engaged as *maestro al cembalo* (his last documented season as such) and composer at Bologna's Teatro del Corso, where he is commissioned to set *L'equivoco stravagante*. In December, he leaves for Venice with a commission for the San

Moisè (*L'inganno felice*). From his pen this year also come a substitute coro and cavatina for Domenico Puccini's *Il trionfo di Quinto Fabio*.

1812   *L'inganno* premieres successfully in Venice on January 8. During this busy year, Rossini accepts the task of setting *Ciro in Babilonia* for Ferrara; it premieres March 14. Because of a contract with the San Moisè, he returns to Venice, where *La scala di seta* opens on 9 May. Nine days later, *Demetrio e Polibio* opens at Rome's Teatro Valle. In Bologna that summer, Rossini receives a commission from La Scala in Milan for *La pietra del paragone*, which premieres on 26 September. Just two months later, he presents *L'occasione fa il ladro* for its debut at the San Moisè.

1813   His contract with the San Moisè continues and, on 27 January, *Il signor Bruschino* premieres there. Rossini makes his debut at Venice's La Fenice ten days later with *Tancredi*. In March, the work is performed in Ferrara with the substitution of a tragic ending. This work brings Rossini international fame, with the aria "Di tanti palpiti" boosting popularity of its composer and performers alike. After the Ferrara production, Rossini returns to Venice where *L'italiana in Algeri* premieres at the Teatro San Benedetto on 22 May. Late in the year, Rossini signs a contract with La Scala for *Aureliano in Palmira*. He returns to Milan in December for that work's premiere and to oversee productions of *Tancredi* and *L'italiana*.

1814   In Spring, Rossini signs a contract for *Il turco in Italia*, which, at its August premiere, Milanese audiences interpret as a mere reversal of *L'italiana*. Rossini composes the cantata *Egle ed Irene* for Count Belgiojoso. By mid-November, he is back in Venice where he prepares *Sigismondo* for the opening of the carnevale season.

1815   In Bologna, Rossini gives music lessons to Napoleon's niece. Following Murat's declaration of the independence of Italy and an ensuing uprising in Bologna, Rossini composes the *Inno dell'indipendenza*, which is performed on 15 April. The following month, he leaves for Naples, where he has been engaged by impresario Domenico Barbaja as musical director of his theaters. There, he meets and composes for his future wife, soprano Isabella Colbran, who sings the lead in his Neapolitan debut opera, *Elisabetta, regina d'Inghilterra*, in October. At the same time, *L'italiana in Algeri* is produced at the Fiorentini. In November, Rossini supervises the Roman premiere of *Il turco in Italia* and the *prima assoluta* of *Torvaldo e Dorliska*, which opens the *carnevale* season at the Teatro Valle. Rossini also signs a contract for an opera for Rome's Teatro Argentina.

1816   Rossini receives the libretto for his next opera: Cesare Sterbini's *Almaviva*, so-called to distinguish it from Paisiello's earlier (and highly popular) setting, *Il barbiere di Siviglia*. The work premieres on 20 February, but when the older composer dies several months later, Rossini's work assumes his title for its Bologna premiere in September. After signing a contract for an opera for *carnevale* at Rome's Valle (*La Cenerentola*), Rossini returns to Naples where he composes the cantata *Le nozze di Teti, e di Peleo* for the marriage of Carolina and Charles-Ferdinand. On 26 September, *La gazzetta* premieres at the Fiorentini. On 4 December, *Otello* premieres with Colbran singing Desdemona. (Newly-discovered correspondence to Rossini's parents suggests that the composer and the singer have by this point begun their relationship.) Rossini returns to Rome at the end of the year to work on a new commission for the Valle.

1817   *Cenerentola* debuts on 25 January. Rossini leaves Rome in mid-February, visits with his parents in Bologna, and heads for Milan where in early March he begins work on *La gazza ladra* for La Scala. The opera premieres on 31 May. In July, Rossini, Colbran, and others vacation on the island of Ischia. By August, Rossini is back in Naples at work on *Armida*, which opens at the San Carlo on 9 November. Returning to Rome, he supervises the 27 December premiere of *Adelaide di Borgogna*.

1818   The early months of the year find Rossini in Naples, working on the *azione sacra Mosè in Egitto* which premieres at the San Carlo on 5 March. Later that month, Rossini informs his parents that he and Colbran, with whom he travels frequently, will visit Bologna. At La Fenice on 2 May, Ester Mombelli performs the cantata *La morte di Didone*, which Rossini had composed for her in 1811. For the June reopening of the Teatro del Sole in Pesaro, Rossini returns in triumph with a production of *La gazza ladra*. While there, he becomes so ill that reports of his death are circulated in Naples and Paris. After his recovery, he returns to Bologna where he receives a commission from Lisbon for *Adina*; although completed and delivered, the premiere is delayed until June of 1826. Rossini's next work, *Ricciardo e Zoraide*, premieres at the San Carlo on 3 December.

1819   Rossini completes a two-act version of *Armida* for Naples. He also composes a cantata for Ferdinando I and revises *Mosè* to include the famous prayer "Dal tuo stellato soglio." The production of the latter work is postponed until 7 March because of Colbran's vocal problems. The early months of the year also see the commission of *Ermione* (27 March) for Naples and *Eduardo e Cristina* (24 April) for Venice. During a visit to Pesaro, he is involved in an incident with the entourage of the Princess of Wales and, as a result of this unpleasantness, leaves his hometown and never returns. Rossini's cantata for the visit of Emperor

Francis I is performed in Naples on 9 May. *La donna del lago* premieres at the San Carlo on 24 October. Two months later, he is back in Milan for the 26 December premiere of *Bianca e Falliero* at La Scala.

1820   On his return to Naples, Rossini stops briefly to visit his parents in Bologna and then proceeds to Rome where he sits for artist Adamo Tadolini, who had been commissioned by authorities in Pesaro to do a bust of the composer. In Genoa, Rossini is feted *in absentia* in conjunction with a production of *Otello*. In Naples, with the assistance of Pietro Raimondi, he composes a *Messa di Gloria* for the Arciconfraternità di San Luigi. Isabella Colbran's father, Giovanni, dies in April, leaving to her some properties Rossini eventually would inherit. In Naples, Rossini sets the *seria* work *Maometto II*, but a political uprising against the reigning Bourbons halts work on the project. (The composer may even have served briefly in some minor capacity in the National Guard.) On December 3, *Maometto* premieres at the San Carlo, and, shortly after, Rossini heads for Rome where he composes *Matilde di Shabran*.

1821   *Matilde* premieres at the Apollo on 24 February. When the impresario discovers that several of the numbers have been set by Giovanni Pacini, whom Rossini, under deadline pressure, has enlisted to help, he refuses to pay Rossini. (Rossini would later reset these numbers). The composer repossesses the score and makes an official complaint to the pontifical office in charge of theaters. After the issue is resolved, *Matilde* reopens in mid-March. At the end of the month, Rossini returns to Naples, where he receives an invitation to compose for the King's Theatre in London. At the end of the year, Barbaja signs a contract to take a company from Naples to Vienna's Kärntnertortheater. Assuming that Rossini will return after his travels, Barbaja releases him to go to London and Paris after their Viennese engagement. In November, Rossini writes to his father of his betrothal to Colbran. In December, the composer premieres the cantata *La riconoscenza* at the San Carlo.

1822   *Zelmira*, Rossini's final opera for Naples, opens at the San Carlo on 16 February. After the opera's final performance, Rossini and Colbran leave Naples and on 16 March, just outside of Bologna, they wed. Barbaja opens his company's visit to Vienna with *Zelmira* on 13 April; in letters, Rossini notes that Colbran suffers stage fright because of increasing difficulties with her voice. Sometime in spring, as he would later relate to Wagner and Hiller, Rossini (supposedly) visits Beethoven. The company remains in Vienna until July when a one-act version of *Ricciardo e Zoraide* is presented as a benefit for its composer. Back in Bologna, Rossini and Colbran sign contracts for the 1822–1823 *carnevale* season. During the summer, he begins work on the *Gorgheggi e solfeggi* vocal exercises. He also purchases a house in the city. After receiving an invitation from Metternich to come to Verona for the Congresso of 1822, he composes the cantatas *La santa alleanza*, performed on 24 November, and *Il vero omaggio*, sung on 3 December. While in Verona, Rossini oversees productions of several of his operas. By 9 December, he and Colbran have traveled to Venice where a slightly revised version of *Maometto II* is produced at La Fenice on 26 December.

1823   Rossini's last Italian opera, *Semiramide*, premieres at La Fenice on 3 February. By mid-March, the Rossinis return to Bologna, where they solidify plans to work with impresario Giovanni Battista Benelli in England; these include the promise of a new work for the London stage. On 1 April, the cantata *Omaggio pastorale* is performed in Treviso. Rossini and his wife leave Bologna on 20 October, reaching Paris by 9 November. A grand picnic held in the composer's honor that month inspires the stage parody *Rossini à Paris ou Le Grand Dîner*. Pro- and con-Rossini debates rage in Paris, but it is apparent that the monarchy wants the composer to remain. Contract obligations with London force the Rossinis to leave, however. They arrive in London on 13 December, and sixteen days later, Rossini is presented to King George IV.

1824   Rossini conducts *Zelmira* at King's Theatre on 24 January, but Colbran's weakening voice ensures its failure. Performances later in the year by Giuditta Pasta help restore Rossini's theatrical fortune in London. Meanwhile, he augments his income by appearing in the salons of wealthy Londoners, even participating in musicales of members of the royal household. He holds two concerts and, at the second, on 11 June, he performs in his cantata, *Il pianto delle muse in morte di Lord Byron*, composed in commemoration of the poet's recent death. In July, Rossini visits Cambridge for the University Music Festival. Later that month, the Rossinis leave for Paris, where on 1 August he begins a contract with the French monarchy. He and Colbran briefly visit Bologna in September so that Rossini can see to his financial affairs. Upon their return to Paris, he renegotiates his contract and is named co-director of the Théâtre Italien with Ferdinand Paër, who resigns in protest. Rossini begins setting *Il viaggio a Reims* for the coronation of Charles X.

1825   *Il viaggio* premieres 19 June. Rossini falls ill shortly thereafter and is unable to work for three months. By September, he is preparing the Paris premiere of Meyerbeer's *Il crociato in Egitto*. On 6 October, *Cenerentola* opens at the Italien, followed by *La donna del lago* and *Semiramide*.

1826   *Zelmira* is produced at the Italien on 14 March. Carl Maria von Weber, on his way to London, visits Rossini, making peace with the young composer whom he had considered an unworthy rival. On 22 June,

Adina, the only one of his premieres at which he was not present, is staged in Lisbon. On 15 September, a pastiche of Rossini music entitled *Ivanhoé* opens, and on 9 October, the composer's first French opera, *Le siège de Corinthe*, premieres. Rossini resigns directorship of the Italien and signs a new contract on 17 October that grants him an annuity of 25,000 francs. Although new talks begin for an opera for the London stage, they come to naught. Rossini begins to revise *Mosè* into its French version: *Moïse et Pharaon*.

1827   Anna Rossini dies on 20 February. A distraught Rossini directs the premiere of *Moïse* on 26 March. At his son's insistence, Giuseppe Rossini arrives in Paris. On 16 July, the cantata for the baptism of the son of banker Alejandro María Aguado is performed. The composer begins work on *Le comte Ory* and, with Antonio Pacini, publishes the vocal exercises *Gorgheggi e solfeggi*.

1828   *Le comte Ory* premieres at the Opéra on 20 August. Rossini begins work on *Guillaume Tell*.

1829   In May, rehearsals of *Tell* begin. The premiere is delayed, however, because of problems with soprano Laure Cinti-Damoreau's voice. Meanwhile, Rossini tries to renegotiate his contract with the French crown allowing for a three-month visit to Bologna every year. Four days after the *Tell* premieres on 3 August, Charles X confers the Légion d'honneur on Rossini. The composer and his wife depart for Bologna, arriving on 6 September. Rossini revises the cantata *La riconoscenza* and prepares productions of his works for the Teatro Comunale.

1830   In March, Édouard Robert, co-director of the Italien, stops in Bologna to seek Rossini's advice about theatrical matters. After a visit to Florence in June, Rossini returns to Bologna the following month, where he gets word of Charles X's dethronement and, consequently, the loss of his annuity. He returns to Paris to settle his affairs in September, leaving Colbran behind with his father; although Colbran and the elder Rossini reside together, the two merely suffer each other's presence.

1831   In February, Rossini and Aguado travel to Spain where Rossini conducts a performance of *Il barbiere* for King Ferdinando VII. He is asked to set the Stabat Mater text, a task he begins but fails to complete due to illness; he seeks the assistance of composer Giovanni Tadolini, who sets the remaining sections. Back in Paris, Rossini suffers from exhaustion coupled with a bout of gonorrhea. A cholera epidemic forces Rossini to flee to Bayonne with the Aguado family.

1832   After returned to Paris, Rossini begins his liaison with Olympe Pélissier. Although no longer its director, Rossini stays active at the Italien, helping young composers, such as Bellini and Donizetti, when their works are premiered at the theater.

1834   Despite appeals from the government, the court finds in favor of Rossini, ruling that his annuity be granted in perpetuity with payments retroactive to 1 July 1830. In June, Rossini returns to Bologna with Robert and Severini. Meanwhile, in Paris, new rumors spread that Rossini has died. Late in August, the composer is back in the French capital, much a part of the city's social and theatrical milieu.

1835   Rossini publishes the *Soirées musicales*. In September, the composer serves as an honorary pallbearer at the funeral of Bellini.

1836   In June, Rossini travels to Belgium and Germany with banker Lionel de Rothschild. In Frankfurt, he meets such composers as Felix Mendelssohn and Ferdinand Hiller. He returns briefly to France and then, in October, leaves for Bologna, where he visits Colbran.

1837   In January, Pélissier makes legal arrangements to move to Bologna where Rossini has purchased property so that they can discreetly set up separate households. There, she meets Colbran, with whom she develops a polite relationship. Meanwhile, Rossini seeks a legal separation from his wife, and, after it is granted, he and Pélissier travel to Milan.

1838   Rossini mourns the loss of Severini, who dies after jumping from the burning Théâtre Italien on 14 January. Although they return to Bologna at the insistence of Giuseppe Rossini in late March, Rossini and Pélissier are off to Milan in September to attend a celebration given by Metternich for Rossini and singer Giuditta Pasta.

1839   Rossini is offered a perpetual appointment as consultant for programs at Bologna's Liceo Musicale. He refuses at first, as his health declines due to urethritis and the onset of nervous disorders. Matters worsen when Giuseppe Rossini dies on 29 April, further plunging the composer into physical and mental collapse. Nevertheless, he and Pélissier travel to Naples in June; both there and in Rome, he is feted. Due to his condition, however, he is unable to attend celebrations in his honor. In September, they return to Bologna.

1840   Having reversed his decision about the position at the Liceo, Rossini presides at the January entrance exams. His ill health continues; he is bled and given recuperative baths, but there is no improvement. Even more debilitating than his physical woes is his depression. For a time, he seems interested in arranging a production of *Tell* as *Rodolfo di Sterlinga* for La Fenice, but nothing comes of the project.

1841   Rossini and Pélissier attend the premiere of Vincenzo Gabussi's opera *Clemenza di Valois* at La Fenice in February. A severe stomach disorder, perhaps from drinking the water, attacks the composer and plagues him for months. At the advice of physicians, he goes to Porretta to take a water cure, but severe weight loss makes him increasingly more weak. To make matters worse, Rossini is forced to enter a legal battle with

French publisher Aulagnier over the rights to the Stabat Mater. In late October, sections of the work, including Rossini's replacements of those by Tadolini, are performed in Paris at the home of Pierre-Joseph-Guillaume Zimmerman.

1842   On 7 January, the Stabat mater is performed at the Salle Ventadour. Still in Bologna, Rossini makes efforts to secure a new director for the Liceo, offering the post to Mercadante, Pacini, and Donizetti. When all refuse, he reluctantly agrees to the appointment of Antonio Fabbri. Donizetti arrives in Bologna to conduct the Italian premiere of the Stabat Mater, performed on 18, 19, and 20 March at the Archiginnasio. Another visitor to the city and to Rossini is Giuseppe Verdi. During this year, Rossini receives various honors, including knighthood in the Prussian Order of Merit in the Sciences and Art as well as the Greek Cross of Knight of the Royal Order of the Savior. A plaque is placed on the house in Pesaro in which he was born.

1843   In May, Rossini conducts a benefit performance of *Otello*, with proceeds going to the Liceo. Ten days later, he leaves for Paris to consult new physicians. Doctors there order isolation, which deepens his depression. At the first sign of physical improvement, he and Pélissier return to Bologna where he once again dedicates himself to activities at the Liceo.

1844   Rossini reworks the "Coro dei bardi" from *La donna del lago* for Turin's celebration of the third centenary of the birth of Tasso. The new chorus is performed on 10 March. In late November, after negotiations with French publisher Troupenas, three choruses, "La Foi," "L'Espérance," and "La Charité" are premiered in Paris.

1845   Via correspondence, Rossini keeps active in theatrical affairs, for example, by writing to Verdi to request a new aria for tenor Nicolai Ivanoff. At the end of August, Rossini receives word that Colbran is dying. On 7 September, he and Pélissier go to Colbran's estate where the composer sees her for the last time. Ten days later, she dies.

1846   Although gaining a reputation as a conservative, Rossini signs his name in June to a petition seeking government reforms, thus placing himself in league with Bolognese liberals whose hopes lie with the new pope, Pius IX. Rossini composes a chorus dedicated to the new pontiff, once again basing it on the "Coro dei bardi"; he conducts it himself in the piazza in front of San Petronio on 23 July. On 16 August, Rossini's name day, he weds Pélissier in a private chapel outside of Bologna. After negotiations with Rossini in that city for a French version of *La donna del lago* for the Opéra, representatives from the theater return to Paris with his blessing on a pastiche called *Robert Bruce*, which premieres on 30 December. The work causes a flurry of criticism, and debate rages in the Parisian press.

1847   On New Year's Day, the *Cantata in onore del Sommo Pontifice Pio Nono*, a pastiche, is performed in Rome.

1848   The political events of this year take a toll on Rossini's condition. Demonstrations in Bologna in April strike Rossini personally, for he is identified as a reactionary by certain elements in the city; others, because of the petition he had signed two years earlier, accuse him of being a liberal. He is verbally attacked and, fearing physical harm, moves to Florence in late April. Friends urge him to return, but, using Pélissier's health as an excuse, he refuses. Although he denies his friends his physical presence, he agrees to set a chorus, which is performed in the city's main piazza on 21 June. Until 1850, Rossini and his wife lead a quiet life in their new city.

1850   In September, Rossini returns to Bologna, only to find the political situation still unsettled. He remains only a few months.

1851   By early January, Rossini is making plans to ship his belongings back to Florence. The issue is settled when he is insulted by friends who refuse to remain in his home when Austrian Count Nobili arrives. Four days later, he departs Bologna, never to return.

1852   Rossini arranges to sell his Bolognese property. He travels frequently to spas in Montecatini and Bagni di Lucca for cures that fail to benefit him. He works sporadically, though, composing a military march for the Sultan of Turkey.

1853   Rossini invests in three adjoining residences in Florence. He learns that, in France, he has been promoted to Commandeur in the Légion d'honneur. Although Rossini attends the production of *Guglielmo Tell* at the Palazzo Pitti in April, Pélissier becomes increasingly concerned about his physical and psychological condition.

1854   Rossini's health is critical. He continues to visit the spas and even attempts a cure with magnetism. Responding to rumors that Rossini has gone mad, Pélissier is quick to spread the word that his health is improving.

1855   Pélissier decides to take Rossini back to Paris, where she feels he will receive more advanced medical care. Leaving on 26 April, they arrive a month later. Rossini will not return to Italy again during his lifetime. In July, he is ordered to take a recuperative trip to Trouville, where he encounters Ferdinand Hiller. Their conversations are recorded in the latter's *Plaudereien mit Rossini*. He returns to Paris in September, where the Théâtre Italien begins a season largely dedicated to his works.

1856   To ensure the improvement of his health, Rossini's doctors prescribe a visit to Wildbad to take the waters. After visits to spas in Kissingen and Baden, he returns to Paris in late September.

1857	Rossini composes *Musique anodine* for Olympe's name day on 5 April. As his health returns, the composer and his wife begin to receive guests, moving to larger quarters to accommodate their entertaining. During this time, Rossini begins to compose the pieces that eventually form the *Péchés de vieillesse*.
1858	Rossini purchases the land for a villa at Passy, where he has spent the past two summers. In town, on 18 December, the Rossinis hold the first of their famous soirées, the *Samedi soirs*, for which invitations are much coveted. These would continue for the next ten years.
1859	On 10 March, with mortar and trowel, Rossini lays the cornerstone for the villa at Passy. His life revolves around socializing and composing, even making the occasional public appearance. His presence at a performance of the Stabat Mater and the finale of *Moïse* in April draws such applause that it reduces the composer to tears. Indeed the Parisians show such appreciation that Rossini has returned to them that the ambitious director at the Italien tries to capitalize on this enthusiasm, announcing a "new" work by Rossini. The composer insists that the opera be identified as the pastiche it is and that the public be informed that he in no way was connected with its production.
1860	In March, Richard Wagner calls on Rossini, and their conversation is recorded by Edmond Michotte; six months later, Eduard Hanslick visits the composer at Passy. On 9 July, the French version of *Semiramide* is performed at the Opéra. Rossini, who has entrusted the project to Michele Carafa, is pleased with production, especially with the performance of the Marchisio sisters as Semiramide and Arsace.
1861	On Good Friday, 29 March, the Stabat mater is performed at Rossini's home. Although the composer refuses an invitation to submit a composition to be played at the opening day ceremonies of the 1862 London Exhibition, he provides the *Chants des Titans* to the Paris Conservatory for performance at a benefit concert for a monument for Cherubini. The work is repeated at the Opéra on 22 December.
1862	Rossini's home continues to attract guests, especially visitors from Italy. Late in the year, Baron Jakob Rothschild asks Rossini for a composition in honor of Napoleon III's visit to his château. He agrees and sets the "Choeur de chasseurs démocrates."
1863	Rossini composes the Petite messe solennelle.
1864	On March 14, the Petite messe is sung at the home of Comte Pillet-Will. Among the guests is Giacomo Meyerbeer, who is extremely moved by the work. The composition is repeated the following day, with Meyerbeer again in attendance along with the Rothchilds, French government officials, and other members of the musical community. Rossini seems not to have been present. After Meyerbeer's death on 2 May, Rossini

composes a choral *Chant funèbre*. Rossini again receives a promotion in the Légion d'honneur, this time to "grand officier." In Pesaro, a festival is held in Rossini's honor, with the participation of composers, including Pacini. Realizing the unlikelihood of a return to Italy, Rossini authorizes the sale of his property in Florence. In December he agrees to cooperate with publisher Tito Ricordi on an edition of his works, although he is bothered about possible criticism of his extensive self-borrowings.

1865   On 24 April, the Petite Messe is performed again at the home of Pillet-Will.

1866   The *Chants des Titans* is sung on 15 April in a concert to raise funds for a statue of Mozart. After initially refusing the challenge, Rossini begins to orchestrate the Petite Messe, which he completes the following year. Wishing to include female voices in its performance, he corresponds with Pius IX, with the help of Latin scholar Luigi Cristostomo Ferrucci. The pope replies with a blessing and vague refusal of the composer's request. Also involved in this issue is Abbé Franz Liszt, who visits Rossini several times during the year. In December, Rossini's health begins to suffer.

1867   Rossini receives guests, including Tito and Giulio Ricordi, composer Emil Naumann, and Hanslick. During the latter's visit, Rossini again relates his remembrance of a meeting with Beethoven. At the 1 July awards ceremony of the Exposition Universelle, Rossini's "Hymn à Napoléon III" is sung. Rossini's physical condition declines.

1868   During this leap year, Rossini's seventy-sixth birthday is celebrated with festivities and commemorations. Most likely as a gesture of thanks for King Vittorio Emanuele's naming him a Grand Knight in the Order of the Crown of Italy, Rossini composes "La Corona d'Italia"; the work will not be performed until 1878, however. On 26 September, the final Saturday soirée is held. Rossini becomes gravely ill and, on Friday, 13 November, he is pronounced dead at 10:45 p.m. The funeral, with more than 4,000 in attendance, is held on 21 November. Burial is in the Cemetery of Pére-Lachaise in Paris.

1869   Three months after Rossini's death, the orchestrated version of the Petite Messe is sung at the Italien.

1878   Olympe Pélissier dies on 22 March. Three months later, a commission in Florence begins to arrange for the transport of Rossini's remains for burial in Santa Croce, a move Pélissier had repeatedly fought. Political issues prevent completion of the plans.

1887   After the Ministry of Public Instruction in Florence resumes the initiative, an escort accompanies Rossini's remains from Paris to Florence. On May 3, he is interred in Santa Croce.

1

Archives and Collections, Bibliographies and Indexes, and Catalogs

ARCHIVES AND COLLECTIONS

Descriptions

1. Bagues Erriondo, Jon. "Rossini y Aranzazu." *Minima: Musica, Danza, Drama* 1 [no. 2] (1992): 9.

   [Not examined.] According to RILM abstract, the author lists Rossini music in this monastery archive.

   *Capitanio, Fabrizio. "L'esecuzione della Stabat Mater di Rossini diretta da Donizetti (Bologna, 1842) in una recensione dell'epoca." See item 794.

2. Carboni, Domenico. "Perché manca là quel foglio? Ossia Rossini nella Biblioteca Musicale 'S. Cecilia.' " In *Rossini a Roma-Rossini e Roma* (see item 289), 203–48.

   The author gives a brief history of the Biblioteca di S. Cecilia and notes its Rossini holdings, which include autograph numbers from *Il viaggio a Reims* (see Johnson, item 754). Following the list of autographs, operas, copyists' scores, and published editions are illustrations of items such as libretti, musical scores and editions, and documents such as Rossini's contract for *La Cenerentola*, exhibited during the conference "Rossini a Rome—Rossini e Roma."

3. *Catalogue of the Allen A. Brown collection of music in the Public Library of the City of Boston: Vol. II. Hi-Rossini.* Boston: Published by the Library Trustees, 1912. 576 pp.

   [Not examined.]

4. Cohen, H. Robert, and Marie-Odile Gigou. *Cent ans de mise en scène lyrique en France (env. 1830–1930)/One Hundred Years of Operatic Staging in France.* Preface by Philip Gossett. Vol. 2 of *Musical Life in 19th-Century France,* Gen. eds. H. Robert Cohen and Yves Gérard. Introduction translated by Donald Gíslason. New York: Pendragon Press, 1986. lviii, 334 pp. ISBN 0-918728-69-X ML128.04 C63 1986.

   In addition to introducing the collection of staging manuals in the archive of the Bibliothèque de l'Association de la Régie Théâtrale, of which this book is a catalogue, this volume presents an introduction to the utilization of staging manuals and the role of the *régisseur,* or stage manager. The Rossini operas represented are *Le barbier de Séville, Le comte Ory, Guillaume Tell, Moïse et Pharaon, Othello, Semiramis,* and *Le siège de Corinthe.* Works in the archive are listed alphabetically; further data gives the source (staging manual, annotated score, or annotated libretto), bibliography and description, pertinent production information (such as details on costumes, scenery, stage furnishings) and archival call numbers. The volume has four indexes, identifying entries by title, composer and librettist, alternate title, and venue. Also see items 317 and 318.

   *Donà, Mariangela. "Un' aria di Rossini per un'opera di Nicolini nella Biblioteca Comunale di Civitanova Marche." See item 225.

5. G[arbelotto], A[ntonio]. "Libri rari e di pregio nella Biblioteca del Conservatorio di Music 'G. Rossini' di Pesaro." *Bollettino del Centro Rossiniano di Studi* 8 [no. 2] (1968): 21–40.

   Briefly recounting the legacy that Rossini bequeathed to his hometown, the author lists the holdings of rare and important music treatises, manuscripts, and scores at Pesaro's Conservatory. Entries include a bibliographic description of each item and its call number. Part 1 of 2 (see item 6), this article's contents range alphabetically from Giuseppe Matteo Alberti to Benedetto Marcello.

6. ———. "Libri rari e di pregio nella Biblioteca del Conservatorio di Music 'G. Rossini' di Pesaro, continuazione" *Bollettino del Centro Rossiniano di Studi* 8 [no. 3] (1968): 41–56.

Conclusion of the listing begun in item 5. Works range alphabetically from Benedetto Marcello to Niccolo Zingarelli. Also notes the collection's three seventeen-century editions of libretti.

7. Genesi, Mario Giuseppe. "La collezione dei libretti d'opera al Teatro Municipale di Piacenza: Documenti di storia ottocentesca." *La vos del campanon* 39 [no.2] (March-April 1997): 34–37.

This theater archive contains the libretto of *Mosè in Egitto* by Andrea Leone Tottola.

*Gerhard, Anselm. "Die französische 'Grand Opera' in der Forschung seit 1945." See item 21.

*Gossett, Philip. "Le fonti autografe delle opere teatrale di Rossini." See item 18.

8. Hunt, Jno L. "Music in the Rosenbloom Collection of Hunt Library at Carnegie-Mellon University." *Notes* 33 [no. 3] (March 1977): 553–62.

Housed in this collection are two Rossini manuscripts: one of numerous settings of "Mi lagnerò tacendo," this one in D major for piano and voice, and a harp sonata in E-flat major. For other settings of the first work, see items 16, 30, and 256.

9. Inventory of *The Rosaleen Moldenhauer Memorial: Music History from Primary Sources: A Guide to the Moldenhauer Archives*, 485–728. Eds. Jon Newsom and Alfred Mann. 733 pp. Washington, D.C.: The Library of Congress, 2000.

In addition to an autograph of a recitative and sketch from Rossini's *Moïse* (see Gossett, item 760), this inventory of the Moldenhauer Archive at the Library of Congress contains Rossini correspondence, including letters to Angelo Mignani and Giovanni Pacini (Box 44) as well as an engraving of the composer (Box 114).

10. Kantner, Leopold, and Michael Jahn, eds. "Fonti rossiniane a Vienna." *Bollettino del Centro Rossiniano di Studi* 33 (1993): 93–120.

Provides a list of Rossini's music and librettos at the Nationalbibliothek in Vienna. Kantner and Jahn have grouped the materials into sections on theatrical, sacred, vocal, and instrumental music. Works in the first section are organized by title (in chronological order of composition) with the date and venue of the each work's Viennese premiere.

11. Lippmann, Friedrich. "Musikhandschriften und -Drucke in der Bibliothek des Furstenhauses Massimo, Rom." *Analecta musicologica* 7 (1976): 254–95.

    Not examined. Lippmann introduces the private library of Prince Massimo, whose collection contains autograph manuscripts of Rossini works.

12. Müller, Reto. "Rossini-Bibliotheken der Welt: Der Fonds Michotte in Brüssel." *La Gazzetta* 11 (2001): 27–28.

    Edmond Michotte was a trusted friend of the Rossinis and executor of Rossini's will (also see items 123 and 160). Müller offers a summary of the contents of the Fonds Michotte at the Royal Conservatory in Brussels, some of which came from Michotte's private collection. The archive contains Rossini autographs, including the score of *Matilde di Shabran*; some 130 published editions of Rossini's music; books from the composer's personal library; iconographic items; correspondence; and memorabilia such as Rossini and Olympe Pélissier's passports and the collection of libretti and dedicatory verse collected by Rossini's father. The most recent discovery in the archive is a collection of the repertoire of Isabella Colbran.

13. ———. "Rossini-Bibliotheken der Welt: Die Sammlung Piancastelli in Forlì." *La Gazzetta* 10 (2000): 28–29.

    Müller briefly describes the holdings of this archive that houses one of the richest collections of Rossini autograph letters as well as correspondence from Isabella Colbran and Olympe Pélissier. Müller also comments on the collection's musical autographs, iconographic items, documents, and books. See also item 100 on the Piancastelli archive.

14. Pico Pascual, Miguel Angel. "La presencia de libros de musica en la vida cotidiana de la alta burguesia valenciana de finales del siglo XVIII y la primera mitad del siglo XIX: Estudio de dos bibliotecas musicales privadas a traves de los protocolos notariales." *Nassarre: Revista aragonesa de musicologia* 16 [no. 2] (2000): 265–87.

    Not examined. The RILM abstract states that the 1834 notarial inventory of a private library in Valencia documents a significant presence of Italian operas, including the works of Rossini.

    *Reich, Nancy. "Liszt's Variations on the March from Rossini's *Siège de Corinthe*." See item 406.

15. Turner, J. Rigbie. "Nineteenth-Century Autograph Music Manuscripts in The Pierpont Morgan Library: A Check List (II). *19th Century Music* 4 [no. 2] (Fall 1980): 157–83.

Turner, the librarian at Pierpont Morgan, notes the collection's ten Rossini autographs, including various cadenzas. Also at this library is a full orchestral score in a copyist's hand of the overture to the pastiche *Ivanhoé*.

*Walker, Frank. "Rossiniana in the Piancastelli Collection." Part 1: "Miscellaneous Unpublished Letters." Item 55. Also see items 13, 61, and 100.

*———. "Rossiniana in the Piancastelli Collection." Part 2: "Correspondence with Michele Costa." Item 61. Also see items 13, 55, and 100.

16. Wright, Craig. "Rare Music Manuscripts at Harvard." *Current Musicology* 10 (1970): 25–33.

Wright lists the manuscripts owned by the Harvard Music Library; included in the collection are three Rossini songs, among them the autograph of an 1852 setting of "Mi lagnerò tacendo." For other settings, see items 8, 30, and 256.

Studies of Archives

*Bini, Annalisa. "Teatro e musica a Roma nell'Ottocento attraverso gli archivi familiari." See item 366.

*Carboni, Domenico. "Perché manca là quel foglio? Ossia Rossini nella Biblioteca Musicale 'S. Cecilia.' " See item 2.

*DiProfio, Alessandro. "Inediti rossiniani a Parigi. Il Fondo Rossini-Hentsch alla Bibliothèque G. Mahler." See item 42.

BIBLIOGRAPHIES AND INDEXES

Primary Sources

17. Fanan, Giorgio. *Drammaturgia Rossiniana: Bibliografia dei libretti d'opera, di oratori, cantate ecc. Posti in musica da Gioachino Rossini. Studi, cataloghi e sussidi dell' Istituto di Bibliografia musicale*, Sussidi Vol. 2. Ed. Giancarlo Rostirolla. Rome: Istituto di Bibliografia musicale, 1997. 1065 p. ML134.R687 F36 1997.

Catalogs 1,659 libretti with information on each one's title page, edition, and physical description; librettist (with variant names) and composer (although most are by Rossini); venue and date of production; cast; structure of libretto by act and scene (with page numbers); artistic collaborators, such as scenographers, choreographers, and orchestra directors; literary source; and lists of libraries, archives, and collections where libretti are located. With separate indexes for librettists and translators, composers, singers, orchestra personnel, production venues, ballets, choreographers and dancers, and publication data. A general index follows. Includes a useful bibliography of theater histories.

18. Gossett, Philip. "Le fonti autografe delle opere teatrale di Rossini." Translated into Italian by Agostino Ziino. *Nuova rivista musicale italiana* 2 [no. 5] (1968): 936–60.

An important example of the early work of one of the major forces in Rossini scholarship. The author explains that theatrical works were revised to suit specific productions and new casts. Thus, a thorough examination of all scores (the theory behind the Rossini Critical Edition) is necessary to produce a complete picture of a work. Gossett then lists the Rossini autographs (located as of the writing of this article), identifying the date and venue of the premiere, location and physical description of the manuscript, and the autograph's relationship to the standard editions published by Ricordi between 1846 and 1864.

Secondary Literature

19. Deutsche Rossini Gesellschaft, Homepage link. "La bibliografia rossiniana di P. Fabbri." (www.rossinigesellschaft.de/members/fabbri/fabbri.html).

A bibliography of the Rossini scholarship of Paolo Fabbri. Includes information on editions, monographs, articles, and translations.

20. Deutsche Rossini Gesellschaft, Homepage link. "*La Gazzetta*-Zeitschrift der Deutschen Rossini Gesellshaft." (www.rossinigesellschaft.de/soc/publd.html#gazz).

An index of articles, research, and reviews in this publication of the German Rossini Society.

21. Gerhard, Anselm. "Die französische 'Grand Opera' in der Forschung seit 1945." *Acta musicologica* 59 [no. 3] (1987): 220–70.

Not examined. The author's RILM abstract lists this source as an annotated bibliography of secondary literature on grand opera, beginning with Rossini's *Le siège de Corinthe*. Also discusses the archive of Eugène Scribe at the Bibliotheque Nationale.

*Loewenberg, Alfred. *Annals of Opera, 1597–1940, Compiled from Original Sources*. See item 293.

22. Monaldini, Sergio, ed. "Indici del 'Bollettino del Centro Rossiniano di Studi' (1955–1991)." *Bollettino del Centro Rossiniano di Studi* 32 (1992): 171–213.

After a brief publication history of the *Bollettino* and its role in inspiring scholarly research, Monaldini lists its contents up through 1991 in four separate indexes: a general listing of contents by issue (pp. 172–189); by authors (pp. 190–97); by the following subject areas: technical, stylistic and poetic topics; biography; correspondence; sources; reception during his career; posthumous reception; posthumous critical commentary; iconography; interpreters; *messa in scena*; works; performance practice; philological topics; contemporary commentaries; musical transcriptions and arrangements (pp. 198–210); and an index of books reviewed (pp. 211–13).

23. Verti, Roberto. *Un almanacco drammatico: L'indice de' teatrali spettacoli: 1764–1823*. 2 Vols. No. 2 in the series *Saggi e fonti*. Pesaro: Fondazione Rossini, 1996. xxvii, 1649 pp.

Not examined. The RILM abstract describes this work as an index of theatrical seasons of Italian opera in theaters throughout Europe during the period specified.

CATALOGS

24. Gossett, Philip. "Catalogo delle opere." In *Gioacchino Rossini* (Rognoni, Item 477), 440–80, 1968 ed.; 440–503, 1977 ed.

This catalog of Rossini works and manuscripts has served as a cornerstone for later Rossini works lists. Gossett divides the catalogue into nine sections: theatrical works, *musiche di scena*, cantatas, *inni* and choruses, sacred music, vocal music, instrumental music, *Péchés de vieillesse*, and miscellaneous works. Each entry includes the title, a brief description, date of composition or date and venue of premiere, original cast (where applicable), and information on the autograph. As a result of Gossett's continued search for sources, the catalogue is expanded in the 1977 edition.

25. Iesuè, Alberto, ed. *"Rossini rivoltato": Incipitario testuale della musica vocale di Gioachino Rossini*. Rome: Istituto di Bibliografia Musicale, 1997. 845 pp. ML134.R687 I37 1997.

Includes text incipits of all of Rossini's vocal music, listed according to the categories in Gossett's catalog (see item 24). Incipit entries for arias, duets, various ensembles and choruses include character, range, work, act and scene (cantata entries by scene). Includes incipits for all French versions of Italian works. Indexes list entries by incipit, genre and title, role, and vocal range. With illustrations.

26. Jones, David Wilson. *An Annotated Catalogue of the Vocal Works of G. Rossini Written between 1857–1868 as Found in the Library of the Fondazione "G. Rossini."* DMA dissertation, University of Iowa, 1972. 146 pp.

    [Not examined.]

27. Messrs. Puttick and Simpson. *Catalogue of the unpublished compositions of Gioachino Rossini . . . which will be sold at auction.* London, 1838. 16 pp.

    Not examined. Abstract based on information from FirstSearch. A catalog of an auction of Rossini's works held in London by the firm Puttick and Simpson, 30 May 1878. A microfilm of this source is available at the New York Public Library.

    *Rossini, Gioachino. Letters, Sotheby's Catalogue for Music Auction, Friday, 7 December 2001. See item 39.

28. Viale Ferrero, Mercedes. "Per Rossini: un primo tentativo di iconografia scenografica." *Bollettino del Centro Rossiniano di Studi* 1–3 (1982): 5–28.

    In hopes of inspiring further research to produce a complete catalog of scenographic iconography of productions of Rossini's operas throughout the composer's career, the author has compiled materials and listed them by design, place and date of publication, and archive catalog information. In addition to indexing these three sections, Viale Ferrero provides an index of the productions included. Four (unnumbered) pages with scenographic and costume illustrations follow the catalog.

2

Correspondence and Documents

GENERAL COLLECTIONS

The Fondazione Rossini Critical Edition

29. Cagli, Bruno, and Sergio Ragni, eds. *Gioachino Rossini: Lettere e documenti*. Vol. 1, 29 February 1792 to 17 March 1822. Pesaro: Fondazione. Rossini, 1992. xxxvii, 682 pp. ISBN 88-7096-072-2 ML410.R8 A4 1992. [Contains letters and documents numbered from 1–316]. Vol. 2, 21 March 1822 to 11 October 1826. Pesaro: Fondazione Rossini, 1996. xx, 732 pp. ML410.R8 A4 1996. [Contains letters and documents numbered from 317–665]. Vol. 3, 17 October 1826 to 31 December 1830. Pesaro: Fondazione Rossini, 2000. xx, 812 pp. ML410.R8 A4 2000. [Contains letters and documents numbered from 666–1014].

These three volumes begin the Fondazione's initiative to publish all Rossini correspondence and biographical and professional documents. In Volume 1, Cagli introduces the project. All volumes include a critical apparatus and list of abbreviations used in nineteenth-century correspondence. Each features indexes of letters and documents; recipients; items dealing with specific compositions; items mentioning specific operas of other composers; references to ballets (with choreographers' names when known); and items noting specific theaters, academies and other musical institutions. Contents are numbered consecutively from volume to volume. Illustrated with engravings and facsimiles.

Other General Collections

30. Allmayer, Alessandro, ed. *Undici lettere di Gioachino Rossini pubblicate per la prima volta in occasione del 1° centenario della nascita di lui, festiggiato in Siena dalla R. Accademia dei Rozzi il giorno II aprile MDCC-CXCII aggiuntivi un brano di musica inedita del sommo maestro e alcuni sparsi sulla musica rossiniana in Siena.* Siena: S. Bernadino, 1892. 50 pp.

Contains transcriptions of Rossini correspondence at Siena's Reale Accademia dei Rozzi. This natal centenary celebration publication also includes a facsimile of a version of "Mi lagnerò tacendo" dated 20 May 1850 in Florence and a chronology of Rossini works performed in Siena from 1814 to 1888. Cited in Schlizter's *Rossini e Siena* (item 53). For other settings of "Mi lagnerò tacendo," see items 8, 16, and 256.

31. Bianchini, Giuseppe Nicolò, ed. *Lettere di Gioaccino [sic] Rossini a Giuseppe Ancillo, speziale Veneziano.* Venice: Ex cordella nell'Orf. Maschile, 1892. xxiv, 35 pp.

[Not examined.]

* *Bollettino del primo centenario rossiniano pubblicato dal comitato ordinatore.* See item 446.

32. Castiglione, Enrico. *Gioachino Rossini: Lettere.* With introductory comments by Giovanni Carli Ballola. Vol. 3 in the series *Musicalia,* ed. Enrico Castiglione. Roma: Logos, 1992. 327 pp. ML410.R8 A4 1992. (N.B.: In the Library of Congress collection, this volume has been assigned the same LC call number as Vol. 1 of the Fondazione Rossini edition, item 29).

Based on the 1902 edition of letters edited by Mazzatinti and the Manises (see item 38), this newly-annotated collection contains 349 letters from Rossini spanning the period between June 1806 to October 1868; fifteen additional letters are undated. The volume also includes a bibliography, an index of recipients, and a general index of names.

33. Cervesato, Michela. "[Venice] Su una sconosciuta raccolta di lettere autografe del Conservatorio B. Marcello di Venezia." *Nuova rivista musicale italiana* 19 [no. 1] (1985): 133–39.

The author introduces this collection of letters, listing its contents by author and inventory number. Among the autograph correspondence are four Rossini items, including a note written in Florence on 7 May 1850 to bass Luigi Lablache recommending an accompanist; Cervesato transcribes the note in her discussion of the archive's contents.

* Inventory of *The Rosaleen Moldenhauer Memorial: Music History from Primary Sources: A Guide to the Moldenhauer Archives*. See item 9.

34. Jarro (Giulio Piccini), ed. *Giovacchino Rossini e la sua famiglia: notizie aneddotiche tolte da documenti inediti*. Florence: R. Bemporad & Figlio, 1902. 37 pp.

   Contains letters to Rossini from his father, Giuseppe, some of which include references to Isabella Colbran with whom the elder Rossini resided in Bologna after her separation from the composer.

35. ———, ed. *Memorie d'un impresario fiorentino [Alessandro Lanari]: Aneddoti inediti, lettere inedite di G. Rossini, G. Donizetti, V. Bellini . . . [ed altri]*. Florence: Loescher e Seeber, ecc., 1892. 156 pp.

   [Not examined.]

36. Klesfisch, Walter. ed. and trans. *Ausgewählte Briefe; mit einer biographischen Skizze von Joseph Marx*. Berlin: P. Zsolnay, 1947. 201 pp. ML410.R8 A35.

   A collection of 186 previously-published letters selected and translated into German. Also includes a brief biography of Rossini.

37. Lippmann, Friedrich. "Briefe Rossinis und Donizettis in der Bibliotek Massimo, Rom." In *Studien zur Italienische-Deutschen Musikgeschichte XII*, 330–35. Ed. Friedrich Lippmann, Vol. 19 of *Analecta musicologica*. Cologne: Arno Volk, 1979.

   Lippmann transcribes the texts of autograph letters in Rome's Bibliotek Massimo. Among the recipients are music publisher Antonio Pacini, tenor Domenico Donzelli, and Joseph Méry of the Paris Opéra. Includes a facsimile.

38. Mazzatinti, G[iuseppe]. *Lettere inedite di Gioacchino Rossini*. Imola, 1890; 2nd ed., *Lettere inediti e rari di G. Rossini*. Imola: Ignazio Galeati, 1892. ix, 207 pp.

   Rev. ed., *Lettere di G. Rossini*, collected and annotated by Mazzatinti with F. [Fanny] and G. Manis, Florence: Barbèra, 1902. vi, 363 pp.; reprinted as Vol. 30, Section 5, of *Bibliotheca musica Bononiensis*. Bologna: A. Forni, 1975. vi, 363 pp. Reprint of 1902 edition: *Rossini Lettere*. Preface by Massimo Mila. Florence: Passigli, 1980. xxvi, 363 pp. ISBN 3-680-038-6.

   A collection of 358 letters from Rossini spanning 1812 to 1868 with annotations that draw on most of the major biographies of the late nineteenth century.

In the 1980 reprint, Mila's preface presents the problems facing those who attempt to decipher Rossini through his correspondence. Garbelotto notes that the letters in this volume have been edited and corrected (see item 44).

* Pougin, Arthur. *Rossini: notes—impressions—souvenirs—commentaires.* See item 130.

* Radiciotti, Giuseppe. *Gioacchino Rossini: Vita documentata, opere ed influenza su l'arte.* See item 164.

* Rognoni, Luigi. *Gioacchino Rossini.* See item 476.

39. Rossini, Gioachino. Letters, Sotheby's Catalogue for Music Auction Friday, 7 December 2001, Lot L01319, 115–23.

The catalogue describes the most important new source for Rossini biographical studies: a bound collection of 249 letters from Rossini's early years as composer. Included in the collection, purchased by the Fondazione Rossini in Pesaro, is correspondence from Rossini to his parents and important letters better documenting the beginning of his relationship with Isabella Colbran. The collection also holds letters in which the composer describes the premieres of his early works, including *L'inganno felice, Ciro in Babilonia,* and the famous account of the first night of *Il barbiere di Siviglia,* now substantiated in Rossini's own words. In addition to revealing his dealings with singers and impresarios, most significant is the new side of the composer unveiled in descriptions of his love for Colbran and his unique relationships with his mother and father. Also auctioned was a letter to the banker Aguado (in the hand of Olympe Pélissier) about Rossini's distress at the sale of the Stabat mater manuscript and a letter of introduction for a baritone who wished to sing in London, sent possibly to Michael Costa (see item 61). Illustrated with facsimiles of several letters in the collection.

40. Titus. "Contributi all'epistolario rossiniano." *Bollettino del Centro Rossiniano di Studi* 3 [no. 1] (1957): 10–13; 3 [no. 2] (1957): 32–34; 4 [no. 3] (1958): 49–50; 4 [no. 4] (1958): 70–73; 4 [no. 5] (1958): 89–91; 4 [no. 6] (1958): 111–13; 4 [no. 1] (1958): 12; 4 [no. 2] (1958): 33–34; 5 [no. 3] (1959): 49–50; 5 [no. 5] (1959): 94–95; 5 [no. 6] (1959): 110–11.

A series that includes Rossini correspondence. See also Schlitzer's earlier series (item 50).

* Zanolini, Antonio. *Biografia di Gioachino Rossini.* See item 138.

STUDIES DRAWN FROM CORRESPONDENCE

The following items are essays on Rossini's correspondence as well as commentaries on archival collections of letters. For information on specific individuals, see the section below, which lists letters by recipient.

41. Alberici, Stefano. "Rossini e Pio IX: Alle luce di documenti inediti dell'Archivio Segreto Vaticano." *Bollettino del Centro Rossiniano di Studi* [no. 1–2] (1977): 5–35.

    Alberici traces his search in the Vatican archives for correspondence between Rossini and Pius IX regarding the composer's request for permission for women's voices in ecclesiastical performances. The author chronicles the agenda by transcribing and commenting on Rossini's correspondence with then-Abbé Franz Liszt, Luigi Ferrucci (Latin scholar who translated and, as Alberici suggests, phrased much of Rossini's missive to the Pope), Nunzio Chigi (whom Rossini asked to deliver the letter to the pontiff) and Padre Placido Abela at Montecassino (to whom Rossini wrote about the Pope's vague reply). Included is a copy in Latin, the Italian translation of the Rossini-Ferrucci letter and Pius IX's reply. Following the article are ten pages of non-paginated plates of facsimiles of Rossini's letter to Pius IX, Nunzio Chigi's presentation letter, and the draft of the Pope's reply.

* Aversano, Luca. "Rossinis französisches Opernschaffen in der Geschäftskorrespondenz deutscher Verleger." In *Rossini in Paris: Eine Veranstaltung des Frankreichzentrums der Universität Leipzig, in Zusammenarbeit mit der Deutschen Rossini Gesellschaft e.V.* See item 290.

42. DiProfio, Alessandro. "Inediti rossiniani a Parigi. Il Fondo Rossini-Hentsch alla Bibliothèque G. Mahler." *Bollettino del Centro Rossiniano di Studi* 35 (1995): 5–59.

    The author introduces and catalogues an important collection of Rossini correspondence and documents donated by the Hentsch family, descendants of Gustave Girod, executor of Olympe Pélissier's estate. The collection contains autographs of Rossini family letters, including some from Rossini to Pélissier; other correspondence, such as letters from Metternich to Rossini; autographs, copies, and publications of the composer's music; other music manuscripts belonging to the composer; iconographic items; and a costume for Figaro purportedly from a production at the Théâtre Italien. The collection also holds Rossini's letters to Franz Liszt and Pius IX requesting the negation of the ban on women singing in church (see Alberici, item 41).

* Fabbri, Paolo. *Rossini nella raccolte Piancastelli di Forlì.* See item 100.

43. ———— and Sergio Monaldini. " 'Delle monete il suon già sento!' Documenti notarili relativi a Gioachino Rossini, possidente." In *Una piacente estate di San Martino: Studi e ricerche per Marcello Conati*, edited by Marco Capra, 77–115. Lucca: Libreria Musicale Italiana, 2000. xiv, 504 pp. ISBN 88-7096-244-X.

The authors examine letters and documents relative to Rossini's business affairs. Included are notarized statements of financial transactions, contracts, and also the dowry arrangements with both Isabella Colbran and Olympe Pélissier. Considers Rossini's property acquisitions and rental properties. The investigation also demonstrates that, contrary to prior belief, Rossini's first name is spelled with one "c" in most legal documents.

44. Garbelotto, Antonio. "Le lettere di Rossini." In *Convegno di studi su Rossini per il Centenario della morte di Gioacchino Rossini*, 156–63. See item 283.

In view of the Fondazione Rossini's plans to publish Rossini's letters, Garbelotto discusses the possibility of discovering Rossini through his letters, passages of which are cited in this article. He also notes the importance of presenting the letters just as Rossini had written them, demonstrating, with an example, that the Mazzatinti-Manis volume (item 38) of the composer's correspondence was edited and corrected.

45. G.[iazotto], R.[emo]. "Due lettere di Rossini." *Nuova rivista musicale italiana* 2 [no. 5] (1968): 970–73.

These two letters offer insight into Rossini's opinion of his operatic works, his finances, and plans for his retirement. The first, written from Paris in November of 1828, replies to an important (but unidentified) recipient in St. Petersburg about possible revisions to *Bianca e Falliero*, which had obviously been selected for production at an important event. Not only does Rossini gracefully refuse the invitation, but he suggests that, of all his operas, only *Guillaume Tell* would be worthy to represent him on this occasion. The second letter, sent from Paris in November of 1856 to his friend, Florentine banker Leopoldo Pini, addresses Rossini's finances and suggests that, at a certain point, he had considered spending his remaining days in Florence.

46. Johnson, Janet. "Rossini in Bologna and Paris during the early 1830s: New Letters." *Revue de Musicologie* 79, [no. 1] (1993): 63–81.

The discovery of the drafts of six letters, found among papers dealing with the Théâtre Italien, helps to document a lacuna in Rossini's biography. The correspondence, dictated to Théâtre Italien's director Édouard Robert, demonstrates that, rather than retiring after *Guillaume Tell*, Rossini not only continued to have an influence in the world of Parisian opera but also had every intention of composing another work for the stage. The six letters (to critics Valentin de Lapelouze and Louis Vitet, Opéra director Émile Lubbert, Vicomte Sosthène de La Rochefoucauld of the Beaux Arts, *Tell* librettist Hipolyte Bis, and a M. Pellot) are transcribed (but not translated) at the end of the article. See also Johnson, item 754.

47. Kallberg, Jeffrey. "Marketing Rossini: Sei lettere di Troupenas ad Artaria." Translated into Italian by Marco Spada. *Bollettino del Centro Rossiniano di Studi*, no. 1–3 (1980): 41–63.

The author suggests that the study of music publishers' correspondence not only yields information about editions and sales of scores but also public taste. Kallberg considers six letters between Rossini's French publisher Eugène Troupenas and Artaria and Co. of Vienna in connection with the rights for *Le siège de Corinth*, *Le comte Ory*, and *Guillaume Tell*. He not only provides a history of their negotiations but also demonstrates that publishers' largest profits came from the sales of arrangements rather than materials for productions. Moreover, Rossini's widespread popularity was due more to the sale of these arrangements than to productions of his works. Includes transcriptions of the Troupenas-Artaria correspondence and a table outlining the negotiations for *Guillaume Tell*.

* Müller, Reto. "Rossini-Bibliotheken der Welt: Der Fonds Michotte in Brüssels." See item 12.

* ———. "Rossini-Bibliotheken der Welt: Die Sammlung Piancastelli in Forlì." See item 13.

48. Schlizter, F[ranco]. "Accenni a Rossini nelle lettere degli altri." *Bollettino del Centro Rossiniano di Studi*, [no. 1] (1956): 13–14; [no. 2] (1956): 31–32; [no. 4] (1957): 67–69; [no. 5] (1957): 88–89; [no. 6] (1957): 107–108.

In this series, the author quotes extracts from the correspondence of composers, singers, theater administrators and impresarios which references Rossini. Among those quoted are Giovanni Pacini, Domenico Barbaja, Giuditta Pasta, Carlo Severini, and Franz Liszt.

49. ———. "Commendatizie, affettuosità, affari, specialità gastronomiche ed altre cose in dieci lettere inedite di Rossini." In *Rossiniana: Contributo all'epistolario di G. Rossini*. Item 52, 17–32.

Schlitzer transcribes and comments on ten Rossini letters in the archive of the Accademia Chigiana in Siena. Among the recipients are Neapolitan impresario Domenico Barbaja; Count Antonio Montanari of the Liceo Musicale in Bologna; banker Luigi Ferrucci and attorney Leopoldo Pini, who both helped Rossini with his affairs in Florence; bassoonist Antonio Zoboli, who had served as a witness when Rossini wed Olympe Pélissier in 1846; Marchese Antonio Busca, who often sent the composer gorgonzola cheese; and several unidentified persons.

50. ———. "Contributo all'epistolario rossiniano." *Bollettino del Centro Rossiniano di Studi* 2 [no. 3] (1956): 43–47; 2 [no. 4] (1956): 63–67; 2 [no. 5] (1956): 83–87; 2 [no. 6] (1956): 109–111; 2 [no. 1] (1956): 13–14; 2 [no. 2] (1956): 29–31.

A series in the early editions of the *Bollettino* in which Schlizter presented the texts and commentaries on Rossini correspondence, most of which had previously appeared in other sources. Volume 2, nos. 4, 5, and 6 (1956) contain correspondence between Carlo Severini, artistic director of the Théâtre Italien, with whom Rossini maintained a close friendship.

51. ———. "Ricordi e lettere in Siena," in *Rossini e Siena e altri scritti rossiniani (con lettere inedite). Quaderni dell'Accademia Chigiana*, 7–16. See item 53.

Schlitzer catalogues Rossini correspondence in the archives of Siena. Included are transcriptions of correspondence from Rossini to Ferdinando Giorgetti, Antonio French, Giuseppe Spada, and from Isabella Colbran and her father, Giovanni. Some letters in the Siena collection are transcribed in Schlizter's *Rossiniana* (item 52). See also Allmayer, item 30.

52. ———. *Rossiniana: Contributo all'epistolario di G. Rossini. Quaderni dell'Accademia Chigiana*, Vol. 35 (1956). 32 pp. ML5.C38 Vol. 35.

Contains two essays, one dealing with a letter Rossini wrote to Charles-Ernest Beulé (see item 58) and a second, with transcriptions and commentaries on Rossini correspondence in the archive of Siena's Accademia Chigiana (see item 49).

53. ———. *Rossini e Siena e altri scritti rossiniani (con lettere inedite). Quaderni dell'Accademia Chigiana*, Vol. 39 (1958) 80 pp. ML5.C38 Vol. 39.

In his first essay, Schlitzer discusses and lists correspondence from and pertaining to Rossini found in archives in Siena (see item 51). Several of the letters are transcribed, and one is partially presented in facsimile. The second documents performances of Rossini's works in Siena, whether in theatrical productions, *accademia* concerts, or recitals. Supported with citations from newspapers and critics, Schlitzer considers casts, individual performers, and theatrical personnel, especially noting local personalities. An appendix catalogues piano/vocal scores and other music of Rossini's housed in the library of the Accademia Chigiana. Schlitzer completes the volume with two character studies: one of Rossini's fellow composer and friend Angelo Catelani (item 218) and the other of Carlo Severini (see item 243), his friend and colleague at the Théâtre Italien.

54. Torrefranca, Fausto. "Parere musicale del 1851." *Bollettino del Centro Rossiniano di Studi* 2 [No. 3] (1956): 41–43.

The author transcribes and comments on a letter in which Rossini corrects the notion that singers "create" roles. Only the composer and the poet create, he maintains; singers interpret.

* Verdi, Luigi, ed. *Rossini a Bologna: Note documentarie in occasione della mostra "Rossini a Bologna,"* 29 Feb.–1 Apr. 2000. See item 104.

55. Walker, Frank. "Rossiniana in the Piancastelli Collection." Part 1: "Miscellaneous Unpublished Letters." *The Monthly Musical Record* 90 (July-August 1960): 138–47.

Walker briefly introduces the Piancastelli collection at the Biblioteca Comunale in Forlí, the contents of which include some 812 autograph letters of Rossini, as well as correspondence of Isabella Colbran and Olympe Pélissier. Letters to and about the composer are also found in this rich archive as are documents, iconographic materials, and press clippings. In Part I, Walker transcribes a sampling of letters, including missives to Domenico Barbaja, letters relating to the death of Giuseppe Rossini, and correspondence about Rossini's illness. See item 61 for Part 2.

LETTERS ORGANIZED BY CORRESPONDENT

Ancillo, Giuseppe
* Bianchini, Giuseppe Nicolò, ed. *Lettere di Gioaccino* [sic] *Rossini a Giuseppe Ancillo, speziale Veneziano.* See item 31.

Arditi, Luigi
* Cagli, Bruno. "Rossini e Luigi Arditi. Una testimonianza e un carteggio." See item 213.

Balocchino, Carlo

56. Schlitzer, Franco. *Un piccolo carteggio inedito di Rossini con un impresario italiano a Vienna.* Florence: Sansoni Antiquariato, 1959. 20 pp. ML410.R8 S2.

Schlitzer introduces the correspondence between Rossini and Carlo Balocchino, impresario at Vienna's Kärtnertortheater from 1836 to 1848. The first letter, written to Rossini in 1836, invited the composer to write an opera for Vienna. The others dealt with singers, five with tenor Nicola Ivanoff, for whom Rossini often interceded, and one recommending Elena Viganò.

Barbaja (Barbaia), Domenico

*Schlitzer, Franco. "Commendatizie, affettuosità, affari, specialità gastronomiche ed altre cose in dieci lettere inedite di Rossini." See item 49.

* ———. "Accenni a Rossini nelle lettere degli altri." See item 48.

* ———. "Ricordi e lettere in Siena." See item 51.

* Walker, Frank. "Rossiniana in the Piancastelli Collection." Part 1: "Miscellaneous Unpublished Letters." See item 55.

Benelli, Giovanni Battista

57. Cagli, Bruno. "Rossini a Londra e al Théâtre Italian di Parigi: Documenti inediti dell'impresario G. B. Benelli." *Bollettino del Centro Rossiniano di Studi* [no. 1–3] (1981): 5–53.

Correspondence to impresario Giovanni Battista Benelli sheds new light on Rossini in London and Paris. Of particular interest are the letters of composer Ferdinando Paër and tenor Giulio Marco Bordogni, who, with Benelli, engaged in spiteful exchanges about Rossini's activities. Benelli's letters also clarify issues about Rossini's London commission, *Ugo, re d'Italia* (see item 784) and the work planned for Giuditta Pasta, *La figlia dell'aria* (see items 754 and 818). Cagli includes an annotated list of the Benelli correspondence as well as transcriptions of the relevant letters from Paër and Bordogni.

Beulé, Charles-Ernest

58. Schlitzer, Franco. "Rossini, Beulé e un 'elogio' di Meyerbeer." In *Rossiniana: Contributo all'epistolario di G. Rossini*, Item 52, 7–18.

A year after the death of Giacomo Meyerbeer, famed archaeologist and secretary of the Académie des Beaux-Arts Charles-Ernest Beulé eulogized the composer. Schlitzer transcribes and comments on Rossini's letter of response, demonstrating the friendship which Rossini shared with Beulé, who several years later would eulogize Rossini as an "Italian maestro, French composer" (see item 394). With a facsimile of the letter's autograph.

* ———. "Ricordi e lettere in Siena." See item 51.

Bis, Hipolyte

* Johnson, Janet. "Rossini in Bologna and Paris during the early 1830s: New Letters." See item 46.

Böhme, Carl Gotthelf (for C.F. Peters)

59. Aversano, Luca. "Brief des Musikverlages C.F. Peters an Rossini." *La Gazzetta* 7 (1997): 8–11.

The text of this letter, found in the correspondence copybook of the German music publishing firm C.F. Peters, details an attempt to procure from Rossini the rights to a piano transcription of *Guillaume Tell*. In his commentary, Aversano cites Jeffrey Kallberg's study (see item 47) which clarifies many of the issues of the composer's negotiations with music publishers. Includes a transcription of the letter and a translation into German.

Braga, Gaetano

60. Braga, Antonio. "La grande amicizia tra Gioacchino Rossini e Gaetano Braga." *Agimus* 14 [no. 4] (April-May 1969): 1–2.

Not examined. The RILM abstract notes that the article contains a transcription and facsimile of a letter from Rossini to cellist Gaetano Braga as well as biography of the musician. See also item 256.

Busca, Marchese Antonio

* Schlitzer, Franco. "Commendatizie, affettuosità, affari, specialità gastronomiche ed altre cose in dieci lettere inedite di Rossini." See item 49.

* ———. "Ricordi e lettere in Siena." See item 51.

Colbran, Giovanni

* Schlitzer, Franco. "Ricordi e lettere in Siena." See item 51.

Colbran, Isabella

* Schlitzer, Franco. "Ricordi e lettere in Siena." See item 51.

* Walker, Frank. "Rossiniana in the Piancastelli Collection." Part 1: "Miscellaneous Unpublished Letters." See item 55.

Costa, Michele (Costa, Sir Michael)

61. Walker, Frank. "Rossiniana in the Piancastelli Collection." Part 2: "Correspondence with Michele Costa." *The Monthly Musical Record* 90 (November-December 1960): 203–13.

A continuation of the discussion of contents in Piancastello archive. Part 2 considers forty-four letters to conductor/composer Michele Costa (later Sir Michael Costa) in England. Walker provides examples of this correspondence, which demonstrate not only Rossini's fatherly concern for Costa but also his generosity in paving the way for performers on their way to London. See items 55 (part 1), 13, and 100.

Donzelli, Domenico

* Lippmann, Friedrich. "Briefe Rossinis und Donizettis in der Bibliotek Massimo, Rom." See item 37.

* Modugno, Maurizio. "Domenico Donzelli e il suo tempo." See item 272.

Ferrucci, Luigi Cristostomo

* Alberici, Stefano. "Rossini e Pio IX: Alle luce di documenti inediti dell'Archivio Segreto Vaticano." See item 41.

* *Bollettino del primo centenario rossiniano pubblicato dal comitato ordinatore.* See item 446.

* Schlitzer, Franco. "Commendatizie, affettuosità, affari, specialità gastronomiche ed altre cose in dieci lettere inedite di Rossini." See item 49.

* ———. "Ricordi e lettere in Siena." See item 51.

Filippu, Filippo

62. "Lettre a un critique musical." *Textuel* 18 (1986): 26.

Not examined. According to the RILM abstract, this article presents the translation of part of a letter, dated 26 August 1868, from Rossini to critic Filippo Filippu.

French, Antonio

63. Müller, Reto. "Brief von Rossini an Antonio French." *La Gazzetta* 1 [no. 2] (1991): 6–8.

In his commentary, on this thank-you note to French for a gift of cigars, the author suggests a history of Rossini's years as a smoker, based on comments made by Ferdinand Hiller (see items 141 and 219). Includes a transcription of the note and a German translation.

* Schlitzer, Franco. "Ricordi e lettere in Siena." See item 51.

Giorgetti, Ferdinando

64. Fabbri, Mario. "Ignoti momenti rossiniani: Contributo all'indagine sul 'lungo silenzio' di Rossini e alla conoscenza dell'attività creativa minore del maestro—Le segrete confessioni a Ferdinando Giorgetti e le sconosciute 'Variazioni' per Alessandro Abate (1817)." *Chigiana* 25 [no. 5] (1968): 265–85.

Fabbri identifies Rossini as the recipient of an 1852 letter from Ferdinando Giorgetti. He then suggests that its contents are linked to the "long silence" in the composer's life when he was tormented by depression and illness. Fabbri explains the references in the letter, in which Giorgetti responded to Rossini's thoughts of death and his grave self-doubts and shame. A post-script in the letter led Fabbri to the discovery of a set of clarinet variations by Rossini. The author spends the remainder of the article discussing the work, supported with score examples from his edition of it. Illustrations include a facsimile of a letter from Rossini to Giorgetti and of the title page of the clarinet variations.

* Schlitzer, Franco. "Ricordi e lettere in Siena." See item 51.

Lablache, Luigi

* Cervesato, Michela. "[Venice] Su una sconosciuta raccolta di lettere auto-grafe del Conservatorio B. Marcello di Venezia." See item 33.

Lanari, Alessandro

* Jarro (Giulio Piccini), ed. *Memorie d'un impresario fiorentino [Alessandro Lanari]: Aneddoti inediti, lettere inedite di G. Rossini, G. Donizetti, V. Bellini . . . [ed altri]*. See item 35.

Liszt, Franz

* Alberici, Stefano. "Rossini e Pio IX: Alle luce di documenti inediti dell' Archivio Segreto Vaticano." See item 41.

* DiProfio, Alessandro. "Inediti rossiniani a Parigi. Il Fondo Rossini-Hentsch alla Bibliothèque G. Mahler." See item 42.

65. "Le donne in chiesa." *Bollettino del Centro Rossiniano di Studi* 1 [no. 2] (1955): 30–31.

This letter from Rossini to Franz Liszt explained the former's desire to have papal permission to allow female voices to sing in churches, specifically in performances of the Petite messe solennelle. See also item 41.

* Schlizter, F[ranco]. "Accenni a Rossini nelle lettere degli altri." See item 48.

Marzari, G.B.
> * Simionato, Giuliano. "Rossini, Canova, e Treviso: I rapporti tra il musicista e la città veneta esaminati attraverso documenti inediti ed un autografo." See item 373.

Méry, Joseph
> * Gautier, Théophile. *La Musique*. See item 759.

> * Lippmann, Friedrich. "Briefe Rossinis und Donizettis in der Bibliotek Massimo, Rom." See item 37.

Metternich, Prince Klemens von
> * DiProfio, Alessandro. "Inediti rossiniani a Parigi. Il Fondo Rossini-Hentsch alla Bibliothèque G. Mahler." See item 42.

Mignani, Angelo
> * Inventory of *The Rosaleen Moldenhauer Memorial: Music History from Primary Sources: A Guide to the Moldenhauer Archives*. See item 9.

66. Müller, Reto. "Brief von Rossini an Angelo Mignani." *La Gazzetta* 1 (1992): 6–7.

> Müller provides a transcription, German translation, and commentary of this letter to Mignani, who, from Rossini's flight from Bologna in 1848 until his death, remained one of the composer's most valuable friends and agents in that city (and later executor of his will). As the author suggests, this letter demonstrates Rossini's obsession with details during his psychological crises and also his nostalgia at the loss of those he held dear.

Montanari, Count Antonio
> * Schlitzer, Franco. "Commendatizie, affettuosità, affari, specialità gastronomiche ed altre cose in dieci lettere inedite di Rossini." See item 49.

> * ———. "Ricordi e lettere in Siena." See item 51.

Morandi, Rosa
> * Schlitzer, Franco. "Ricordi e lettere in Siena." See item 51.

Pacini, Antonio
> * Lippmann, Friedrich. "Briefe Rossinis und Donizettis in der Bibliotek Massimo, Rom." See item 37.

Pacini, Giovanni
> * Inventory of *The Rosaleen Moldenhauer Memorial: Music History from Primary Sources: A Guide to the Moldenhauer Archives*. See item 9.

* *Le mie memorie artistiche (edite ed inedite): Autobiografia del Maestro Cav. Giovanni Pacini riscontrata sugli autografi e pubblicata da Ferdinando Magnani*. See item 129.

The appendix includes transcriptions of eight letters from Rossini to Pacini. Among their topics are Rossini's thoughts on Pacini's published memoirs, Pacini's role in the repatriation of Bellini's remains for reburial in Sicily, and the oft-cited comments on Rossini's retirement from the musical stage.

* Schlizter, F[ranco]. "Accenni a Rossini nelle lettere degli altri." See item 48.

Pasqui, Leopoldo

67. Müller, Reto. "Brief von Rossini an Lepoldo [sic] Pasqui." *La Gazzetta* 4 [no. 1] 1994: 11–12.

In this letter, dated 2 July 1852, Rossini wrote to Florentine cartographer and architect Leopoldo Pasqui, excusing himself for not visiting Pasqui prior to leaving for Montecatini (whence the letter was sent). The composer states his intentions to see Pasqui upon his return to Florence. Most likely, the subject of the visit was Rossini's intention of purchasing a house there since he had recently—and definitively—left Bologna. Although a later hand identified a certain "Sig. C." as historian Gino Capponi, Müller proposes that Rossini may have been making a crude reference to a third party. Includes a transcription of the letter and a German translation.

Pasta, Giuditta

* Schlizter, F[ranco]. "Accenni a Rossini nelle lettere degli altri." See item 48.

Pélissier, Olympe

68. Cambi, Luisa. "Bellini—un pacchetto di autografi." In *Scritti in onore di Luigi Ronga*, 53–90. Milan-Naples: R. Ricciardi, 1973. ix, 669 pp. ML55.R63 1973.

Although the main subject of this essay is the correspondence of Vincenzo Bellini, Cambi briefly discusses a letter, probably dating from 1855, written by Olympe Pélissier to Pietro Folo, a Roman attorney seeking biographical information on Bellini. Responding for her husband, Pélissier comments on Bellini's final days and Rossini's role in the production of *I puritani*.

* DiProfio, Alessandro. "Inediti rossiniani a Parigi. Il Fondo Rossini-Hentsch alla Bibliothèque G. Mahler." See item 42.

69. "Lettere della Pélissier." *Bollettino del Centro Rossiniano di Studi* 8 [no. 4] (1967): 70–72.

Four undated letters written by Olympe Pélissier are transcribed in this brief article; its anonymous author suggests that they demonstrate a certain ostentatiousness as well as a desire to rise to the social and intellectual level of the people with whom she corresponded on Rossini's behalf.

70. "Perplessità della Pélissier per la traslazione della salma di Rossini." *Bollettino del Centro Rossiniano di Studi* [no. 1] (1955): 10–12.

This article gives the background and text of a letter that Rossini's widow wrote to the Minister of Public Instruction in Florence. In it, Pélissier argues against the transfer of her husband's remains to Italy, maintaining that, because of demonstrations against him in Bologna in 1848, he had expressed the desire to be buried in France.

* Riboli, Bruno. "Profilo medico-psicologico di Gioacchino Rossini." See item 194.

71. Schlizter, F[ranco]. "Nozze di Rossini." *Bollettino del Centro Rossiniano di Studi* 2 [no. 6] (1956): 112–13.

In this letter to her friend Hector Couvert in Paris, Olympe Pélissier announces her marriage to Rossini, 16 August 1846. Schlitzer comments on the letter, providing details on how Rossini met his second wife.

* Walker, Frank. "Rossiniana in the Piancastelli Collection." Part 1: "Miscellaneous Unpublished Letters." See item 55.

Pini, Leopoldo
* G.[iazotto], R.[emo]. "Due lettere di Rossini." See item 45.

72. Müller, Reto. "Brief von Rossini an Leopoldo Pini." *La Gazzetta* 6 (1996): 10–14.

In this letter, previously presented by Schlitzer (see item 73), Rossini gives lawyer Leopoldo Pini authorization to access funds and instructions to prepare items from Rossini's household in Florence for transport to his villa in Passy. Pini, who worked as Rossini's agent in Florence, is told what items are to be shipped and what is to be sold. Müller includes a transcription of the original letter and a German translation.

* Schlitzer, Franco. "Commendatizie, affettuosità, affari, specialità gastronomiche ed altre cose in dieci lettere inedite di Rossini." See item 49.

73. ———. *Mobili e immobili di Rossini, lettere inedite a un avvocato.* Florence: L. Lapiccirella, 1957. 22 pp.

This volume contains correspondence, dating from 1857 to 1858, from Rossini to lawyer Leopoldo Pini who handled the composer's real estate and business affairs in Florence. An illustration shows two of the three houses that Rossini owned on the Via Larga.

* ———. "Ricordi e lettere in Siena." See item 51.

Pius IX

* Alberici, Stefano. "Rossini e Pio IX: Alle luce di documenti inediti dell'Archivio Segreto Vaticano." See item 41.

74. "Una lettera della Pélissier al Papa e la risposta della Segreteria di Stato." *Bollettino del Centro Rossiniano di Studi* 1 [no. 2] (1955): 28–30.

Item 70 presents a letter in which Rossini's widow protested the attempt to move her husband's remains to Florence. The letters transcribed herein are Pélissier's attempt to engage Pius IX in her crusade and the draft of a response by the Vatican's Secretary of State, noting that the composer had left her with the right to decide where he would be buried.

Ricordi, Giovanni

75. M[ila], M[assimo]. "Un 'Miserere' sconosciuto di Rossini." *Nuova rivista musicale italiana* 2 [no. 5] (1968): 973–75.

In a letter to Giovanni Ricordi, dated 26 February 1848, Rossini discusses the existence of a "Misererino," a youthful composition whose autograph had been given to a certain Grimani (identified by Guido Johannes Joerg as Filippo Grimani—see item 788). Mila also mentions the composer's 1847 "Tantum ergo," the publication of which Ricordi had delayed. Includes a facsimile of the letter.

76. Müller, Reto. "Brief von Rossini an Giovanni Ricordi." *La Gazzetta* 1 (1993): 10–12.

This 1843 missive to music publisher Giovanni Ricordi deals with two issues: Polish composer Franciszek Mirecki's interest in the post of professor at the Liceo Musicale in Bologna and the publication of music by Parisian publisher Aulagnier. Rossini, who had tried to recruit composers such as Gaetano Donizetti, Saverio Mercadante, and Giovanni Pacini for the Liceo post, felt that Mirecki's reputation was not illustrious enough. He also assured Ricordi that the pieces announced by Aulagnier were not his but rather the work of another composer.

Robert, Édouard

* Johnson, Janet. "Rossini in Bologna and Paris during the early 1830s: New Letters." See item 46.

Rossi, Gaetano

* Cavazzocca Mazzatinti, Vittorio. "Rossini a Verona durante il Congresso del 1822." See item 817.

Rossini, Giuseppe

* Jarro (Giulio Piccini), ed. *Giovacchino Rossini e la sua famiglia: notizie aneddotiche tolte da documenti inediti.* See item 34.

Santocanale, Filippo

77. De Rensis, Raffaello. "Rossini intimo: Lettere all'amico Santocanale." *Musica d'oggi* 13 [no. 8–9] (August-September 1931): 343–53.

The author transcribes letters from Rossini to Filippo Santocanale, an attorney in Palermo. Aside from their friendship, the two were connected by Isabella Colbran's legal affairs in Sicily. Topics of the letters include efforts toward Italian unification, in which Santocanale was involved; Vincenzo Bellini; and Rossini's final illness.

* Grembler, Martina. *Rossini e la patria: Studien zu Leben und Werk Gioachino Rossinis vor dem Hintergrund des Risorgimento.* See item 200.

78. Müller, Reto. "Brief von Rossini an Filippo Santocanale." *La Gazzetta* 8 (1998): 19–21.

In this 1842 letter to the Sicilian lawyer who handled the legal affairs the composer inherited from Colbran, Rossini discusses business and health issues. The letter demonstrates the emotional crisis the composer was suffering during this period. Includes a transcription of the letter and a German translation.

Sayn-Wittgenstein, Carolyne

79. Müller, Reto. "Ein Brief aus Weimar an Rossini in Wildbad." *La Gazzetta* 9 (1999): 16–21.

This letter, dated 16 July, was written by Princess Carolyne Wittgenstein on behalf of Franz Liszt. Sent to Rossini, then in Wildbad taking a cure of medicinal baths, the letter not only invited the composer to visit Liszt in nearly Weimar but also mentioned Liszt's piano transcriptions of the Stabat mater and of the chorus "La charité," which should have been delivered to Rossini in Paris by Wittgenstein's nephew. The princess also reminds Rossini that he had been voice teacher to her mother, Countess Pauline Podeska, while he was in Vienna in 1822. Müller notes that Richard Pohl, a journalist in the camp of the New German school, who had been entrusted with delivering the letter to Rossini, may not have been successful, for the composer may have left Wildbad before the letter arrived. Contains a transcription of the letter, a translation into German, and Müller's commentary.

Severini, Carlo

* Schlizter, F[ranco]. "Accenni a Rossini nelle lettere degli altri." See item 48.

* ———. "Contributo all'epistolario rossiniano." See item 50

* ———. "Severini e la 'Severiniana.'" See item 243.

Spada, Giuseppe

* Schlitzer, Franco. "Ricordi e lettere in Siena." See item 51.

Treitschke, Georg Friedrich

80. Müller, Reto, and Bernd-Rüdiger Kern. "Rossinis Verhandlungen mit dem Darmstädter Hoftheater." *La Gazzetta* 5 (1995): 3–7.

Müller introduces a letter from Rossini to Friedrich Treitschke, Ludwig I of Hessen-Darmstadt's theatrical agent, in which the composer acknowledges a request to perform *Zelmira* at the granducal theater. The composer gives his authorization for the production at a price of 20 ducats. Kern then presents a receipt signed by Rossini for 30 ducats, his price for the opera's score. Both the letter and receipt are transcribed, translated into German, and discussed in the commentary, which also examines Rossini's relationship with the Darmstadt theater. See also item 263.

Verdi, Giuseppe

* Gossett, Philip. "A new Romanza for *Attila*." See item 276.

* Petrobelli, Pierluigi. "Rossini nell'opera e nella vita di Verdi." See item 423.

Zoboli, Antonio

* Schlitzer, Franco. "Commendatizie, affettuosità, affari, specialità gastronomiche ed altre cose in dieci lettere inedite di Rossini." See item 49.

* ———. "Ricordi e lettere in Siena." See item 51.

ROSSINI'S STYLE AND LANGUAGE IN CORRESPONDENCE

81. Macinante, Umberto. "Francesismi d'ambito teatrale e metafore di tradizione figurativa nel carteggio Verdi-Boito." In *Le parole della musica*,

I: Studi sulla lingua delle letteratura musicale in onore di Gianfranco Folena, 287–309. Vol. 21 of *Studi di Musica Veneta*. Eds. Fiamma Nicolodi and Paolo Trovato. Florence: Leo S. Olschki, 1994 viii, 424 pp. ISBN 88-222-4284 X ML63.P26 1994 Vol. 1.

Although the majority of his study deals with Verdi, the author concludes, from a sampling of 246 letters, that Rossini, too, adopted French terms in correspondence, although the composer was more likely to use that vocabulary colloquially than in reference to theatrical matters.

3

Iconographies and Exhibition Catalogs

BIOGRAPHICAL ICONOGRAPHY

* Alverà, Pierluigi. *Rossini*. Item 170.

* Bruson, Jean-Marie. "Rossini in der Karikatur." In *Rossini in Paris: Eine Veranstaltung des Frankreichzentrums der Universität Leipzig, in Zusammenarbeit mit der Deutschen Rossini Gesellschaft e.V.* See item 290.

* —— and Martine Kahane. *Rossini et Paris*. Item 321.

82. Diotallevi, Daniele. "Le 'miserie' cavalleresche di Rossini." *Bollettino del Centro Rossiniano di Studi* 37 (1997): 69–119.

   Rossini was the recipient of numerous decorations and titles, including those of Commendatore and Cavalliere. Often, information about these honors has been gleaned from the composer's correspondence or from contemporary iconography in which he is depicted wearing decorations (one such painting is featured on the *Bollettino*'s cover). According to the author, lists of Rossini's honors, including the one compiled by Giuseppe Radiciotti (see item 164), often misidentify the title accompanying the award or even the reason Rossini received it. Limiting the scope of this essay to the twenty decorations at the Tempietto Rossiniano in Pesaro, the author offers a physical description of each medal (illustrated by a color photo of its verso and recto), along with the general history of the decoration and, when known, the date it was conferred.

83. Joerg, Guido Johannes, and Rüdiger Krüger. "Plaudereien über Rossini." *La Gazzetta* 3 (1993): 5–27.

An iconographic narrative of Rossini portraits from Reto Müller's private collection (see also item 85). The authors not only consider the composer's life as told through the pictures but also the histories of the portraits themselves.

* Maione, Paologiovanni, and Francesca Seller, eds. *Gioachino Rossini*. See item 358.

84. Melica, Ada. "La casa di Rossini, oggi." *Bollettino del Centro Rossiniano di Studi* [no. 1] (1955): 4–9.

Melica lists the contents of the items on exhibit in the various rooms of Rossini's birth house in Pesaro. Items include portraits of the composer, his family, and fellow composers and interpreters of his music, as well as letters and documents collected by the Fondazione Rossini. See item 97 for a more recent description of the house's contents.

85. Müller, Reto, ed. *Hommage an Rossini: Katalog zur Ausstellung*. Vol. 3 of the *Schriftenreihe der Deutschen Rossini Gesellschaft e.V.* Leipzig: Leipziger Universitätsverlag, 1999. 160 pp. ISBN: 3-933240-80-8.

A catalog of Rossini iconography from lithographs, engravings, caricatures, photographs, and postcards in the collection of the editor. Arranged chronologically from an 1814 lithograph to Gustave Doré's deathbed sketch, the pictures are accompanied by the editor's ample commentary, which, when known, gives the history of the entries.

* Museo di Casa Rossini (www.fondazione.scavolini.com/iniziativo/casa_rossini/). See item 361.

86. Pagan, Victor. *Rossini en la Villa y Corte: Estudio iconografico*. Madrid: n.p., 1992.

[Not examined.]

87. ———. "Un italiano en Madrid: Gioacchino Rossini (estudio de iconografia)." *Revista de musicologia* 18 [no. 1–2] (1995): 229–45.

Pagan demonstrates that Madrid reveled in "Rossini fever" along with the rest of Europe. This reaction can still be measured by the presence of numerous iconographic remembrances throughout the city. Also includes brief discussions about the artists who created these works (sculpted busts, paintings, and decorative fans). Pagan maintains that no other Italian composer left so lasting an imprint on the city.

* Radiciotti, Giuseppe. *Gioacchino Rossini: Vita documentata, opere ed influenza su l'arte*. See Vol. 4, Appendix 4 (item 164).

88. Ragni, Sergio. "Il problema del ritratto." In *Rossini 1792–1992* (item 95), pp. 17–42.

   Ragni considers the question of Rossini iconography in this essay, illustrated with pictures of portraits, busts, sketches, engravings, and photographs. Ragni notes how the works not only demonstrate how Rossini appeared physically but also how he was represented as a man and an artist.

   * Scherliess, Volker. *Gioacchino Rossini mit Selbstzeugnissen und Bilddokumenten*. See item 184.

SCENOGRAPHIC ICONOGRAPHY

   * Bartlet, M. Elizabeth C. "Rossini e l'Académie Royale de Musique a Parigi." Item 316.

89. Bartlet, M. Elizabeth C. with Mauro Bucarelli. *Guillaume Tell di Gioachino Rossini: fonti iconografiche*. Vol. 1 in the series *Iconografia Rossiniana*. Pesaro: Fondazione Rossini, 1996. 227 pp.

   [Not examined.]

90. Biggi, Maria Ida, and Carla Ferraro, eds. *Rossini sulla scena dell'Ottocento. Bozzetti e figurini dalla collezioni italiane*. Vol. 2 in the series *Iconografia rossiniana*. Pesaro: Fondazione Rossini, 2001. xix, 269 pp.

   A collection of illustrations from Italian archives of stage sets and costumes for premieres and subsequent mountings of Rossini operas. Includes French productions as well as the *pasticci Ivanhoé* and *Robert Bruce*.

91. Cagli, Bruno, and Franco Mariotti. *Il teatro Rossini: Le nuove edizioni e la messinscena contemporanea*. Testimonies by Gae Aulenti, Roberto de Simone, Emanuele Luzzati, Pier Luigi Pizzi, Jean-Pierre Ponnelle, Luca Ronconi, and Luigi Squarzina. Historical and critical notes by Marco Spada. Milan: Ricordi, 1992. 269 pp. ISBN 88-7592-365-5 ML410.R8 T43 1992.

   A volume of illustrations from modern productions of twenty of Rossini's operas. Contains a brief discussion of the "Rossini Renaissance" and comments from directors. Concludes with a chronology of Rossini's life and a works list based on the critical edition of Rossini's works.

92. Cohen, H. Robert, with Sylvia L'Écuyer Lacroix and Jacques Léveillé. *Les Gravures dans "L'Illustration."* 3 vols. Quebec: Les Presses de L'Université Laval, 1983. Vol. 1—1843–1863, xcv, 521 pp.; Vol. 2—1864–1899,

522–1162; Vol. 3—Critical Apparatus, li, 173. ISBN 2-7637-6833-4
ML270.4.G7 1983 Vols. 1–3.

A catalog of engravings of musical and operatic subjects from the weekly
French news magazine *L'Illustration*. The volume features portraits of
famed Rossini interpreters and a photograph of the composer himself taken
shortly before he died. Vol. 3 includes an index; appendices with lists of
artists and sculptors, photographers, engravers, and references to issue numbers and corresponding years. A supplement contains engravings of musical
items of minor importance.

* Viale Ferrero, Mercedes. "Per Rossini: un primo tentative di iconografia
scenografica." See item 28.

EXHIBITION CATALOGS

93. Bibliothèque-Musée de l'Opéra. *Rossini a l'Opéra*. Paris: Bibliothèque
    Nationale de France—Opéra National Vuitton, 1992. 16 pp.

    A catalog of an exhibition held from 29 October 1992 to 3 February 1993 at
    the Bibliothèque-Musée de l'Opéra. Includes a list of Rossini operas per-
    formed at the Salle Le Peletier and the Palais Garnier.

94. Bruson, Jean-Marie, ed. *Rossini à Paris, Musée Carnavalet, 27 October– 31
    December 1992*. Paris-Alençonnaise, 1992. 207 pp. ISBN 2-90-1414-43-5
    ML141.P18R67 1992.

    This exhibition catalog features ample illustrations, many in color, which
    document Rossini's relationships with the Théâtre Italien, the interpreters of
    his Paris productions, the music composed during his tenure in France, and
    the famous *soirées chez Rossini*. An excellent treatment of Rossini and his
    place in the cultural and social milieu during his Parisian tenure. Rossini is
    depicted in both portraits and photographs in this bicentennial exhibition
    catalog.

95. Bucarelli, Mauro, ed. *Rossini 1792–1992: Mostra storico-documentaria*.
    Perugia: Electa Editori Umbri, 1992. 397 pp. ISBN 88-435-3959-0
    ML141.P47 R68 1992.

    A sumptuously illustrated catalog of the Rossini exhibition held in Pesaro
    from 27 June to 30 September 1992. Also contains essays by major Rossini
    scholars on various aspects of the composer's life and career (see items 88,
    139, 173, 187, 261, 266, 302, 307, 316, 323, 338, 351, 356, 360, 363, 370,
    376, 607, and 867); topics include iconography, Rossini's rapport with cities
    in which he lived and worked, his singers, and editions of his music. The

book contains a catalog of items in the exhibit. With an introduction by Bruno Cagli, Bucarelli, and Fabrizio Scipioni.

96. ———, ed. *Rossini e Firenze: Immagini e note*. Florence: Silvana, 1993. 102 pp. ISBN 88-366-0416-1 ML141.F6 R67 1993.

A catalog, with text commentary by Bruno Cagli and Vittorio Emiliani, from an exhibit at the Palazzo Strozzi held from 15 April to 5 June 1993. Highlights Rossini's relationship with the city that became his final resting place, discussing the productions of his operas there and the compositions connected with the city. Considers Rossini's flight from Bologna and his refuge in Florence during the years he suffered from his nervous disorder. Includes photographs of the arrival of Rossini's remains at Santa Croce in 1887. The final section, with illustrations of sets and costume designs, deals with productions of Rossini's operas for Florence's Il Maggio Musicale.

97. Cagli, Bruno, and Mauro Bucarelli, eds. *La casa di Rossini: Catalogo del museo*. Modena: Panini, 1989. 197 pp. ISBN 88-768-6136-X ML141.P47 R63 1989.

A catalog of items on exhibit in the Pesaro home in which Rossini was born. Cagli offers the preface, including a history of the house (see also Panzini, item 362). Bucarelli describes the various sections of the exhibit, including memorabilia on various singers and productions, particularly those in France. The catalog includes various portraits and photographs of Rossini; some of the illustrations are in color. An appendix lists a chronology of the composer's works in Paris. See also item 84.

98. ———, Paolo Fabbri, and Paolo Micalizzi. *Rossini: Dentro la scena: Mostra di costumi, gioielli, bozzetti e scenografie di opere rossiniane*. Ferrara: Ferrara Arte, 1995. 123 pp.

A catalog of an exhibition of costumes and set designs for productions of Rossini works in Italy from 1970 to 1995.

99. Emiliani, Vittorio. *Raffaello, Rossini e il bello stile*. Urbino: Quattroventi, 1993. v, 96 pp. ISBN: 88-3920-379-X ML141. U73 R67 1993.

An exhibition catalog published under the auspices of the Fondazione Rossini and the Accademia Raffaello, this volume contains illustrations as well as the following essays: "Raffaello 'maestro' del giovane Rossini" (Vittorio Emiliani); "Da Carpani a Balzac: un itinerario estetico rossiniano" (Bruno Cagli); and "Mito del classicismo a cultura delle legazione" (Andrea Emiliani).

100. Fabbri, Paolo. *Rossini nelle raccolte Piancastelli di Forlì*. Lucca: Libreria Musicale Italiana, 2001. lvi, 354 pp. ISBN: 88-7096-298-9 ML141.L85 R67 2001.

This catalog of an exhibition held from 5 May through 3 June 2001 at the Palazzo Trisi in Lugo contains a listing of the contents of the Piancastelli archive. With illustrations and bibliography. See also item 13.

101. Ferrari, Luigi, ed. *Viaggio a Rossini*. Bologna: Nuova Alfa, 1992. 224 pp. ISBN 88-777-9351-1 ML141.B65 R67 1992.

This catalog of an exhibition held from 13 November 1992 to 14 February 1993 at the Museo Civico Archeologico in Bologna is illustrated with color plates of Rossiniana as well as art works, facsimiles, and excerpts of musical scores. The book also contains brief essays on Rossini's life, his connections with Bologna and Paris, and sections on both the Italian orchestra and the pianoforte in Rossini's day and also features a discussion of the parallels between the composer and contemporary art, especially the paintings of Antonio Canova. For more on Rossini and Canova, see item 373.

102. *Il teatro di Rossini a Roma 1812–1821: Debutti, musiche, artisti, librettisti, teatri*. Gaeta: Edizioni il Geroglifico, 1992. 351 pp. ML141.R64 R67 1992.

Catalog of a bicentennial exhibit at Rome's Biblioteca Vallenciana. Text commentaries consider Rossini's activities in Rome, contemporary reviews (with excerpts), and the librettists of Rossini's Roman operas. Illustrations from the exhibit include portraits of Rossini and contemporary singers and librettists (Vincenzina Viganò Mombelli, Cesare Sterbini, Giovanni Schmidt, Jacopo Ferretti). Included also are facsimiles of publications and autograph manuscripts. Also contains diagrams of the Valle, Argentina, and Apollo theaters, along with a bibliography of theater histories.

103. Jocteur-Montrozier, Yves. *Cimarosa, Mozart, Rossini: Stendhal et la musique: Exposition, Grenoble, juin-novembre 1992*. Grenoble, Musée Stendhal and Maison Stendhal, 1992. 1 unpaginated volume.

[Not examined.]

104. Verdi, Luigi, ed. *Rossini a Bologna: Note documentarie in occasione della mostra "Rossini a Bologna," 29 February–1 Apr. 2000*. Bologna: Pàtron, 2000. 185 pp. 88-555-2533-6 ML410.R8 R79 2000.

This volume catalogs an exhibit held at various venues in Bologna, including the Accademia Filarmonica (of which Rossini was a member) and the Archiginnasio. Items, which include documents, letters, and illustrations chronicling Rossini's links with the city, are divided into the following chapters: Years of Study (1799–1812); Great Operatic Successes (1812–1822); Rossini's First Marriage (1822–1829); Time between Bologna and Paris (1829–1838); "The Golden Years of the Bologna Stay" (1845–1848); and Rossini's Farewell to the City (1848–1851).

4

Biographies and General Studies of Rossini's Career

NINETEENTH-CENTURY BIOGRAPHIES AND PERSONAL ACCOUNTS

105. Azevedo, Alexis. *G. Rossini: sa vie et ses ouevres*. Paris: Heugel et Cie., 1864. 310 pp. ML410.R8 A9.

This biography, the work of an acquaintance of the composer, is an insider's look at Rossini's dealings with theaters and publishers in the French musical milieu. Citing contemporary reviews, Azevedo discusses the French premieres of Rossini's work, mentioning, as well, Castil-Blaze and his translations (see items 330 and 658). In his account of the inner workings and politics of the French theatrical arena, he comments on the initial antagonism of Ferdinand Paër at the Théâtre Italien (see item 57). The volume includes sample facsimiles of Rossini autographs, including that of the "O salutaris" for four voices as well as a facsimile of a letter to the Mayor of Pesaro on the occasion of the dedication of a statue of the composer at his birthplace (with French translation).

106. Bellaigue, Camille. *Etudes musicales et silhouettes de musiciens*. Paris: C. Delagrave, 1896. 302 pp. ML390.B43; other editions: 1898, 423 pp. ML60.B42; 1903, 516 pp. ML60.B424; 1907; 394 pp. ML60.B425.

Published in English as *Portraits and Silhouettes of Musicians*. Trans. Ellen Orr. New York: Dodd. Mead and Co., 1897. 302 pp.; reprinted in 1900 (375 pp.) and 1901 (302 pp.); latest reprint, Boston: Longwood Press, 1978, 302 pp. ISBN: 0-8934-1424-7 ML390.B43 1978.

In a brief six pages (pp. 258–63), Bellaigue sums up Rossini's life and career, concluding, in line with most contemporary criticism, that the composer had succumbed to laziness and gluttony. Illustrated with an engraved portrait of Rossini.

107. Bennett, Joseph. *Gioacchino Rossini*. London: Novello/Ewer, 1884. 84 pp.

[Not examined.]

108. Bussenius, Arthur Friedrich, and Wilhelm von Lenz. *Gioachino Rossini*. Vol. 11 of the series *Die Componisten der neueren Zeit*. Cassel: E. Balde, 1854–1857. Available also on microfiche: Leiden: IDC, 2000.

[Not examined.]

109. Camaiti, V[enturino]. *Gioachino Rossini: notizie biografiche, artistiche e aneddotiche (Ricordo del 3 maggio 1887)*. Florence: Coppini e Bocconi, 1887. 48 pp. ML410.R8 C16.

A brief biography that draws upon previously-published works, including Silvestri (item 133), Stendhal (item 135), and Zanolini (item 138). The author also has compiled a section of anecdotes and one of defenses of Rossini's music. Includes a list of Rossini's compositions.

110. Checchi, Eugenio. *Rossini*. Florence: G. Barbèra, 1898. 200 pp. ML410.R8 C43.

The author begins by reminiscing about how, as a child, he often saw Rossini in Florence. Briefly comparing Rossini with Verdi, Checchi then commences a fairly anecdotal biography in which he calls Rossini a "fortunate improviser" and the essence of the Italian character. This work serves as a good example of early Rossini biographies as it contains only six chapters, the final chapter beginning with *Semiramide*. No emphasis is placed on the composer's life after *Guillaume Tell*, after which Rossini entered "live" into the temple of immortality, according to Checchi.

111. Damme, Jean van. *Vie de G. Rossini, Célèbre compositeur, Membre de l'institut, Directeur du chant de l'Académie Royale de Musique, a Paris, Chevalier de la Légion d'Honneur, et d'une quantité d'ordres impériaux et royaux, membre de la Grande Harmonie de Bruxelles, et de toutes les institutions harmonique de l'Italie. Dédiée aux vrais adorateurs du célèbre Maître, par un dilettante*. Anvers: Librairie nationale et étrangère, 1839. 215 pp. ML410.R8 D16.

Perhaps the subtitle of this volume best describes the writer's intent: to laud Rossini as a great man and composer. As often with early biographies,

Damme chose to present Rossini's life in conjunction with his works. The nine operas before *Tancredi*, however, are mentioned briefly in the first chapter. More significant works, in the author's view, merit greater space. After the chapter on *Guillaume Tell*, Damme relates Rossini's trip to Belgium and Germany with Rothschild. The volume ends with a chapter of anecdotes and a works list. The author promises that, if his book has a second edition, he will devote chapters to analyses of works such as *Otello*, *La gazza ladra* and *Elisabetta, regina d'Inghiterra*.

112. Dole, Nathan Haskell. *A Score of Famous Composers*. New York: Thomas Y. Crowell & Co., 1891. 540 pp. ML390.D65; reprint, 4th ed. with appendix by David Ewen. Freeport, N.Y.: Books for Libraries Press, 1968. ML390.D66 1968.

The chapter on Rossini (pp. 237–57) is, for the most part, a summary of Rossini's life comparable to other biographical accounts of the late nineteenth century. The author begins by comparing Rossini to Napoleon, claiming that both were Italians who became French and that both came to dominate Europe, engaging devoted followers. Dole's account confirms that Rossini, while still considered an important force in Western music history, was no longer actively in the repertoire. " 'The Italian bon-bon dealer,' " he maintains, "is forgotten." The author cites comments by Ambros (item 460).

113. Duprez, G[ilbert-Louis]. *Souvenirs d'un chanteur*. Paris: Calmann Lévy, 1880; reprint, 1888.

Duprez, master of chest high "C's" and successor to Adolphe Nourrit, creator of the role of Arnold in *Guillaume Tell*, recalls Rossini in his memoirs. In addition to *Tell*, Duprez notes other Rossini roles he performed in Italy. He concludes his volume with an account of Wagner's visit to Rossini in Paris (see Michotte, item 160 and Rognoni, item 476). For more on Duprez, see items 273 and 274.

114. Edwards, H[enry] Sutherland. *The Life of Rossini*. London: Hurst and Blackett, 1869. 344 pp. ML410.R8 E2.

In his introduction, Edwards writes that no one had yet attempted to document Rossini's life by demonstrating the "modifications, developments, and new combinations in opera due to him." Avoiding unnecessary technicalities, the author first presents a history of opera beginning with Monteverdi. He then offers chapters on Rossini's reforms in serious and comic opera and in vocal writing. Edwards dedicates several chapters to *Il barbiere*, and although his history is by today's standards inaccurate, he does attempt to place Rossini in the contemporary artistic milieu. The author also notes the composer's relationship with the English theater. The book concludes with a chapter on the Stabat mater, mentioning Heine's views on the work (item 805).

* ———. *Rossini and His School*. Item 522.

115. Escudier, Leon. *Mes souvenirs*. Paris: E. Dentu, 1863. 352 pp. ML390.E7.

In Chapter One of his book (pp. 1–31), the author discusses Rossini's career in context with other Italian composers of the early nineteenth century. Escudier considers his development from a composer of buffa works to grandiose serious pieces, culminating in the creation of his masterpiece, *Guillaume Tell*, after which, Escudier notes, he "rested, like God after He created the universe." Escudier also mentions Rossini's "inferiors," Donizetti, Mercadante, and Pacini, and contrasts them to Bellini. Rossini's music, he notes, is lively, spontaneous, and original, but Bellini's is Italian melody "at its most sweet and most tender." Escudier lauds Rossini's vigorous orchestration and claims that in *Il barbiere di Siviglia*, the composer accomplished a revolution in opera buffa. He concludes his thoughts on Italians by stating that with Rossini silent and Bellini deceased, the way was clear for the "Caesar of the Triumvirate"—Giuseppe Verdi.

116. Escudier, Leon and Marie. *Rossini: sa vie et ses ouevres, avec une introduction de M. Méry*. Paris: E. Dentu, 1854. 338 pp.

The Escudiers describe Rossini as the "Homer of Music" and the Prince Crusader who conquered the "Jérusalem melodiques." This laudatory volume considers Rossini's life in connection with his compositions. Although praising his work in the French theatrical arena, the authors note Rossini's formative years in Italy, commenting on the various schools of Italian music. Contains a chronological table of Rossini's works as well as a chapter on "Mme. Colbrand-Rossini," (pp. 273–80), which paints an erroneously positive picture of the composer's relationship with his first wife (see item 205).

117. Ferris, George T. *Great Italian and French Composers*. New York: D. Appleton & Co., 1879. 248 pp. ML390.F394.

In this volume, which purports to devote space to "composers of the higher rank," Rossini garners some thirty-seven pages (pp. 48–85), more than any of the other composers included. Ferris deems Rossini the "most gifted composer" Italy ever produced, although he condemns his retirement. The account is mostly biographical and anecdotal, citing sources such as Stendhal (item 135), Righetti-Giorgi (item 131), and Mount Edgcumbe (item

306). Ferris notes that Wagner's followers were unwarranted in their narrow approach to Rossini and claims that Rossini can be credited with perfecting the forms and structures he inherited.

118. Hiller, Ferdinand. "Nachruf an Rossini." In *Aus dem Tonleben unserer Zeit. Gelegentliches van Ferdinand Hiller. Neue folge*, 87–94. Leipzig F.E.C. Leuckart (C. Sander), 1871. 194 pp. ML63.H65.

This brief essay follows up on Hiller's accounts of his conversations with Rossini (see item 119), further explaining the friendship between the two men and Hiller's estimate of Rossini as a composer. For a critical edition and commentary, see item 120.

119. ———. "Plaudereien mit Rossini." In *Aus dem Tonleben unserer Zeit*, Vol. 2, 1–84. Leipzig: Hermann Mendelssohn, 1868. 271 pp. ML60.H65.

Hiller's accounts of his conversations with Rossini. The German composer relates Rossini's comments on music, aesthetics, and various aspects and personalities of the contemporary musical world. Considered one of the most significant contemporary sources on Rossini's views.

120. ———. *Plaudereien mit Rossini*. Edition and commentary by Guido Johannes Joerg. Afterward by Reto Müller. Vol. 1 of *Schriftenreihe der Deutschen Rossini Gesellschaft*, eds. Guido Johannes Joerg and Rüdiger Krüger. Stuttgart: Deutsche Rossini Gesellschaft, 1993. 104 pp. ML410.R8 H55 1993.

Includes the texts of both Hiller's "Plaudereien" (item 119) and "Nachruf an Rossini" (item 118) along with a critical apparatus and comments on the relationship between Hiller and Rossini. With illustrations from the original publications.

121. Kohut, Adolph. *Rossini*. Vol. 14 of the series *Musiker-Biographien*. Leipzig: Philipp Reclam, [1892]. 103 pp. ML410.R8 K6.

This diminutive volume, issued in commemoration of the centennial of the composer's birth, exemplifies Rossini biography for the average reader at the end of nineteenth century. As usual, most of the book deals with Rossini's life through 1828. A single chapter traces the years from *Guillaume Tell* until his death. A final section considers Rossini, the man, through citations of anecdotes, attributed sayings, and correspondence.

122. Loménie, L[ouis] L[eonard] de. *Galerie des Contemporains Illustres, par un homme de rien*: *M. Rossini*. Paris: A. René et Co., 1842. 36 pp. ML410.R8 L7.

The author writes his commentary on Rossini when the composer, at fifty, has seemingly abandoned Paris to reside in Bologna. Before commenting on the composer's career, Loménie questions Rossini's retreat from composing. Although he admits to the importance of the Stabat mater, he seems to be of the opinion that religious music is less significant than opera. He also claims that Rossini is a composer who lives in the musical past; hence, he has retreated from the current scene. Like many of Rossini's contemporary commentators, he points to the composer's laziness, but resolves that it remains to be seen whether Rossini's decision to leave the stage was wise.

123. Michotte, Edmond. *Souvenirs: Une Soirée chez Rossini à Beau-Sejours (Passy)* 1858. Published privately sometime after 1893. 31 pp.; English translation, see Weinstock, item 161.

Michotte recalls the conversation among Rossini and his guests at one of the composer's famous *soirèes*; others in attendance were contralto Marietta Alboni and music critic Alexis-Jacob Azevedo (item 105). Includes samples of Rossini's witty banter (such as his account of the night following the premiere of *Il barbiere di Siviglia*). A significant element of these reminiscences comprises the composer's comments on bel canto singing and his disdainful remarks about contemporary vocal practices. When discussing specific singers, Rossini notes that the greatest was his first wife, Isabella Colbran, and the most unique was Maria Malibran.

124. Mirecourt, Eugène de. *Rossini*. Paris: Gustave Havard, 1855. 95 pp. ML410.R8 M4.

An anecdotal biography, which takes a hard stance on Rossini's request for a stipend from the French government. The author maintains that Rossini does not recognize or appreciate the hospitality accorded him by the French; he calls the composer a materialist who has transformed "the temple of art into a boutique."

125. Montazio, Enrico. *Giovacchino Rossini*. Turin: Dall'Unione Tipografico-Editrice, 1862. 127 pp.

[Not examined.]

126. Montrond, Maxime de. *Rossini: étude biographique sur cet illustre maestro*. Lille: J. Lefort, 1870. xii, 144 pp.

[Not examined.]

127. Mordani, Filippo. *Della vita privata di Giovacchino Rossini: memorie inedite*. Edited by Romualdo Cannonero. Imola: Ignazio Galeati, 1871. vi, 28 pp.

[Not examined.]

128. Naumann, Emil. *Italienische Tondichter von Palestrina bis auf die Gegen-wart.* Berlin: Robert Oppenheim, 1876; 2nd ed., 1883. x, 570 pp. ML390.N292.

In the book's final chapter, Naumann briefly sketches Rossini's life and traces his career from the early *farse* through *Guillaume Tell*, which he deems a masterpiece of orchestral and vocal color. Naumann claims that the highpoints in Rossini's career were *Il barbiere di Siviglia*, *Semiramide*, and *Tell*; after noting Rossini's influence in Paris, he recounts his meeting with him there in 1867 when they discussed Wagner and Mozart.

129. Pacini, Giovanni. *Le mie memorie artistiche.* Florence: G.G. Guidi, 1865; expanded and published as *Le mie memorie artistiche (edite ed inedite): Autobiografia del Maestro Cav. Giovanni Pacini riscontrata sugli autografi e pubblicata da Ferdinando Magnani.* Florence: Le Monnier, 1875; reprint, edited by Luciano Nicolosi and Salvatore Pinnavia, Lucca: Maria Pacini Fazzi, 1981. lxxvii, 346 pp. ISBN L20000. ML410.P11 A3 1981.

In his memoirs, first published in serial form in the Florentine newspaper *Boccherini* (1863–1865), Pacini included incidents—some spurious—from the career of his friend and colleague, Rossini. Chapter 2 includes several escapades connected to Rossini's early operas. In the next chapter, Pacini recalled how Rossini, under deadline pressure, asked him to set several numbers for the premiere of *Matilde di Shabran*. In Chapters 20–22, Pacini discussed his part in the 1864 celebration held in Rossini's honor by the *Società Rossini* in Pesaro (which the honoree did not attend), and, in Chapter 23, notes Rossini's role on the commission to erect a monument to Guido d'Arezzo (famous for Verdi's disdainful refusal to participate). Pacini, usually dismissed as an imitator of Rossini, lauded his colleague throughout the book, noting, in an oft-quoted passage, that if any composer were to survive, he had to follow the style of "the great reformer."

130. Pougin, Arthur. *Rossini: notes—impressions—souvenirs—commentaires.* Paris: A. Claudin and Alf. Ikelmer et Cie., 1871. 91 pp. ML410.R8 P8.

The author states that it is not his intention to write a complete biography of Rossini, as have Carpani [sic] and Stendhal. Rather he wishes to create a "biographical study," with anecdotes and excerpts from correspondence that portray Rossini's character through his relationships with others. Pougin, writing in the first person and offering his personal opinions throughout, gives his account of important events in the composer's life, ending his volume with transcriptions of letters to and from Rossini.

131. Righetti-Giorgi, Geltrude. *Cenni di una Donna cantante sopra il Maestro Rossini, in risposta a ciò che ne scrisse nell'estate dell'anno 1822 il giornalista inglese in Parigi, e fu riportato in una Gazzetta di Milano dell stesso anno.* Bologna: Sassi, 1823; reprinted in Rognoni, item 476.

In addition to being the first "Rosina" and "Angiolina (Cenerentola)," contralto Geltrude Righetti-Giorgi was Rossini's childhood friend in Bologna. The "English journalist" to whom her title refers was Stendhal [Henri Beyle] whose article on the composer had appeared in 1822 in *The Paris Monthly Review* (later republished in *The Blackwood's Edinburgh Magazine, The Gallignani's Monthly Review*, in German in *Literarisches Konversationsblatt*, and in Italian in the *Gazzetta Musicale*). Righetti-Giorgi methodically responds to Stendhal by first quoting from his writing and then correcting its inaccuracies. Particularly valuable are her comments on the two works in which she performed. Just as Rossini would later deny any friendship with Stendhal (see Hanslick, item 161), Righetti-Giorgi demonstrated that the "English journalist knew about as much about Rossini as [she] did about the Emperor of China."

132. Rovani, Giuseppe. *La mente di Gioachino Rossini.* Florence: Ricordi, 1871. 29 pp.

[Not examined.]

133. Silvestri, Lodovico Settimo. *Della vita e delle opere di Gioachino Rossini: notizie biografico-artistico-aneddotico-critiche compilate su tutte le biografie di questo celebre italiano e sui giudizi della stampa italiana e straniera intorno alle sue opere.* Milan: Fratelli Biatti G. e Minacca, 1874. vii, 354 pp. ML410.R835.

Written in 1869, but, as the author notes, published after several years' delay, this biography relies heavily on previously-published biographies; the author admits to an almost literal quoting of Zanolini, for example (item 138). The first section of the book is dedicated to Rossini's life, the second, to a chronological list of works, which includes information on premiere date and venue, librettist, cast, excerpts from reviews, and subsequent production history in Milan. Silvestri quotes liberally from correspondence and also reprints Rossini's will. Appendices contain poems and honors, including the dedication of Rossini's statue in Pesaro in 1864; elogies; details on the Stabat mater and the Petite messe solennelle; a selection of writings on Rossini and his music; biographical sketches of Isabella Colbran and Domenico Barbaja; an engraving of the statue of Rossini at LaScala; and facsimiles of two letters.

134. Stendhal [Henri Beyle]. *Rome, Naples et Florence en 1817*. Paris: M. Lévy Frères, 1854; Paris: Calmann Lévy [1872?]. 435 pp. DG426.B5. Published in English as *Rome, Naples, and Florence*. Trans. Richard N. Coe. London: Calder, 1959. DG426.B57 1959; also New York: G. Braziller, 1960. xxii, 562 p. DG426.B57 1960.

The author's reminiscences of—or, as translator Coe points out—his ideal of the Italy he toured. Stendhal offers a vision of the cultural, social, and political climate in Italy, taking delight in describing the operas he attended and the singers he heard. Among the works he discusses are various Rossini operas. Even though he claimed to enjoy a friendship with Rossini (which the composer denied), Stendhal never missed an opportunity to criticize Rossini for idleness and dishonesty.

135. ————. *Vie de Rossini*. Paris: Auguste Boulland et Cie., 1824. viii, 623 pp. ML410.R8 B5; published first as *Memoirs of Rossini: By the Author of the Lives of Haydn and Mozart*. London: T. Hookham, 1824. xlii, 287 pp. ML410.R8 B53.

Vie de Rosini [sic], printed as a second edition, 1824; *Vie de Rossini, nouvelle édition*. Paris: Michel Lévy Frères, 1854. 375 pp.; *Vie de Rossini, nouvelle édition entièrement revue*. Paris: Michel Lévy Frères, 1864. 375 pp.; *Vie de Rossini, nouvelle édition*. Calmann Lévy, 1876. 375 pp.; *Vie de Rossini, nouvelle édition entièrement revue*. Paris: Calmann Lévy, 1892. 375 pp. ML410.R8 B51 1892.

Stendhal, Vie de Rossini, edited and annotated by Henry Prunières (with his foreword and afterword). 2 vols. In *Oeuvres Complètes de Stendhal*, under the direction of Paul Arbelet and Edouard Champion. Paris: Librairie ancienne Honoré Champion, 1922. lxiv, 380 pp. and 506 pp. PQ2435.A1 1913.

Vie de Rossini, ed. Henri Martineau. 2 vols. Paris: Le Divan, 1929. xxxvii, 337 pp. and 341 pp.

Vie de Rossini, ed. V. Del Litto. Lausanne: Editions Rencontre, 1960.

Vie de Rossini, revised and edited, translated and annotated by Richard N. Coe. London: John Caldar, 1956. xxiii, 566 pp.; reprint, New York: Orion Press, 1970. xxiii, 566 pp. ISBN 0-6704-2790-X ML410.R8. B513 1970; 2nd edition, London: Calder & Boyars, 1970. xxiv, 566 pp. ISBN 0-71450341-X ML410.R8 B513 1970b; reprint, Seattle: University of Washington Press, 1972 xxiii, 566 pp. ISBN 0-295951893 ML410.R8 B513 1972; reprint, London: John Caldar Press and New York: Riverrun Press, 1985. xxiv, 566 pp. ISBN 0-7145-0632-X ML410.R8 S735 1985. Facsimile edition, edited and annotated by Pierre Brunel, *Vie de Rossini*. No. 2433 in the Series Folio/Essais. Paris: Gallimard, 1992. 575 pp.

The most famous of Rossini's early biographies, Stendhal's work is more fiction than fact. Despite its inaccuracies, the book, originally intended to be a history of Italian music from 1800 to 1823, offers a look—often ironic—at the theatrical arenas in Italy and Paris in which Rossini worked. Completing the volume in 1823 and publishing it the following year, Stendhal dedicates chapters to specific operas through *Semiramide* (which is included in a chapter dedicated to "minor" operas). In addition to these critiques and musical commentaries, the author discusses various personages important in Rossini's professional career, including Isabella Colbran, Domenico Barbaja, Giuditta Pasta, and the castrato Giovanni Battista Velluti. The volume includes chapters on other topics, such as Italian and German music, composers who preceded Rossini, and Mozart and his impact in Italy.

136. Wagner, Richard. "Eine Erinnerung an Rossini." In *Allgemeine Zeitung* [Augsburg], no. 352, 17 December 1868, 5375–76; reprinted in *Gesammelte Schriften und Dichtungen*, Vol. 8. Leipzig, 1873; 6/1914 as *Sämtliche Schriften und Dichtungen*.

English translation by William Ashton Ellis. "A Remembrance of Rossini." In *Art and Politics*, 269–71. Vol. 4 of *Richard Wagner's Prose Works*. London: Kegan Paul, Trench, Trüber & Co., 1895 ML410.W1 A127; reprint, St. Claire Shores, Mich.: Scholarly Press, 1972. ISBN 0-40-300255-9 ML410.W1 A127 1972.

Wagner admitted to hearing comments about him attributed to Rossini, a topic of discussion that came up when the two met in 1860 (see also Michotte's account, item 160). In this remembrance, Wagner recalled Rossini as "the first truly great and reverable man I had as yet encountered in the world" (Ellis's translation), and claimed that his estimate of Italian opera was guided by Rossini's comments during their visit. Wagner was urged on various occasions to revisit Rossini, but, as he noted here (and as did Michotte), he constantly refused. Written after Rossini's death, this interesting commentary ends with a prophetic comment in terms of Rossini studies: Wagner calls for a "competent historian" to undertake a study of his Italian colleague's place in contemporary music.

137. Wendt, Amadeus. *Rossinis Leben und Treiben, vornehmlich nach den Nachrichten des hrn. v. Stendhal geschildert und mit Urtheilen der Zeitgenossen über seinen musikalischen Charakter begleitet.* Leipzig: Leopold Voss, 1824. xvi, 440 pp. ML410.R8 W4.

In addition to Rossini's biography, the author offers a discussion of his works, including the opinions of his contemporaries, among them Carpani

(Item 483), Majer (item 486), Zingarelli, Berton (item 481), Stendhal (item 135), Spohr (417), and Weber.

138. Zanolini, Antonio. *Biografia di Gioachino Rossini*. Bologna: Nicola Zanichelli, 1875. vi, 298 pp. ML410.R8 Z2.

Zanolini, a friend of Rossini's from the 1830s, addresses the composer's life and works in this volume. Its most famous contribution is the section entitled "Una passeggiata in compagnia di Rossini." Originally published in 1836 in Paris in *L'Ape italiana redivia*, it is a record of a conversation in which Rossini shared his musical philosophy. Zanolini includes transcriptions of documents and letters as well as a catalog of the composer's works, divided into eight categories: operas (with premieres, librettists, casts, and price of piano-vocal score), cantatas, instrumental music, sacred music, chamber music and works composed for private performance, other compositions, unedited works, and manuscripts in various archives. See item 463 for a commentary on Rossini's music addressed to Zanolini.

COMMENTARIES ON NINETEENTH-CENTURY STUDIES

139. Ciarlantini, Paola. "Il ritratto umano e artistico di Gioachino Rossini nelle sue prime biografie." In *Rossini 1792–1992* (item 95), pp. 367–384.

The author offers a summary of the earliest biographies and commentaries on Rossini. Among those cited are Alexis-Jacob Azevedo (item 105), Stendhal (item 135), Geltrude Righetti-Giorgi (item 131), Edmond Michotte (items 123 and 160), Stendhal (item 135), Giuseppe Radiciotti (items 163 and 164), Amadeus Wendt (item 137), and Antonio Zanolini (138).

140. Lippmann, Friedrich. "Sull'estetica di Rossini." In *Convegno di studi su Rossini per il Centenario della morte di Gioacchino Rossini*, pp. 62–69. See item 283.

Hiller, Ferdinand

141. Joerg, Guido Johannes, ed. "Gli scritti rossiniani di Ferdinand Hiller." *Bollettino del Centro Rossiniano di Studi* 32 (1992): 63–155.

Joerg presents an edition and parallel Italian translation of the major writings of Hiller dedicated to Rossini: *Plaudereien mit Rossini* (item 119), *Nachruf an Rossini* (item 118), the letter concerning Rossini entitled "Briefe an eine Ungannte," and the *Besuche in Jenseits*. Joerg begins with the publication history of the works and then explains his critical method.

Following the text of *Plaudereien*, the author includes an index of names and subjects that refers to the pages in the original work.

Stendhal [Beyle, Henri]

142. Burroughs, Bruce. "Stendhal on Rossini: Excerpts from the 1823 *Life* as translated by Richard N. Coe." *The Opera Quarterly* 9 (Summer 1993): 4–22.

Burroughs briefly introduces Stendhal's biography and then cites passages from Coe's translation (both item 135). Excerpts include Stendhal's comments on the differences between Rossini's and Mozart's music ("Rossini is more *dramatic* than Mozart") as well as his impressions of the Italian impresarial system, the castrato Giovanni Battista Velluti (see item 270), and Rossini's *Tancredi*, *Il barbiere*, *La gazza ladra*, and *Mosè*. A taste of Stendhal's style. Illustrated with two engravings of the composer.

143. Dado, Stéphane and Philippe Vendrix. "Stendhal e Rossini: uno studio documentario." Translated from French into Italian by Reto Müller and Mauro Tosti-Croce. *Bollettino del Centro Rossiniano di Studi* 39 (1999): 21–69.

The authors meticulously chart references to Rossini in the various writings of Stendhal. Dividing the writer's career into his years in Milan and as a novelist, journalist, and reviewer in Paris, Dado and Vendrix note that Stendhal's account of Rossini's life must be taken cautiously; they contend, however, that his writings on theater during the late 1820s pioneered modern music criticism. In addition to the *Vie de Rossini*, the authors address Stendhal works including *Rome, Naples, et Florence en 1817*, *L'Italie en 1818*, *Promenades dans Rome*, *Lucien Leuwen*, and his writings in the *Journal* and *La corrispondenza*. Includes charts with references to citations about Rossini and their location in modern editions. See items 134 and 135 for works by Stendhal.

* Durbe, Dario. "Rossini e Stendhal." In *Atti del convegno di studi: Rossini, edizioni critiche e prassi esecutiva*, 19–29. See item 282.

* Rognoni, Luigi. "Una cantante bolognese in polemica con Stendhal." See item 279.

144. Saccenti, Mario. "Rossini fra Stendhal e Bacchelli." Archiginnasio 66–68 (1971–73): 623–37; reprinted in *Rossini fra Stendhal e Bacchelli*, 7–29. Vol. 15 of *Letture e notizie dall'Otto al Novecento*. Bologna: Massimiliano Boni, 1975. 229 pp. PQ4085.S2.

Saccenti considers the Rossini biographies written by Stendhal in 1823 and by Riccardo Bacchelli in 1941. Both authors were fiction writers, and, according to Saccenti, the single link between these works is music. Saccenti demonstrates that each author's interpretation of Rossini is driven by cultural and historical differences. Nonetheless, he argues, Rossini was a symbol for both men: for Stendhal, he became his personal vision of Italy, and for Bacchelli, a necessary wartime image of Italy's greatness.

145. Sala di Felice, Elena. "Stendhal spettatore euforico." In *Le parole della musica II: Studi sul lessico della letteratura critica del teatro musicale in onore di Gianfranco Folena*, 147–81. Vol. 22 in *Studi di Musica Veneta*. Ed. Maria Teresa Muraro. Florence: Leo S. Olschki, 1995. 334 pp. ISBN 88-222-4340-4 ML63.P26 1994 Vol. 2.

The author states that Stendhal's writings on music in general and on composers like Rossini and Mozart stem not from intellect or reason but rather from hedonistic sentiment. Stendhal's subjective style, therefore, lends itself to both metaphor and simile often based in art and literature. In addition, Stendhal introduces socio-political and cultural commentary into his writings, expressing himself in a manner he admits is decidedly partisan. Cites examples of Stendhal's prose. See item 135.

* Spina, Giuseppe. "Stendhal aveva ragione?" See item 652.

* Vecchi, Giuseppe. "Stendhal, la musica e Bologna." See item 342.

Wagner, Richard
* Grondona, Marco. "Rossini e Wagner negli scritti: Il problema dell'-opera." See item 491.

Wendt, Amadeus
146. Müller, Reto. "La prima monografia tedesca su Rossini: *Rossini's Leben und Treiben* di Amadeus Wendt." Translated from German into Italian by Mauro Tosti-Croce. *Bollettino del Centro Rossiniano di Studi* 40 (2000): 5–147.

Müller addresses the criticism that Amadeus Wendt's *Rossini's Leben und Treiben* is merely a translation of Stendhal's *Vie de Rossini*. Contending that Wendt's adaptation is quite different, Müller compares both, demonstrating that, while Stendhal's is a mélange of anecdotes and observations, Wendt's is an organized presentation of Rossini's life and career. The author lists the sources Wendt consulted and gives a sample passage in which he shows how Wendt adapted the original French text in three ways: correction, integration, and objection. The author then gives numerous examples of each type of adaptation, citing the passages from both Stendhal and Wendt (with an Italian translation of the later) and a brief commentary. Finally, Müller provides Wendt's text with a parallel Italian translation. For further discussion of Wendt's musical criticism and analysis, see item 147.

147. ———. "Rossini nel giudizio di Amadeus Wendt." Translated from German into Italian by Mauro Tosti-Croce. *Bollettino del Centro Rossiniano di Studi* 39 (1999): 71–109.

The contributions of Amadeus Wendt to Rossini literature are often overlooked, according to the author. In this essay, Müller presents examples of the writings of Wendt, author of *Rossini's Leben und Treiben*. Following a brief biography of Wendt, the author offers an annotated sampling of Wendt's works on music. Müller then provides seven examples of Wendt's critical writings on Rossini, presented in both the original German and a parallel Italian translation. For Müller's full discussion of Wendt's *Leben und Treiben*, see item 146.

Zanolini, Antonio

* Grondona, Marco. "Rossini e Wagner negli scritti: Il problema dell'-opera." See item 491.

BIOGRAPHICAL STUDIES PUBLISHED BETWEEN 1900 AND 1950

148. Amico, Lele [Fedele] d'. *Gioacchino Rossini*. Turin: Rotocalco Dagnino, 1938. 86 pp. ML410.R8 A5.

A fifty-three-page summary of Rossini's life followed by twenty-eight plates of illustrations, which include photographs, caricatures, documents, and score facsimiles.

149. Bacchelli, Riccardo. *Gioacchino Rossini: Con 14 tavole in rotocalco*. Turin: Unione Tipografico-Editrice Torinese, 1941. 298 pp. ML410.R8 B2; corrected reprint published as *Rossini con quattordici tavole fuori testo*. Vol. 16 in the series *I grandi italiani*. Turin: Tipografia Torinese, 1945 ML410.R8B2 1945.

Published with additional sections of the author's personal thoughts as *Rossini e Esperienze Rossiniane*. Verona: Arnoldo Mondadori, 1959. 337 pp. ML410.R8 B2; reprint: *Rossini*. Florence: Passigli, 1987. 318 pp. ML410.R8 B27 1987.

Also published as *Rossini e saggi musical. Verdi, Beethoven, Monteverdi*, pp. 11–330. Vol. 16 in *Tutte le opere di Riccardo Bacchelli*. Milan: Mondadori, 1968. 589 pp. ML60.B128.

This biography, written by a famed Italian literary figure, considers Rossini's life along with the author's conception of his stylistic development. Although he does not read music, as he admits in his *Esperienze*, Bacchelli's understanding of his subject makes this volume noteworthy; although not a musicologist or musician, he clearly sees the need for more serious study of Rossini as well as for reexamination of his music through scholarly endeavor. The 1941 edition is illustrated, as the title states, with fourteen plates of engravings. *Esperienze* includes the essay "Chi sa Rossini non lo sa . . . ," which also appears in item 465.

150. Bevan, W. Armine. *Rossini*. London: George Bell & Sons, 1904. 70 pp. ML410.R8 B4.

Part of *Bell's Miniature Series of Musicians*, this diminutive volume represents Rossini biographical studies at the turn of the century. Citing as his sources the nineteenth-century standards, such as Zanolini (see item 138), Edwards (items 114 and 522), Pougin (130), Carpani (483), Stendhal (135) and Azevedo (105), Bevan traces Rossini's career through *Guillaume Tell* and then dismisses his later years as a period that holds "little interest for the student." Illustrated, this volume contains an alphabetized list of operas, an incomplete slate of other works, and an advertisement for vocal and piano scores of Rossini's "standard" operas available in England.

151. Caussou, Jean-Louis. *Gioachino Rossini: L'homme et son oeuvre*. In the series *Musiciens de Tous les Temps*. Paris: Seghers, 1967. 192 pp. ML410.R8 C3.

A brief biography told in context of his works. Caussou also addresses the operas individually, giving information on the original performance and cast, the libretto and its history, a plot summary, and comments on the composition. The non-operatic works are then considered. Brief sections deal with Rossini's character, his approach to singing, his meeting with Wagner, Stendhal's presentation of the composer, and quotations from admirers and detractors. The volume concludes with a works list, bibliography, and discography of recordings through the mid-1960s. Illustrated.

152. Cowen, Sir Frederic H. *Rossini*. Volume in the series *Masterpieces of Music*, ed. E. Hatzfeld. New York: Frederick A. Stokes Co., 1912. 63 pp. ML410.R8 C8.

A thirty-page biography beginning with the accusation that even though Rossini had composed forty [sic] operas, he suffered from laziness. Cowen's account is more fictional than real and is aimed at the general reader. Following the text are transcriptions of pieces from the Stabat mater,

Guillaume Tell (including an abridged version of the overture) and *The Barber of Seville*; the vocal selections also provide an English text.

153. Curzon, Henri de. *Rossini*. In the series *Les Maîtres de la Musique*. Paris: Librairie Félix Alcan, 1920. 207 pp. ML410.R8 C9.

Curzon divides his study into a section on Rossini's life (told in strict connection with his compositions) and another on his music. The latter includes commentaries on individual works and specific numbers therein, on libretti and plots, and on the author's impressions of Rossini's style. With musical examples and a chronological works list (with page references to text discussions).

154. Dauriac, Lionel. *Rossini*. Paris: Henri Laurens, 1906. In the series *Les Musiciens Célèbres*. 123 pp. ML410.R8 D2.

This biography, as the author mentions, is a study of Rossini's life through his works. Includes a chapter on the author's judgment of Rossini's compositions, style, and musical legacy. Has a chronological works list and a brief annotated bibliography with the standard late nineteenth-century sources, such as Stendhal (item 135), Carpani (item 483), Azevedo (item 105), and Zanolini (item 138).

155. Fara, Giulio. *Genio e ingegno musicale: Gioachino Rossini*. Turin: Fratelli Bocca, 1915. 140 pp. ML410.R8 F2.

A psychological look at Rossini's character. Fara's stated purpose is to clear Rossini from mud slinging; thus, he answers charges that the composer had a split personality, megolomania, and hypochondria. He mentions some of the anecdotes leading to the commonly held picture of Rossini as suffering from a nervous or psychological disorder. Fara places the composer's behavior under the guise of genius. For example, he depicts Rossini as a man hiding under a mask of a superman, affecting indifference, and responding to life with irony. As to his "lazy" silence after *Guillaume Tell*, Fara responds that the successful composer had a fear of his own greatness. He questions whether geniuses can be classified as normal in the psychological and physical functions, leaving the decision up to his readers.

156. Fraccaroli, Arnaldo. *Rossini*. Verona: Mondadori, 1941; 2nd ed., 1941; 3rd ed., 1942; 4th ed., 1944. 369 pp. ML410.R8 F7.

Translated into Spanish by Concepción de Bofarull. Barcelona: Luis de Caralt, 1944. 399 pp. ML410.R8 F73.

A biography presented as a fictional account, related in episodes. With illustrations.

157. Giacobbe, Juan Francisco. *Rossini*. Buenos Aires: Ricordi Americana, 1942. 151 pp. ML410.R8 G5.

A brief biography of Rossini with comments on his style. Includes a discography of the early recordings by singers such as Caruso and Björling and conductors such as Furtwängler and Toscanini. With illustrative plates.

158. Lancellotti, Arturo. *Gioacchino Rossini, 1772*[sic]*–1868*. Rome: Fratelli Palombi, 1942. 232 pp. ML410.R8 L3.

This basic biography also includes chapters on the character of Rossini's music, Rossini's rapport with colleagues, and his two wives. Lancellotti ends his volumes with a discussion of Rossini's assistance in founding the Liceo in Pesaro. With illustrations.

159. Malerbi, Giuseppe. *Gioacchino Rossini: pagine segrete*. Bologna: Pizzi e C., 1921. 16 pp. ML410.R8 M15.

This descendant of Giuseppe and Luigi Malerbi demonstrates the importance of their influence and teachings on Rossini before he began musical studies in Bologna. He also documents Rossini's connections with Lugo (see also item 346).

160. Michotte, Edmond. *Souvenirs personnels: la visite de R. Wagner a Rossini (Paris 1860); details inedits et commentaires*. Paris: Fischbacher, 1906. 53 pp. ML410.W11 M4; Italian translation by Marzio Pieri and Benedetta Origo. Rome: Edizione dell'elefante, 1988. 152 pp.; English translation, see Weinstock, item 161; new English translation (not examined): "Wagner and Rossini," in *Wagner* 13 [no. 3] (September 1992): 122–38.

Based on notes taken during the historic meeting of Rossini and Wagner, Michotte, an amateur composer/pianist and close friend of Rossini, recounts the two composers' discussion. Among the topics were fellow composers, including Carl Maria von Weber, Antonio Salieri, and Felix Mendelssohn. After sharing with Wagner his recollections of his visit to Beethoven in Vienna, Rossini discussed his study of German scores, including those of Mozart and Bach. In addition to sharing their philosophies on musical composition, melody, and "the music of the future," both spoke of the art of singing, which Rossini claimed had declined since the disappearance of the castrato. Michotte concludes his narration with comments on the disparate nature of both geniuses.

161. ———. *Richard Wagner's visit to Rossini (Paris 1860)*; and, *An evening at Rossini's in Beau-Sejours (Passy) 1858*. Translated and annotated, with introduction and appendix, by Herbert Weinstock. Chicago: University of Chicago Press, 1968. xi, 144 pp. ML410.W11 M42.

Single-volume English translation of items 123 and 160. In his appendix, Weinstock includes translations of Eduard Hanslick's comments on two visits to Rossini, published as "Musical Recollections of Paris (1860)" and "Musical Letters from Paris (July 18, 1867)" in Hanslick's *Aus dem Concert-Saal* (Vienna, 1897) and of Emil Naumann's 1867 meeting with Rossini, published in Naumann's *Italienische Tondichter, von Palestrina bis auf die Gegenwart* (1876) (see item 128). With index and illustrations.

162. Pfister, Kurt. *Das Leben Rossinis: Gesetz und Triumph der Oper*. Vienna: Gallus, 1948. 162 pp. ML410.R8 P5.

A study of Rossini's career in Italy and his subsequent theatrical triumph in Europe. The author includes accounts of the composer's stay in Vienna and his meeting there with Carl Maria von Weber and Beethoven. He continues with Rossini's stay in London, his move to Paris, and his return to Italy after *Guillaume Tell*, where he met tenor Adolphe Nourrit in Milan in 1838. Pfister not only cites excerpts from Wagner's writings about Rossini (see item 136) but also quotes from Michotte's narration of the meeting of the two composers (item 160). In addition to describing Rossini's physical appearance, Pfister also considers his artistic and cultural image. Illustrated.

163. Radiciotti, Giuseppe, compiler. *Aneddoti rossiniani autentici*. Rome: A.F. Formíggini, 1929. 168 pp. ML410.R8 R24.

Radiciotti relates some 153 anecdotes about Rossini's life, habits, career, and personal relationships. Contains an index of the reminiscences as well as a list of contributors, among them Charles Gounod, Eduard Hanslick, Victor Hugo, Tito and Giulio Ricordi, Camille Saint-Saëns (see item 166), and Edmond Michotte (see items 123, 160, and 161).

164. ———. *Gioacchino Rossini: Vita documentata, opere ed influenza su l'arte*. 3 vols. Tivoli: Arti Grafiche Majella di Aldo Chicca, 1927–1929. ML410.R8 R22.

The monumental biography upon which much subsequent Rossini scholarship was based. Volume 1 (1927; xii, 502 pp.), spans the years from the composer's childhood to the end of his artistic activity in Italy. It contains Part I, with information on Rossini's early years and musical studies, and the beginning of Part II, which traces his career from the earliest operas to

Semiramide. Volume 2 (1928; 567 pp.) concludes Part II, which follows Rossini from his invitation to London up until his death and the translation of his remains from Paris to Florence in 1887. Volume 3 (1929; 362 pp.) contains both Parts III (a physical and psychological portrait of Rossini) and IV, which considers the artistic ambiance from 1800 to 1810; Rossini's artistic characteristics; his influence on the art of singing; the development and evolution of the Rossinian style; the influence of his music; and his place in music history. The third volume also contains six appendices. The first is a works list, including information on the operas' premieres and casts, librettists, score editions, and subsequent productions; following this are lists of cantatas and hymns, vocal chamber and instrumental music, sacred music, didactic works, pieces contained in *Peccati di vecchiezza (Péchés de vieillesse)*, pasticci, and other autograph works. The first appendix also lists the volume and page number where the works are discussed. Appendix 2 gives page references to observations from Rossini's artistic colleagues that appear in the volume; additional comments not in the text appear here. Appendix 3 lists mention of Rossini made in other stage works, such as *Rossini à Paris).* Appendix 4 is an iconography. Appendix 5 lists all of the composer's honors (see also Diotallevi, item 82), and Appendix 6 is a bibliography. An index of all names in the three volumes as well as a fifteen-page index to the complete work follow. As an additional aid, each chapter in the three volumes is divided into numbered sections, which are listed at the beginning of the chapter; also, each volume is indexed separately. Correspondence, abundant musical examples, and illustrations of the composer's family and contemporaries are included throughout the entire work.

165. Roncaglia, Gino. *Rossini: L'Olympico.* Milan: Fratelli Bocca, 1946. 557 pp. ML410.R8 R75.

A biography as well as a commentary on Rossini's works and a chapter on the aesthetics of his music, citing Mazzini (item 487). The author includes musical examples to support his comments on the operas. With a works list and illustrations.

166. Saint-Saëns, Camille. *École buissonnières.* Paris: P. Lafitte & Cie, 1913. viii, 366 pp. ML60.S14.

Translated by Edwin Gile Rich as *Musical Memories.* Boston: Small, Maynard & Co., 1919. 282 pp. ML60.S14R4; reprint, New York: Da Capo, 1969. 282 pp. ML60.S14 R4 1969; reprint of 1919 edition, New York: AMS Press, 1971. 282 pp. ISBN 0-404-05502-8 ML60.S14R4 1971.

Fellow composer Saint-Saëns describes Rossini in his retirement, which the author likens to "musical suicide." Also discusses Rossini as host of the famous *soirées*, at which the young Saint-Saëns played piano. He depicts Rossini as an idol worshipped by all of Paris even though his music "belonged to the past." Contains the story of Adelina Patti singing for Rossini and his comments on her embellishments. The composer's remembrances of Rossini are on pages 201 to 210 in all editions.

167. Toye, Francis. *Rossini: A Study in Tragi-Comedy*. London: William Heinemann, 1934, 269 pp.; also published in New York: A.A.Knopf: 1934, 269 pp. ML410.R8T73 1934; reprint (with fewer, different, illustrations and new preface), London: Arthur Barker Ltd., 1954, 269 pp. ML410.R8T73 1954; reprint, New York: W.W. Norton, 1963, 269 p. ML410.R8T73 1963.

Toye offers a chronological mix of biography and commentary on Rossini's career, ending the volume with his views on the composer's influence on nineteenth-century contemporaries and on Rossini as innovator and composer. Although Toye demonstrates a knowledge of contemporary Rossini scholarship, because many scores were unavailable for his examination, he bases some of his comments on the music on Radiciotti's discussions (item 164). Toye's approach is often unfairly critical.

168. ———. *Rossini: The Man and His Music*. New York: Dover Publications, Inc., 1987. 268 pp. ISBN 0-486-25396-1 ML410.R8T73.

A slightly revised and enlarged republication of Item 167. Includes the preface and illustrations from the 1934 edition as well as the preface from 1954 edition.

BIOGRAPHICAL STUDIES PUBLISHED BETWEEN 1950 AND THE PRESENT

169. Albarelli, Giuseppe. "L'infanzia di Gioacchino Rossini (da documenti inediti dell'Archivio storico del Comune di Pesaro: 1) Vicende della famiglia Rossini a Pesaro dal 1789 al 1797." *Bollettino del Centro Rossiniano di Studi* 4 [no. 6] (1958); 103–106; and 2) "Dalla rivoluzione del 21 dicembre 1797 alla fine dell'anno 1800," 4 [no. 1] (1958): 6–9 and [no. 2] (1958): 28–31.

Using archival documents in Pesaro that were unedited at the time of this article, in this three-part series, Albarelli traces the history of Rossini's family during the composer's early years. For a confirmation and completion of this study, see Loschelder, item 179.

170. Alverà, Pierluigi. *Rossini*. Trans. by Raymond Rosenthal. In *Portraits of Greatness* series. New York: Treves Publishing Co., 1986. 87 pp. ISBN 0-918367-11-5 ML410.R8 A4613 1986.

A light and romanticized narrative, the book is mostly an illustrative treatment of Rossini's career and professional environment. Contains photographs of some twentieth-century productions and a reprint of a portion of Rossini's visit with Wagner (see items 160 and 161). Includes a section by Marco Spada on Rossini's works.

171. Baricco, Alessandro. "Rossini e la malattia come grembo originario." In *Intorno a Massimo Mila: Studi sul teatro e il novecento musicale. Atti del Convegno di studi promosso dal Centro studi musicale Feruccio Busoni. Empoli 17–19 February 1991,* 87–97, edited by Talia Pecker Berio. Vol. 32 of *Quaderni della Rivista Italiana di Musicologia, Società Italiana di Musicologia.* Florence: Leo S. Olschki, 1994. x, 216 pp. ISBN 88-222-4176-2 ML423.M613 I57 1994.

Baricco uses as inspiration what he calls Massimo Mila's "silence" about Rossini's illness (see item 540). After citing an account of an ill Rossini given by poet Felice Romani's wife, Emilia Branco (included in Radiciotti, item 163), Baricco suggests that Rossini may have always lived with this nervous hypochondria; therefore, rather than using this illness as an excuse for his inability to compose, one should see it as the cause of all the music which preceded it. Suggesting that Rossini's perception of the world was based on this disorder, he relates it to what he calls Rossini's irrational, illogical, and incoherent theater. The law of Rossini's universe, he maintains, is one of fear. He suggests that our understanding of such disorders makes Rossini the first "modern" composer, more readily comprehensible to the twentieth century than to the nineteenth.

172. Bassi, Adriano. *Gioacchino Rossini.* Padua: Franco Muzzio, 1992. 295 pp. ISBN: 88-7021-599-7 ML410.R8 B33 1992.

Bassi's multifaceted work deals with various aspects of Rossini's life and career. Although a biography, the volume also considers Rossini's musical development and his works. Other chapters examine the composer's relationships with his colleagues and comments from contemporaries and twentieth-century writers. Bassi also quotes excerpts from the composer's correspondence and offers a list of Rossini interpreters listed by vocal range as well as a discography.

173. Cagli, Bruno. "L'ultima stagione." In *Rossini 1792–1992* (item 95), pp. 317–40.

The author traces Rossini's life after *Guillaume Tell* from his illness in Italy in the 1850s to his death in 1868. Considers the composer's years at Passy with his second wife, Olympe Péllisier, and their popular *soirées*. Also mentioned are Rossini's last works: the *Péchés de vieillesse* and the Petite messe solennelle. Illustrated with portraits, engravings and Gustave Doré's rendering of Rossini on his deathbed.

174. ————. "Rossini tra Illuminismo e Romanticismo." *Bollettino del Centro Rossiniano di Studi* 12 [no. 1](1972): 7–11.

Cagli begins by noting that the use of the term "classical" refers to items with universal, lasting appeal. He continues by considering the "classical" or formal side of Rossini, one that he maintains the composer left behind when he went to France. The "romantic" element in Rossini's music can be heard in *Guillaume Tell*. After further discussing the two sides of Rossini's musical personality, Cagli concludes that with the Petite messe solennelle, Rossini actually reached out to the future.

175. Camosci, Arnaldo. *Gioachino Rossini dai ritratti e dalle scritture*. Vol. 12 of the series *Raccolta di studi sui beni culturali ed ambientali delle Marche*. Rome: Paleani, 1985. 274 pp. ML410.R8 C18 1985.

Camosci, a graphologist, attempts to portray Rossini's character through an analysis of his handwriting taken from various periods of the composer's life. The author also analyzes Rossini from portraiture. Camosci considers the roles of the women in Rossini's life, noting their influences (often negative) on his personality and career, and specifically examines Olympe Pélissier through her handwriting.

176. Guandalini, Gina. *Rossini*. Milan: Ricordi, 1995. 78 pp. ISBN: 88-759-2460-0.

[Not examined.]

177. Keitel, Wilhelm and Dominik Neuner. *Gioachino Rossini*. Munich: Albrecht Knaus, 1992. 320 pp. ISBN 3-8135-0364-X ML410.R8 K4 1992.

This German contribution to Rossini biography devotes chapters to his childhood in Pesaro, his studies in Bologna, his early operatic experiences in Venice, the Neapolitan years, his operas in Rome and Milan, the Viennese visit, and his time in London. Two chapters deal with the early years in Paris; following these are sections on the composer's final visit to Italy, and his return to and remaining years in Paris. The authors also include a discussion of Rossini's meeting with Richard Wagner as related by Michotte (see item 160). In addition to a chronological outline of the composer's life, the book contains a biographical dictionary of his fellow composers, and a works list. Information on operas includes the names of librettists, details on premieres, a list of main characters and their vocal ranges, and a summary of the plot.

178. Kendall, Alan. *Gioacchino Rossini: The Reluctant Hero*. London: Victor Gollancz, 1992. xi, 276 pp. ISBN 0-575-05178-7 ML410.R8 K43 1992.

Written, as he notes in his introduction, when the "long overdue reappraisal of Rossini" was underway, Kendall's biography considers the enigmas in Rossini studies: how, he asks, could so prized a composer be forgotten so quickly? Considers Rossini's personality as well as his works and compares him stylistically with Bellini, Donizetti, Verdi, and Meyerbeer. Contains illustrations and a catalog of works.

* Kern, Bernd-Rüdiger. "Biographischer Überblick." In *Rossini in Paris: Eine Veranstaltung des Frankreichzentrums der Universität Leipzig, in Zusammenarbeit mit der Deutschen Rossini Gesellschaft e.V.* See item 290.

179. Loschelder, Josef. "L'infanzia di Gioacchino Rossini. Conferme e completamenti dello scritto di Albarelli: Part 1." *Bollettino del Centro Rossiniano di Studi* 12 [no. 1]: 45–63; "L'infanzia di Gioacchino Rossini: Sulle trace di Albarelli—Conferme, Lacune, Complementi," Part 2. 12 [no. 2] (1972): 33–52.

The author attempts to confirm the facts and fill in lacunae in the archival study of Rossini's earliest years by Giuseppe Albarelli (see item 169). Loschelder begins the first of this two-part series with documents concerning Giuseppe Rossini's employment as a musician and his political activities; the second part continues with documents concerning Rossini's father's trial, imprisonment, and release, his move to Lugo, and young Gioachino's activities there, including his studies with the Malerbis. See also items 159, 346, and 787.

180. Nicolao, Mario. *La maschera di Rossini*. Milan: Rizzoli, 1990. 237 pp. ISBN: 88-1784-034-3.

[Not examined.]

181. Osborne, Richard. *Rossini. Master Musicians* series. London: J.M. Dent, 1986, 330 p. ISBN 0460031791. ML410.R8 O9 1986; reprint, Boston: Northeastern University Press, 1990, xiii, 330 pp. ISBN 1-55553-088-5. ML410.R8 O9 1990. Reprint, New York: Oxford University Press, 2000. ISBN 0-1981-6490-4 ML410.R8 O9 2000. Translated into German by Grete Wehmeyer as *Rossini: Leben und Werk*. Munich: Drömer Knauer, 1992. 383 pp.

Osborne's purpose is to fill what he terms a fifty-year gap in "full length" English-language studies of Rossini's life and works. He repairs this oversight with a detailed chronological narrative that traces the composer's artistic development from childhood to his final years as mentor of the Italian musical establishment in Paris; following the biography, the author offers commentaries on Rossini's operas as well as the sacred music and compositions for voice and piano. Because Osborne draws heavily on the research and critical editions published by the Fondazione Rossini, this volume reflects current scholarship for its time. Although he demonstrates a knowledge of Rossini's career, Osborne ignores relationships between the composer and his colleagues. The resulting picture of Rossini is often isolated from the contemporary Italian theatrical milieu. The volume includes musical excerpts, illustrations, a chronological outline of Rossini's life, works list, annotated index of significant contemporaries, and bibliography.

182. ———. "Rossini's Life: An Overview." In *The Cambridge Companion to Rossini*. See item 478.

183. Rosselli, John. "Verdi e la storia della retribuzione del compositore italiano." *Studi verdiani* 2 (1993): 11–28.

Rosselli demonstrates how the position of the composer changed between the time of Rossini and Verdi. One issue he considers is earnings. Rossini's income increased after he arrived in Naples, not only because his operas gained popularity but because his stipend included his duties as director of music as well as a percentage of the gambling fees earned by Domenico Barbaja (see item 241). Eventually, however, Rossini's success did ensure higher pay for composers as did the money they earned from publication of their music.

184. Scherliess, Volker. *Gioacchino Rossini mit Selbstzeugnissen und Bilddokumenten*. Hamburg: Rowohlt, 1991. 158 pp. ISBN 3-499-50476-6 ML410.R8 S17 1991.

An illustrated biography of the composer that places him in the theatrical arena of his day and considers his impact and influence on his contemporaries as well as those who followed in the second half of the century. Also considers the impresarios, singers, and librettists who worked with Rossini. Chapters are devoted to his early years, the Italian works, the serious works for the Paris stage, his later years in Paris, and his church music. Includes an outline of the composer's life, comments about the composer from contemporaries, a works list, and a discography citing Modugno (see items 845, 846, and 847) as a source.

185. Till, Nicholas. *Rossini: His Life and Times.* New York: Hippocrene Books, 1983, and Tunbridge Wells, England: Midas Books, 1983. 143 pp. ISBN 0-88254-668-6 ML410.R8 T54 1983. Later published as *Rossini* in *The Illustrated Lives of the Great Composers* series. London: Omnibus Press, 1987. 143 pp. ISBN 0-7119-0988-1 ML410.R8 T54 1987.

A general biography that, amply supported by illustrations of important venues and contemporaries, places Rossini in the theatrical and cultural milieu of his day. A book for general readership.

186. Tubeuf, André. "Rossini: Le plaisir, et ses travaux forces." *Revue des deux mondes* [no. 3] (March 1992): 151–59.

[Not examined.]

187. Vingradito, Fabrizio. "Ahi cotta e vergognosa morte!" In *Rossini 1792–1992* (item 95), pp. 341–43.

This bicentennial exhibit catalog includes this brief section on Rossini the gourmand.

188. Weinstock, Herbert. *Rossini: A Biography.* New York: Alfred A. Knopf, 1968. xviii, 560 pp. ML410.R8 W35: London: Oxford University Press, 1968. xviii, 561 pp. ML410.R68 W35; 1968b; reprint, New York: Limelight Editions, 1987. xviii, 560 pp. ML410.R8 W53 1987.

Weinstock's aim, in his words, is to provide a "life and times" of Rossini. Although the most substantial and best documented biography of its day, the work still echoes a share of myth and misinformation that had traced its way down from the earliest histories. Weintock divides Rossini's life into small chronological segments, discussing them in light of corresponding musical works. An epilogue considers the days immediately following the composer's death in 1868 until the celebration in Florence of the 1892 centenary of his birth. Several appendices follow: the text of the contract commissioning *Il barbiere di Siviglia*; an 1842 report from Rossini's physician; the composer's will and codicils; an equivalency chart comparing currency in Rossini's day with the value of the U.S. dollar in 1967; ninety-four pages of notes and citations; and four annotated sections, which form a chronological works list of the operas, vocal music, instrumental music, and *Péchés de vieillese* (this latter section cross-references pieces that also appear as vocal and instrumental works). A twenty-five-page bibliography, general index, and index of references to compositions complete the volume.

SPECIALIZED STUDIES

Rossini and Art

189. Parigi, Luigi. "Rossini e le arti figurative." *La rassegna musicale* 24 [no. 3] (July-September 1954): 255–69.

Considers Rossini's talents in and understanding and appreciation of the graphic arts. Parigi uses as examples the composer's designs for a sculpture in memory of Giovanni Colbran, Isabella's father, and of the silhouettes the composer made. The author also considers the *objets d'art* Rossini owned, concluding that, by understanding this side of Rossini, one may flesh out a better conception of him as a complete artist.

Rossini's Health

* Baricco, Alessandro. "Rossini e la malattia come grembo originario." See item 171.

190. Cagli, Bruno. "Il risveglio magnetico e il sonno della ragione: Variazioni sulla calamita, l'oppio e il sonnambulismo." *Studi musicali* 14 (1985): 157–70.

Cagli begins with references to Anton Mesmer in Mozart's *Così fan tutte*, then notes similarities in its libretto with that of *Turco in Italia*, a forerunner of Rossini's opera written by poet Caterino Mazzolà. Although these operas (as well as Rossini's version of the latter) fell out of favor with the advent of Romanticism, the author notes that pseudomedical theories in line with Mesmer's did not. After connecting the process of magneticism and the "sonnambula," found, of course, in Bellini's opera, the author quotes from a letter demonstrating that Olympe Pélissier sent a lock of her husband's hair to Florence so that a "sonnambula" in a state of trance might diagnosis and treat his illness. A facsimile of the letter is included.

191. Franken, Franz Hermann. *Der Krankheiten grosser Komponisten. II.* Vol. 105 in the series *Taschenbücher der Musikwissenschaft*. Wilhelmshaven: Heinrichshofen, 1988. 303 pp.

Not examined. For an earlier study by this author on Rossini's health, see item 192.

192. ———. *Krankheit und Tod grosser Komponisten.* Baden-Baden: Gerhard Witzstrock, 1979. viii, 279 pp. ISBN 3-87921-123-X ML390.F82.

Drawing information from biographies and studies of Rossini's personality and illnesses, the author considers Rossini's life in terms of his physical condition, reconstructing a history of his illnesses, medical diagnoses, and treatments. Specific conditions discussed include the composer's gonorrhea, hemorrhoids, emphysema-bronchitis and related heart ailments, and his final illness, rectal cancer. Also considers Rossini's depression. See also item 191.

193. Riboli, Bruno. *Malattia de Gioacchino Rossini secondo una relazione medica di 1842*. Pesaro: Federici, 1956. 7 pp. Extracted from *Note e riviste di psichiatria*, 3–4 (July-December 1955).

[Not examined.]

194. ———. "Profilo medico-psicologico di Gioacchino Rossini." *La rassegna musicale* 24 [no. 3] (July-September 1954): 292–303.

The author examines letters of Olympe Pélissier and a report that describe symptoms and treatments for Rossini's illnesses, such as the urinary ailment from which he suffered during much of the 1840s. Also considers the possibility that the composer had cyclothymia, a mild form of what was once known as manic-depression. Riboli suggests that perhaps Rossini's physical and mental health could be connected to his activities as a composer.

195. Schwartz, Daniel W. "Rossini: A Psychoanalytic Approach to 'the Great Renunciation.' " *Journal of the American Psychoanalytic Association* 113 [no. 3] (July 1995): 551–69; reprinted in *Psychoanalytic explorations in music*, 423–40. Madison, Conn.: International Universities, 1990.

Dr. Schwartz states that, to date, excuses for Rossini's renunciation of his career have been insufficient explanations for his decision. The author takes a psychoanalytical look at the composer's personality, concluding that Rossini's action resulted from his inability to deal with the death of his mother. Maintaining that composing had given Rossini an outlet for sublimating his feelings for his mother (*Tell*, the author claims, reflects oedipal feelings), Schwartz suggests that after her death, Rossini submitted to narcissistic withdrawal and depression. After recovering from anorexia and depression in Italy, Rossini returned to France in 1855 and survived by becoming obsessively orderly. Having never been able to create for himself a mature image of his mother, Rossini spent the remainder of his days in a dependent and sadomasochistic relationship with Olympe Pélissier.

* Volk, Peter. "Der Krankheitsverlauf bei Rossini." In *Rossini in Paris: Eine Veranstaltung des Frankreichzentrums der Universität Leipzig, in Zusammenarbeit mit der Deutschen Rossini Gesellschaft e.V.* See item 290.

Rossini, Politics, and Patriotism

* Bellaigue, Camille. "Un chef d'oeuvre patriotique; le second acte de *Guillaume Tell.*" See item 769.

196. Berti, Marcello. *Da Rossini a Verdi lungo i sentieri del Risorgimento.* Lugo di Romagna (Ravenna): Walberti, 2001. 228 pp.

    [Not examined.]

    * Betzwieser, Thomas. "A propos de l'exotisme musical de Rossini." See item 534.

197. Cheskin, Jonathan L. "Catholic-Liberal Opera: Outline of a Hidden Italian Musical Romanticism." Ph.D. dissertation, University of Chicago, 1999. xv, 514 pp.

    Cheskin bases his thesis on the work of Neapolitian critic Francesco De Sanctis, who divided Italian Romantic literature into the Democratic and Catholic-Liberal schools. The latter was based on Catholicism and an ideology of endurance. Cheskin argues that, although Italian opera is normally viewed in light of Democratic theories, Catholic-Liberalism also can be seen in the text and music of compositions by Rossini, Bellini, Donizetti, and Verdi. Cheskin examines how Rossini's *Maometto II* and *Mosè in Egitto* foreshadow the aesthetics of this literary movement.

198. Gerhard, Anselm. *Die Verstädterung der Oper: Paris und das Musiktheater des 19. Jahrhunderts.* Stuttgart: J.B. Metzler, 1992. 491 pp. ISBN 3-476-00850-9 ML1727.8.P2 G38 1992; published in English as *The Urbanization of Opera: Music Theater in Paris in the Nineteenth Century.* Chicago: University of Chicago Press, 1998. xxi, 503 pp. ISBN 0-226-28857-9 ML1727.8.P2 G313 1998.

    Gerhard includes a chapter, "Rossini and the Revolution" (pp. 61–100 in the German edition and pp. 63–121 in the English), in which he considers *Le siège de Corinth* and *Guillaume Tell.* The author looks at the revolutionary elements in *Le siège,* which breaks with the traditions of trágedie lyrique and introduces musical innovations. He notes problems caused by Rossini's transfer of Italian compositional techniques to French opera and comments on the historicism of the subject. *Tell,* too, offered its share of political overtones, such as the oath-taking scene, he says. Includes a chapter on Victor-Joseph Etiénne Jouy, librettist of *Tell,* and his *Essai sur l'opera français* (item 395). Gerhard suggests that the success of Meyerbeer's operas was the cause of Rossini's retirement. Before the discussion of each opera, the author lists information on the librettist, the premiere, characters and their vocal ranges, plot synopsis, editions, and recommended recordings.

199. Gossett, Philip. "Becoming A Citizen: The Chorus in *Risorgimento* Opera." *Cambridge Opera Journal* 2 [no. 1] (1990): 41–64.

Examining works from Rossini to Verdi, Gossett traces the evolution of the chorus as a political statement in nineteenth-century Italy. Rossini's early operas, the author maintains, are normally so neutral in expression that they are perfect for self-borrowing, fitting one text as well as another. However, in the accompaniment of a chorus in *L'italiana in Algeri*, Gossett notes, Rossini set an instrumental reference to "La Marseillaise." Thereafter, the author sees the chorus emerging as a more forceful dramatic group representative of "a people"—the Scots—in *La donna del lago* (the "Coro dei Bardi" took on a different risorgimental role as a hymn to Pope Pius IX), and finally, in *Giullaume Tell*, the fully developed chorus signifies those under the political domination of a foreign power, a message clear to northern Italian audiences. Gossett continues his study with Verdi, demonstrating Rossini's influence on his younger colleague, for example, by indicating the musical links between the Act II finale of *Guillaume Tell* and the Act III Knights of Death chorus in Verdi's *La battaglia di Legnano*.

200. Grembler, Martina. *Rossini e la patria: Studien zu Leben und Werk Gioachino Rossinis vor dem Hintergrund des Risorgimento*. Vol. 195, Kölner Beiträge zur Musikforschung. ed., Dietrich Kämper. Kassel: Gustav Bosse, 1996. 241 pp. ISBN 3-7649-2627-9 ML410.R8 G74 1996.

Grembler examines Rossini's career in connection with contemporary politics. Works considered include the Inno dell'indipendenza (1815), the cantatas for the Bourbons (1815–1822), the Cantata for the Congress of Verona (1822), compositions for Pius IX, and Parisian works with political overtones (*Il viaggio a Reims* and "La corona d'Italia"). The author also looks at selections from operas, such as *L'italiana in Algeri*'s "Pensa alla patria," and their political overtones. She places the composer in the politically-charged periods during which he lived, connecting his music and correspondence to the revolutionary views of his day (see pp. 23–35 in which letters to Sicilian lawyer Filippo Santocanale are discussed). An appendix lists the major political events during Rossini's life.

* O'Grady, Deirdre. "La fonction du choeur dans l'opéra patriotique du XIXe siècle." See item 778.

* Walton, Benjamin. *Romanticisms and Nationalisms in Restoration France*. See item 328.

5

Studies of Rossini's Contemporaries

ROSSINI'S PARENTS: GIUSEPPE AND ANNA (GUIDARINI) ROSSINI

* *Bollettino del primo centenario rossiniano pubblicato dal comitato ordinatore*. See item 446.

* Fabbri, Paolo. "Alla scuola dei Malerbi: altri autografi rossiniani." Item 346.

201. ———. "I Rossini, una famiglia in arte." *Bollettino del Centro Rossiniano di Studi* [no. 1–3] (1983): 125–51.

Gleaning information from Rossini biographies, theater histories, and archival materials, Fabbri documents the professional activities of Rossini and his parents from the late 1790s until the young composer's first operatic commission in 1810. Of importance is Fabbri's demonstration that Anna Rossini's stage career actually began before her husband's imprisonment in 1800. Also significant are the details of young Rossini's appearances as a singer as well as of his employment as an orchestra violist and *maestro al cembalo*. In addition to clarifying details about Rossini's parents' careers, Fabbri describes Rossini's apprenticeship in the theater. Includes a facsimile and the program of a concert organized by Rossini in Imola in 1804, in which he performed with his mother; included is the text of the *buffa cavatina* "Se mia moglie crepasse una volta" he sang. Also gives the texts of the original aria from Weigl's setting of *L'amor marinaro* and the substitute number Rossini composed for tenor Antonio Chies.

202. ———. *"Minima rossiniana*: ancora sulle carriere dei Rossini." *Bollettino del Centro Rossiniano di Studi* [no. 1–3] (1987): 5–23.

Sheds new light on the professional activities of Rossini and his parents before 1810. In addition to citing sources documenting Rossini's roles as singer and *maestro al cembalo*, Fabbri corrects information about Anna Rossini's singing career, placing her debut in Ancona's 1797–1798 *Carnavale*. This new date corresponds with the arrival of the French and the sanction of women on stage by one year. It also substantiates Rossini's account of his mother performing during his father's imprisonment for political activism. Includes theatrical programs and lists Anna Rossini's career both by season and repertoire of buffa operas. Illustrated with a poster documenting her Ancona debut.

* Jarro (Giulio Piccini), ed. *Giovacchino Rossini e la sua famiglia*: *notizie aneddotiche tolte da documenti inediti*. See item 34.

* Ragni, Sergio. "Isabella Colbran: Appunti per una biografia." See item 205.

* Schwartz, Daniel W. "Rossini: A Psychoanalytic Approach to the "Great Renunciation." See item 195.

* Walker, Frank. "Rossiniana in the Piancastelli Collection." Part 1: "Miscellaneous Unpublished Letters." See item 55.

ROSSINI'S WIVES: ISABELLA COLBRAN AND OLYMPE PÉLISSIER

Colbran, Isabella [Colbrand]

* Appolonia, Giorgio. *Le voci di Rossini*. See item 265.

* Bucarelli, Mauro. "Rossini Fever." See item 307.

* Cagli, Bruno. "All'ombra dei gigli d'oro." See item 356.

* Celletti, Rodolfo. "Il vocalismo italiano da Rossini a Donizetti. Parte I: Rossini." See item 562.

* De Rensis, Raffaello. "Rossini intimo: Lettere all'amico Santocanale." See item 77.

* Fabbri, Paolo, and Sergio Monaldini. "Delle monete il suon già sento! Documenti notarili relativi a Gioachino Rossini, possidente." See item 43.

* Lancellotti, Arturo. *Gioacchino Rossini, 1772* [sic]*–1868*. See item 158.

203. Lazzari, Daniela. "L'anima della Colbran." *Rassegna veneta di studi musicali* 2–3 (1986–87): 389–91.

[Not examined.]

* "Mme. Colbrand-Rossini." Chapter 25 (pp. 273–80) in Leon and Marie Escudier's *Rossini: sa vie et ses oeuvres, avec une introduction de M. Méry.* See item 116.

204. Montero Alonso, José. *Isabel Colbrand: la madrileña que enamoró a Rossini.* Madrid: Artes Gráficas Municipales, 1992. 20 pp. ISBN: 8-4781-2143-9 ML410.C65.

[Not examined]

* Müller, Reto. "Rossini-Bibliotheken der Welt: Der Fonds Michotte in Brüssels." See item 12.

205. Ragni, Sergio. "Isabella Colbran: Appunti per una biografia." *Bollettino del Centro Rossiniano di Studi* 38 (1998): 17–55.

Gleaning particulars from Rossini biographies, theater histories, and period news items and reviews, the author presents details from the life and career of Isabella Colbran, both before and after she became Rossini's first wife. Citing correspondence, Ragni also presents a portrait of Colbran's declining years in Bologna, under the control of Rossini's father, while the composer (with his new companion, Olympe Pélissier) worked in Paris. Mentions Colbran's own activities as a composer. Along with a facsimile of the singer's baptismal record, the article features a chronology of Colbran's concerts and operatic career, with data on performances, venues, and, in the case of operas, roles and fellow cast members.

206. ———. "Isabella Colbran, soprano con obbligo di primadonna." See *Gioachino Rossini*, item 358.

207. Ricci, Corrado. *Rossini, le sue case e le sue donne.* Milan: G. Ricordi & C, 1891. 10 pp.

[Not examined.]

* Rossini, Gioachino. Letters, Sotheby's Catalogue. See item 39.

* Schlitzer, Franco. "Ricordi e lettere in Siena." See item 51.

* Silvestri, Lodovico Settimo. *Della vita e delle opere di Gioachino Rossini.* See item 133.

* Stendhal. *Vie de Rossini.* See item 135.

* Walker, Frank. "Rossiniana in the Piancastelli Collection." Part 1: "Miscellaneous Unpublished Letters." See item 55.

Pélissier, Olympe

* Atwood, William G. *The Parisian Worlds of Frédéric Chopin*. See item 310.

208. Bruson, Jean-Marie. "Olympe, Pacini, Michotte e altri: la vendita dei *Péchés de vieillesse* e le sue vicende." *Bollettino del Centro Rossiniano di Studi* 34 (1994): 5–68. Translated from French to Italian by Reto Müller and Paolo Fabbri.

Traces the attempts of Rossini's widow to sell and publish the manuscripts of the *Péchés de vieillesse*. Citing correspondence and articles from the contemporary press, Bruson documents Olympe Pélissier's legal battles with Emilien Pacini over rights to some of the texts and with family friend Edmond Michotte (see items 123 and 160), whose relationship with the widow ended bitterly when he had several of the pieces performed without permission. An appendix includes letters between Pélissier, Michotte, and their lawyers; letters regarding Pacini's claim; the sale contract of the *Péchés* to Albert Grant; documentation of return of the works from Michotte to Pélissier; and the court's rendering in the widow's case against Michotte.

* ———. "Olympe Pélissier." In *Rossini in Paris: Eine Veranstaltung des Frankreichzentrums der Universität Leipzig, in Zusammenarbeit mit der Deutschen Rossini Gesellschaft e.V.* See item 290.

* Cagli, Bruno. "Il risveglio magnetico e il sonno della ragione: Variazioni sulla calamita, l'oppio e il sonnambulismo." See item 190.

* Cambi, Luisa. "Bellini—un pacchetto di autografi." See item 68.

* DiProfio, Alessandro. "Inediti rossiniani a Parigi. Il Fondo Rossini-Hentsch alla Bibliothèque G. Mahler." See item 42.

* Fabbri, Paolo, and Sergio Monaldini. "Delle monete il suon già sento! Documenti notarili relativi a Gioachino Rossini, possidente." See item 43.

209. "Il testamento di Madame Pélissier." *Bollettino del Centro Rossiniano di Studi* 4 [no. 5] (1958): 92–93.

A transcription of the will of Olympe Pélissier dated 26 January 1837, deposited with Hector Couvert (see also item 71) when she was making legal arrangements prior to her move to Bologna to reside near Rossini.

* Lancellotti, Arturo. *Gioacchino Rossini, 1772* [sic]*–1868*. See item 158.

* "Lettere della Pélissier." See item 69.

* "Perplessità della Pélissier per la traslazione della salma di Rossini." See item 70.

* Ricci, Corrado. *Rossini, le sue case e le sue donne.* See item 207.

* Schlizter, F[ranco]. "Nozze di Rossini." See item 71.

* ———. *Rossini e Siena e altri scritti rossiniani (con lettere inedite).* See item 53.

* Schwartz, Daniel W. "Rossini: A Psychoanalytic Approach to 'the Great Renunciation.' " See item 195.

* "Una lettera della Pélissier al Papa e la risposta della Segreteria di Stato." See item 74.

* Walker, Frank. "Rossiniana in the Piancastelli Collection." Part 1: "Miscellaneous Unpublished Letters." See item 55.

ROSSINI'S ACQUAINTANCES AND COLLEAGUES

General Studies

210. Stecchina, Giuliana. *Rossini e dintorno.* Trieste: Lint, 1992. 159 p. ISBN: 88-85083-89-7.

    [Not examined.]

COMPOSERS

211. Conati, Marcello. "Florimo e Mercadante." In *Atti Francesco Florimo e l'Ottocento musicale del convegno: Morcone, 19–21 aprile 1990,* Vol. 1, 121–33. Edited by Rosa Cafiero and Marina Marino. Reggio Calabria: Jason Editrice, 1999. ISBN: 88-8157-069-0 ML423.F63 F73 Vol. 1.

    Although the focus of this essay is on the professional rapport between Francesco Florimo and Saverio Mercadante, Conati mentions Rossini's position in the Neapolitan musical arena dominated by composers trained by Niccolò Zingarelli, whose disdain for Rossini is legend. Conati considers how Mercadante purposely attempted to create a style and direction which differed from that established by Rossini.

212. Weinstock, Herbert. "Rossini, Donizetti, Bellini, and Verdi." *Opera* 19 (1968): 865–71.

    With quotations from correspondence, a capsulized summary of Rossini's relationships with these three composers. Based on material from Weinstock's *Rossini: A Biography* (see item 188).

Studies of Specific Composers

> N.B. Items in this section relate to Rossini's relationships with various col-
> leagues, ways in which he was compared or contrasted to his contempo-
> raries, and their influence on his music. Studies of how Rossini's music
> influenced that of other composers can be found in Chapter 8.

Arditi, Luigi

213. Cagli, Bruno. "Rossini e Luigi Arditi. Una testimonianza e un carteggio."
Bollettino del Centro Rossiniano di Studi [no. 1–3] (1978): 31–44.

> Cagli describes the friendship between Rossini and Arditi, best known as
> the composer of the popular song "Il bacio." Abstracting passages from
> Arditi's memoirs, Cagli helps to document their relationship; his inclusion
> of transcriptions of six letters (one from Arditi to Rossini and the others
> from Rossini to Arditi) demonstrates their closeness. In addition to men-
> tioning compositions such as Arditi's mazurca, "La farfalletta," dedicated to
> Rossini, Cagli notes that the younger man, also a conductor, did much to
> keep Rossini's music alive by programming it during the second half of the
> nineteenth century. Includes a facsimile of a card and letter in Rossini's
> hand. The collection of letters is located in the Fondo Piancastelli: for more
> on that archive, see Walker, items 55 and 61.

Beethoven, Ludwig van

> * Krones, Hartmut. "1805–1823: Vier Opern—ein Vokabular. Musiksprach-
> liche Bedeutungskonstanten in *Fidelio, Il Barbiere di Siviglia, Der Freis-
> chütz*, und *Fierrabras*." See item 665.

214. Sandelewski, Wiaroslaw. "Beethoven e gli operisti italiani del suo tempo."
Rivista italiana di musicologia 6 (1971): 246–76.

> According to Sandekewski, Beethoven became familiar with Italian opera as a
> young man in Bonn. His views on its composers prove interesting; for exam-
> ple, Beethoven felt that Italians were responsible for the rivalry existent
> between the two national schools. The author considers Beethoven's relation-
> ship with various Italian composers, including Rossini. The author proposes
> that Rossini may never have visited Beethoven in 1822, as Rossini later
> asserted. According to Anton Schlinder, Beethoven claimed to be busy the two
> times Rossini attempted to call. Rossini, on the other hand, recounted the visit
> to Ferdinand Hiller (item 119) and Richard Wagner (item 160), saying that
> Giuseppe Carpani had arranged the meeting. Sandelewski notes that
> Beethoven's resentment of the Italians may have come from envy of their pop-
> ular operas, for the Viennese had been lukewarm in their acceptance of his
> *Fidelio*.

215. Sponheuer, Bernd. "Beethoven vs. Rossini: Anmerkungen zu einer asthetis-
chen Kontroverse des 19. Jahrhunderts." 398–403. *In Bericht über den
Internationalen Musikwissenschaftlichen Kongress Bayreuth*, edited by
Christoph-Hellmut Mahling and Sigrid Wiesmann, 1981. Kassel: Bärenreiter, 1984. xvi, 642 pp. ISBN: 3-7618-0750-3 ML38.K5 G4.

Sponheuer considers the aesthetic debate surrounding the so-called "epoch
of Beethoven and Rossini" (1800–1832) and the development of the notion
of "higher" and "lower" music. The author traces the argument linking
Beethoven with harmony and, on a higher level, with Truth, while Rossini
came to symbolize melody and Beauty. Sponheuer demonstrates how these
aesthetic judgments were nurtured by national differences, forcing one
composer to somehow be deemed the antithesis of the other. This argument,
built upon abstracts, can be seen as a result of certain elements in nineteenth-century culture.

* Zeman, Herbert. "Treue Liebe wahrt die Seele sorgend in verschwig'ner
Brust: Zur Libretto-Gestaltung der deutschen Oper im frühen 19. Jahrhundert (Beethoven, Rossini, Weber und Schubert)." See item 675.

Bellini, Vincenzo
* Cambi, Luisa. "Bellini—un pacchetto di autografi." See item 68.

216. Fabbri, Paolo. "Rossini e Bellini a paragone." In *Music franca: Essays in
Honor of Frank A. D'Accone*, edited by Irene Alm, Alyson McLamore, and
Colleen Reardon, 283–95. Festschrift Series No. 18, Kristina Kwacz, general editor. Stuyvesant, N.Y.: Pendragon Press, 1996. x, 656 pp. ISBN 0-
945193-92-0 ML55.D15 1996.

Considers several examples of primo Ottocento "epidemic parallelomania,"
as Marchese di S. Jacinto put it (see item 489). Although this exercise in
contrast was quite common, not all participants in the debate agreed *how*
these two composers differed. Some heard Bellini as sentimental and more
true to setting poetry, while others felt that Rossini was monumental and
sublime. Fabbri's appendix contains a statement by Henri Blaze De Bury,
suggesting that while Rossini made virtuosi, Bellini made singers.

Berlioz, Hector
217. Cohen, H. Robert. "Rossini in Paris As Depicted in the Uncollected Criticisms of Hector Berlioz." In *La recezione di Rossini ieri e oggi* (item 288),
38–53.

Citing excerpts from Berlioz's writings about Rossini for the French press,
Cohen demonstrates that the Italian composer was one of the writer's musical heroes, primarily because of his ability to link drama to music, one of

the chief tenets of Berlioz's musical philosophy. Praise apart, Berlioz was critical of Rossini's instrumentation, particularly his use of the bass drum, and of his seeming indifference when his scores were modified or altered. Berlioz, however, was well aware of Rossini's influence on the next generation of composers. Works mentioned in these press excerpts (cited without translation) include *Le barbier*, *Le siège de Corinthe*, *Moïse*, *Le comte Ory*, and the opera about which Berlioz wrote most, *Guillaume Tell*. In discussing the contemporary stage, Cohen proposes that lack of financial success and poor quality performances may have contributed to Rossini's retirement from the French stage (see Johnson, item 754, for another perspective on this part of Rossini's career). Includes an illustration of Danton Jeune's 1860 bust of Rossini.

Catelani, Angelo

218. Schlitzer, Franco. "Colui che rubò una penna a Rossini." In *Rossini e Siena e altri scritti rossiniani (con lettere inedite)*, 57–62. See item 53.

Documents the friendship of Rossini with composer Angelo Catelani, which lasted from their meeting in 1841 until the latter's death in 1866. Includes letters from Rossini to his younger colleague as well as Catelani's anecdotes, including his tale of stealing the pen with which Rossini worked on the Stabat mater.

Donizetti, Gaetano

* Capitanio, Fabrizio. "L'esecuzione della Stabat Mater di Rossini diretta da Donizetti (Bologna, 1842) in una recensione dell'epoca." See item 794.

Hiller, Ferdinand

219. Müller, Reto. "Rossini e Hiller attraverso i documenti e gli scritti." Translated from German into Italian by Maria Letizia Catenaro. *Bollettino del Centro Rossiniano di Studi* 32 (1992): 33–62.

The author describes the relationship between Rossini and Hiller by examining the latter's writings. (See also items 118 and 119). Müller concludes that Hiller's narration of Rossini's life is faithful to the account he was given. If there are inaccuracies, he says it is the fault of Rossini's attempts to mask the reality. This issue of the *Bollettino* includes eight illustrations (without pagination) that precede Müller's essay. They depict the views of the seashore at Trouville, where Rossini had his chats with Hiller; portraits of both composers; and photographs of a note from Rossini to Hiller and of Rossini autographs collected in an album of pieces owned by Hiller.

Liszt, Franz

220. Risaliti, Riccardo. "Rossini e Liszt." *Bollettino del Centro Rossiniano di Studi* 12 [no. 3]: 40–46.

Risaliti notes how composers of instrumental music in the nineteenth century were influenced by Italian opera. The author considers the transcriptions and paraphrases of Rossini's music composed by Franz Liszt. The period of these works—between 1835 and 1837—makes Rossini the first opera composer from whose works Liszt drew inspiration. The author introduces the Liszt pieces, noting whether they are strict quotations or elaborations of themes. With a score excerpt. See also items 41, 42, and 48.

Morlacchi, Francesco

221. Ciliberti, Galliano. "Morlacchi e i suoi rapporti con Rossini nel panorama musicale europeo della prima metà dell'Ottocento." *Bollettino del Centro Rossiniano di Studi* 33 (1993): 73–91.

Albeit several years apart, composer Francesco Morlacchi and Rossini both studied at Bologna's Liceo Filarmonico. The author traces their professional encounters, noting that even though Morlacchi was Kapellmeister in Dresden, he never seemed at a loss to criticize Rossini and those who followed his style. Ciliberti points out the irony that Morlacchi, a defender of "German" music, was often accused of sounding like Rossini. He also demonstrates that, despite Morlacchi's feelings toward Rossini, he regularly programmed his operas. The author includes reviews, correspondence, and a list of Rossini operas performed under Morlacchi's direction in Dresden.

222. Franchi, Saverio. "*Il barbiere di Siviglia*: Confronti, suggestioni, linguaggio." In *Francesco Morlacchi e la musica del suo tempo (1784–1841): atti del convegno internazionale di studi, Perugia, 26–28 ottobre 1984*, 39–51, edited by Biancamaria Brumana and Galliano Ciliberti. Florence: Olschki, 1986. ix, 412 p. ML410.M78 F7 1986.

Although this essay deals primarily with the settings of *Il barbiere* by Paisiello and Morlacchi, Franchi briefly contrasts the latter's setting with Rossini's. Citing Paolo Gallarati (see items 590 and 591), Franchi notes that these works differ in the composers' use of the orchestra and the librettists' presentation of the characters. He points out that the audiences were also dissimilar, as were the cultural environments for which the works were created, Rossini's for Italy and Morlacchi's for Dresden.

223. Marino, Marina. "Morlacchi e Pavesi: Due occasioni di confronto." In *Francesco Morlacchi e la musica del suo tempo*, 29–38, item 222.

In her comparison of Francesco Morlacchi's and Stefano Pavesi's operas entitled *Corradino* (1818 and 1809, respectively), the author considers both Ètienne Mehul's earlier treatment of the subject (*Euphrosine*, 1790) and

Rossini's later *Matilde di Shabran* (1821). Suggesting that Rossini's is dramatically the most disjointed of the works, she examines the different distribution of the scenes and the presentation of the characters. Includes charts of the points of comparisons.

224. Pascale, Michelangelo. "Le lettere veneziane di Morlacchi." In *Francesco Morlacchi e la musica del suo tempo*, 131–62, item 222.

Although he gives no exact citations from the letters, Pascale notes that in letters to the Venetian Francesco Peluti, composer Francesco Morlacchi made references to his artistic contemporaries, one of whom was Rossini.

* Tartak, Marvin. "Matilde and Her Cousins: A Study of the Libretto Sources for Rossini's *Matilde di Shabran*." See item 744.

Nicolini, Giuseppe

225. Donà, Mariangela. "Un'aria di Rossini per un'opera di Nicolini nella Biblioteca Comunale di Civitanova Marche." In *Studien zur Italienische-Deutschen Musikgeschichte XII*, edited by Friedrich Lippmann, 320–29. Vol. 19 of *Analecta musicologica*. Cologne: Arno Volk, 1979.

The author discusses the manuscript of the *scena ed aria* "Guidò Marte i nostri passi," which Rossini composed for insertion into a production of Giuseppe Nicolini's opera, *Quinto Fabio* for the 1817 *carnevale* season at Rome's Teatro Argentina. Donà fills in gaps in the opera's history, stating that Rossini's music seems only to have been used for the Roman production of the work. After describing the music, with score excerpts, she goes on to discuss other important manuscripts in the archive.

Offenbach, Jacques

226. Huber, Hans Rudolf. "Rossini zitiert Offenbach." *La Gazzetta* 9 (1999): 11–15.

One of Rossini's *Péchés de vieillesse* is the "Petit Caprice (Style Offenbach)." Rossini also made use of the French composer's music in "La chanson du bébé." Huber demonstrates with score examples that Rossini quoted from Offenbach's *Barbe-Bleue* in this vocal character piece, modifying Offenbach's original work rather than copying it exactly. Huber also demonstrates the word play in Emilien Pacini's text, with references to theater singer Hortense Schneider and cafe singer Thérésa (Emma Thérèse Valadon). Transcribing texts by both Rossini and Pacini, Huber suggests that the content of the song was actually the composer's idea.

Paër, Ferdinando

227. Aversano, Luca. "Eine Paërische Quelle für di *Cavatina di Rosina*." *La Gazzetta* 6 (1996): 4–9; published in Italian in *Rossini, Paër e il classicismo musicale*, pp. 5–12. Rome: Il Calamaio, 1993.

Aversano suggests that the aria "Io morirò d'affanno" from Paër's opera *Sofonisba* was the source for "Una voce poco fa" from *Il barbiere di Siviglia*. With musical examples, the author demonstrates the similarities in orchestral introduction, melodic motives, vocal range, tempo, meter, and key between the two numbers. Rossini may have been introduced to Paër's opera in Bologna in 1805 or through the 1809 piano-vocal edition; Aversano concludes that, as he often did with his own self-borrowings, Rossini used Paër's music in a completely different dramatic situation.

* Cagli, Bruno. "Rossini a Londra e al Théâtre Italian di Parigi: Documenti inediti dell'impresario G. B. Benelli." See item 57.

Paganini, Niccolò

228. Neill, Edward. "Paganini e Rossini." *Bollettino del Centro Rossiniano di Studi* [no. 1–3] (1986): 15–32.

Traces Paganini's friendship with Rossini and speculates when the violinist might have heard the operas that inspired his variations on Rossinian themes and transcriptions of arias for his concerts. Briefly mentions Paganini's meeting with Isabella Colbran, who agreed to intercede for him with impresario Domenic Barbaja. Illustrated with facsimiles of a letter from Paganini and a page from Rossini's manuscript of "Un mot à Paganini." For more on that composition, see Redditi, item 229.

229. Redditi, Aldo. "Un mot a' Paganini." *Bollettino del Centro Rossiniano di Studi* [no. 1] (1973): 5–7.

The author discusses this "elégie" for violin and piano (Vol. 9 of the *Péchés de vieillesse*), which Rossini composed in memory of Paganini. Describing the piece's characteristics and comparing it with Paganini's first concerto, Redditi demonstrates how Rossini echoed the virtuoso's own technique. After tracing their encounters, Redditi concludes that, rather than providing artistic inspiration, their friendship enriched both of their styles. With score examples.

Paisiello, Giovanni

230. Henze-Döhring, Sabine. "La tecnica del concertato in Paisiello e Rossini." Translated into Italian by Leonardo Cavari. *Nuova rivista musicale italiana*. 22 [no. 1] (Jan.-Mar. 1988): 1–23.

The author examines the changing aesthetics in opera buffa from the eighteenth to the nineteenth century, suggesting that the text was given more importance in the later period. A comparison is made between the three-movement quintet in Paisiello's setting of *Il barbiere di Siviglia* and the four-movement structure in Rossini's. The author analyzes the harmony and instrumentation in connection with the text, suggesting that such examinations lead to a better historical understanding of buffa works. For more on concertato movements, see items 541, 546, 549, 590, 591, and 602. Further comparison of Paisiello and Rossini is covered in Lippmann, item 634.

* Kunze, Stefan. "Ironie des Klassizismus: Aspekte des Umbruchs in der musikalischen Komodie um 1800." See item 592.

231. Scherliess, Volker. "*Il Barbiere di Siviglia*: Paisiello und Rossini." In *Colloquium "Die Stilistische Entwicklung der italienischen Musik zwischen 1770 und 1830 und ihre beziehungen zum Norden (Rome 1978)*," edited by Friedrich Lippmann, 100–127. Vol. 21 of *Analecta Musicologica*. Arno Volk: Laaber, 1982. viii, 461 pp. ISBN 3-9215-1866-0 ML290.3.C64 1978.

Offers a look at the history and musical analysis of aspects of Paisiello's and Rossini's *Barbers*. Concluding with the question of which setting is better, the author proposes that it is useful to consider Paisiello's work as representative of late eighteenth-century opera buffa. One can then consider the musical and dramatic development of that genre and the works' reception histories. With musical examples and an extract from the libretto of Paisiello's 1787 Neapolitan production that reflect changes from the original 1782 version.

Pavesi, Stefano

* Marino, Marina. "Morlacchi e Pavesi: Due occasioni di confronto." See item 223.

* Tartak, Marvin. "Matilde and Her Cousins: A Study of the Libretto Sources for Rossini's *Matilde di Shabran*." See item 744.

Raimondi, Pietro

232. Rosenberg, Jesse. "The Experimental Music of Pietro Raimondi." Ph.D. dissertation, New York University, 1996. 2 vols., x, 790 p.

While the major focus of this dissertation is on the experimental scores of this Rossini contemporary, Rosenberg examines the relationship between the two composers. See also item 791 in which Rosenberg proposes that Rossini had Raimondi's aid in composing a movement of the Messa di Gloria.

Schubert, Franz

* Erickson, Raymond, ed. *Schubert's Vienna.* See item 300.

* Krones, Hartmut. "1805–1823: Vier Opern—ein Vokabular. Musiksprachliche Bedeutungskonstanten in *Fidelio, Il Barbiere di Siviglia, Der Freischütz,* und *Fierrabras.*" See item 665.

* Zeman, Herbert. "Treue Liebe wahrt die Seele sorgend in verschwig'ner Brust: Zur Libretto-Gestaltung der deutschen Oper im frühen 19. Jarhhundert (Beethoven, Rossini, Weber und Schubert)." See item 675.

Spontini, Gaspare

233. Loschelder, Josef. "Spontini und Rossini. Wesen und Werk, Wirkung und Nachleben." *Bollettino del Centro Rossiniano di Studi* 15 [no. 1–2]: 65–81; Italian translation, 98–110.

The author compares the lives and careers of Gaspare Spontini and Rossini, tracing the beginnings of their musical careers, their professional lives, and their eventual influences on their contemporaries. Loschelder also cites contemporary authors, including Heinrich Heine and Eduard Hanslick, in their opinions of both composers. He concludes that, although Spontini has not enjoyed the lasting fame that Rossini has, both composers' works merit stage revivals.

Verdi, Giuseppe

234. G[arbelotto], A[ntonio]. "Un acquerello Rossiniano inedito: Giuseppe Verdi alla Scala di Milano." *Bollettino del Centro Rossiniano di Studi* [no. 3] (1968): 57–60.

The first publication of a watercolor depicting Verdi as conductor of the La Scala concert held on 8 April 1892 in occasion of the centennial of Rossini's birth. The author includes the program performed and notes discrepancies between the cast as recorded historically and that printed on the watercolor.

235. Schlizter, Franco. *Mondo teatrale dell'Ottocento: episodi, testimonianze, musiche e lettere inedite.* Naples: Fausto Fiorentino, 1954. 220 pp. ML1733.S35.

Contains a section (pp. 176–80) in which, by citing their comments, the author describes the opinions Rossini and Verdi held of each other's music.

Wagner, Richard

236. Bischoff, Friedrich. " 'Dire que maintenant . . . ': Eine Daumier-Karikatur von Berlioz, Wagner, und Rossini." *Die Musikforschung* 38 [no. 1] (1985): 22–26.

The author traces the history of an Honoré Daumier cartoon in which Berlioz appears as a wine merchant, Wagner as a grocer, and Rossini as a butcher. The cartoon played off a vaudeville entitled *L'Ecole des Epiciers*, and the caption, noting that one must weigh things properly, sell good wine, and not pass off bones as meat, reflected a recent theatrical scandal in Paris. As the author notes, it ironically foreshadowed Wagner's woes with *Tannhäuser*.

* Grondona, Marco. "Rossini e Wagner negli scritti: Il problema dell'-opera." Item 491.

237. Gui, Vittorio. "La visita di Wagner a Rossini." *Bollettino del Centro Rossiniano di Studi* 1–3 (1985): 19–25.

In this brief essay, a renowned conductor and advocate of the "Rossini Renaissance," Vittorio Gui examines the meeting between Wagner and Rossini from various angles. Basing his conclusions on Michotte's account (see item 160) and on biographical information, Gui analyzes both men, decidedly favoring Rossini. He concludes that their encounter was more than a meeting of minds: it was a confrontation of two epochs and two styles of operatic music.

* Keitel, Wilhelm, and Dominik Neuner. *Gioachino Rossini*. See item 177.

238. Melica, Ada. "Parallelo: grandezza e sofferenza di Rossini e di Wagner." In *Convegno di studi su Rossini per il Centenario della morte di Gioacchino Rossini*, 119–29. See item 283.

239. Mila, Massimo. "Wagner moralista." *La rassegna musicale* 31 [no. 3] (1961): 171–74; reprint in *Brahms e Wagner*, edited by Alberto Batisti, 220–24. Turin: Einaudi, 1994. xix, 443 pp. ISBN 88-06-13506-6 ML390.M53 1994.

Even though Wagner's desire was dramatic reform, Mila contends that his true achievement was in transforming music; after Wagner, states the author, music was not composed in the same way. Mila contends that Wagner's music appeals to the introvert because of the pyschological depth of his works; extroverts, he maintains, return to the lighter music of Rossini.

* Zimmermann, Michael. "Rerum concordia discors. Musik und Drama bei Rossini, Schopenhauer und Richard Wagner." See item 506.

Weber, Carl Maria von
* Edler, Arnfried. " 'Glanzspiel und Seelenlandschaft': Naturdarstellung in der Oper bei Weber und Rossini." See item 771.

* Krones, Hartmut. "1805–1823: Vier Opern—ein Vokabular. Musiksprachliche Bedeutungskonstanten in *Fidelio, Il Barbiere di Siviglia, Der Freischütz,* und *Fierrabras.*" See item 665.

* Zeman, Herbert. "Treue Liebe wahrt die Seele sorgend in verschwig'ner Brust: Zur Libretto-Gestaltung der deutschen Oper im frühen 19. Jarhhundert (Beethoven, Rossini, Weber und Schubert)." See item 675.

IMPRESARIOS AND THEATRICAL ADMINISTRATORS

General Studies

240. Rosselli, John *The Opera Industry in Italy from Cimarosa to Verdi: The Role of the Impresario.* Cambridge: Cambridge University Press, 1984. viii, 214 pp. ISBN 0-521-25732-8 ML 1733 .R78 1984; expanded Italian translation: *L'impresario d'opera: Arte e affari nel teatro musicale italiano dell'Ottocento.* Biblioteca di cultura musicale. Turin: Edizioni di Torino, 1985. ix, 279 pp. ISBN 88-7063-037-4. ML 1733 .R7813 1985.

Although Rosselli's scope is broader than the *primo Ottocento,* he goes in detail into the Italian theatrical arena in which Rossini worked. Briefly mentioning the composer's involvement with the *impresa* of the Teatro San Carlo, Rosselli's major emphasis (developed even more in the Italian translation) is on the careers of impresarios such as Domenic Barbaja, with whom Rossini worked. The volume's strong point is its considerable coverage of the business aspects of opera, including data, much of which pertains to Rossini's years in Italy, on subscription prices, admission fees, singers' salaries, and orchestra and chorus membership. Other topics include censorship and government control, the theater-going public, and theatrical agents and journalists. Rosselli uses several Rossini operas (*Il barbiere di Siviglia, Cenerentola, La donna del lago, Mosè in Egitto* and *Semiramide*) to demonstrate various aspects of production history. Includes charts, tables and illustrations, as well as a section suggesting further readings in this area of opera history.

Balocchino, Carlo

* Schlitzer, Franco. *Un piccolo carteggio inedito di Rossini con un impresario italiano a Vienna.* See item 56.

Barbaja (Barbaia), Domenico

* Bini, Annalisa. "Teatro e musica a Roma nell'Ottocento attraverso gli archivi familiari." See item 366.

241. Maione, Paologiovanni, and Francesca Seller. "Domenico Barbaia a Napoli (1809–1840): meccanismi di gestione teatrale." In *Il testo e la scena* (item 286), 403–329.

The beginnings of an archival investigation into the activities of impresario Domenico Barbaja take him out of the world of anecdotal tales. Maione and Seller introduce him as he functioned first under the French, who demanded gambling "pleasure palaces," and then under the reinstated Bourbons, who sought traditional theatrical entertainment. The essay highlights the intricate financial arrangements with both governments, his dealings with failed impresario Joseph Glossop, and his relationships with artists in his employ, including Rossini. An appendix contains correspondence relating to issues presented by the authors.

* ————, eds. *Gioachino Rossini*. See item 358.

* Rossi-Espagnet, Andrea. "Attività spettacolari al Teatro S. Carlo di Napoli nella prima metà dell'Ottocento." See item 355.

* Silvestri, Lodovico Settimo. *Della vita e delle opere di Gioachino Rossini*. See item 133.

* Walker, Frank. "Rossiniana in the Piancastelli Collection." Part 1: "Miscellaneous Unpublished Letters." See item 55.

Benelli, Giovanni Battista

* Bini, Annalisa. "Teatro e musica a Roma nell'Ottocento attraverso gli archivi familiari." See item 366.

* Cagli, Bruno. "Rossini a Londra e al Théâtre Italian di Parigi: Documenti inediti dell'impresario G. B. Benelli." Item 57.

Cortesi, Giuseppe

* Kern, Bernd-Rüdiger. "Aspekte der Vertrages." In *Rossinis Eduardo e Cristina*. Item 731.

* Ragni, Sergio. "Eine Tochter namens Eduardo." In *Rossinis Eduardo e Cristina*. Item 731.

Lanari, Alessandro

242. De Angelis, Marcello. *Le carte dell'impresario: Melodramma e costumi teatrale nell'Ottocento*. Florence: Sansoni, 1982. 283 pp. ML1733.4 .D4 1982.

DeAngelis reconstructs the career of impresario Alessandro Lanari. Included are references to Lanari's productions of Rossini's operas and his correspondence with and about the composer. A view of theater through the profession of impresario and a look at which Rossini's works remained in the repertoire throughout Lanari's career.

Severini, Carlo

243. Schlitzer, Franco. "Severini e la 'Severiniana." In *Rossini e Siena e altri scritti rossiniani (con lettere inedite)*, 63–80. See item 53.

Schlitzer documents the friendship and working relationship between Rossini and Carlo Severini, artistic director of the Théâtre Italien in Paris. The author quotes their correspondence dealing with the administration of the theater, Rossini's purchase of land for Severini in Italy, and Severini's care of Olympe Pélissier in Paris while Rossini visited his father and wife Isabella Colbran in Bologna. Illustrated with a portrait of Severini. For more on Severini, see items 46, 50, 319, and 320.

LIBRETTISTS

Aventi (Avventi), Francesco

244. Antolini, Bianca Maria. "Il *Mentore teatrale* di Francesco Avventi e l'organizzatione teatrale in Italia nel primo Ottocento." In *Il testo e la scena* (item 286), 385–402.

Antolini summarizes the contents of the *Mentore teatrale* (1845), an anthology of sorts dealing with issues of theatrical administration, compiled by Francesco Avventi, librettist of *Ciro in Babilonia*. Among the issues considered in the work are censorship; the behavior of the public and the role of the military in keeping order; the duties of the first violin (see also item 515); contracts between artists and the impresario and between the *imprese* and the public, and business aspects such as ticket sales and control over the season's repertory. In a section dedicated to young composers, Rossini's music is described variously as grandiose, fearsome, epic, and festive.

245. Fabbri, Paolo. "Il Conte Aventi, Rossini e Ferrara." *Bollettino del Centro Rossiniano di Studi* 34 (1994): 91–157.

Fabbri offers a brief biographical sketch of the life and military career of Francesco Aventi, librettist of *Ciro in Babilonia*. The author also notes Aventi's theatrical interests and activities, mentioning the *Mentore teatrale* (see also item 244). Noting that Rossini may first have encountered Aventi when the composer's mother sang at Ferrara and he himself was employed as *maestro del cambalo*, Fabbri documents the various occasions upon which the two would have met and worked together. Although Aventi may have given Rossini the libretto for *Ciro*, Fabbri demonstrates that he was not the original author but undertook the task from someone who proved less than able. A listing of Aventi's librettos is provided as well as a copy and facsimile of his libretto for the cantata *La gratitudine*, set to music by Rossini in 1815. For further information on Rossini and his connections with Ferrara, see also items 202 and 360.

Berio di Salsa, Francesco

* Grondona, Marco, and Guido Paduano, eds. *I quattro volti di Otello*: *William Shakespeare, Arrigo Boito, Francesco Berio di Salsa, Jean-François Ducis*. Item 682.

Ferretti, Jacopo

246. Bini, Annalisa. " 'Altro è l'Arcadia, altro è poi Valle': *Jacopo*, un *divertissement* letterario di Jacopo Ferretti a proposito di *Cenerentola*." *Bollettino del Centro Rossiniano di Studi* (1996): 5–43.

Bini examines the background of *Jacopo*, a personal satire by Jacopo Ferretti. After analyzing references in the libretto, located among Ferretti's papers at the Accademia Nazionale di Santa Cecilia in Rome, Bini confirms that the *farce* was written following the 1817 premiere of *Cenerentola* and cites evidence that the librettist, also possibly one of the journalists reporting on the opera, was alone in deeming the opening a "fiasco." The author then demonstrates that, rather than dealing with detractors of Rossini and his music, *Jacopo* confirms a breach between Ferretti and conservative Roman adversaries such as poet Gaetano Celli and librettist Michelangelo Prunetti. In addition to the text of the libretto (which portrays Rossini in a constant state of somnolence), there is an appendix that includes the sketch of an incomplete discourse to the "Arcadians," which not only contains material Ferretti used in his libretto but also praise for fellow poet Felice Romani.

247. Cametti, Alberto. *Un poeta melodrammatico romano*: *Appunti e notizie in gran parte inediti sopra Jacopo Ferretti e musicisti del suo tempo*. Milan: G. Ricordi, 1898. xv, 269 pp. ML423.F38.

This biography of the librettist of *La Cenerentola* and *Matilde di Shabran* was reprinted from the *Gazzetta musicale di Milano* (1897). Cametti documents Ferretti's life and theatrical activities with Rossini, Donizetti, and other composers for whom he wrote. Cametti includes information on theaters, singers, and productions of works in which Ferretti had a hand. Makes mention of Ferretti's satirical libretto *Jacopo* (see Bini, item 246). Illustrated with reproductions of two oil paintings of the poet; facsimiles include copies of texts and notes in Ferretti's hand. Cametti also reprints a signed copy of Rossini's contract for *Cenerentola*. In the appendices are letters to the poet from Rossini and lists of Ferretti's libretti and their premieres.

248. Ferretti, Jacopo. "Alcune pagine della mia vita: Delle vicende della poesia melodrammatica in Roma. Memoria seconda." Edited by and introduction by Francesco Paolo Russo. *Recercare* 8 (1996): 157–94.

This commentary on theatrical poetry in Rome during the *primo Ottocento* was cited in part by Alberto Cametti in his study of Ferretto's career (item 247). Herein, Russo presents the work in its entirety for the first time. Partly autobiographical, the work describes the theatrical world in Rome during the first two decades of the nineteenth century and the active role Ferretti had in creating and adapting works for its stage. Finally, the poet considers the state of contemporary poetry, speaking out against the borrowing of French Romanticism and invoking the name of Felice Romani as the savior of the Italian stage. In addition to citing Rossini's role in Rome during this period, Ferretti narrates the oft-cited history of the genesis of the libretto of *La Cenerentola*. Includes a facsimile of Ferretti's autograph, libretto covers, and a plan of Rome's Teatro Apollo.

* *Il teatro di Rossini a Roma 1812–1821: Debutti, musiche, artisti, librettisti, teatri*. See item 102.

* Mauceri, Marco. "F.F. Padre ignoto dell'*Agatina* di Pavesi." See item 698.

* Tartak, Marvin. "Matilde and Her Cousins: A Study of the Libretto Sources for Rossini's *Matilde di Shabran*." See item 744.

Jouy, Victor-Joseph Étienne de
* Jouy, Victor-Joseph Étienne de. "Essai sur l'opéra français." See item 395.

Lechi, Luigi
* Gossett, Philip. "The Tragic Finale of Tancredi." See item 632.

Mombelli, Vincenzina Viganò
* *Il teatro di Rossini a Roma 1812–1821: Debutti, musiche, artisti, librettisti, teatri*. See item 102.

* Russo, Francesco Paolo. "Alcune osservazioni sul *Demetrio e Polibio* di Rossini." See item 620.

* ———. "La prima 'differita' (maggio 1812) di *Demetrio e Polibio*." See item 621.

Palomba, Giuseppe
* Mauceri, Marco. "*La Gazzetta* di Gioachino Rossini: fonti del libretto e autoimprestito musicale." Item 676.

Romani, Felice

* Bini, Annalisa. " 'Altro è l'Arcadia, altro è poi Valle': *Jacopo*, un *divertissement* letterario di Jacopo Ferretti a proposito di *Cenerentola.*" Item 246.

* Mauceri, Marco. "F.F. Padre ignoto dell'*Agatina* di Pavesi." Item 698.

249. Roccatagliati, Alessandro. "Derivazioni e prescrizioni librettistischi: come Rossini intonò Romani." In *Il testo e la scena* (item 286), 163–182.

Felice Romani wrote libretti for Rossini's *Aureliano in Palmira*, *Il turco in Italia*, and *Bianca e Falliero.* After discussing the role of librettists and how their verse reflects contemporary theatrical practices, Roccatagliati considers Romani's collaboration with Rossini. With the aid of comparison tables, the author specifically examines the sources of *Aureliano* along with Romani's text, noting how the poet expanded Mazzolà's libretto for *Il turco.* Includes examples from poetic texts discussed. For more on Romani, see items 250 and 251.

250. ———. "Felice Romani, drammaturgo in musica: Caratteri e limiti della prescrizione librettistica nel processo compositivo del melodramma italiano di primo Ottocento." *Revista de musicologia* 16 [no. 6] (1993): 3147–62.

Romani, one of the greatest librettists of the *primo Ottocento*, was especially able to construct a libretto that could be judged both on its own literary merits and its adaptability to the musical stage. Roccatagliati considers how Romani's sense of drama influenced composers, including Rossini. See also items 249 and 251.

251. ———. *Felice Romani librettista.* Vol. 37 of the Quaderni *Musica/Realtà*, ed. Luigi Pestalozza. Lucca: Libreria Musicale Italiana, 1996. 458 pp. ISBN: 88-7096-157-5 ML423.R66 R63 1996.

This award-winning study of Romani contains not only a biography of the poet but a description of the profession of librettist, based on the author's examination of documents. Significant as well is the second part of the volume, which is an analysis of Romani's approach to writing *melodrammi* and an explanation of Italian versification and the structure of operatic "numbers." Appendices contain a catalog of Romani's works and transcriptions of documents and correspondence, some of which contain references to Rossini. See also items 249 and 250.

Rossi, Gaetano

* Fabbri, Paolo. "Gioachino Rossini uno e due." See item 629.

* Goldin, Daniela. *La vera Fenice: Librettisti e libretti tra Sette e Ottocento.* See item 577.

* Gossett, Philip. "The Tragic Finale of Tancredi." See item 632.

252. Henze-Döhring, Sabine. " 'Combinammo l'ossatura . . . ' Voltaire und die Librettistik des fruhen Ottocento." *Die Musikforschung* 36 [no. 3] (1983): 113–27.

Part of this article deals with Gaetano Rossi's adaptation of Voltaire's *Tancrède* and *Semiramis* for Rossini. In addition to briefly addressing Rossi's working methods, in particular his outlining of his dramatic models, the author concludes that he and his fellow librettists considered the necessities of constructing poetry to fit operatic structures more important than remaining faithful to literary sources. For more on Voltaire and *Tancrède*, see item 632; for Voltaire and *Semiramis*, see item 752.

* Mauceri, Marco. "*La Gazzetta* di Gioachino Rossini: fonti del libretto e autoimprestito musicale." Item 676.

253. Miggiani, Maria Giovanna. "Termini e concetti prescrittivi in Gaetano Rossi." In *Le parole della musica*: *Studi sulla lingua delle letteratura musicale in onore di Gianfranco Folena*, 225–58. Vol. 1. *Studi di Musica Veneta*, Vol. 21. Edited by Fiamma Nicolodi and Paolo Trovato. Florence: Leo S. Olschki, 1994 viii, 424 pp. ISBN 88-222-4284-X ML63.P26 1991 Vol. 1.

Along with a series of letters, Miggiani examines an autograph libretto for a work entitled *Maria di Brabante* (1830), written for an inexperienced composer named Albert Guillion. In his correspondence and in annotations in the libretto, Rossi, who had written three libretti for Rossini, attempted to assist Guillion in setting the work. Miggiana considers Rossi's terminology (some of which appears as well in Abramo Basevi's *Studio sulle opere di Giuseppe Verdi* of 1859—see Powers, Item 425) and how it demonstrates that the veteran librettist envisioned a modern musical treatment that highlighted the overall drama, not just his verse.

Schmidt, Giovanni

* *Il teatro di Rossini a Roma 1812–1821*: *Debutti, musiche, artisti, librettisti, teatri.* See item 102.

* Spada, Marco. "*Elisabetta, regina d'Inghilterra* di Gioachino Rossini: fonte letterarie e autoimprestito musicale." See item 651.

254. ———. "Giovanni Schmidt librettista: biografia di un fantasma." In *Il testo e la scena* (see item 286), 465–90.

After listing the difficulties frequently encountered in researching the careers of librettists, Spada notes the few biographical details gleaned from archival materials about Giovanni Schmidt, who from 1802 to 1841 wrote for the major composers in the Neapolitan arena. Spada traces Schmidt's activity by examining the titles of his works and his annual productivity. Also looking at the poet's self-borrowings, Spada concludes that in addition to the libretti for *Elisabetta, regina d'Inghilterra, Armida*, and *Adelaide di Borgogna*, Schmidt may have written Act I of *Matilda di Shabran*, citing verse to support his theory. Includes a catalog of libretti written by and attributed to Schmidt. See also item 651.

Sterbini, Cesare

255. Bini, Annalisa. " 'Insomma, mio signore, chi è lei, si può sapere?': Note biografiche su Cesare Sterbini, poeta romano." *Bollettino del Centro Rossiniano di Studi* 38 (1998): 5–15.

Documents details of the life of the librettist of *Torvaldo e Dorliska* (1815) and *Almaviva ossia l'inutil precauzione* (or *Il barbiere di Siviglia*) (1816). Bini lists other librettos by Sterbini, including *Il gabbamondo* (set by Pietro Generali) and *Finto molinaro ossia Il credulo deluso* (Giovanni Tadolini). Bini also describes the relationship between the poet and fellow librettist Jacopo Ferretti (see also item 246).

* Goldin, Daniela. *La vera Fenice: Librettisti e libretti tra Sette e Ottocento.* See item 577.

* *Il teatro di Rossini a Roma 1812–1821: Debutti, musiche, artisti, librettisti, teatri.* See item 102.

* König, Rosemarie. "Beaumarchais und Sterbini." In *Gioacchino Rossini: Der Barber von Sevilla*, 267–74. See item 668.

Tottola, Andrea Leone

* Castelvecchi, Stefano. "Walter Scott, Rossini e la *couleur ossianique*: il contesto culturale della *Donna del lago*." See item 735.

* Raffaelli, Renato. "Tracce di allattamento filiale nella *Zelmira* di Tottola per Rossini." See item 746.

MUSICIANS

Braga, Gaetano

256. Ortolani, Carla, and Francesco Zimei. "Memorie rossiniane dei diari di Gaetano Braga." *Bollettino del Centro Rossiniano di Studi* 40 (2000): 149–63.

The authors transcribe sections from letters and reminiscences of cellist/composer Gaetano Braga, who met Rossini in Paris and to whom the composer dedicated "Une larme," theme and variations for cello and pianoforte (No. 10 in Volume 9 of the *Péchés de vieillesse*). Among the "rossiniana" furnished by Braga is an account of how Rossini composed the setting *Mi lagneró tacendo* (*sopra una sola nota*); Braga's transcription of this piece, in fact, is the sole source. Also related is fellow cellist Rossini's comment on a composition by Braga in which he stated that "the cello must always cry and never laugh." In addition to transcribing relevant writings by Braga (illustrated with facsimiles), the authors include Vincenzo Bindi's account of how Rossini and Braga met and Rossini's comments on Wagner. See also items 60 and 580.

Höpler, Gaetano

257. Kantner, L[eopold] M. "Klapptrompeten und schmertzige Wäsche." *Bollettino del Centro Rossiniano di Studi* [no. 3] (1973): 31; Italian translation, 45.

The author presents a brief account of Austrian military band trumpeter Gaetano Höpler's meetings with Rossini in Naples in 1821. Höpler noted Rossini's fascination with the valve trumpet. After once seeing the composer in bed, the trumpeter expressed disgust at the dirty state of his lodgings and linens.

PUBLISHERS

General Studies

258. Antolini, Bianca Maria. "Copyists and Publishers in Italy Between 1770 and 1830." In *The Dissemination of Music: Studies in the History of Music Publishing*, edited by Hans Lenneberg, 107–15. Vol. 14 in *Musicology: A Book Series*. Lausanne, SW: Gordon and Breach, 1994. xii, 146 pp. ISBN 2-88449-117-1 ML112.D57 1994.

Antolini begins with a brief geographical summary of publishers' activities (both score sales and rentals) during the period specified. She attributes Italian publishers' increased activity in the 1820s to the success of Rossini's music.

259. Seller, Francesca. "Editoria musicale a Napoli: la Stabilimento Musicale Partenopeo." In *Atti Francesco Florimo e l'Ottocento musicale del convegno: Morcone, 19–21 aprile 1990*, Vol. 2, 469–81. Edited by Rosa Cafiero and Marina Marino. Reggio Calabria: Jason Editrice, 1999. ISBN: 88-8157-069-0 ML423.F63 F73 Vol. 2.

Seller gives a history of the Neapolitan publishing house owned by the Cottrau family. In the appendix, she lists the Rossini works published by the

Stabilimento Musicale Partenopeo, which include twenty-five operas and the Stabat Mater.

260. Zanetti, Emilia. "L'editoria musicale a Roma nel secolo XIX: Avvio di una ricerca." *Nuova rivista musicale italiana* 18 [no. 2] (April-June 1984): 191–99.

Zanetti considers the activity of Roman publishers after the introduction of the lithographic developments of Giovanni Dall' Arma. Includes information on the Roman firms who published Rossini's operas.

Studies Specific to Rossini and His Publishers

261. Antolini, Bianca Maria. "Le edizioni rossiniani." In *Rossini 1792–1992* (item 95), 355–66.

Rossini's immense popularity resulted in a demand for scores of his works. Antolini considers the editions offered for sale by publishing houses such as Ricordi, Artaria, Pacini, Schott, and Simrock. She explains how different editions of the same work often reflected local productions and concludes with mention of the Opera Omnia project under the auspices of the Fondazione Rossini, noting that this edition increases scholarly and performance knowledge of Rossini and contributes to a greater understanding of music publication in the nineteenth century. Illustrated with facsimiles of title pages for scores issued by some of the publishing houses addressed in the essay.

262. Giazotto, Remo. "Alcune ignote vicende riguardanti la stampa e la diffusione della 'Semiramide.'" *Nuova Rivista Musicale Italiana* 2 [no. 5] (1968): 961–73.

Rossini's commission with La Fenice for the composition of *Semiramide* required that the autograph score would become the property of the theater. Artaria of Vienna subsequently received exclusive rights to publish the score, protesting the pieces Ricordi had begun to market. Giazotti presents correspondence documenting the battle between the two publishers and the intervention each sought from La Fenice. Significant is Ricordi's powerfully phrased response to charges of fraud, which, as the author notes, raised questions about an author's rights to intellectual and artistic property.

* Gossett, Philip. *The Operas of Rossini: Problems of Textual Criticism in Nineteenth-Century Opera.* See item 582.

* Kallberg, Jeffrey. "Marketing Rossini: Sei lettere di Troupenas ad Artaria." See item 47.

263. Kern, Bernd-Rüdiger. "Rossinis Umgang mit urheberrechtlichen Fragen." *La Gazzetta* 10 (2000): 4–16.

Kern deals with aspects of performance and publication rights that Rossini faced during his career. Citing specific operas and their contracts, the author explains that such agreements were complicated by issues of location. For example, rights at the premiere venue were not the same as those beyond the political boundaries of the region in which the work was first produced. Foreign publishers also sought individual contracts for score publication rights within their own countries. Kern comments on Rossini's agreements with impresarios, theater owners, and publishers, including, as an example, the composer's negotiations with Darmstadt theatrical agent Friedrich Treitschke (see item 80) and French publisher Eugéne Troupenas (see also item 47). In a general comment about such legal dealings during Rossini's lifetime, Kern notes the composer's works were best protected in France.

SINGERS

General Studies

264. Adkins Chiti, Patricia. *Una voce poco fa, ovvero Le musiche delle prime donne rossiniane*. Rome: Garamond, 1992. 212 pp. ISBN: 88-86180-00-4.

[Not examined.]

265. Appolonia, Giorgio. *Le voci di Rossini*. Preface by Giorgio Gualerzi. Turin: Edizioni Eda, 1992. 499 pp. ML1733.A66 1992.

After brief comments on the composer's vocal writing, Appolonia offers capsule biographies of Rossini interpreters, among them Luigi Raffanelli, Ester and Anna Mombelli, Filippo Galli, Adelaide Malanotte, Manuel García, Teresa Belloc, Isabella Colbran, Geltrude Righetti-Giorgi, Domenico Donzelli, Giovanni David, Luigi Lablache, Laure Cinti-Damoreau, Adolph Nourrit, Giuditta Pasta, Maria Malibran, and Marietta Alboni. Includes several twentieth-century artists as well. With tables for each singer, listing roles, performance data, and source of information. An appendix includes letters from several of the book's subjects. Illustrated.

266. Bucarelli, Mauro. "I divi rossiniani. Avventure biografiche di alcuni campioni." In *Rossini 1792–1992* (item 95), 268–284.

Bucarelli profiles singers important in Rossini's operas. Included, with reproductions of portraits, are Isabella Colbran, Giovanni David, Giuditta

Pasta, Giovanni Battista Rubini, Joséphine Fodor-Mainvielle, Giuseppina Ronzi-DeBegnis, Maria Malibran, Luigi Lablache, Adolphe Nourrit, Laure Cinti-Damoreau, Giulia Grisi, and Marietta Alboni.

267. Gara, Eugenio. "La redentrice vocalità rossiniana." In *Convegno di studi su Rossini per il Centenario della morte di Gioacchino Rossini*, 106–110. See item 283.

268. Ortkemper, Hubert. *Engel wider Willen: Die Welt der Kastraten*. Berlin: Henschel, 1993. 415 pp. ML1460.O78 1993 ISBN 3-89487-006-0.

Dedicated to the history of castrati. Contains a short section on Rossini and Giovanni Battista Velluti, who sang Arsace in *Aureliano in Palmira*. Cites comments from Stendhal's biography (see item 135). Also mentions Girolamo Crescentini, the castrato who, for a time, taught Rossini's first wife, Isabella Colbran. The book includes thumbnail sketches of famous castrati and lists of works in which castrati performed.

* Pinamonti, Paolo. "Da 'ornamento dell'Italia' a 'dominator musicale del mondo': Rossini nella vita teatrale veneziana." Item 376.

269. Pirrotta, Nino. "Rossini eseguito ieri e oggi." *La recezione di Rossini ieri e oggi* (item 288), 2–13.

Rossini's Italian career is explained in the context of the contemporary theatrical organization as well as the personalities who, according to Pirrotta, helped to shape his compositional output. Establishing Rossini's origins as a singer himself and commenting on his intuitive sense of how to write for the voice, Pirrotta then links the growth of the composer's professional reputation with his dealings with performers such as Domenico Mombelli, Giovanni and Rosa Morandi, Filippo Gallo, Maria Malibran, Geltrude Righetti-Giorgi, and Isabella Colbran. Included also in this professional network were impresarios such as Domenico Barbaja who, the author notes, steered Rossini towards serious subjects. Maintaining that Rossini also had his "years in the galley," as Verdi would comment about himself, Pirrotta notes that Rossini had an "artisan mentality" and was concerned with immediate success rather than artistic immortality.

270. Rosselli, John. *Singers of Italian Opera: The History of a Profession*. Cambridge: Cambridge University Press, 1992. xvi, 272 pp. ISBN 0-521-41683-3 ML1460.R68 1992. Italian translation by Paolo Russo: *Il cantante d'opera: Storia di una professione (1600–1900)*. Bologna: Società Editrice Il Mulino, 1993. 305 pp. ISBN 88-15-0-4175-3. ML1460.R6816 1993.

Although this history covers the singing profession from the seventeenth to the twentieth centuries, much of it deals with the professional lives, training, and careers of opera singers in Rossini's day. Specific references are made to performers who sang for Rossini, including his first wife, soprano Isabella Colbran; the castrato Giovanni Battista Velluti, who premiered the lead role in *Aureliano in Palmira* in 1813; and the tenor, Nicola Ivanoff, whom the composer held in almost filial affection. Includes illustrations and tables of singers' salaries as well as a four-page essay suggesting further readings.

Studies about Specific Singers

Bordogni, Giulio Marco
* Cagli, Bruno. "Rossini a Londra e al Théâtre Italian di Parigi: Documenti inediti dell'impresario G. B. Benelli." See item 57.

Cinti-Damoreau, Laure
* Appolonia, Giorgio. *Le voci di Rossini*. See item 265.

271. Caswell, Austin. "Mme Cinti-Damoreau and the Embellishment of Italian Opera in Paris: 1820–1845." *Journal of the American Musicological Society* 28 [no. 3] (Fall 1975): 459–92.

Caswell begins with a brief biography of Laure Cinti-Damoreau, the *diva* whom Rossini employed as one of the few French singers trained in the Italian style and for whom he composed roles such as the Comtesse in *Le comte Ory* and Matilda in *Guillaume Tell*. The author then discusses the embellishments and cadenzas for which she was famous. These were found in her *Méthode de chant*, written for her students at the Conservatoire, and in seven manuscript notebooks, some of them intended for Rossini's music. Includes indices and a discussion of the content of the volumes as well as facsimiles and musical examples.

Colbran, Isabella
See items in this chapter in the section under Rossini's family.

Cortesi, Carolina
* Ragni, Sergio. "Eine Tochter namens Eduardo." In *Rossinis Eduardo e Cristina*. Item 731.

Donzelli, Domenico
272. Modugno, Maurizio. "Domenico Donzelli e il suo tempo." *Nuova rivista musicale italiana* 18 [no. 2] (April-June 1984): 200–16.

Modugno traces the career of this tenor, noting his relationship with *primo Ottocento* composers, including Rossini. The author also documents the roles Donzelli sang, including his Parisian debut in *Otello* in 1825. Includes excerpts from the singer's correspondence.

Duprez, Gilbert-Louis

273. Beghelli, Marco. "Il do di petto: Dissacrazione di un mito." *Il saggiatore musicale* 3 [no. 1] (1996): 105–49.

Gilbert Duprez was touted in his day as master of the "do di petto," or production of high "C" with his chest voice, a sound Rossini did not necessarily enjoy. Beghelli engages semantics to demonstrate that the incorrect use of the term "falsetto" as synonymous with "head voice" led to this myth. He also suggests that such comments about Duprez's voice were merely promotional hype since, physiologically, such sound production is close to impossible. *If* the singer were able to produce such notes from his chest voice, he contends, he was a musical rarity. With illustrations of Duprez.

* Duprez, G[ilbert-Louis]. *Souvenirs d'un chanteur.* See item 113.

274. Landini, Giancarlo. "Gilbert Louis Duprez ovvero l'importanza di cantar Rossini." *Bollettino del Centro Rossiniano di Studi* [no. 1–3] (1982): 29–54.

Traces the career of tenor Gilbert Duprez, especially his years in Italy. Landini suggests that performing Rossini's music enabled singers like Duprez to develop the vocal techniques and abilities necessary to sing the great Romantic roles through early Verdi. Includes ample musical examples demonstrating the repertoire for which Duprez was famous.

Galli, Filippo

* Appolonia, Giorgio. *Le voci di Rossini.* Item 265.

275. Mioli, Piero. "Duce di tanti eroi: il primo basso Filippo Galli." In *Il testo e la scena* (item 286), 491–542.

The author presents the career of one of the most important *basso* singers of Rossini's day. Galli, who premiered Rossini roles such as Tarabotto in *L'inganno felice*, Asdrubale in *La pietra del paragone*, Mustafà in *L'italiana in Algeri*, Selim in *Il turco in Italia*, Il Duco d'Ordow in *Torvaldo e Dorliska*, Fernando in *La gazza ladra*, Maometto II in *Maometto II*, and Assur in *Semiramide*, also performed numerous other Rossini roles on stages throughout Europe and in Mexico. Through his influence, Galli also was able to help Rossini get commissions during his early years as a composer. Following the singer's life from his years of stardom until the critics attacked his aging voice, Mioli reconstructs Galli's career from numerous sources, cited in the appendix, which also lists Galli's performances by theatrical season, city, and theater, opera and genre; librettist and composer; date of premiere, if a subsequent production; role sung; and source from which the data was taken.

García, Manuel

* Ahlquist, Karen. *Democracy at the Opera*: *Music, Theater, and Culture in New York City, 1815–60*. See item 386.

* Pahlen, Kurt. "Manuel García, der erste 'Almaviva.' " In *Gioacchino Rossini: Der Barber von Sevilla*, 275–55. See item 668.

* Preston, Katherine K. *Opera on the Road*: *Traveling Opera Troupes in the United States*. See item 385.

Ivanov (Ivanoff), Nicolai

276. Gossett, Philip. "A new Romanza for *Attila.*" *Studi verdiani* 9 (1993): 13–35.

Gossett addresses the friendship between Russian tenor Nicolai Ivanov (later Ivanoff) and Rossini, demonstrating, with the support of correspondence, the composer's efforts on the singer's behalf. Rossini made one such request to Verdi, asking for a new aria for Ivanov for a production of *Attila* in Trieste in 1846. Gossett provides an edition of the new piece, a *romanza*.

* Petrobelli, Pierluigi. "Rossini nell'opera e nella vita di Verdi." Item 423.

* Schlitzer, Franco. *Un piccolo carteggio inedito di Rossini con un impresario italiano a Vienna*. See item 56.

Malibran, Maria

277. Giazotto, Remo. *Maria Malibran (1808–1836): Una vita nei nomi di Rossini e Bellini*. Turin: ERI, 1986. ML420.M2 G5 1986.

Rossini thought that one of the greatest singers of his time was Maria Malibran, who performed many of his roles, including Desdemona in *Otello*. This biography not only relates her brief life but describes the cultural and professional environment in which she worked. Appendices includes biographical documents, a family history, excerpts from reviews and commentaries on her life and work, and samples of her own compositions. Illustrated with facsimiles of correspondence, musical programs, and portraits of the singer as well as engravings of her in Rossini roles. With musical excerpts.

Raffanelli, Luigi

* Appolonia, Giorgio. *Le voci di Rossini*. Item 265.

278. Paissa, Roberto. "La carriera di un cantante di *farsa*: Luigi Raffanelli." In *La farsa musicale veneziana*, 567–96. Vol. 2 of *I vicini di Mozart*. See item 287.

Luigi Raffanelli, the *basso* who premiered the role of Bruschino senior as well as roles in *La cambiale di matrimonio* and *L'inganno felice*, was a master of the conventions of the *farsa*. Paissa traces his career with comments from contemporaries and demonstrates that Raffanelli had the credible acting and intelligent interpretation to make him a perfect exponent of the new sentimental style popular with Venetian audiences (see items 600 and 602 for comments on the sentimental and Venetian taste). Describes the typical "letter reading" scene at which Raffanelli excelled and includes a facsimile of such a scene from his role in *Una fatale supposizione*. Includes a preliminary chronology of Raffanelli's career.

Righetti-Giorgi, Geltrude

* Appolonia, Giorgio. *Le voci di Rossini*. Item 265.

* Ciarlantini, Paola. "Il ritratto umano e artistico di Gioachino Rossini nelle sue prime biografie." See item 139.

* Righetti-Giorgi, Geltrude. *Cenni di una Donna cantante sopra il Maestro Rossini*. See item 131.

279. Rognoni, Luigi. "Una cantante bolognese in polemica con Stendhal." *Archiginnasio: Bollettino della Biblioteca Comunale di Bologna,* 56–57 (1971–1973): 638–47.

[Not examined.] For Righetti-Giorgi's defense of Rossini, see item 131.

Tacchinardi, Nicola
280. Ciarlantini, Paola. "Una testimonianza sul teatro musicale degli inizi dell'Ottocento: il saggio *Dell'opera in musica* di Nicola Tacchinardi." *Bollettino del Centro Rossiniano di Studi* 19 (1989): 63–135.

Ciarlantini chronicles the life of Nicola Tacchinardi, a frequent interpreter of Rossini tenor roles such as Otello. Drawing information from the singer's correspondence, the author defines Tacchinardi's career on stage as well as his association with impresario Alessandro Lanari and his work as a stage director, scenographer, writer, and pedagogue. The essay highlights his book, *Dell'opera in musica sul teatro italiano e de' suoi difetti* (1833), which, Ciarlantini notes, offers a practical rather than a theoretical view of the contemporary Italian musical stage. Appendices include the author's edition of Tacchinardi's book and a chronology of the tenor's theatrical career, citing season, venue, work, role, and source citation.

Velluti, Giovanni Battista

* Ortkemper, Hubert. *Engel wider Willen*: *Die Welt der Kastraten*. See item 268.

OTHER CONTEMPORARIES

281. Kern, Bernd-Rüdiger. "Rossini e Metternich." Translation into Italian by Enrico Luigi Siepi. *Bollettino del Centro Rossiniano di Studi* 39 (1999): 5–20.

Kern traces the nearly forty-year friendship between Rossini and Metternich, surmising that the stateman first became acquainted with the composer's music in 1815 or 1816. Although Metternich surely heard Rossini'a works while he traveled through Italy, the two did not meet until Rossini visited Vienna in 1822. Kern discusses their meeting in Verona that same year, when at Metternich's invitation, the composer wrote the *La santa alleanza* and *Il vero omaggio*. He also considers their correspondence during the late 1850s. The author concludes that their relationship was based on mutual admiration rather than on political issues and opinions.

6

Conference and Congress Reports

282. *Atti del convegno di studi*: *Rossini, edizioni critiche e prassi esecutiva—Siena, 30 agosto–1 settembre 1977*. Florence: Olschki, 1981. 215 pp.

Not examined. This volume contains the following papers: "Rossini e Stendhal" (Dario Durbe), "Appunti su Gautier critico rossiniano" (Raffaele Monti), "Sui rapporti tra teatro e politica negli anni delle 'prime' veneziane di Rossini" (Nicola Mangini), "*Le Rossiniane*, lettere musico-teatrali di Giuseppe Carpani, ed altri scritti epistolari" (Margherita Sergardi), "Rossini con le dande" (Lorenzo Tozzi), "Una ouverture per *Il barbiere di Siviglia*" (Mario Rinaldi), "La prima italiana dello Stabat Mater: Precisazioni e documenti" (Marcello DeAngelis), "Riflessioni su alcuni aspetti della vocalitá francese di Rossini" (Giancarlo Landini), "Vicende novecentesche del teatro rossiniano" (Giorgio Gualerzi), "Rossini's *Péchés*: 'blague sous l'aisselle' " (Sergio Martinotti), and "Problemi di esecuzione della Petite Messe solennelle" (Piero Rattalino).

283. *Convegno di studi su Rossini per il Centenario della morte di Gioacchino Rossini, Pesaro, 13–16 June 1968. Bollettino del Centro Rossiniano di Studi* 8 [no. 4–6] 1968. 177 pp.

This special issue features papers on a variety of topics, although not all annotated the papers are indexed under their appropriate subject headings as items 44, 140, 238, 267, 397, 467, 508, 532, 616, 628, 802, 844, and 871.

284. *Convegno italo-tedesco "Mozart, Paisiello, Rossini e l'opera buffa." Rome,* 1993. Ed. Markus Engelhardt and Wolfgang Witzenmann. Vol. 31 of

Analecta musicologica. Arno Volk: Laaber, 1998. vii, 386 pp. ISBN 3-89007-404-9 ML1704.C66 1998

Papers on Rossini are listed separately as items 638 and 696.

285. *Di si felice innesto*: *Rossini, la danza, e il ballo teatrale*. Pesaro: Fondazione Rossini, 1996. 200 pp.

[Not examined.]

286. *Gioachino Rossini, 1792–1992*: *Il testo e la scena*. Convegno internazionale di studi, Pesaro, 25–28 giugno 1992. Ed. Paolo Fabbri. Pesaro: Fondazione Rossini, 1994. xvi, 701 pp. ML410.R8 G57 1994. [N.B.: In the text, this work will be referred to as *Il testo e la scena* to differentiate it from item 95, *Rossini 1792–1992*]

The acts of this Rossini bicentennial conference include papers in the following five areas: Rossini's epoch, the contemporary stage, text and the libretto, Rossini in the theatrical context of his day, and Rossini in Paris. In addition to indices of names, of Rossini's works, and of musical examples, there is an index to the volume, to works referred to within the essays, and to musical examples. (Individual papers from this volume are annotated separately as items 241, 244, 249, 254, 275, 315, 322, 331, 332, 335, 344, 393, 492, 512, 515, 534, 546, 549, 589, 590, 598, 687, 705, 708, 719, 732, 767, 795, 865, 866).

287. *I vicini di Mozart*. Atti del convegno internazionale di studi promosso dalla Fondazione Giorgio Cini (Venice, 7–9 Sept. 1987), *Studi di Musica Veneta*, 15. Vol. 1, *Il teatro musicale tra Sette e Ottocento*. Ed. Maria Teresa Muraro. Florence: Leo S. Olschki, 1989. ix, 428 pp. ISBN 88-222-3685-8 ML1794.V5 1989. Vol. 2, *La farsa musicale veneziana (1750–1810)*. Ed. David Bryant. Florence: Leio S. Olschki, 1989. 279 pp., xvi. ISBN 88-222-3685-8 ML1794.V5 1989.

Papers on Rossini are listed as items 278, 542, 599, 600, 601, 602, and 603.

288. *La recezione di Rossini ieri e oggi*. Convegno organizzato con la collaborazione della Accademia Nazionale di Santa Cecilia, Fondazione Giorgio Cini, Fondazione Gioacchino Rossini, [e] Società Italiana di Musicologia, Roma, 18–20 febbraio 1993. Atti dei Convegni Lincei, no. 110. Rome: Accademia Nazionale dei Lincei, 1994. 284 pp. ISBN 0391-805X. ML410.R8 R4 1994.

These fourteen conference papers deal not only with the reception of Rossini and his music in nineteenth-century Europe, but also with the twentieth-century perception and acceptance of the composer and his works. Relevant essays are annotated as items 217, 269, 291, 292, 296, 301, 423, 432, 433, 435, 436, 496, 505, and 718.

289. *Rossini a Roma—Rossini e Roma.* Convegno di studi, Roma, 25 marzo 1992. Ed. Francesco Paolo Russo. Rome: Fondazione Marco Basso, 1992. 251 pp. ML410.R8 C66 1992.

The acts of this conference include eight papers dealing with aspects of Rossini's relationship with and work within the Roman musical establishment. This item also includes a catalog and illustrations of period publications in the conference exhibition. Relevant papers are annotated as items 2, 369, 372, 518, 621, and 823.

290. *Rossini in Paris: Eine Veranstaltung des Frankreichzentrums der Universität Leipzig, in Zusammenarbeit mit der Deutschen Rossini Gesellschaft e.V.* Edited by Reto Müller with foreword by Bernd-Rüdiger Kern. Forthcoming in Spring 2002.

This volume containing the acts of this series of three symposiums held at the University of Leipzig under the auspices of the Deutsche Rossini Gesellschaft includes papers dealing with Rossini's personal and professional relationships with Paris. The papers, organized according to session (which are not presented chronologically, however), are as follows: From the roundtable held 1 June 1999: "Biographischer Überblick" (Bernd-Rüdiger Kern), "Rossini-Rezeption im Paris der 1820-Jahre" (Paolo Fabbri), " 'Wilhelm Tell'—Eine Werkanalyse "(Gerhard Rienäcker), and "Rossinis 'Reise nach Reims' " (Reto Müller); from the session held from 17 to 19 October 1997: "Reichtliche Auseinandersetzungen um das 'Stabat Mater' " (Christian Sprang), "Der Krankheitsverlauf bei Rossini" (Peter Volk), "Olympe Pélissier" (Jean-Marie Bruson), "Rossinis Opern in Paris unter Gattungsgesichtspunkten" (Sabine Henze-Döhring), " 'Stabat Mater'—Eine Werkanalyse" (Gerhard Rienäcker), " 'Péchés de vieillesse' " (Ralf Rohmann), and "Die Rossinirezeption in der französischen Literatur" (Edward Reichel); from the session held from 16 to 18 April 1999: "Rossini in der Karikatur" (Jean-Maris Bruson), "Rossinis französisches Opernschaffen in der Geschäftskorrespondenz deutscher Verleger" (Luca Aversano), "Rossini und die französisch-italienische Politik" (Martina Grempler), "Gedanken zu den drei Fassungen der 'Petite Messe solennelle' " (Norbert Pritsch), "Die Klavieralben Rossinis" (Ulrike Teske-Spellerberg), and "Wilhelm Hauffs Rossini-Rezensionen in Paris" (Bernd-Rüdiger Kern). See also item 326.

7

Performance History, Reception, and Locative Studies

PERFORMANCE HISTORY

291. Antolini, Bianca Maria. "Rappresentazioni rossiniane e dibattito critico in Italia nel decennio 1860–70." In *La recezione di Rossini ieri e oggi* (item 288), 121–48.

Antolini looks at the press images of Rossini's work during a time when Italy was divided culturally between a reaffirmation of its melodic roots and the need to assimilate foreign musical elements. She considers the productions of Rossini's music during the decade under study, demonstrating that they often were hasty substitutions, which were frequently so modified that critics called them unrecognizable "mutilations." The author notes that Rossini was depicted in different ways during this time: as the emblem of old-fashioned and outmoded music models, a composer who had fused the past and the present, and the creator of a modern masterpiece, *Guillaume Tell*. Antolini also mentions the founding of the Società rossiniana to encourage young composers to continue in the Classical tradition. Her appendix includes a list of reviews of Rossini's music from Milan's *Gazzetta musicale* and *Perseveranza*.

292. Conati, Marcello. Appendices in *La recezione di Rossini ieri e oggi* (item 288), pp. 229–84.

Conati offers a chronology of Rossini productions in Italian theaters from 1810 to 1823 compiled from published libretti and theater chronicles (pp. 229–50). He also includes an anthology of press excerpts from 1812–1825 (pp. 251–84) and a transcription of "Rossini a Milano" from *Il censore universale dei teatri*, 2 September 1829 (pp. 280–84).

293. Loewenberg, Alfred. *Annals of Opera, 1597–1940, Compiled from Original Sources*. Introduction by Edward J. Dent. Cambridge, U.K.: W. Heffer; New York: Broude Bros., 1943. xxiii, 879 pp. ML102.O6 L6.

Second edition, revised and corrected by Frank Walker. Geneva: Societas Bibliographica, 1955. 2 vols. xxv, 1756 columns. ML102.O6 L6 1955; this edition later published by St. Clair Shores, Mich.: Scholarly Press, 1971. ML102.O6 L6 1971.

Third edition revised. Totowa, N.J.: Rowman and Littlefield, 1978. xxv, 1756 columns. ISBN: 0-87471-851-1 ML102.O6 L6 1978.

Lists operas chronologically by year and date of premiere. Includes information on librettists and their sources, number of acts, revivals and revisions, and often on manuscripts and editions. Although similar (and updated) information on Rossini's works can be found in other sources, Loewenberg provides significant data on productions up through 1940.

* Verti, Roberto. *Un almanacco drammatico: L'indice de' teatrali spettacoli: 1764–1823*. See item 23.

294. Viale Ferrero, Mercedes. "Staging Rossini." In *The Cambridge Companion to Rossini*. See item 478.

RECEPTION

295. Bianconi, Lorenzo. "Reception and Image." In *The Cambridge Companion to Rossini*. See item 478.

* Carvalho, Mario Vieira de. "Belcanto-Kultur und Aufklärung: Blick auf eine widersprüchliche Beziehung im Lichte der Opernrezeption." See item 537.

* Chorley, Henry Fothergill. "Signor Rossini's Operas: Characteristics" in *Thirty Years' Musical Recollection*. See item 304.

* Conati, Marcello. Appendices in *La recezione di Rossini ieri e oggi*. See item 292.

296. ———. " ' . . . Una certa malattia, la quale può denominarsi *contagio fantastic*.' " In *La recezione di Rossini ieri e oggi* (item 288), 101–119.

Conati examines reviews and commentaries in lesser-known nineteenth-century periodicals, noting that, at first, Rossini was seen as a disciple of his predecessors but later was viewed as a trailblazer. The author also suggests that Italian musical theater was often seen through the eyes of literary critics; thus the libretto received more attention than did the music. Conati devotes sections of his essay to other issues addressed in the periodicals, including Rossini's self-borrowings and use of his music as substitutions in operas of other composers. He also comments on the composer's faulty harmony and attempts to place him in historical context. Conati concludes that critics' review of singers provide an invaluable key to understanding Rossini since his music can best be viewed as vocal creations for specific artists.

297. Loschelder, Josef. "Rossinis Bild und Zerbild in der Allgemeinen Musikalischen Zeitung Leipzip: Part I." *Bollettino del Centro Rossiniano di Studi* 13 [no. 1] (1973): 23–42; Italian translation, 43–57; Part II, 13 [no. 2] (1973): 23–42; Italian translation, 43–55.

Loschelder examines the treatment Rossini received in this important German music periodical. Part I of the series contains citations from reviews of Rossini's earliest works through *Elisabetta, regina d'Inghilterra*. Noting that the newspaper had critics who reported on theatrical activity in Italy as well as in Germany, Loschelder demonstrates that often reports on Italian productions were more harsh than reviews of productions in Germany. Despite any criticism, though, the newspaper consistently stated that Rossini was the best of contemporary Italian composers. Part 2 deals with productions through 1820. Loschelder notes that the German critics often offered different reports than their Italian colleagues about the same performances. Also, more and more, these reviewers struck out at what they heard as homogeneity in Rossini's opera; that is, if audiences knew one of his works, they knew them all. See item 298 for the series' conclusion.

298. ———. "Rossinis Bild und Zerrbild [sic] in der Allgemeinen Musikalischen Zeitung Leipzig." *Bollettino del Centro Rossiniano di Studi* 17 [no. 3] (1977): 17–40; Italian translation, 41–57.

A continuation of Loschelder's two-part examination published in 1973 (see item 297), this survey of Rossini reviews in this periodical begins with the composer's introduction to Vienna and concludes with citations of news items about the Petite messe solennelle. The author demonstrates with citations from articles that these reviewers differed greatly in their opinions of Rossini and his music. He also notes that these journalists often had no basis or knowledge for commenting on the composer's scores. Loschelder includes reviews of publications of Rossini's music as well as productions of his works.

LOCATIVE STUDIES

Studies in this section are commentaries on Rossini's first-hand experiences in places where he lived and worked as well as venues where his works were produced.

Australia

299. Irvin, Eric. "Australia's First Public Concerts." *Studies in Music* 5 (1971): 77–86.

> Not examined. According to the RILM abstract of this article, the author notes that the earliest public concerts in Sydney in 1826 included Rossini overtures on the programs.

Austria

Vienna

General Cultural Studies

300. Erickson, Raymond, ed. *Schubert's Vienna*. An Aston Magna Academy Book. New Haven: Yale University Press, 1997. xvi, 283 pp. ISBN: 0-300-07080-2 ML410.S3 29975 1997.

> This book of essays on Viennese society and culture during the time of Schubert describes the world into which Rossini and his music were introduced in 1822 and the city's subsequent "Rossini fever."

Rossini in Vienna

> * Joerg, Guido Johannes. "Zur Verwendung des Volkslied "Freut euch des Lebens" in den Werken Gioachino Rossini." Item 751.

301. Kantner, Leopold. "Rossini nello specchio della cultura musicale dell'Impero Asburgico." In *La recezione di Rossini ieri e oggi* (item 288), 215–22.

> Kantner discusses Rossini's reception in the Hapsburg Empire, especially in Vienna, attributing his success not only to the composer's genius but to the Viennese predilection for Italian music. He also cites statistics of period and modern productions of Rossini. In addition to a copy of "Addio per Maestro Rossini ai Viennese," sung by tenor Giovanni David in 1822, the article includes illustrations of the title page of *Un viaggio a Vienna*, the 1854 Viennese remake of *Un viaggio a Reims,* and of an 1832 poster for a Viennese production of *Le siège de Corinthe (Die Bestürmung von Corinth).* Mentions the relationship between Metternich and Rossini (see also items 42, 751, and 817).

* ———, and Michael Jahn, eds. "Fonti rossiniane a Vienna." See item 10.

302. ———. "Il viaggio a Vienna." In *Rossini 1792–1992* (item 95), 197–204.

The authors offer an account of Rossini's professional and personal contacts during his stay in Vienna under contract to impresario Domenic Barbaja. Includes illustrations as well as a table of Rossini's operas produced in Vienna from 22 March until 24 July 1822.

303. Szmolyan, Walter. "Rossinis Opern in Wien." *Österreichische Musikzeitschrift* 28 [no. 5–6] (1973): 220–32.

Szmolyan suggests that the "Rossini Renaissance" revitalized scholarly interest in the composer's works. With excerpts from contemporary reviews and the writings of commentators such as Eduard Hanslick (see item 161), the author examines Rossini's importance in Vienna from the earliest productions of his operas to his visit with Isabella Colbran in 1822. Not only were Rossini works performed in Italian in Vienna, but there also existed German versions and parodies. In addition, the proliferation of piano transcriptions supports the claim that Rossini was a favorite in Vienna. Includes a chart of Rossini's operas with dates of premieres and, where applicable, data on Viennese productions.

England

Contemporary Accounts of the London Stage
304. Chorley, Henry Fothergill. "Signor Rossini's Operas: Characteristics" in *Thirty Years' Musical Recollection*, Vol. 1, 34–43. London: Hurst and Blackwell, 1862. 2 vols. ML423.C55 C5;

pp. 24–29, 2nd ed., New York and London: A.A. Knopf, 1926. xxv, 411 pp. ML423.C55 C5 1926;

Reprint of second edition, with introduction by Ernest Newman, New York: Vienna House, 1972. xxv, 411 pp. ISBN 0-844-30026-8 ML423.C55C5 1972;

Reprint of 1862 edition, New York: Da Capo Press, 1984. ISBN 0-306-76216-1 ML1731.C58 1984.

Comments on Rossini's then-waning popularity and on the composer after his retirement from the stage after *Guillaume Tell* (see items 46 and 754 for another view of Rossini's "retirement"). The author's opinions are significant in that they defend Rossini (save for his choice of librettos) from contemporary English prejudices favoring what Chorley calls the German "scientific school of stage composition."

305. Ebers, John. *Seven Years of the King's Theatre*. London: William Harrison
     Ainsworth, 1828; Philadelphia: Carey, Lea & Carey, 1828. PN2596.L7 K4;

     Reissued, London and New York: Benjamin Blom, 1969. xxviii, 395 pp.
     PN2596.L7 K4.

     This history by Ebers, manager of King's Theater in Haymarket, documents
     the important role Rossini's works played in bringing Italian opera to Lon-
     don in the early nineteenth century. Not only was *La gazza ladra* chosen to
     reopen the theater in 1821, but, based on the lists of annual productions
     given by the author, Rossini operas made up at least half of the repertoire in
     any given season. The author also relates the history (albeit often anecdotal)
     of Rossini and Colbran's visit to London. In addition to comments on Col-
     bran's performances of Zelmira and Zoraide, Ebers discusses the issue of
     the unfinished opera, *Ugo, re d'Italia* (see item 784). Ebers writes of his
     visit to Paris to bring Rossini back to London and of the composer's assis-
     tance in procuring singers for the English stage. Also discusses the King's
     Theatre under Benelli's management (see item 57). Appendices include
     administrative details, such as a list of box subscribers, pay records of
     singers and dancers, and Giuditta Pasta's contract with the theater in 1826.

     * Edwards, H[enry] Sutherland. *The Life of Rossini*. See item 114.

306. Mount Edgcumbe, Richard. *Musical Reminiscences chiefly respecting the
     Italian Opera in England From the Year 1773 to the Present Time*. London:
     George Clark, 1824; 3rd ed., 1828. xvi, 192 pp. ML1731.3.E23.

     This early-nineteenth-century English writer bemoans all the faults of Ital-
     ian opera, citing examples from Rossini for each of his criticisms. No
     longer, he writes, is there a difference between *opera seria* and *opera
     buffa*—in fact, the same singers perform both. He also loathes the "mon-
     grel" genre of *semi-seria* works and dislikes the disappearance of arias in
     favor of "interminable" ensembles and accompanied recitative. Although he
     admits to liking *Il turco in Italia*, Edgcumbe finds faults in *La gazza ladra*.
     His chief criticism is that Rossini sets too much stock in his orchestra and
     leaves the singer unsupported. He predicts that Rossini will be quickly
     "thrown aside."

Rossini in London
307. Bucarelli, Mauro. "Rossini Fever." In *Rossini 1792–1992* (item 95),
     205–20.

     In this discussion of Rossini and Colbran's stay in London, Bucarelli con-
     siders the composer's dealings with impresario G.B. Benelli (see item 57)

and professional commitments such as private concerts, productions at The King's Theatre, and the London compositions: the opera *Ugo, re d'Italia* (see item 784) and "Il pianto delle Muse" (item 818). With illustrations.

* Cagli, Bruno. "Rossini a Londra e al Théâtre Italian di Parigi: Documenti inediti dell'impresario G. B. Benelli." See item 57.

308. Fenner, Theodore. *Opera in London: Views of the Press 1785–1830*. Carbondale, Ill.: Southern Illinois University Press, 1994. xv, 788 pp. ISBN 0-8093-1912-8 ML1731.8.L7 F4 1994.

This volumes treats the London periodical press as well as English musical theater and Italian opera, with consideration of their respective theaters, audiences, repertoire, and performance history. A section on Rossini in London (pp. 144–57) capsulizes the productions of his works, substantiated by relevant comments from leading critics. Fenner documents the beginning of Rossini's popularity and its heyday from 1821 to 1824. The section on English opera considers the adaptations of Rossini's works by Henry Rowley Bishop (see items 655) and Michael Rophino Lacy (item 694 and 699). The Italian opera section contains appendices on seasonal listings of performances and reviews, comic and serious productions (premieres and revivals), productions by composers in three-year periods, operas listed by composer and librettist, and singers.

309. McVeigh, Simon. "The Benefit Concert in Nineteenth-Century London: From 'tax on the nobility' to 'monstrous nuisance.' " In *Nineteenth-Century British Music Studies*. Vol. 1, 242–66. Ed. Bennett Zon. Aldershot, U.K.: Ashgate, 1999. xix, 324 pp. ISBN: 1-84014-259-6 ML285.4.N56 1999 Vol. 1.

The author demonstrates the presence of Rossini's music in concert programs and specifically notes how, based on ticket prices, his own two benefit concerts in 1824 initially were aimed at the highest social audience possible.

* Walker, Frank. "Rossiniana in the Piancastelli Collection." Part 2: "Correspondence with Michele Costa." See item 61.

Specific Works
* Bucarelli, Mauro. "Rossini Fever." See item 307.

* Joerg, Guido Johannes. "Rossini a Londra e la cantata *Il pianto delle Muse in morte di Lord Byron*." See item 818.

English Adaptations of Rossini Works
* Carnevale, Nadia. " ' . . . That's the barber!': Henry Rowley Bishop e l'adattamento del *Barbiere* rossiniano." See item 655.

* Fenner, Theodore. *Opera in London: Views of the Press 1785–1830*. See item 308.

France

General Cultural Studies

310. Atwood, William G. *The Parisian Worlds of Frédéric Chopin*. New Haven: Yale University Press, 19999. vii, 470 pp. ISBN: 0-3000-07773-4 ML410.C54 A78 1999.

References within this work comment on Rossini in the salons of Paris. Also considers Olympe Pélissier's role in this society prior to meeting Rossini. Illustrated.

311. Mongrédien, Jean. *La Musique en France des Lumières au Romantisme (1789–1830)*. Paris: Flammarion, 1986. In the series *La Musique en France*, Jean-Michel Nectoux, ed. 370 pp. ISBN 2-08-064651-6 ML270.4.M65 1986; published in English as *French Music from the Enlightenment to Romanticism 1789–1830*. Trans. Sylvain Frémaux. Reinhard G. Pauley, general editor. Portland, Ore.; Amadeus Press, 1996. 394 pp. ISBN 1-57467-011-5 ML270.4.M6513 1996.

The author offers an overview of the French musical world from the 1780s to the 1830s, demonstrating the gradual cultural developments that occurred during this period. Citing at relevant points of the discussion the significance of Rossini's activities, Mongrédien covers the following topics: standardization of musical education, music and politics, the French musical stage, sacred music, public and private concert life, shifting aesthetics and instrumental music, and the influence of the German school. Includes illustrations and a section giving modern equivalent dates for the French revolutionary calendar.

Studies of French Theater

312. Barbier, Patrick. *La vie quotidienne à l'Opéra au temps de Rossini et de Balzac: Paris, 1800–1850*. Paris: Hechette, 1987. 295 p. ML1727.8.P2 B3 1987 ISBN 2-01-012187-2; translated by Robert Luoma and reprinted as *Opera in Paris, 1800–1850: A Lively History*. Portland, Ore.: Amadeus Press, 1995. vii, 243 pp. ML 1727.8.P2 B313 1995 ISBN 0-931340-83-7.

A nonscholarly look at French opera history from the era of Napoleon through the beginning of the Second Empire. The author mentions Rossini frequently throughout the text but dedicates specific sections to his retirement after *Guillaume Tell* (see also item 754) and to his direction of the Théâtre Italien. The English translation is illustrated.

* Cohen, H. Robert, and Marie-Odile Gigou. *Cent ans de mise en scène lyrique en France (env. 1830–1930)/One Hundred Years of Operatic Staging in France*. See item 4.

* ——— with Sylvia L'Écuyer Lacroix and Jacques Léveillé. *Les Gravures dans "L'Illustration."* See item 92.

* Dauriac, Lionel. *La psychologie dans l'Opéra Français (Auber-Rossini-Meyerbeer)*. See item 533.

313. Fauré, Michel. "Opéra historique et problematique sociale en France, du premier au second Empire." In *La musique et le pouvoir*, edited by Hugues Dufourt and Joël-Marie Fauquet, 87–101. Paris: Aux amateurs de livres, 1987. 203 pp. ML270.M87 1987.

The author considers a definition and history of historic opera and the social problems encountered in its librettos. Concentrating on works between 1800 and 1860, *Tancredi* and *Elisabetta, regina d'Inghilterra* are among those discussed.

* Gautier, Théophile. *La Musique*. See item 759.

314. Johnson, James. *Listening in Paris: A Cultural History*. Berkeley: University of California Press, 1995. xvi, 384 pp. ISBN 0-520-08564-7 ML270.J64 1995.

Johnson presents the social history of the Théâtre Italien and traces how Rossini's works became favorites in Paris, particularly among the so-called "mélomanes," or musical dilettantes. Johnson also considers how Rossini's music was heard by audiences and critics, and how *Guillaume Tell* revitalized grand opera and became popular fare in the concerts at the Conservatoire. The book is illustrated and features musical examples; it also contains a list of contemporary French periodicals.

* Jouy, Victor-Joseph Étienne de. "Essai sur l'opéra français." See item 395.

315. Schmierer, Elisabeth. "L'esthétique française de l'opéra italien à Paris avant Rossini." In *Il testo e la scena* (item 286), 589–97.

The author traces artistic controversies in Paris in the eighteenth century, suggesting that, in order to understand the aesthetic that controlled the reception of the earliest productions of Rossini in Paris, one must know the development of prevailing artistic theories prior to his arrival.

Studies of Specific Theaters

L'Opéra

316. Bartlet, M. Elizabeth C. "Rossini e l'Académie Royale de Musique a Parigi." In *Rossini 1792–1992* (item 95), 245–66.

Considers the composer and his association at the Opéra with *Guillaume Tell* and *Le siège de Corinthe*, demonstrating his influence on the Parisian stage. With illustrations of costumes and set designs. Also features caricatures and statuettes from this period in Rossini's career.

* ———, with Mauro Bucarelli. *Guillaume Tell di Gioachino Rossini: fonti iconografiche.* See item 89.

317. Cohen, H. Robert. *The Original Staging Manuals for Ten Parisian Operatic Premières 1824–1843/Dix Livrets di Mise en Scène Lyrique Datant des Créations Parisiennes 1824–1843.* Vol. 6 in *Musical Life in 19th-Century France.* H. Robert Cohen, general editor. Stuyvesant, N.Y.: Pendragon Press, 1998. xxii, 218 pp. ISBN 0-945193-61-0 ML1727.8.P2 D58 1998.

Contains facsimiles of Parisian staging manuals, including those for the productions of *Le siège de Corinthe* (9 October 1826) and *Moïse et Pharaon* (26 March 1827) at the Opéra. Cohen's introduction explains the significance of staging manuals, particularly for provincial productions of works premiered in Paris. See also items 4 and 318.

318. ———. *The Original Staging Manuals for Twelve Parisian Operatic Premiéres/Douze livrets de mise en scène lyrique datant des créations parisiennes.* Preface by Maria-Odile Gigou. Vol. 3 in *Musical Life in 19th-Century France.* H. Robert Cohen and Yves Gérard, general editors. Stuyvesant, N.Y.: Pendragon Press, 1991. xxxiv, 282 pp. ISBN 0-918728-70-3 ML1727.8.P2 O7 1991.

Includes a facsimile of the staging manual from the Opéra's premiere of *Guillaume Tell* (3 August 1829). Cohen's introductory remarks outline the use of staging manuals in France and their adoption in Italian theaters. See also items 4 and 317.

Le Théâtre Italien

* Cagli, Bruno. "Rossini a Londra e al Théâtre Italian di Parigi: Documenti inediti dell'impresario G. B. Benelli." See item 57.

319. Castil-Blaze [François Henri Joseph Blaze]. *L'Opéra-Italien de 1548 à 1856.* Paris: Castil-Blaze, 1856. 543 pp. ML1727.8.P22 T52.

The author, known for his adaptations of Rossini's operas (see items 328, 330, and 658), details 307 years of Italian opera in France; he divides his history in epochs, noting Rossini's arrival (Epoch 9) and details of his career in France (Epoch 10). In addition to mentioning the singers who performed Rossini's works in Paris, he discusses the efforts of Eduoard Robert and Carlo Severini in the administration of the Italien and the former's attempts to have Rossini return there. Castil-Blaze is loath to attribute any innovations to Rossini, assigning credit elsewhere whenever possible. He relates a conversation with Rossini in which the composer noted the selections in the Petit Messe solennelle that were self-borrowings from operas.

* Gautier, Théophile. *La Musique*. See item 759.

* Johnson, James. *Listening in Paris: A Cultural History*. See item 314.

* Johnson, Janet. "Rossini, Artistic Director of the Théâtre Italien, 1830–1836." See item 322.

* ———. "Rossini e le sue opere al Théâtre Italien a Parigi." See item 323.

* ———. "Rossini in Bologna and Paris during the early 1830s: New Letters." Item 46.

* Schmierer, Elisabeth. "L'esthétique française de l'opéra italien à Paris avant Rossini." See item 315.

320. Soubies, Albert. *Le Théâtre-Italien de 1801 a 1913*. Paris: Fischbacher, 1913. iv, 186 pp. ML1727.8.P2 S77.

Very much a history of the theater's administration. The author maintains that Castil-Blaze's history of the Italien (see item 319) is full of errors. Soubies considers Rossini's initial engagements at the theater and the contractual arrangements he made when he became its director in 1824. He also mentions the politics with Ferdinand Paër (see item 57). Quoting correspondence and documents, he deals also with the direction of Eduoard Robert and Carlo Severini (see items 46 and 50) and the specific productions of Rossini's works. Although the material is dominated by Rossini's presence at the theater, Soubies acknowledges the importance of Robert and Severini, especially in engaging top-notch singers. Includes details on government subventions and the repertoire performed.

Rossini and Paris

* Bailbè, Joseph-Marc. "Rossini et la sensibilité française." See item 435.

* Beulé, Charles Ernest. *Éloge de Rossini*. See item 394.

321. Bruson, Jean-Marie, and Martine Kahane. *Rossini et Paris*. Paris: Tête d'Affliche, 1993. 62 pp. ISBN 2-909139-06-9 ML410.R8 B77.

A capsulized narrative of Rossini's years in Paris. While Bruzon deals with biographical details, Kahane centers on production history at the Opéra. The major part of this volume is iconographic, with color plates of portraits of Rossini and his circle, lithographs of nineteenth-century Paris, and illustrations of set and costume designs from productions at the Opéra.

* Cagli, Bruno. "L'ultima stagione." See item 173.

* ———, and Mauro Bucarelli, eds. *La casa di Rossini: Catalogo del museo*. See item 97.

* Fabbri, Paolo. "Rossini-Rezeption im Paris der 1820-Jahre." In *Rossini in Paris: Eine Veranstaltung des Frankreichzentrums der Universität Leipzig, in Zusammenarbeit mit der Deutschen Rossini Gesellschaft e.V.* See item 290.

* Ferrari, Luigi, ed. *Viaggio a Rossini*. See item 101.

* Grempler, Martina. "Rossini und die französisch-italienische Politik." In *Rossini in Paris: Eine Veranstaltung des Frankreichzentrums der Universität Leipzig, in Zusammenarbeit mit der Deutschen Rossini Gesellschaft e.V.* See item 290.

* Henze-Döhring, Sabine. "Rossinis Opern in Paris unter Gattungsgesichtspunkten." In *Rossini in Paris: Eine Veranstaltung des Frankreichzentrums der Universität Leipzig, in Zusammenarbeit mit der Deutschen Rossini Gesellschaft e.V.* See item 290.

322. Johnson, Janet. "Rossini, Artistic Director of the Théâtre Italien, 1830–1836." *Il testo e la scena* (item 286), 599–622.

Citing new documents that portray the politics and theatrical intrigue in Paris, Johnson demonstrates that the traditional charges of inactivity and opportunism leveled against Rossini were part of what can be termed a "campaign of disinformation." After explaining that the composer's career was embroiled not only in the politics of the Restoration but also in the often questionable dealings of Théâtre Italien entrepreneurs Eduoard Robert and Carlo Severini, the author goes on to define the roles of those in charge at the theater. She describes Rossini's "artistic authority" as including responsibilities such as the recruiting of singers, reconstitution of the orchestra under a new conductor, selection of repertoire, and casting. She also confirms, despite criticism in contemporary French sources such as Fétis, that Rossini actually maintained a continuous level of participation in the theater's affairs from 1824 until 1836. Cites police reports, correspondence, and contemporary commentaries. See also Johnson, item 46.

323. ————. "Rossini e le sue opere al Théâtre Italien a Parigi." In *Rossini 1792–1992* (item 95), 221–244.

Johnson examines Rossini's early years in Paris at the Italien, the productions of his works, and his growing influence in theatrical affairs. See also Johnson 46, 322, and 754.

* ————. "Rossini in Bologna and Paris during the early 1830s: New Letters." Item 46.

324. Kern, Bernd-Rüdiger. "Meister der Verhandlungstaktik: Gioachino Rossinis Vertrage mit der Krone Frankreichs." *Neue Zeitschrift für Musik 153* [no. 3] (March 1992): 13–18.

Kern examines the history of Rossini's contracts with the French crown and his appointment as "compositeur du Roi et Inspecteur Géneral du chant." The author highlights Rossini's talent at business negotiations. Illustrated with facsimiles of contracts.

* ————. "Wilhelm Hauffs Rossini-Rezensionen in Paris." In *Rossini in Paris: Eine Veranstaltung des Frankreichzentrums der Universität Leipzig, in Zusammenarbeit mit der Deutschen Rossini Gesellschaft e.V.* See item 290.

* Landini, Giancarlo. "Riflessioni su alcuni aspetti della vocalità francese di Rossini." In *Atti del convegno di studi: Rossini, edizioni critiche e prassi esecutiva*, 153–72. See item 282.

* Ortique, Joseph d'. *De la guerre des dilettanti, ou De la révolution opérée par M. Rossini dans l'Opéra françois [sic] et des rapports qui existent entre le musique, la littérature et les arts.* See item 396.

325. Prod'homme, J.G. "Rossini and His Works in France." *Musical Quarterly* 17 (1931): 110–37.

Traces "Rossinism" in Paris from the earliest reactions to his Italian operas prior to his first visit in 1823 until his assumption of the status of "living legend" after the success of *Guillaume Tell*. The author mentions Rossini's various professional duties at the Théâtre Italien and the Académie Royale de Musique, his position as Director of Music and Composer to the King, and finally his five-year contractual battle with the government of Louis Philippe. Includes brief stage histories of many of the Parisian productions and mentions the two Rossini parodies: *Le grand Dîner ou Rossini à Paris* and *Le Siège de l'Opera*. Illustrated with a caricature of Rossini by Charles Gilbert Martin.

326. Rohmann, Ralf. " 'Rossini in Paris': eine 'Table Ronde' am 1. Juni 1996 in Lepizig, verantaltet von Frankreichzentrum der Universität Leipzig in

Zusammenarbeit mit dem Institut français Leipzig un der Deutschen Rossini Gesellschaft e.V." *La Gazzetta* 6 (1996): 18–20.

Rohmann offers a report on this conference, which featured papers on Rossini's years in Paris, reception of Rossini's works in the 1820s, an analysis of *Guillaume Tell*, and a history of *Il viaggio a Reims*. For the list of published conference papers, see item 290.

* *Rossini in Paris: Eine Veranstaltung des Frankreichzentrums der Universität Leipzig, in Zusammenarbeit mit der Deutschen Rossini Gesellschaft e.V.* See item 290.

327. Vani, Mario. "Rossini e le sue dimore parigine." *Bollettino del Centro Rossiniano di Studi* [no. 3] (1973): 28–30.

The author chronicles the various residences in which Rossini lived during his years in Paris.

328. Walton, Benjamin. *Romanticisms and Nationalisms in Restoration France.* Ph.D. dissertation, University of California Berkeley, 2000. 334 pp.

Walton looks at the complex relationship between opera, culture, and nationalism in France between 1824 and 1830, that is, during the reign of Charles X. In his first chapter, he examines Rossini's *Il viaggio a Reims*, performed for Charles's coronation in 1825. He turns again to Rossini's works in his final chapters, considering both *Le siège de Corinthe* and *Guillaume Tell*, suggesting that both can be seen as nationalistic statements in which the composer was intimately involved. Also considers the works of Castil-Blaze and Weber on the French stage.

329. ———. "Rossini and France." In *The Cambridge Companion to Rossini.* See item 478.

French Adaptations of Rossini's Works Outside of Paris
    * Everist, Mark. "Lindoro in Lyon: Rossini's *Le Barbier de Séville.*" See item 658.

330. Loubinoux, Gerard. "Gli adattamenti francesi di Rossini: Il caso Castil-Blaze." In *Il testo e la scena* (see item 286), 649–67.

The author looks at the adaptations of Rossini's operas by François-Henri-Joseph Blaze (Castil-Blaze) and proposes that an understanding of his theories as a translator demonstrates the logic behind works that were often considered "massacres" of the originals. Loubinoux explains that Castil-Blaze attempted to use a system of versification that would standardize poetry, allowing a simple transfer of one language for another (isorhythmic parallels). Thus, he strove not for exact translation but for an "osmosis" between the spirit of the music and the words. The author also suggests that Castil-Blaze's adaptions, often done in provincial cities such as Lille and Lyon, made Rossini available to a wider audience and contributed to the overall diffusion of his music. See also item 658.

Germany

General Studies
331. Brauner, Charles S. " 'No, No, Ninetta': Observations on Rossini and the Eighteenth-Century Vocabulary of Opera buffa." In *Il testo e la scena* (item 286), 25–47.

The essay's title comes from critics' divergent views on whether the sung repetition of "no" in Rossini's works was stylistically comic or serious. Brauner examines the comic vocabulary of the eighteenth century, looking at a German treatise on high comedy and farce in opera. In light of their aesthetics, Brauner maintains, Germans often criticized Rossini for not having the correct tone (for more on Rossini and the Germans, see items 297, 298, and 332). Choosing the Act I finale *La gazza ladra*, actually a *semiseria* work, Brauner compares and contrasts comments by the Milanese critic for the *Allgemeine Musikalische Zeitung* (see items 297 and 298) and Stendhal (see item 135). He concludes by citing Arthur Schopenhauer's view that music, as an expression of the Will, speaks it own language. Seen thusly, Rossini's style is neither comic nor serious, but purely musical. Includes musical examples.

332. Döhring, Sieghart. "Rossini nel giudizio del mondo tedesco." Translated from German into Italian by Paola Riesz. In *Il testo e la scena* (item 286), 93–104.

Traces German views on Rossini from the arrival of the composer's music in Germany and Vienna in 1816 through the twentieth-century discussions of Friedrich Lippmann (see, for example, items 538 and 579) and Carl Dahlhaus (526). Initially, Rossini's popularity was seen as a threat to a German national style by critics such as Louis Spohr. When productions of Rossini's works declined and those of Giacomo Meyerbeer's increased, however, the author states that many Germans chose to view Rossini solely in terms of opera buffa, thus as typically Italian. Yet Germans lacking any knowledge of *bel canto* had no means to judge Rossini, and frequently the same issues were praised by some and criticized by others (see, for example, discussions of comedy in Brauner, item 331). Lippmann's studies (such as items 473 and 539) of Rossini initiated serious scholarly dialogue to which Dahlhaus, among others, have contributed.

333. Wittmann, Michael. "Das Bild der italienischen Oper im Spiegel der Kritik der 'Leipziger Allgemeine Musikalische Zeitung.' " In *Le parole della musica II*: *Studi sul lessico della letteratura critica del teatro musicale in onore di Gianfranco Folena*, 195–226. Vol. 22 in *Studi di Musica Veneta*. Ed. Maria Teresa Muraro. Florence: Leo S. Olschki, 1995. 334 pp. ISBN 88-222-4340-4 ML63.P26 1994 Vol. 2.

In his examination of German musical criticism of Italian opera in the *Allgemeine Musikalische Zeitung*, Wittmann considers comments about Rossini, many from the pens of Peter Lichtenthal and Gottfried Wilhelm Fink. Even though Germans acknowledged the composer's talent, his works were usually judged less worthy than Italian operas by Mozart and others in their own musical tradition. In particular, critics often felt that Rossini's settings failed to match the tone of their libretti. Wittmann concludes that only in the twentieth century, with the scholarship of Frederick Lippmann and Carl Dahlhaus, did Germans reconsider their opinion of the Italian repertoire. Also comments on nineteenth-century German opinion of Rossini's major contemporaries and considers the criticisms of Robert Schumann, Karl Franz Brendel, and Eduard Hanslick.

Studies of Rossini's Music in Specific Locales

Darmstadt
334. Kern, Bernd-Rüdiger. "Das Darmstädter Hoftheater und Rossini." In *Archiv für Hessische Geschichte und Alterkumskunde* New Series 42 (1984): 149–83.

[Not examined.]

* Müller, Reto, and Bernd-Rüdiger Kern. "Rossinis Verhandlungen mit dem Darmstädter Hoftheater." See item 80.

Frankfurt
335. Didion, Robert. "Le rappresentazioni di opere rossiniane a Francoforte nell'Ottocento: repertorio e materiale d'esecuzione." Translated from German into Italian by Reto Müller and Paolo Fabbri. In *Il testo e la scena* (item 286), 325–31.

Addresses Rossini's popularity at the Frankfort Opera, where he was one of the most produced composers, with *Il barbiere*, *Guillaume Tell*, and *Otello* in the theater's repertory by 1850. Didion explains that performance materials indicate that several of Rossini's operas were performed with spoken dialogue in the *Singspiel* tradition, with singers learning their roles from both a musical score and printed script. The author discusses the possible provenance of these and other sources, such as the librettos of censors and stage and technical directors. Includes a table of Rossini productions at the Frankfurt Opera from 1817 to after 1945.

Munich

336. Bolongaro-Crevenna, Hubertus. "Die italienische Oper in München." In *Musik in Bayern*, Vol. 1, 179–89. Edited by Robert Munster and Hans Schmidt. Tutzing: Schneider, 1972. 411 pp. ML277.M9 Vol. 1.

The author gives a history of Italian musical theater in Munich, noting that, after the eighteen-year ban on the production of Italian carnival operas, Rossini's works were among those produced until Italians productions were terminated in 1825.

Italy

337. Rosselli, John. *Music & Musicians In Nineteenth-Century Italy*. London: B.T. Batsford, 1991. 160 pp. ISBN 0-7134-6153-5; Portland, Ore.: Amadeus Press, 1991. ISBN 0-931340-40-3. ML290.4.R65 1991; Italian translation by Paolo Russo, *Sull'ali dorate*: *Il mondo musicale italiano dell'ottocento*. Bologna: Società Editrice Il Mulino, 1992. 176 pp. ISBN 88-15-03250-9. ML 290.4.R68 1992.

A readable work about the nineteenth-century Italian musical arena and its participants. Although he does not develop Rossini's role to any great extent, Rosselli cites the composer and his works as examples in developing a portrait of artistic life before and after the Unification. Contains illustrations as well as suggestions for further reading.

Studies of Rossini and His Music in Specific Locales

Bologna

338. Beghelli, Marco. "Bologna, nobile patria di aggressioni e di mortadelle." In *Rossini 1792–1992* (item 95), pp. 71–98.

Traces Rossini's connections to Bologna and his experiences there, beginning with his performances as a boy soprano through his years of study and early professional life. Cited are the remembrances of his childhood friend, Geltrude Righetti-Giorgi (see item 131). The essay concludes with the history behind Rossini's bitter decision to leave Bologna permanently. With illustrations.

* Capitanio, Fabrizio. "L'esecuzione della Stabat Mater di Rossini diretta da Donizetti (Bologna, 1842) in una recensione dell'epoca." See item 794.

* Collita, Carlo. *Il Palazzo dell'Archiginnasio e l'antico studio bolognese: con il Teatro Anatomico, le Funzioni dell'Anatomia; prima esecuzione dello Stabat Mater di Rossini.* See item 809.

339. Dioli, Arrigo. "Origini e vicende dell'Accademia Filarmonica di Bologna." In *Festschrift Ferdinand Haberl zum 70. Geburtstag: Sacerdos et cantus gregoriani magister*, edited by Franz A. Stein, 85–88. Regensburg: Bosse, 1977. 325 pp. ML55.H2 1977.

Dioli recounts the history of the Accademia Filarmonica and its offer to make Rossini its president and "consulente onorario perpetuo" in January of 1843. Initially, the composer declined for reasons of poor health; after he later accepted, he spent years in dedication to the institution.

* Ferrari, Luigi, ed. *Viaggio a Rossini*. Item 101.

340. Gallino, Nicola. "Lo 'scuolaro' Rossini e la musica strumentale al Liceo di Bologna." *Bollettino del Centro Rossiniano di Studi* 33 (1993): 5–55.

New archival research has yielded a fuller reconstruction of Rossini's years as a student at the Liceo Filarmonica. After demonstrating the importance of instrumental and vocal concerts in the rich musical life of Bologna in the early nineteenth century, Gallino traces how Rossini's early compositions fit into this artistic milieu. Liceo records not only present an idea of what Rossini studied and when he attended (including absences most probably explained by work he took on as *maestro al cembalo* in theatrical seasons) but also suggest that perhaps some of these early compositions may have later been operatic self-borrowings, such as a vocal-instrumental quartet which appears in *Demetrio e Polibio*. An appendix features documents, reviews, and facsimiles of programs discussed in the essay.

* Johnson, Janet. "Rossini in Bologna and Paris during the early 1830s: New Letters." See item 46.

* Tozzi, Lorenzo. "Rossini con le dande." In *Atti del convegno di studi: Rossini, edizioni critiche e prassi esecutiva*, 69–84. See item 282.

341. Vatielli, Francesco. *Rossini a Bologna*. Bologna: Cooperativa tipgrafica Azzoguidi, 1918. 54 pp.

[Not examined.]

342. Vecchi, Giuseppe. "Stendhal, la musica e Bologna." *Archginnasio: Bollettino della Biblioteca Comunale di Bologna* 56–58 (1971–1973): 573–86.

[Not examined.]

* Verdi, Luigi, ed. *Rossini a Bologna*: *Note documentarie in occasione della mostra "Rossini a Bologna,"* *29 Feb.–1 Apr. 2000*. See item 104.

Florence

* Bucarelli, Mauro, ed. *Rossini e Firenze*: *Immagini e note*. See item 96.

343. De Angelis, Marcello. "Presenza di Rossini a Firenze e in Toscana durante l'epoca granducale." *Bollettino del Centro Rossiniano di Studi* [no. 1–2] (1977): 37–60.

The author presents a chronology of performances of Rossini's music in Florence, Siena, and Lucca from 1812 to 1854. Data is gleaned from theatrical records and the contemporary press. The latter references include not only details on performances of Rossini's works but also articles on his music, such as several abstracted from Giuseppe Mazzini's *Filosofia della musica* (item 487). Information on operas includes lists of cast members and, where applicable, notes other productions in which they repeated their roles.

* G.[iazotto], R.[emo]. "Due lettere di Rossini." See item 45.

Forlì

* Fabbri, Paolo. *Rossini nella raccolte Piancastelli di Forlì*. See item 100.

* Müller, Reto. "Rossini-Bibliotheken der Welt: Die Sammlung Piancastelli in Forlì." See item 13.

* Walker, Frank. "Rossiniana in the Piancastelli Collection." Part 1: "Miscellaneous Unpublished Letters." See item 55.

* ———. "Rossiniana in the Piancastelli Collection." Part 2: "Correspondence with Michele Costa." See item 61.

Genoa

344. Ivaldi, Armando Fabio. "Tra impero francese e regno sardo: repertorio rossiniano e teatri genovesi d'inizio Ottocento." *Il testo e la scena* (item 286), 543–64.

Ivaldi chronicles the productions of Rossini operas in Genoa from 1814 to 1836. In addition to mentioning which of the composer's works were given poor, mediocre, or enthusiastic reception, the author demonstrates that the judgment of the audiences was quite often at odds with that of the city's theatrical critics, who on several occasions did not even deign to review a production. Ivaldi also includes three appendices: a list of Rossini operas tabulated by years of production; a chronological table of productions, noting both season and theatrical venue; and a sampling of seven reviews from the *Gazzetta di Genoa*.

Lucca

345. Barberio, Francesco. "La regina d'Etruria e Rossini." *Rivista Musicale Italiana* 55 (1953): 64–74.

Barberio recounts the history of a commission Rossini accepted in 1820 for an opera to be premiered at the Teatro del Giglio in Lucca. Citing correspondence between Carlo Carafa in Naples and agents for Maria Luisa di Borbone in Lucca, the author demonstrates that, no matter what excuses the composer made, Rossini completed neither the opera nor a Mass he had promised the Lucchesi as a peace offering.

* De Angelis, Marcello. "Presenza di Rossini a Firenze e in Toscana durante l'epoca granducale." See item 343.

Lugo

346. Fabbri, Paolo. "Alla scuola dei Malerbi: altri autografi rossiniani." *Bollettino del Centro Rossiniano di Studi* [1–3] (1980): 5–37.

Rossini's youthful musical training is most often ascribed to his teachers in Bologna. Fabbri demonstrates the importance of the composer's earlier instruction by Giuseppe Malerbi in Lugo. Examining autographs attributed to Malerbi, the author identifies some in Rossini's hand, all sacred, five of which were parts of Rossini's Messa di Ravenna. Fabbri, crediting Malerbi with introducing his pupil to counterpoint and imitation, also notes Rossini's continued connection to this teacher, given that the dateable autographs come from 1808, after Rossini had begun his studies in Bologna. Also mentions Rossini's early activities as a performer. Includes score examples, and a catalog and facsimile plates of the manuscripts. See also items 159, 179, and 787.

* ———. "Die Sakralmusik aus Lugo und die Jugendwerke Rossinis." See item 787.

347. *La casa paterna di Gioacchino Rossini*. Lugo: W. Berti, 1990. 92 pp. ML410.R8 C25 1990.

This volume celebrates the composer's links to Lugo, the town where his father was born and where Rossini spent formative years studying with Giuseppe Malerbi before going to Bologna. Brief essays deal with topics such as the Rossini home and efforts to restore it, the composer's friendship with Luigi Ferrucci (see items 41, 49, and 446), and Giuseppe Rossini's Lughese heritage. With illustrations and schematics of the house.

* Malerbi, Giuseppe. *Gioacchino Rossini: pagine segrete*. See item 159.

348. Rambaldi, Silvia. "I fratelli Malerbi e il giovane Rossini: Vita musicale a Lugo di Romagna tra Sette e Ottocento." *Hortus musicus: Trimestrale di musica antica* 1 [no. 2] (April-June 2000): 51–54.

[Not examined.]

349. Rossini a Lugo (www.teatrorossini.it/rossini_HTML/storia/Rossini.html).

Considers Rossini's connections with Lugo and the Malerbis. Also notes Rossini manuscripts at the town's Biblioteca Trisi. Accessed 27 December 2001.

Milan

350. Arruga, Lorenzo. *La Scala; con una testimonianza di Mario Labroca*. Milan: Electa, 1975. 317 p. ML1733.8.M5 A9; published in English as *La Scala, with an introduction by Paolo Grassi and Testimony to Times Past by Mario Labroca*. New York: Praeger, 1975. 314 pp. ML1733.8.M5 A93.

This history of Milan's most famous theater includes a chapter on Rossini's relationship to the theater and to the Milanese. Mentions the composer's five Scala premieres: *La pietra del paragone, Aureliano in Palmira, Il turco in Italia, La gazza ladra*, and *Bianca e Falliero*. Illustrated. See also item 351.

351. Quattrocchi, Arrigo. "Rossini alla Scala: ascese e cadute." In *Rossini 1792–1992* (item 95), 117–38.

After his initial successes in Venice, Rossini needed to build a reputation in other important opera centers. The author considers Rossini's dealings with La Scala and the premieres of his works for Milan. The essay is supported by excerpts from correspondence and contemporary reviews. With illustrations. See also item 350.

Naples

General Studies of Music in Naples

352. Florimo, Francesco. *La scuola musicale di Napoli e i suoi conservatorii con uno sguardo sulla storia della musica in Italia*. 4 vols. First published in 2 volumes as *Cenno storico sulla scuola musicale di Napoli, 1869–1871*. 2nd ed., 3 vol, 1881–1883. Reprint, Section 3, No. 7 of the series *Biblioteca musica bonoiensis*. Bologna: Forni, 1969. ML290.8.N2 F6 1969.

Vol. 1—*Come venne la musica in Italia ed origine della scuole italiane,* 209 pp.

Vol. 2—*Cenno storico sulla scuola musicale di Napoli e suoi Conservatorii, con le Biografie dei Maestri usciti dai medesimi,* ix, 471 pp.

Vol. 3—*Cenno storico sulla scuola musicale di Napoli e suoi Conservatorii, con le Biografie dei Maestri usciti dai medesimi,* 650 pp.

Vol. 4—*Elenco di tutte le opere in musica rappresentate nei teatri di Napoli dal 1651 al 1881 con cenni sui teatri e sui poeti melodrammatici,* xxiv, 605 pp.

Although this history of music and theaters in Naples deals peripherally with Rossini, certain aspects of Florimo's study merit mention for they chronicle the theatrical arena in which the composer worked during his years with Domenico Barbaja. Vol. 2 begins with a letter from the author dedicating the book to Rossini (v); the composer's acceptance is also transcribed (vi). Florimo also includes a letter from Olympe Pélissier acknowledging his condolences upon Rossini's death (viii). Vol. 3 includes Florimo's comments on Rossini and Bellini (pp. 230–1), a letter from Rossini about Neapolitan composer Carlo Conti (p. 169), and Florimo's opinion that Conti imitated Rossini too much (see section on Conti, pp. 153–71). Vol. 4 is a useful history of theater in Naples. Florimo not only gives histories of the various musical and dramatic stages but also lists all of the operas presented at these houses from 1651 to 1881. Information includes the works title, librettist, composer, venue and date, cast and comments on the production. For essays on Florimo, see items 211, 259, and 560.

Music Publishing in Naples
    * Seller, Francesca. "Editoria musicale a Napoli: la Stabilimento Musicale Partenopeo." See item 259.

Studies of the Teatro San Carlo
353. Henze-Döhring, Sabine. "Das Melodramma serio am Teatro San Carlo unter Napoleonischer Herrschaft (1808–1815)." In *Napoli e il teatro musicale in Europa tra Sette e Ottocento: Studi in onore di Friedrich Lippmann,* 247–66. Edited by Bianca Maria Antolini and Wolfgang Witzenmann. Vol. 28, *Quaderni della Rivista Italiana di Musicologia, Società Italiana di Musicologia.* Florence: Leo S. Olschki, 1993. 448 pp. ISBN 88-222-4026-X ML1720.N36 1993.

The author considers Rossini's serious works for Naples in line with those of his predecessors at the San Carlo. Also considers the French influence on the San Carlo repertory. Among the works examined are Mosca's *Il salto di*

Leucade, Manfroce's *Ecuba*, and Farinelli's *Caritea, regina di Spagna*. Henze-Döhring concludes that one can not understand the early works of Rossini without fitting them into this tradition. Includes musical examples and text excerpts. Also mentions librettists and singers.

* Maione, Paologiovanni, and Francesca Seller, eds. *Gioachino Rossini*. See item 358.

354. Mancini, Franco. *Il teatro di San Carlo, 1737–1987*. Vol. 2: *L'opera, il ballo*. Eds. Bruno Cagli and Agostino Ziino. Naples: Electa, 1987. 344 pp. ML290.8.N2 M3 1987 Vol. 2.

Cagli's chapter ("Al gran sole di Rossini," pp. 133–70) offers an account of Rossini's tenure in Naples under impresario Domenico Barbaja. Includes information on business aspects of the theatrical administration and of Rossini's specific duties. Details are also given on the production of Rossini's and his colleagues works in the Neapolitan arena. Touches upon the operas Rossini composed for Rome during his years with Barbaja in Naples; illustrations of singers and memorabilia from the seasons at the San Carlo. There is no specific discussion of Rossini in the other two volumes in this series: Vol. 1 deals exclusively with the theater's history and construction, and Vol. 3 treats scenography and costume design.

* Piperno, Franco. " 'Effetto Mosè': Fortuna e recezione dell *Mosè in Egitto* a Napoli e in Italia (1818–1830)." Item 718.

* ———. "Il *Mosè in Egitto* e la tradizione napoletana di opere bibliche." Item 719.

* ———. " 'Stellati sogli' e 'immagini portentose': Opere bibliche e stagioni quaresimali a Napoli prima del *Mosè*." See item 359.

355. Rossi-Espagnet, Andrea. "Attività spettacolari al Teatro S. Carlo di Napoli nella prima metà dell'Ottocento." *Nuova rivista musicale italiana* 30 [no. 1–2] (January-June 1996): 99–118.

The author considers the theatrical activity in Naples from 1810 to 1840. From 1815 to 1822, Rossini was active in this arena, working for Domenico Barbaja, and his works continued to be produced there after he left. Although the article does not deal directly with Rossini (save for citing a review of a production of *Guglielmo Tell* in 1833), the author provides a picture of the social and political environment in which he worked. In addition to noting the hierarchy of theaters by social class and genre, Rossi-Espagnet notes the vigilance of the censors, who accounted for every slight modification to a libretto or production.

Other Neapolitan Theaters

    * Maione, Paologiovanni, and Francesca Seller. "Domenico Barbaia a Napoli (1809–1840): meccanismi di gestione teatrale." See item 241.

    * ———, eds. *Gioachino Rossini*. See item 358.

Studies Specific to Rossini and Naples

    * Cagli, Bruno. "Al gran sole di Rossini." In *Il teatro di San Carlo, 1737–1987*, 133–70. See item 354.

356. ———. "All'ombra dei gigli d'oro." In *Rossini 1792–1992* (item 95), 161–96.

Cagli documents Rossini's years in Naples, with attention to his professional connections to impresario Domenico Barbaja (on Barbaja, see also item 241). Also considers his compositions for Isabella Colbran, his first wife. With illustrations.

357. Gossett, Philip. "History and works that have no history: Reviving Rossini's Neapolitan operas." In *Disciplining music: Musicology and its canons*, edited by Katherine Bergeron and Philip V. Bohlman pp. 95–115. Chicago: University of Chicago Press, 1992. xi, 220 pp. ISBN 0-226-04368-1 ML3797.1.D5 1992.

Because many of Rossini's works had fallen out of the repertory, they were merely considered in historical context and were not deemed worthy of analysis or study. According to the author, other reasons for this lack of interest included a scarcity of accurate editions and the numerous negative myths surrounding the composer's persona. By pointing to a study of the libretti and large-scale musical structures in the Neapolitan works, Gossett demonstrates their importance not only in understanding Rossini but also in documenting the development of nineteenth-century Italian opera. Includes tables of premieres and literary sources of the Neapolitan works and a chart of structural models for the librettos.

    * ———. "Rossini in Naples: Some Major Works Recovered." See item 814.

    * Isotta, Paolo. "I diamante della corona. Grammatica del Rossini napoletano." See item 586.

358. Maione, Paologiovanni, and Francesca Seller, eds. *Gioachino Rossini*. Volume in the series *Protagonisti nella storia di Napoli: Grandi napoletani*, ed. Saverio Ricci, et al., 68 pp. Naples: Elio de Rosa, 1994.

Primarily an iconography, this volume introduces readers to aspects of Rossini's career in Naples. In addition to illustrations of Rossini, his family and colleagues, Neapolitan theaters and panoramas, autograph manuscripts, and representative art work of the primo Ottocento, the volume includes brief essays for a general readership on Naples and its place in Rossini's career; its theaters and musical style; musicians, singers, and impresarios; the Naples Conservatory (all by Maione and Seller); Rossini as protagonist in the Neapolitan kingdom (Giuseppe Tortora); Isabella Colbran (Sergio Ragni); scenographer Antonio Niccolini and neoclassicism (Pier Luigi Ciapparelli); and the literary salon life in Naples (Tobia R. Toscano). Includes a chronology of Rossini's life and a bibliography.

* Piperno, Franco. " 'Effetto Mosè': Fortuna e recezione dell *Mosè in Egitto* a Napoli e in Italia (1818–1830)." Item 718.

* ———. "Il *Mosè in Egitto* e la tradizione napoletana di opere bibliche." Item 719.

359. ———. " 'Stellati sogli' e 'immagini portentose': Opere bibliche e stagioni quaresimali a Napoli prima del *Mosè*." In *Napoli e il teatro musicale in Europa tra Sette e Ottocento: Studi in onore di Friedrich Lippmann*, 267–98. Edited by Bianca Maria Antolini and Wolfgang Witzenmann. Vol. 28, *Quaderni della Rivista Italiana di Musicologia, Società Italiana di Musicologia*. Florence: Leo S. Olschki, 1993. 448 pp. ISBN 88-222-4026-X ML1720.N36 1993.

Piperno has demonstrated elsewhere (items 718 and 719) that *Mosè* reestablished the prerevolutionary Lenten biblical operas in Naples. In this essay, the author examines works in this tradition from 1785 to 1807. In addition to looking at structural models and production history, Piperno touches upon the possible connections Freemasonry may have had with this repertoire. Along with a list of productions, Piperno includes a table demonstrating instances of the use of choral prayers.

Pesaro

360. Fabbri, Paolo. "I Rossini a Pesaro e in Romagna." In *Rossini 1792–1992* (item 95), 53–70.

Offers a look at the composer's parents and their activities during Rossini's early years as a student and professional. Mentions the early compositions, including works associated with places important in his youth, such as those associated with the Conventello (see Fabbri, item 364). Illustrated.

361. Museo di Casa Rossini (www.fondazione.scavolini.com/iniziativo/casa_rossini/).

A single page featuring photographs of the Museo di Casa Rossini in Pesaro. Accessed 31 December 2001.

362. Panzini, Franco. "La casa natale di Rossini." *Bollettino del Centro Rossini- ano di Studi* 28 (1988): 47–76.

Details the construction and ownership history of the house in which Rossini was born. Illustrative plates include a site map of Pesaro, drawings of the building's facades, diagram of the house's various stages of construc- tion, and photographs of the exterior and interior.

363. Uguccioni, Riccardo Paolo. "Gli anni francesi. Pesaro dal 1797 al 1799." In *Rossini 1792–1992* (item 95), 45–52.

Presents a study of the political climate in the town of Rossini's birth during the volatile years of republican turmoil. With illustrations.

Ravenna

364. Fabbri, Paolo. "Luoghi rossiniani: Villa Triossi al Conventello." *Bollettino del Centro Rossiniano di Studi* [nos. 1–3] (1984): 43–51.

Fabbri notes the archival discovery that links two compositions from Rossini's youth with his summer stays at the Conventello near Ravenna. Owned by Agostino Triossi, the property was visited frequently by musical amateurs who presumably were the original performers of these works: the *Sinfonia scritta al Conventello* and the *Sinfonia obbligata a contrabasso* (composed for contrabassist Triossi). With illustrations, Fabbri describes the property and history of its ownership. Also in the Ravenna archive were partbooks for the Messa di Ravenna, which Fabbri maintains was not com- posed at the Conventello but points to Rossini's connections there. The author suggests that these works, "the experiments of an apprentice com- poser," foreshadow Rossini's mature style. See also item 360.

365. ———. "Presenza rossiniane negli archivi ravennati. Due inediti, un auto- grafo ed altro." *Bollettino del Centro Rossiniano di Studi* [nos. 1–3] (1978): 5–30.

Fabbri considers Rossini's musical connections with Ravenna, especially manuscripts in the archive of the Istituto Musicale Parregiato "G. Verdi," which recently had been rediscovered. Among these were autograph of the "Gratias agimus tibi" from the Gloria of the tenor version of the Ravenna Mass (see also item 787) and copies of two scores that link to Rossini's association with the Triossi family and his visits at the Conventello (see item 364). After describing the manuscripts and their music with score examples, including later instances of thematic self-borrowings, the author recounts details of the lives of Triossi and the other amateurs who would have performed these works or inspired their composition. Includes facsimiles of pages from the "Gratias" and maps of the Conventello.

Rome

General Studies of Theater in Roma

366. Bini, Annalisa. "Teatro e musica a Roma nell'Ottocento attraverso gli archivi familiari." In *La musica a Roma attraverso le fonti d'archivio: Atti del convegno internazionale, Roma 4–7 giugno 1992*, 237–86. Edited by Bianca Maria Antolini, Arnaldo Morelli, and Vera Vita Spagnuolo. Vol. 2 in the series *Strumenti della ricerca musicale* of the Società italiana di musicologia. Lucca: Libreria Musicale Italiana, 1994. xiii, 644 pp. ISBN: 88-7096-050-1 ML290.8 .R79 M94 1994.

After examining materials in the Archivi Lante Della Rovere and Capranica, Bini takes a look at theatrical activity in Rome from the early- to mid-nineteenth century. Her examination of the business aspect of theatrical production and the rapport between the various impresarial families and their theaters offers an overview of the environment in which Rossini's Roman works were produced. Mentions the composer's contacts with G.B. Benelli, Domenico Barbaja, and other influential theatrical administrators.

367. Cametti, Alberto. *"La musica teatrale a Roma cento anni fa."* In *Annuario della R. Accademia di Santa Cecilia 1915–1916*, 44–97. Rome: n.p., 1916. MT5.R6 A35 1916.

The first in a series of annual lectures in which Cametti discussed the history of significant productions in Roman theaters a century prior. Although one opera usually was highlighted in the talk, Cametti also included information about theaters, composers, impresarios, singers, and librettists. The lecture in 1916 included information of productions of Rossini operas and of the premiere in 1816 of *Il barbiere di Siviglia*. Other lectures in this series are listed as individual entries (see items 679, 692, 711, 727, 734, 743, 747, and 756.

368. Celani, E. "Musica e musicisti in Roma (1750–1850)." *Rivista musicale italiana* 22 (1915): 257–300.

The author examines production and contract details, some of which relate to performances of Rossini's works in Rome, such as *Il barbiere* in 1816. Celani cites the diary of Prince Mario Chigi, which lists productions in the city during the period in question; he also gives excerpts from the correspondence of Cesare Sterbini and from Geltrude Righetti-Giorgi's defense of Rossini (see item 131).

Specific Studies of Rossini's Music in Rome

369. Bini, Annalisa. "Echi delle prime rossiniane nella stampa romana dell'epoca." In *Rossini a Roma—Rossini e Roma*, item 289, 165–98.

Bini excerpts comments from the Roman press documenting reactions to Rossini's operas presented in Rome, both those that were *prime assolute* and productions. Her essay, which offers a look at the history of Roman theaters, imprese, and press, suggests that Rome served as a stimulus for the composer and proved to be a city that helped to spread his music, even after his move to France. (See also item 372).

370. ———. "Rossini a Roma, ossia le comicità." In *Rossini 1792–1992* (item 95), 139–60.

Describes the theatrical milieu in which Rossini composed his Roman premieres, including *Cenerentola*, *Il barbiere di Siviglia*, and *Matilde di Shabran*. Includes mention of the composer's numerous personal and professional contacts there. With illustrations. See also item 102.

* *Il teatro di Rossini a Roma 1812–1821: Debutti, musiche, artisti, librettisti, teatri*. See item 102.

371. Mauceri, Marco. "Rossini a Roma nel 1821: nuovi documenti su un'opera mai scritta." *Bollettino del Centro Rossiniano di Studi* 28 (1998): 27–46.

Introduces correspondence demonstrating that Rossini had entered into an agreement to compose an opera buffa for the 1821–1822 *carnevale* season in Rome. However, he was legally bound to Naples and to impresario Domenico Barbaja, who at first seemed to have agreed to release him. Barbaja subsequently refused to release Rossini since he then would have been without a composer as Ferdinando Päer had decided to remain in Paris. The letters printed here illustrate aspects of the professional relationship between the impresario and Rossini. More important, they disprove the theory that Rossini had abandoned opera buffa after *Cenerentola*. Includes transcriptions of the correspondence between the Roman theater authorities and Barbaja, and facsimiles of two of the impresario's letters.

372. Quattrocchi, Arrigo. "Le accademie romane e Rossini." In *Rossini a Roma—Rossini e Roma*, item 289, 87–102.

In addition to giving the histories of Rome's three *accademie*, the Congregazione di Santa Cecilia, the Accademia Filarmonica, and the Accademia Antifilarmonica, Quattrocchi explains Rossini's professional rapport with them during the period of this study (1822–1842). Because of the rivalry between the institutions, they often fought to gain the rights to perform Rossini's works before Rome's high society. Such was the case in 1844 when the Filarmonica vied with the Congregazione di Santa Cecilia for the Roman debut of the Stabat mater. The author also includes information on a censored production of *Guglielmo Tell* at the Filarmonica in 1835. Quattrocchi considers the versions of these works as reflected in the libretti and also questions the level of performance by musical dilettantes. He concludes that such research demonstrates the cultural ambitions of Roman musical societies. Includes a table of Rossini's works at the Accademie and copies of relevant correspondence.

Siena

* De Angelis, Marcello. "Presenza di Rossini a Firenze e in Toscana durante l'epoca granducale." See item 343.

* Schlitzer, Franco. *Rossini e Siena e altri scritti rossiniani (con lettere inedite).* See item 53.

Treviso

373. Simionato, Giuliano. "Rossini, Canova, e Treviso: I rapporti tra il musicista e la cittá veneta esaminati attraverso documenti inediti ed un autografo." *Bollettino del Centro Rossiniano di Studi* [no. 3] (1975): 13–25.

Considers Rossini's contributions for the 1823 memorial celebration for artist Antonio Canova. Simionato cites contemporary reports of the ceremonies and the musical program, which featured, among other selections by Rossini, an overture (the so-called Sinfonia per Treviso or the Sinfonia per il busto di Canova) and a pastoral cantata. After describing the score, comprised of the overture, a terzetto, recitative, and duet, Simionato demonstrates that only the recitative was original for the Treviso ceremony. The other two vocal movements were from the cantata "La Riconoscenza" and the Sinfonia, as identified by Philip Gossett, was the overture written for the 1822 Venice production of *Maometto II*. Includes the cantata text and transcriptions of correspondence between G.B. Marzari, president of the Treviso Ateneo, and the composer.

Turin

* Gualerzi, Giorgio. "Il 'Rossiniano' Gui a Torino." See item 618.

Venice

Studies of Specific Theaters in Venice

La Fenice

* Giazotti, Remo. "Alcune ignote vicende riguardanti la stampa e la diffusione della 'Semiramide.' " See item 262.

374. Martinotti, Sergio. "Rossini, Venezia e La Fenice." Essay in *La Fenice*. Introduction by Floris L. Ammannati. Milan: Nuove Edizioni, 1972. 353 pp. ML1733.8 V42 F4 Case.

Not only does the author consider Rossini's relationship with La Fenice, the subject of this illustrated volume of essays, but also with other theaters in which he premiered as a young composer. Included is a discussion of Rossini's *farse* for the smaller Venetian houses. Martinotti also offers a brief production history and a look at the reception of Rossini's works in Venice. Illustrated with period scenographic sketches, libretto and score facsimiles, a portrait of Rossini interpreter Maria Malibran, and an oil of the composer.

San Moisè

375. Miggiani, Maria Giovanna. "Il Teatro di San Moisè (1793–1818)." *Bollettino del Centro Rossiniano di Studi* 30 (1990): 5–44.

This entire volume is dedicated to Miggiani's extensive history of the Venetian theater, which gave a start to the young Rossini with his five early *farse*: *La cambiale di matrimonio* (1810), *L'inganno felice*, *La scala di seta*, and *L'occasione fa il ladro* (all 1812), and *Il signor Bruschino* (1813). The author traces the social and production history of the San Moisè. Following the rise of the *farsa* as a genre, she notes that its decline in Venice paralleled Rossini's rise as a star composer so popular at the Moisè that productions of his works made up most of the repertoire of the theater's final eight years. She also includes the role of *opera serie*, spoken drama, ballet, and instrumental concerts in her history. A complete chronology follows (pp. 45–177) as do indexes of productions and concerts; librettists and playwrights; composers; operatic and dramatic roles; singers, actors, dancers, and musicians; choreographers, set and costume designers, impresarios and other production personnel (pp. 181–213). Includes tables of productions by acts and of the operatic repertoire. Illustrated with plates of the theater's design and of advertisements for performances of Rossini's works.

* Mangini, Nicola. "Sui rapporti tra teatro e politica negli anni delle 'prime' veneziane di Rossini." In *Atti del convegno di studi: Rossini, edizioni critiche e prassi esecutiva*, 41–52. See item 282.

Rossini in Venice
* Miggiani, Maria Giovanna. "Il Teatro di San Moisè (1793–1818)." See item 375.

376. Pinamonti, Paolo. "Da 'ornamento dell'Italia' a 'dominator musicale del mondo': Rossini nella vita teatrale veneziana." In *Rossini 1792–1992* (item 95), 99–116.

Considers Rossini's theatrical connections with Venetian theaters from the early *farse* to *Semiramide*. In addition to illustrations of singers and set designs, the essay features a chronology of the Venetian works.

Verona
* Cavazzocca Mazzatinti, Vittorio. "Rossini a Verona durante il Congresso del 1822." See item 817.

Poland

377. Sandelewski, Wiaroslaw. "Sulle prime esecuzioni rossiniane in Polonia." *Rivista italiana di musicologia* 2 [no. 1] (1967): 152–61.

The author documents the popularity of Rossini's works in Poland, specifically in Warsaw, where *Tancredi* was produced in 1818. Noting that these operas were performed by Polish singers rather than by traveling Italian companies, Sandelewski proposes that Warsaw was one of the few cities that consistently accepted and enjoyed Rossini's works. The author supports his study with excerpts from contemporary reviews, noting, however, that much archival material was destroyed during World War II. Includes a list of Rossini productions in Warsaw.

Puerto Rico

378. Thompson, Donald. "Nineteenth-Century Musical Life in Puerto Rico." *Die Musikkulturen Lateinamerikas im 19.Jahrhundert*, 327–32. Vol. 57 in the series *Studien zu Musikgeschichte des 19.Jahrhunderts*, ed. Robert Gunther. Regensburg: Bosse, 1982. 463 pp. ML199.4. M88 1982.

Thompson examines the arrival of European art music in Puerto Rico. Noting that Rossini's *Il barbiere* was the first Italian opera presented on the island, Thompson discusses the history of the Compañía Filarmonica, who performed the opera in 1835. Later productions of Rossini's works were directed by Stefano Busatti, whose company arrived in Puerto Rico in 1842.

Russia

379. Imanalieva, Kumusc. "Rossini nel giudicio di un critico russo." *Bollettino del Centro Rossiniano di Studi* 40 (2000): 195–209.

In the face of Russian nationalism, composer-critic Alexander Serov wrote favorably of Rossini and his music, publishing an essay on the composer in which he placed him above Mozart. Serov stressed that Hiller's account of his conversations with Rossini (see item 119) was the key to the composer's true beliefs. Along with this introduction to Serov, the author provides an Italian translation of Serov's essay "Rossini," published shortly after the Italian composer's death in 1868. With illustrations.

Spain

* Bagues Erriondo, Jon. "Rossini y Aranzazu." See item 1.

380. Ester-Sala, María, and Josep Maria Vilar. "La presencia de Rossini en la vida cotidiana en la Catalunya del ochocientos." *Nassarre: Revista Aragonesa de Musicología* 8 [no. 2] (1992): 69–82.

After mentioning the popularity of Rossini's operas in the theaters in Barcelona in the nineteenth century, the authors go on to surmise that his reputation came from the spread of transcriptions of his music (see also item 405). Tracking the presence of copies of Rossini arrangements catalogued as "domestic music" in some thirty archives, the authors contend that, both for entertainment and musical training, Rossini's music was a significant part of the musical life of nineteenth-century Catalonian society. The authors match a list of operas produced in Barcelona with arrangements in local archives, identified and located on an accompanying map.

* Pagan, Victor. *Rossini en la Villa y Corte: Estudio iconografico.* See item 86.

* . ———. "Un italiano en Madrid: Gioacchino Rossini (estudio de icono-grafia)." See item 87.

* Pico Pascual, Miguel Angel. "La presencia de libros de musica en la vida cotidiana de la alta burguesia valenciana de finales del siglo XVII y la primera mitad del siglo XIX: Estudio de dos bibliotecas musicales privadas a traves de los protocolos notariales." See item 14.

381. Rizzuti, Alberto. "La fortuna del teatro rossiniano a Madrid (1816–24)." *Bollettino del Centro Rossiniano di Studi* 31 (1991): 77–95.

Tracing the production history of Rossini operas in Madrid from the earliest (1816) through the "Rossini fever" of the 1820s, Rizzuti describes the incredible impact the composer's music had on the cultural, social, and even political life of the Spanish capital. Also introduces Ramón Carmier, who not only composed in Rossini's style but also wrote various substitute numbers, at least one of which Rossini himself authorized for use. Includes performance statistics of Rossini premieres in Madrid during the 1823–1824 season.

382. Ruiz Tarazona, Andres. "Musicos extranjeros en España: Gioachino Rossini." *Temporadas de la musica* 6 [no. 19] (1988): 51–55.

[Not examined.]

United States

General Studies

383. Dizikes, John. *Opera in America: A Cultural History*. New Haven and London: Yale University Press, 1993. 612 pp. ISBN: 0-300-05496-3 ML1711.D6 1993.

Within this larger study, Dizikes deals with the role Rossini's works played in the introduction of opera to America. Chapter one is devoted to the García troupe and their productions, including *The Barber of Seville*. The author also discusses performances of *Semiramide* in America.

384. Norris, Renee L. " 'Black Opera': American Blackface Minstrelsy and European Opera." Ph.D. dissertation, University of Maryland, 2001. ix, 230 pp.

Norris demonstrates that the audiences of opera and minstrelsy were shared; thus, differences between high and low art did not exist during the antebellum period. In fact, the audiences' appreciation of opera helped minstrels to create successful parodies. The author considers the popular adaptations of Rossini's *Cenerentola* and *Ivanhoé*, *Cinderella* and *The Maid of Judah*, both by Michael Rophino Lacy (see items 694 and 699), as well as a parody of *La gazza ladra* (*The Gass Ladder*). Such works, she argues, demonstrate the popularity of Italian opera before the Civil War.

385. Preston, Katherine K. *Opera on the Road: Traveling Opera Troupes in the United States*. Urbana and Chicago: University of Illinois Press, 1993. xvii, 479 pp. ISBN 0-252-01974-1 ML1711.4.P73 1993.

Preston demonstrates the popularity of opera in nineteenth-century America, brought about by traveling English and Italian companies. Among the works performed by these troupes was *The Barber of Seville*. First staged in English in New York in 1812 and 1813, this work was a staple of the repertory until mid-century. Preston also notes the adaptations and pastiches of

Rossini's works such as those by Michael Rophino Lacy (see also items 384, 694 and 699). Ample citations from the contemporary press substantiate this study. Illustrated. See also item 386.

New York

386. Ahlquist, Karen. *Democracy at the Opera: Music, Theater, and Culture in New York City, 1815–60*. Urbana and Chicago: University of Illinois Press, 1997. xvii, 248 pp. ISBN 0-252-02272-6 ML1711.8.N3 A45 1997.

Ahlquist examines the musical scene in early nineteenth-century New York, noting the role of Rossini's operas in that city's artistic culture. *Il barbiere*, for example, was the first Italian opera to be performed there. In addition, the first opera on the New York stage featuring a tragic ending was Rossini's *Otello*. Introducing Rossini's works to New York was a company led by Manual García, who had premiered the role of Almaviva for Rossini at the Roman debut of *Il barbiere*. The author compares the reception of Rossini's music to that of Bellini and Verdi, demonstrating that despite its popularity, it was short-lived in the repertoire. With musical examples. See also item 385.

387. Lawrence, Vera Brodsky. *Strong on Music: The New York Music Scene in the Days of George Templeton Strong, 1836–1875*.

Vol. 1—*Resonances, 1836–1849*. New York: Oxford University Press, 1988. ISBN: 0-19-504199-2; reprint, Chicago: University of Chicago Press, 1995. lvi, 686 pp. ISBN: 0-226-47009-1. Vol. 2—*Reverberations, 1850–1856*. Chicago: University of Chicago Press, 1995. xxii, 863 pp. ISBN: 0-226-47010-5. Vol. 3—*Repercussions, 1857–1862*. Chicago: University of Chicago Press, 1999. xxviii, 630 pp. ISBN: 0-226-47015-6. ML200.8.N5 L4 1995 Vol. 1, 2, and 3.

Lawrence transcribes and adds commentary to the journal of George Templeton Strong, a record of the musical scene in New York through much of the nineteenth century. Includes accounts of both English and Italian productions of Rossini's works in New York and of popular pastiches. See also item 386 and 388.

388. McKnight, Mark Curtis. *Music Criticism in the New York Times and the New York Tribune, 1851–1876*. Ph.D. dissertation, The Louisiana State University and Agricultural and Mechanical College, 1980. 434 pp.

Not examined. The author's abstract notes that this study, which highlights a period of transition in America, permits an examination of the cultural life of this growing city. Relevant to Rossini studies, the dissertation traces the change in taste from Italian opera to French *opéra bouffe* and Wagner. See also items 386 and 387.

Specific Studies of Rossini's Music in America
389. Jennings, Harlan F. "Rossini Re-visited: Nineteenth-Century Opera Performances in the American Heartland." *The Sonneck Society for American Music Bulletin* 19 [no. 1] (Spring 1993): 5–6.

Using period newspapers, the author traces the popularity of Rossini operas in Missouri, Kansas, Nebraska, and Colorado, noting that the majority of these works were produced in St. Louis. Jennings also reports on the singers and companies who brought these works to this four-state region. Sung in both Italian and English, the most frequently performed opera was *The Barber of Seville*. Also staged were *William Tell* and *Semiramide*. One production of the latter featured world-famous singers Adelina Patti and Sofia Scalchi.

English Language Adaptations in America
* Graziano, John, ed. *Italian Opera in English: Cinderella (1831)*. See item 694.

8

Rossini's Historical Position and Influence

GENERAL STUDIES

390. Barblan, Guglielmo. "Rossini e il suo tempo." *Chigiana* 35 [no. 5] (1968): 143–79.

During his visit to Vienna in 1822, according to Rossini, Beethoven praised him for his comic abilities; in 1860, Wagner lauded Rossini, then long retired from the stage, for his serious works. Barblan uses these comments to initiate a discussion about Rossini as a product of his Italian opera heritage and as the forerunner of new style of the later nineteenth century. Tracing the impact of Rossini's works, Barblan suggests that Beethoven's and Wagner's comments are not really antithetical but rather complementary. He also suggests that even though Rossini has been called a conservative composer of the political Restoration, the musical transformation with which he can be credited is worthy of a revolutionary. This article reflects older Rossini scholarship; see, for example, Caswell (items 271 and 568) on a newer approach to the question of Rossini and vocal embellishment. In addition to commenting on Rossini's major works, Barblan also mentions Rossini's relationship with Carl Maria von Weber.

391. Mila, Massimo. "La fortuna di Rossini." *Bollettino del Centro Rossiniano di Studi* 8 [no. 1] (1968): 1–10.

In this speech, which opened the commemoration in Pesaro of the centennial of Rossini's death, Mila considers Rossini's significance both in modern times and in his own day. The author links Rossini with the very nature of Italians—what he terms "Italianità." Mila then cites Stendhal's oft-quoted comment comparing Rossini with Napoleon, stating that the composer did indeed conquer his world on three levels—locally, nationally, and internationally. Mila examines Rossini's career between that of Cimarosa and Weber, noting both of his "faces"—that of a revolutionary and of a reactionary. In contrast to earlier composers, Mila suggests, Rossini can only be seen as a progressive, but when placed with Weber, Wagner and Verdi, he appears conservative. Although it was Rossini who took Italian opera out of "Arcadia," Mila pays tribute to the composer's predecessors, urging a study of the works of Mayr and his contemporaries (for research in this area, see items 541 and 542).

392. Nicastro, Aldo. "Il ruolo dell'intellettuale e del musicista tra Rivoluzione e Restaurazione." *Chigiana: rassegna annuale di studi musicologici* 33 [no. 13] (1976; publ. 1979): 199–210.

Not examined. According to the RILM abstract, the article addresses the Italian opera composer within the contradictory framework of the Enlightenment and Romanticism. The specific cultural roles of Rossini and Verdi are considered.

393. Zoppelli, Luca. "Intorno a Rossini: sondaggi sulla percepzione della centralità del compositore." *Il testo e la scena* (item 286), 13–24.

Through the eighteenth century, operas tended to be identified by various "authors": composer, librettist, scenographer, and choreographer. Limiting his investigation to the Venetian political press, which reflected news from all over Italy, Zoppelli attempts to determine Rossini's influence in the move to identify operas solely by their composer. The study concentrates on three periods: 1808–1810 (pre-Rossini), 1818, and 1824–1825 (after the composer left Italy). Graphs which represent the statistical results demonstrate that during these years, the composer came to be the sole "author" associated with a work, while mention of the librettist—and indeed any other aspect but the music—declined significantly.

CONTEMPORARY ASSESSMENTS OF ROSSINI

Although these studies may touch upon biography, their purpose was to judge Rossini's place in the cultural environment of his day. Contemporary biographical studies may be found in Chapter 4 and aesthetic commentary and arguments about his music in Chapter 9.

394. Beulé, Charles Ernest. *Éloge de Rossini*. Paris: Académie des Beaux Artes, 1869. 28 pp. ML410.R8 B38.

In the text of this speech delivered at the Académie des Beaux Arts on 18 December 1869, Beulé compares Rossini to Mozart. Then, briefly tracing Rossini's life via his operas, the author states that the composer thought only of theater throughout his compositional career. Beulé contends that Rossini imitated no one and that each opera was an exercise in his development. Praising the composer's new forms, rich harmonies, and enchanting rhythms, Beulé proposes that, although Rossini gave Paris *Guillaume Tell*, it was Paris that made Rossini great.

* Chorley, Henry Fothergill. "Signor Rossini's Operas: Characteristics" in *Thirty Years' Musical Recollection*. See item 304.

395. Jouy, Victor-Joseph Étienne de. "Essai sur l'opéra français." In Volume 12 of Jouy's *Oeuvres complètes*, 226–82. Paris: Didot, 1826; Reprint: "Essai sur l'opéra français." Edited by Anselm Gerhard in *Bollettino del Centro Rossiniano di Studi* 1–3 (1987): 61–91.

Jouy, who worked on the librettos of *Moïse et Pharaon* and *Guillaume Tell*, defines opera as a collection of four elements: poetry, music, dance, and art (costumes and set design). Of those responsible for an opera, he believes that the poet is the most important. In the ensuing discussion, which considers French opera and some aspects of Italian, Jouy expounds on all four of opera's components, using as examples works as old as those of Jean-Baptiste Lully. Includes a discussion of the "marvelous" in opera and extols the happy ending. In the section on music, Jouy mentions Rossini's current popularity and his talent in setting finales. He eschews lengthy comment, however, since, as he puts it, Rossini's place in the French musical world has yet to be defined. For a commentary on Jouy's essay, see Gerhard's comments in the *Bollettino* reprint and item 497.

396. Ortique, Joseph d'. *De la guerre des dilettanti, ou De la révolution opérée par M. Rossini dans l'Opéra françois {sic} et des rapports qui existent entre le musique, la littérature et les arts*. Paris: Librairie de Ladvocat, 1829. 77 pp. ML410.R8 O8.

The author compares Rossini with Voltaire in this look at the music and the arts. He notes that Rossini's music is not for everyone and that, although the composer has been touted as revolutionary, his expression is rather artificial and facile. Although the work's preface was written before *Guillaume Tell*, Ortique considers the work in a postscript.

ROSSINI'S INFLUENCE ON THE MUSIC OF OTHERS

General Studies

397. Guaccero, Domenico. "Ironia di Rossini e dell'avanguardia." In *Convegno di studi su Rossini per il Centenario della morte di Gioacchino Rossini*, pp. 111–18. See item 283.

398. Jou, Jeng-Jong Jonathan. "Bel Canto: Its Effect on Piano Repertoire of the Nineteenth Century." D.M.A. dissertation, University of Washington, 1997. 120 pp.

    This performance practice study demonstrates how the bel canto singing techniques in operas such as Rossini's influenced both pedagogy and performance during the nineteenth century. Considered, with musical examples, is the production of the so-called singing tone.

399. Litschauer, Walburga, and Walter Deutsch. " 'Es reiten drei Schneider', oder, Rossini im Volkslied." *Jahrbuch des Österreichischen Volksliedwerkes* 41 (1992): 39–48.

    [Not examined.]

400. Vlad, Roman. "Rossini e i compositori moderni." *Nuova rivista musicale italiana* 26 [no. 1] (January-March 1992): 72–84; originally published in *Rassegna musicale* 24 (1951): 65–90.

    Vlad considers Rossini's role in the evolution and development of music into the twentieth century as well as his influence on composers such as Alfredo Casella, Ottorino Respighi (see item 430), Darius Milhaud, François Poulenc, and Igor Stravinsky. The author suggests that the cultural environment in Rossini's day was, in many ways, similar to that in which these modern composers worked.

Studies of Specific Nineteenth-Century Composers

Items in this section relate to how Rossini's music influenced his contemporaries. For studies of Rossini's relationships with various colleagues, ways in which he was compared or contrasted to his contemporaries, and their influence on his music, see Chapter 5.

Beethoven, Ludwig van

401. Massenkeil, Günther. "Einige überlegungen zu Beethovens Italianità." In *Colloquium Die Stilistische Entwicklung der italienischen Musik zwischen*

1770 und 1830 und ihre beziehungen zum Norden (Rome 1978), edited by Friedrich Lippmann, 410–19. Vol. 21 of *Analecta Musicologica*, Arno Volk: Laaber, 1982. viii, 461 pp. ISBN 3-9215-1866-0 ML290.3.C64 1978.

The author considers the influence of Rossini, Paisiello, and Salieri on Beethoven's music. Specific examples demonstrate that Beethoven's instrumental music was indeed inspired by Italian opera. With score excerpts.

Bellini, Vincenzo
402. Conati, Marcello. "La novella scuola musicale." *Studi musicali* 21 [no. 1] (1992): 191–208.

Even though Rossini codified the concept and structures of *melodramma*, Conati notes that its development was far from linear. Looking beyond Rossini, the author sees what he terms the "discontinuità" of Bellini's music in respect to Rossini's. Citing production statistics, Conati demonstrates that, even though *Il barbiere di Siviglia*'s popularity continued through the 1840s, Rossini's domination of the Italian stage declined a decade earlier. Conati then cites Carlo Ritorni's *Ammaestramenti alla composizione* (see also item 543) in which Bellini is touted as the founder of a "new school." Conati examines Ritorni's comments, concluding that Bellini absorbed Rossini's musical experience, taking it into new dramatic dimensions.

Berlioz, Hector
403. Langford, Jeffrey. "Berlioz, Cassandra, and the French operatic tradition." *Music & Letters* 57 [no. 3–4] (July-October 1981): 310–17.

Langford traces Berlioz's creation of Cassandra as operatic heroine in *Les Troyens*, suggesting that when the composer was faced with resolving his heroine's fate, he turned to Rossini's *Le siège de Corinthe* for a model. The author compares Cassandra and Pamyra; both are princesses who defy their conquerors by ending their own lives. Although Berlioz may have borrowed this plot device, Langford notes that his music differs radically from its Rossinian forerunner.

Donizetti, Gaetano
   * Bini, Annalisa. "Esiti ottocenteschi della farsa in Rossini e Donizetti." See item 598.

404. Petrobelli, Pierluigi. "Dulcamara e Berta: Storia di una canzone." In *Lied-studien: Wolfgang Osthoff zum 60. Geburstag*, 307–12. Edited by Martin Just and Reinhard Wiesend. Tutzing: Schneider. 1989. viii, 538 pp. ISBN: 3-7952-0613-8.

The author demonstrates that, even though it is entitled "Barcarola," the song sung by Dulcamara and Adina in *L'elisir d'amore* was actually based on Berta's aria "Il vecchietto cerca moglie" from *Il barbiere di Siviglia*. Petrobelli suggests that Donizetti was influenced by Rossini's setting because of its similar dramatic purpose.

Giuliani, Marco

405. Castelvecchi, Stefano. "Le *Rossiniane* di Mauro Giuliani." *Bollettino del Centro Rossiniano di Studi* [no. 1–3] (1986): 33–72.

The author examines the composition and publication history of guitar virtuoso Mauro Giuliani's *Rossiniane* (1822–1828). With score excerpts, Castelvecchi demonstrates the techniques used in transforming the original opera selections into these instrumental versions, citing Giuliani's talent at imitating contemporary vocal techniques and recreating orchestral elements, such as the famed crescendo. Identifies the theme of a Giuliano transcription formerly identified as one from Pietro Generali's *I Baccanali di Roma* as identical to one from *Armida*. The article also suggests the import of such transcriptions in contemporary musical life. Concludes with a thematic catalogue of the *Rossiniane* with incipits of both the transcriptions and the originals, a list of editions, and a discography.

Liszt, Franz

406. Reich, Nancy. "Liszt's Variations on the March from Rossini's *Siège de Corinthe*." *Fontes artis musicae* 23 [no. 3] (July-September 1976): 102–106.

Reich notes the discovery of a manuscript of the "Introduction des variations sur une marche du 'Siège de Corinthe' " signed by Franz Liszt, in the Manhattanville College Library (Purchase, N.Y.). She recounts the history of the piece and notes how the manuscript, which Liszt had dedicated to Alois Fuchs, most likely came into the latter's possession in 1851. Includes a facsimile illustration. See also items 79 and 407.

407. Saffle, Michael. "Little-known Liszt 'Sheet Music' Letters." *The Journal of the American Liszt Society* 28 (July-December 1990): 69–72.

One of the letters described by the author deals with Liszt's piano transcription of Rossini's *Soirées musicales*. Written to Andreas Schott of music publisher B. Schotts Söhne in Mainz, the letter discusses Liszt's transcription, which was "written as it were under the eyes of the Master." The letter proves curious in Liszt scholarship because it would seem that the composer had had prior dealings with this publisher. For another letter on Liszt transcriptions of Rossini, see Müller, item 79.

Meyerbeer, Giacomo

408. Huebner, Steven. "Italianate Duets in Meyerbeer's Grand Operas." *Journal of Musicological Research* 8 [no. 3–4] (March 1989): 203–58.

The author suggests that Meyerbeer's opera experiences in Italy influenced his composition of grand opera. Huebner points out that the composer's instructions to librettist Eugène Scribe on writing verse reflects Meyerbeer's own sense for setting Italian verse. Huebner also looks at prototypical Italian operatic structures such as four-part duets and how these relate to Meyerbeer's French works. As examples, Huebner uses *Semiramide*, *Ricciardo e Zoraide*, and *Elisabetta, regina d'Inghilterra*. He concludes that forms shared by Rossini and Meyerbeer then influenced later French composers, suggesting that consideration of this "coupe italienne" will help clarify studies of nineteenth-century French stage music.

Pacini, Giovanni

409. Carli Ballola, Giovanni. "I pianeti e l' 'Astro maggiore': due fasi del rossinismo di Pacini." *Nuova rivista musicale italiana* 30, [no. 3–4] (July-December 1996): 323–31.

In his memoirs (see item 129), Giovanni Pacini admitted that, in order to be popular, he and other composers adopted the techniques of Rossini. Carli Ballola looks at how Rossini affected Pacini's career in the 1820s and in the 1840s, after the latter's brief retirement from the theatrical arena. He concludes that Pacini and others retreated into the safety of Rossinian forms while Verdi was developing in new directions. See also item 411.

410. Gallo, Denise. "Giovanni Pacini's *Giuditta*: The Dramatic Possibilities of the Oratorio." Ph.D. dissertation, The Catholic University of America, Washington, D.C., 1997. 560 pp.

In addition to demonstrating how Pacini was perceived as a lesser figure in the orbit of Rossini, this edition of the oratorio *Giuditta* demonstrates Pacini's reliance on so-called Rossinian operatic forms and structures.

411. Lippmann, Friedrich. "Giovanni Pacini: Bemerkungen zum Stil seiner Opern. *Chigiana*: *rassegna annuale di musicologici* 24 [no. 4] (1967): 111–24.

In his autobiography (see item 129), Giovanni Pacini wrote that any composer who wanted to make a living learned to imitate Rossini, the "Astro maggiore." Lippmann offers examples of Pacini's compositions, demonstrating his close reliance on Rossini as a model. See also item 409.

Schubert, Franz

412. Bisogni, Fabio. "Rossini e Schubert." *Nuova rivista musicale italiana*. 2 [no. 5] (September-October 1968): 920–35.

After summarizing Schubert scholarship, the author criticizes those who denigrate Rossini's influence or dismiss it as merely a faddish phase in Schubert's career. Bisogni attributes such ideas to scholars' association of Rossini with opera buffa; he maintains that Schubert knew Rossini rather as composer of *seria* works. After demonstrating that Schubert was influenced by the Italian style from his teacher, Antonio Salieri, the author mentions similarities in Schubert's and Rossini's education and compositional interests. He concludes by listing works, other than the two Italian overtures, in which Schubert was inspired by the music of Rossini. With musical examples.

413. Dahlhaus, Carl. "Franz Schubert und das 'Zeitalter Beethovens und Rossinis.' " In *Franz Schubert: Jahre der Krise, 1818–1822: Bericht über das Symposium Kassel 30 September bis 1 Oktober 1982. Arnold Feil zum 60. Geburtstag am 2 Oktober 1985*, 22–28. Edited by Aderhold Werner, Walther Dürr, und Walburga Litschauer. Kassel: Bärenreiter, 1985. 144 pp. ISBN: 3-7618-0758-9 ML410S3 F83 1985.

Dahlhaus demonstrates that, in addition to Beethoven's influence, Schubert worked under that of Rossini in his symphonies as well as his operas.

414. Denny, Thomas A. "Archaic and Contemporary Aspects of Schubert's *Alfonso und Estrella*: Issues of Influence, Originality, and Maturation." In *Eighteenth-Century Music in Theory and Practice: Essays in Honor of Alfred Mann*, edited by Mary Ann Parker, 241–61. Festschrift Series No. 13. Stuyvesant, N.Y.: Pendragon Press, 1994. ISBN: 0-945193-11-4 ML55.M25 1994.

Denny discusses the possible influences of Rossini's music on Schubert's decision to set *Alfonso und Estrella* without spoken dialogue. He examines the three large ensembles in Schubert's opera and points to features shared with Rossini: tonal closure, dramatic coherence, multisectional form in several tempi, and general formal pattern. He suggests, though, that the opera moved beyond the Rossinian model into a realm of Schubert's own making. See also 412, 415, and 416.

415. Jahrmarker, Manuela. "Schuberts Beziehungen zur italienischen Oper: Form-Modelle in *Des Teufels Lustschloss und Alfonso und Estrella*. In *Bericht von der Tagung Schubert-Aspekte*, edited by Klaus Gotthard Fischer and Christiane Schumann, 95–109. Kassel: Bärenreiter, 1996. 152 pp. ISBN: 3-7618-1295-7.

Not examined. See also 412, 414, and 416.

416. McKay, Elizabeth Norman. "Rossinis Einfluss auf Schubert." Trans. Rudolf Klein. *Österreichische Musikzeitschrift* 18 [no. 1] (1963): 17–22.

The author first considers Schubert and Rossini as contemporaries and then traces Schubert's introduction to Rossini's operas in Vienna. With the aid of musical examples, McKay demonstrates how Schubert's own operas, such as *Alfonso und Estrella*, were influenced by Rossini's melodies, rhythms, and structures, as in his finales. McKay concludes that despite this influence, Schubert's own strengths with vocal music would have made him a great opera composer in his own right. See also 412, 414, and 415.

Spohr, Louis
417. Tosti-Croce, Mauro. "Rossini nelle *Lebenserinnerungen* di Spohr." *Bollettino del Centro Rossiniano di Studi* 38 (1998): 57–96.

Tosti-Croce capsulizes Louis Spohr's place in music history. Then, citing passages from the composer's *Lebenserinnerungen*, he demonstrates that although Spohr was a vocal part of the German anti-Rossini camp, he freely programmed Rossini's works and admitted that his own opera, *Zemire und Azor*, was influenced by Rossini's style. Includes two selections (with musical examples) from Spohr's memoirs, as edited by Folker Göthel, along with a parallel Italian translation. Illustrated with Spohr's self-portrait.

Sullivan, Sir Arthur
418. Nelson, John Christopher. "Tonal and Structural Design in the Finales of the Savoy Operas, With Some Suggestions as to Derivation." *Indiana Theory Review* 13 [no. 2] (Fall 1992): 1–22.

[Not examined.]

419. Saremba, Meinhard. *Arthur Sullivan: Ein Komponistenleben im viktorianischen England.* Wilhelmshaven: Nötzel, 1993. xviii, 437 pp. ISBN: 3-7959-0640-7.

[Not examined.]

Verdi, Giuseppe
420. Balthazar, Scott L. "Analytic contexts and mediated influences: The Rossinian *convenienze* and Verdi's middle and late duets." *Journal of Musicological Research* 10 [no. 1–2] (October 1990): 19–46.

Balthazar, whose work has examined alternate methods of tracing the development of operatic forms in the *primo Ottocento* (see, for example, items

541 and 542), suggests that rather than interpreting the duets in works of Verdi's middle and late periods as extensions of Rossinian convention, analysis demonstrates the younger composer's more innovative approaches to dramatic structure, vocal settings, and musical form. With musical examples.

421. Girardi, Michele, and Pierluigi Petrobelli. *Messa per Rossini: la storia, il testo, la musica*. Parma: Istituto di studi verdiani and Ricordi, 1988. 166 pp. ISBN 88-85065-08-2 ML410.V4 A8 Vol. 5. Published in German as *Messa per Rossini: Geschichte, Quellen, Musik*. Ed. Ulrich Prinz. Vol. 1 in the series *Schriftenreihe der Internationalen Bachakademie Stuttgart*. Kassel: Bärenreiter, 1988. 189 pp.

A collection of eight essays dealing with the compositional history and music of the Requiem for Rossini, conceived by Giuseppe Verdi as a joint effort by various Italian composers. The completed work, planned for the first anniversary of Rossini's death, was not performed, however. Compiled as a contribution to Verdi scholarship, of significance to Rossini studies is Philip Gossett's piece (see item 422). The volume features illustrations and score examples.

422. Gossett, Philip. "Omaggio a (liberazione da) Rossini." In *Messa per Rossini*, 7–10. See item 421.

The Requiem Mass for Rossini was composed by Giuseppe Verdi and a group of others to honor their deceased colleague. Gossett proposes that the work was also a liberation for composers who no longer felt the need, as had Giovanni Pacini, to imitate Rossini in order to succeed (see item 129). In addition, the author demonstrates that even though Verdi may have respected the memory of his older colleague, he did not always espouse his artistic philosophy.

423. Petrobelli, Pierluigi. "Rossini nell'opera e nella vita di Verdi." *La recezione di Rossini ieri e oggi* (item 288), 15–25.

Petrobelli traces the Italian artistic heritage as passed from Rossini to Verdi. The author claims that the younger composer learned Rossini's works from productions of French versions of his operas performed in Milan; he cites *Un giorno di regno* and *Nabucco* as Verdi works influenced by Rossinian designs. Petrobelli notes that Verdi soon went beyond Rossini's musical moments, conceiving an opera as an organic whole in which the voice is subservient to drama. Aware of this, Rossini carefully framed his requests on behalf of tenor Nicola Ivanoff, who had asked for the composer's intercession in obtaining substitute arias from Verdi.

Respecting Rossini as a symbol of Italian musical tradition, however, Verdi proposed a "utopian" project upon the death of his older colleague—a multi-authored requiem. Rejection of the Rossinian tradition, however, killed Verdi's plan, which finally found voice in the Manzoni requiem. Quotes Rossini's correspondence to Verdi on Ivanoff's behalf (item 276). See item 422, for more on Rossini's influence on Verdi.

424. Pirrotta, Nino. "Semiramis e Amneris, un anagramma o quasi." In *Il melo-dramma italiano dell'Ottocento: Studi e ricerche per Massimo Mila*, 5–12. No. 575 in the series *Saggi*, edited by Giorgio Pestelli. Turin: Einaudi, 1977. xv, 653 pp. ML 1733.4.M5.

Beginning by pointing out the anagrammic possibility between the names "Semiramis" and "Amneris," Pirrotta then examines the musical antecedents of *Aida* in Rossini's *Semiramide*. Demonstrating that these women are alike in that they are the most vigorously portrayed characters in both scores, Pirrotta also indicates plot, conflict, and scene parallels. Includes musical examples from both operas.

425. Powers, Harold S. " 'La solita forma' and 'The Uses of Convention.' " *Acta musicologica* 59 [no. 1] (Jan.-Apr.1987): 65–90; also in *Nuove prospettive nella ricerca verdiana: Atti del Convegno Internazionale in Occasione della Prima del "Rigoletto"* in *Edizione Critica*, Vienna, 12–13 marzo, 1983, 74–105. Eds. Marisa Di Gregorio Casati and Marcello Pavarani. Parma: Istituto di Studi Verdiani and Milan: Ricordi, 1987. xii, 137 pp. ISBN 88-85065-03-1. ML410.V4 C68 1983.

Although this article is primarily Powers's response to analyses of the works of Verdi, particularly by Julian Budden, the author also looks at possible developments from the Rossinian models for the duet and finale described by Philip Gossett in "Verdi, Ghislanzoni, and *Aida*: The Uses of Convention" [*Critical Inquiry* I (1974): 291–334] (not cited) and "The 'candeur virginale' of *Tancredi*" (see item 631).

Wagner, Richard

426. Bonaccorsi, Alfredo. "Paragone per una marcia funebre (fra Rossini e Wagner). *Bollettino del Centro Rossiniano di Studi* 1 [no. 2] (1955): 21–23; also in the *Bollettino* 8 [no. 4–6] (1968): 70–72.

The author suggests a similarity between the "motto-theme" in Rossini's *Marche et Réminiscences pour mon dernier voyage* (No. 7 in Vol. 9 of the *Péchés de vieillesse*) and the Funeral March for Siegfried in Wagner's *Götterdämmerung*, begun by Wagner in 1869, one year after Rossini's death.

Bonaccorsi notes that, while Rossini's use of the material remains constant, Wagner's undergoes rhythmic change. With musical examples.

427. Lippmann, Friedrich. *"Die Feen* und *Das Liebesverbot,* oder Die Wagner-isierung diverser Vorbilder."* In *Wagnerliteratur, Wagnerforschung: Bericht über das Wagner-Symposium, München 1983,* edited by Carl Dahlhaus and Egon Voss, 14–46. Mainz and New York: Schott, 1985. 239 pp. ML410.W131 W22 1983.

With musical examples, Lippmann demonstrates the influence Italian com-posers such as Rossini had on Wagner's early operas. The author suggests that works such as *Semiramide, Mosè* and later *Tell* inspired Wagner to bor-row aria forms such as the cantabile and cabaletta. Lippmann also notes that although Wagner attempted to hide this influence by utilizing more complex harmonies, his melodic lines are similar to Rossini's in their chromaticism.

Other Composers' Arrangements or Quotations of Rossini's Music

428. Melica, Ada. "Rossini nella musica degli altri." *Bollettino del Centro Rossiniano di Studi* [no. 1] (1955): 16; [no. 2] (1955): 36–37; [no. 3] (1956): 56–57; [no. 4] (1956): 76–78; [no. 5] (1956): 98–99; [no. 6] (1956): 118; [no. 1] (1956): 17–19; [no. 2] (1956): 37–39; [no. 3] (1957): 57–58; [no. 4] (1957): 77–78; [no. 5] (1957): 96–97; [no. 6] (1957): 117–119; [no. 1] (1957): 15–17; [no. 2] (1957): 38–39; [no. 3] (1958): 58; [no. 4] (1958): 77–78; [no. 5] (1958): 97–98; [no. 6] (1958); 119; [no. 1] (1958): 17.

Melica, one of the founding contributors to the *Bollettino,* wrote this early series to cite quotations of Rossini's music as well as arrangements and transcriptions of his compositions. Includes brief commentaries on the pieces, their composers, and publication information.

429. Murphy, Edward. "A programme for the first movement of Shostakovich's fifteenth symphony: 'A debate about four musical styles.' " *Music Review* 53 [no. 1] (February 1992): 47–62.

Murphy suggest that the five Rossini quotations, placed symmetrically in the first movement, represent simple, tonal music in contrast to the other three styles: Shostakovich's own tonal system, twelve-tone music, and what the author terms "a contrived, artificial style." The Rossini quotations pro-voke different reactions, ranging from humorous to ironic. Murphy provides a formal chart of the movement and illustrates his points with musical examples.

430. Pritsch, Norbert. "Die musikalischen Quellen des Balletts 'La boutique fan-tasque'—ein Beitrag zur Rossini-Rezeption durch Ottorino Respighi." *La Gazzetta* 8 (1998): 9–15.

Often, the works of a composer become better known through arrangements than from the original works. Pritsch addresses several popular transcriptions of Rossini's music, focusing on Respighi's use of music from the *Péchés de vieillesse* and the *Soirées musicales* in *La boutique fantasque* and the orchestral suite *Rossiniana*. Pritsch demonstrates how, in these works, Respighi either remained true to the model or chose different keys, dynamics, or tempi. Includes a breakdown of the Respighi work and lists of the Rossini works cited and how they appear in the fourteen movements.

431. Schröther, Franz. "Rossini und die deutsche Militärmusik." *La Gazzetta* 7 (1997): 12–15.

The author discusses the adaptation of themes from Rossini's operas that were transcribed for use by German military bands, noting that these marches were among the repertoire played during the First and Second World Wars. In addition to works of other composers whose music was similarly transcribed, Schröther lists Rossini's own military marches. Includes a discography.

Rossini's Influence on Twentieth-Century Composers

432. Guarnieri Corazzol, Adriana. "La recezione dell'ultimo Rossini e le avanguardie novecentesche." In *La recezione di Rossini ieri e oggi* (item 288), 195–214.

The author indicates that Rossini's later works demonstrate a change in compositional style from public works to private chamber pieces. After demonstrating a closer consideration of text in his compositions, even down to the irony and satire of the titles given to *Les Péchés de vieillesse*, she notes that these works obviously were meant for a reader as well as a listener. She links this music, created for an elite audiences, to that of Erik Satie and to the artistic philosophies of avant-garde poets and the members of the "scapigliati," such as Arrigo Boito. She concludes that Rossini's later works depict an artist who has been resurrected after years of silence and one who exists in a state of creative happiness. See also item 433.

433. Sala, Emilio. "Di alcune 'rossiniane' novecentesche." In *La recezione di Rossini ieri e oggi* (item 288), 81–99.

The author cites twentieth-century comments about Rossini and the "youth" and freshness in his music. Calling the composer the first Neoclassicist, the author indicates Rossini's influence on Erik Satie, François Poulenc, Darius Milhaud, Igor Stravinsky, and Camille Saint-Saëns. Sala also discusses specific works inspired by Rossini such as Respighi's *La boutique fantastique*, Zanelli's orchestral arrangements of Rossini's music, and Britten's *Soirées* and *Matinées musicales*; also mentioned are dance and ballet compositions based on Rossini and his music. A table demonstrates the connection between of *La boutique* to the original pieces in *Les péchés de vieillesse* and the Rossinian Suite to *Les Riens*. See also item 432.

ROSSINI AND LITERATURE

General Studies

434. Lindenberger, Herbert S. "Rossini, Shelley, and Italy in 1819." In *Opera in History From Monteverdi to Cage*, 81–106. Stanford, Calif.: Stanford University Press, 1998. x, 364 pp. ISBN 0-8047-3104-7 ML1700.L54 1998.

Rossini met the poet Shelley in 1819. Lindenberger demonstrates the various comparisons between the two artists. Although both achieved fame in the first half of the century, both later suffered the neglect of audiences and critics alike. In the twentieth century, though, their works challenged critical principles, and both have achieved myth status. Lindenberger considers the "performability" of Rossini's music and Shelley's poetry. He concludes by suggesting that they can be seen as models for the fin-de-siècle postmodernism. See also items 432 and 433.

Consideration of Rossini's Music in Literature

435. Bailbè, Joseph-Marc. "Rossini et la sensibilité française." In *La recezione di Rossini ieri e oggi* (item 288), 27–36.

Considers Rossini's effect on the French from the early years in Paris when he was perceived merely as a representative of Italian music to his later years as a cultural icon. Cites passages from contemporary literature, journalism, and culture criticism in which the composer and his music were represented.

436. Fabbri, Paolo. "Un compositore in cerca d'autore: Rossini come personaggio letterario nell'Ottocento." In *La recezione di Rossini ieri e oggi* (item 288), 149–63.

Because of the popularity of Rossini's operas, it was common for novelists and playwrights to employ them as allusions or when creating settings of the contemporary cultural milieu. Fabbri considers writers' uses of Rossini himself as a literary character. Includes excerpts from several of these works.

437. Joerg, Guido Johannes. "Conte Fosco alias Gioacchino Rossini?—Eine Skizze." *La Gazzetta* [no. 1–2] (1991): 3–5.

The author notes similarities between Rossini and the character of Count Fosco in Wilkie Collins's novel *The Woman in White*. After drawing parallels, though, Joerg suggests that Fosco was rather representative of personalities associated with mid-nineteenth century music culture and would have been recognized immediately by readers as such. Nonetheless, the references to Rossini's music again demonstrate his widespread popularity.

438. Ley, Klaus. *Die Oper im Roman: Erzählkunst und Musik bei Stendhal, Balzac und Flaubert.* Vol. 83 in the series *Studia romantica.* Heidelberg: Winter, 1995. 445 pp. ISBN: 3-8253-0283-0 PQ653.L49 1995.

Ley suggests a link between the development of the novel and of opera in the nineteenth century, especially in the relationships between literary narrative and melody, and prose description and harmony. After considering Stendhal's *Vie de Rossini* (item 135), Ley proposes Balzac's *Massimilla Doni* and its inclusion of Rossini's *Mosè* as an example of this literary-musical connection. Also mentions works by Walter Scott and Gustave Flaubert as well as the contemporary debate over Italian and German music.

* Reichel, Edward. "Die Rossinirezeption in der französischen Literatur." In *Rossini in Paris: Eine Veranstaltung des Frankreichzentrums der Universität Leipzig, in Zusammenarbeit mit der Deutschen Rossini Gesellschaft e.V.* See item 290.

Heine on Rossini

439. Sharp, Elizabeth, trans. *Heine in Art and Letters.* London: Walter Scott, Ltd., 1895 xv, 250 pp. PT2316.A5 S4.

Sharp explains in her preface that, in his criticism of art and music, Heine wrote from a literary perspective. Among the essays included in her translations is Heine's commentary on Rossini and Meyerbeer (1837), in which the author addresses the futility of defining or analysing music. He then gives reasons why he inclines more toward Rossini's music and character. Rich in melody, he writes, Rossini is a composer of the Restoration; Meyerbeer, a master of harmony, is one of Revolution. He discusses the German in Rossini and the Italian in Meyerbeer. Of operas, Heine briefly mentions *Il barbiere*, concentrating more on *Robert le diable* and *Les Huguenots*. See also item 440.

440. Wehrmann, Harald. "Heines Musikanschauung." *Acta Musicologica* 70 [no. 1] (January-June 1998): 79–107.

The author compiles observations on music from Heine's correspondence and writings. Of the poet's discussions of Rossini, Wehrmann cites Heine's contrasting the Italian melodic nature of Rossini's operas with the German harmonies of Meyerbeer's. Heine felt that Rossini's orchestration was full of colors, describing his "signature" sound as "Italian sunshine and the scent of oranges." Also includes comments on the Stabat mater, which Heine felt was a true representation of Christian music. See also item 439.

Balzac and Rossini—Mosè in Egitto *in* Massimilla Doni

441. Brunel, Pierre. *"Mosè* dans *Massimilla Doni." L'année balzacienne* 15 (1994): 39–54.

Brunel suggests that Rossini's portrayal of drama in music (specifically in *Mosè*) inspired Balzac's style as a literary realist. Considers the character depiction of Massimilla. See also items 438, 713, and 715.

* Brzoska, Matthias. "Mosè und Massimilla: Rossinis *Mosè in Egitto* und Balzacs politische Deutung." See item 713. See also 438 and 715.

* Glascow, E. Thomas. "Rossini's *Mosè* According to Balzac: Excerpts from *Massimilla Doni.*" See item 715. See also 438 and 713.

* Ley, Klaus. *Die Oper im Roman: Erzahlkunst und Musik bei Stendhal, Balzac und Flaubert.* See item 438.

Gautier and Rossini

442. Corapi, Giorgio. "Théophile Gautier e il marmo rossiniano." *Bollettino del Centro Rossiniano di Studi* [no. 1–3] (1984): 21–41.

Poet, novelist, journalist, critic, and creator of the libretto for the ballet *Giselle*, Gautier idolized Rossini, notes Corapi. He maintains that, aside from the obvious respect for Rossini's music, Gautier saw in the composer a kindred artistic spirit in such things as his use of the contralto voice and *travestimento* roles, which Corapi links to Gautier's 1835 novel, *Mademoiselle de Maupin*. Corapi also suggests that the writer's references to marble as a poetic image can be equally connected to his view of the immortality and permanence of Rossini's genius. Appendices, in the original French, include Gautier's articles on the Parisian premiere of the Stabat Mater (see Adam, 803, for comments on another performance), on the performance of three choruses for female voices, and a copy of Gautier's poem "Contralto" (inspired by his love for the singer Ernesta Grisi). See also Gautier, item 759.

* ———. *La Musique.* See item 759. See also item 442.

* Monti, Raffaele. "Appunti su Gautier critico rossiniano." In *Atti del convegno di studi: Rossini, edizioni critiche e prassi esecutiva*, 31–40. See item 282.

Fictional Works Featuring Rossini

The following items treat a sampling of works in which Rossini appears as a character.

* Bailbè, Joseph-Marc. "Rossini et la sensibilité française." See item 435.

443. Fauchois, René. *Rossini, Comédie en Trois Actes*. Lyon: Gellerat, 1922. 252 pp. PQ2611.A8 R6 1922; 2nd ed., Paris: Berger-Levrault, 1950. 206 pp. 4PQ Fr 1480.

René Fauchois, who penned, among other works, the libretto for Gabriel Fauré's lyric drama *Pénélope*, took the role of Rossini when this comic script premiered on 27 January 1920 at the Théâtre des Célestin. Sarah Bernhardt played Anna Rossini. These fictional scenes from the composer's life are constructed into three acts, with the first set at a hotel on Lake Como. Act 2 takes place in Rome on 27 December 1816, the day after the debut of *Il barbiere* (the actual premiere was on 20 February of that year), and Act 3 depicts a visit from the composer to his ailing mother in Bologna in 1816.

444. Ghislanzoni, Antonio. *Gli artisti da teatro*. Milan: Editore Daelli, 1865; new edition edited by Ernesto Scialpi. Volume 9 in the series *Ghirlanda Romantica Rara Universale*. Milan: Ultra, 1944. 508 pp. PQ4692.G46 A8 1944.

Ghislanzoni's readable novel tells the tale of Emilia Redenti, a young singer whose parents are bent on her theatrical success although she is tempted to abandon her career for true love. Ghislanzoni paints a true picture of the theatrical milieu in which his characters function, using real personalities as minor characters; among these is Rossini, who is depicted as he was after his return to Paris in 1865. Typically, Ghislanzoni calls Rossini the "Napoleon of music" and portrays him as a *maestro* whose favor [or disfavor] determined public opinion.

445. Moscato, Italo. *Rossiniana: Nove specchi per Gioacchino/ L'aria del sorbetto*. No. 388 in the series *Biblioteca di Cultura*. Rome: Bulzoni, 1989. 103 pp. ISBN 88-7119-058-0 MLCS 90/03718.

Moscato's *Nove specchi*, broadcast on Italian radio (Raiuno) in 1979, is a script of nine scenes depicting Rossini's life, career, and public and private persona. *L'aria del sorbetto* is a comedy first presented in 1986 at the Festival di Benevento. According to Moscato's introduction, the play, while never naming Rossini, describes his trials during the production of *Otello* in Naples. The author notes that his impressions of Rossini were developed by reading the work of Riccardo Bacchelli (item 149) and Paolo Isotta (for example, item 586).

COMMEMORATIVE PUBLICATIONS AND STUDIES

* Beulé, Charles Ernest. *Éloge de Rossini*. See item 394.

446. *Bollettino del primo centenario rossiniano pubblicato dal comitato ordinatore*. Pesaro: Feb. 29 to Sept. 15, 1892. (Library of Congress editions are bound together in a single volume, 144 pp., continuous pagination. ML410.R8 B57).

The eighteen issues of this newsletter feature articles about Rossini's life and career and notices of activities and festivals held in celebration of the 100th anniversary of his birth. Items of historical interest include the text of Giuseppe Rossini's appointment as town trumpeter in Pesaro (p. 117) and the transcript of his interrogation during the so-called political Processo Vivazza (pp. 130–33). Also published are several of Rossini's letters, including correspondence to Luigi Cristostomo Ferrucci about Rossini's request to Pius IX to allow female voices in ecclesiastical choirs (see also item 41).

* Bonafé, Félix. *Rossini et son oeuvre*. See item 466.

447. Cagli, Bruno. "Un nostro contemporaneo suo malgrado." *Bollettino del Centro Rossiniano di Studi* 32 (1992): 9–15.

Cagli delivered this address in Pesaro at the commemoration of the centenary of the composer's birth. In briefly summing up Rossini's life and fortunes as a composer, Cagli notes that, thanks to renewed interest in the composer's works, Rossini can be called our contemporary.

448. *Celebrazioni rossiniane*. Pesaro: Tipo Nobili, ?1963. [50 pp.]. ML410.R8 F56.

A commemorative volume of a performance of *Il barbiere di Siviglia* for the 171st anniversary of Rossini's birth, held in August 1963 in Pesaro. Includes a plot summary in Italian, French, English, and German, as well as a facsimile from the original libretto, a section of photographs of important Rossini locales in Pesaro, and a list of Rossini's works.

449. *Celebrazioni rossiniane*. Pesaro: Tipo Nobili, ?1964. [28 pp.]. ML410.R8 F6.

A book commemorating the 172th anniversary of Rossini's birth, held from 23–25 August 1964, in Pesaro. The program included a performance of *Guglielmo Tell*. The booklet features a plot summary in Italian, French, English, and German as well as a brief commentary by Giuseppe Pugliese.

* *Convegno di studi su Rossini per il Centenario della morte di Gioacchino Rossini, Pesaro, 13–16 June 1968*. See item 283.

450. D'Amico, Fedele. "Questo compleanno." *Bollettino del Centro Rossiniano di Studi* 31 (1991): 9–19.

In preparation for the centenary of Rossini's birth, the author summarizes the state of affairs in Rossini scholarship. Not only has Rossini's music returned to the stage but activity in the scholarly camp portends well for Rossini's second century.

451. Graves, Perceval. "Homage to Rossini." *Opera* 19 (1968): 858–64.

The author describes not only his visit to Pesaro for the centenary commemorations of Rossini's death, but also the contents of the exhibitions held at the ducal palace and the Casa Rossini. Illustrated with portraits of Rossini's parents (including one of his mother, Anna Guidarini, as a young girl), Maria Malibran, and Britain's George IV, who sang duets with Rossini at the Royal Pavilion in Brighton during the composer's visit in 1823. Also illustrated with a photograph of the Casa Rossini and of the festival's production of *Mosè*.

* Kohut, Adolph. *Rossini*. See item 121.

452. Mazzi, Maria Chiara. "Il primo centenario della nascita di Gioacchino Rossini." *Annuario del Conservatorio Statale di Musica Gioacchino Rossini* 1990–1991.

[Not examined.]

453. Ronga, Luigi. *Gioacchino Rossini nel I centenario della morte: Celebrazione indetta d'intesa con l'Accademia di S. Cecilia*. Rome: Accademia Nazionale dei Lincei, 1969. 17 pp. ML410.R8 R76.

A transcription of an address given by Ronga on 19 November 1968 for the beginning of the academic year 1968–1969, attended by guests including the president of the Republic of Italy. The speech traces Rossini's career, extolling him as a composer as well as an important figure in Italian music history.

454. Vanzolini, Giuliano. *Relazione delle pompe funebri fatte in Pesaro in onore di Gioacchino Rossini nel suo giorno onomastico 21 di agosto 1869 e de' trattenimenti musicali che le seguirono*. Pesaro: A. Nobili, 1869. 65 pp. ML410.R8 V3.

This volume documents the program held in Pesaro on Rossini's name day in the year following his death. Transcribes not only the events and speeches of these ceremonies but also recounts the activities of the delegation from Pesaro that attended Rossini's funeral in Paris nine months earlier.

9

Studies of Rossini's Music

GENERAL STUDIES

455. Dean, Winton. "Rossini." In "Italian Opera" in *The Age of Beethoven (1790–1830)*, pp. 403–26. Vol. 8 of the *New Oxford History of Music*, ed. Gerald Abraham. London and New York: Oxford University Press, 1994. ML160.N44 1994 Vol. 8.

Dean's comments on Rossini's role in Italian opera history are primarily a summary of the composer's theatrical career with specific commentary on *La gazza ladra*. Dean considers the early *buffa* works and the *seria* operas, Rossini's Neapolitan productions, and the composer's method of structuring his scores. In his chapter on French opera, Dean also briefly mentions *Guillaume Tell* and *Le comte Ory*, noting Rossini's influence of the French musical stage (pp. 104–12). With score examples.

456. Della Corte, Andrea. *Disegno storico dell'arte musicale*. 5th ed. revised. Turin: G.B. Paravia, 1944. 233 pp. ML160.C79 1944.

In a brief section on Rossini (pp. 199–202), Della Corte echoes historians like Massimo Mila (see item 540) who envisioned the composer as a classicist. In fact, claims Della Corte, Rossini is not anti-Romantic, but "a-Romantic," incapable of the passion with which Bellini would write. He lauds Rossini's creative imagination, however, citing several of his operas. He calls *Guillaume Tell* an expression of humanity, which parallels the similar expression Rossini made in the field of comedy. Its hero is to tragedy what Figaro is to comedy. Such studies demonstrate contemporary views on

Rossini prior to the "Rossini Renaissance" of the 1950s. (On the "Rossini Renaissance," see items 608, 609, and 610).

457. Della Seta, Fabrizio. *Italia e Francia nell'Ottocento*. Vol. 9 in the Società Italiana di Musicologia's series *Storia della musica*. Turin: E.D.T., 1993. xvii, 409 pp. ISBN 88-7063-113-3 ML196.D45 1993.

This music history contains sections on Rossini and the age in which he lived and composed. Discusses Rossini's codification of *primo Ottocento* musical structures. Places the composer culturally as well as historically and includes an explanation of the aesthetic principles that governed much early criticism and defense of his works. In the "Readings" section, the author provides one of the letters from Carpani's *Le Rossiniane* (see item 483).

458. Gossett, Philip. "Gioachino Rossini," in *The New Grove Masters of Italian Opera: Rossini, Donizetti, Bellini, Verdi, Puccini*, 1–90. In the Composer Biography Series. New York: W.W. Norton, 1983. ISBN 0-3930-1685-4. ML390.N466 1983.

Masters of Italian Opera: Rossini, Donizetti, Bellini, Verdi, Puccini, 1–90. In *The New Grove Composer Biography* series. London: Macmillan, 1983. 353 pp. ISBN 0-333-35823-6; translated in German by Annette Holoch and published as *Meister der italienischen Oper: Rossini, Donizetti, Bellini, Verdi, Puccini*. In the series *The New Grove: Die Grossen Komponisten*. Stuttgart: Metzler, 1993. 393 pp. ISBN: 3-476-00928-9. A slightly modified and updated version of the entry on Rossini in *New Grove Dictionary of Music and Musicians*, 16:226–251. Ed. Stanley Sadie. London: Macmillan, 1980 (see item 459 for the latest edition of *The New Grove*); translated by Lorenzo Bianconi and published in Italian in *Rossini, Donizetti, Bellini*. In the series *Guida alla musica*. Florence: Ricordi, 1995. 220 pp. ISBN: 88-7592-454-6. [Not examined.]

Beginning with the caveat that much work yet remains to be done on the composer's biography, Gossett provides a solid introduction to Rossini studies. A discussion of Rossini's career is divided into the following sections: the early years, the first period (1810–1813), from *Tancredi* to *La gazza ladra*, Naples and the opera seria (1815–1823), Europe and Paris (1822–1829), retirement, and "A new life," or the composer's last years. Following is a complete works list (operas, sacred music, cantatas, incidental music, hymns and choruses; miscellaneous vocal; and instrumental works); the final section enumerates the contents of the composer's *Péchés de vieillesse* (*Sins of Old Age*—1857–1868). The works list includes information on, among other things, manuscript locations, publishing data, and performing forces. Includes illustrations, score excerpts, and a bibliography.

459. ———. "Rossini, Gioachino (Antonio)." In *The New Grove Dictionary of Music and Musicians*, 2nd ed., edited by Stanley Sadie, 21:734–68. London: Macmillan, 2001. ISBN: 1-56159-239-0 ML100.N48 2000.

(Available online to subscribers at http://www.grovemusic.com)

An updated version of item 458.

* Osborne, Richard. *Rossini*. See item 181.

NINETEENTH-CENTURY COMMENTARIES

460. Ambros, August Wilhelm. "Rossini und das Prinzip des sinnlichen Genusses in der Musik." In *Culturhistorische Bilder aus dem Musikleben der Gegenwart*, 33–41. Leipzig: Heinrich Matthes (E.D. Schurmann), 1860; 2nd ed. 1865. 260 pp. ML60.A52.

As his title suggests, composer/critic Ambros describes Rossini's music as gratifying the senses. Citing his uncle, the musicologist Kiesewetter, he suggests that the period of 1800 through 1832 can be called the epoch of Beethoven and Rossini (see Dahlhaus, item 526, for a similar statement). Yet the two composers were exact opposites, he notes, with Beethoven's music coming from the spirit and Rossini's from the senses. Although he seems at times to speak in favor of Rossini, his discourse repeats typical cliches applied to Rossini's music: that it is like champagne from a bottle or the scent of Italian oranges. In his musical discourse, moreover, he notes that Rossini's music is monotonous, following unchanging forms. Yet there is no outright condemnation. He praises *Tell*, for example, and notes that, had Beethoven lived to hear that work, he might have been pleased to meet Rossini a second time.

461. Asioli, Bonifazio. *Il maestro di composizione ossia séguito del Trattato di armonia*. Milan: Ricordi, 1836. xxxix, Book 1: 111 pp.; Book 2: 95 pp.; Book 3: 223 pp. MT50.A86 (bound together as one volume at the Library of Congress).

Book 1, the *Trattato di armonia* of 1813, is followed by a treatise on composition, which includes instruction in imitation, counterpoint, fugue, and canon. Score examples are from the music of Haydn, Handel, Marcello, Mattei (Rossini's teacher in Bologna), and Clementi, among others. Book 3 begins with lessons on instruments and their uses; on musical phrases and poetic metrics, with examples of how to correctly set Italian verse forms; on voicing various instruments against the voice, another solo instrument or various instrumental ensembles; and how to orchestrate. In this last section, Asioli reproduces the overture to Rossini's *La Cenerentola*; in an analysis of its musical form and harmonies, the author comments that this overture demonstrates that Rossini is both a great dramatic and instrumental composer. See also item 542 for an excerpt of this work.

462. Bettoni, Nicolò. *Rossini e la sua musica*. Milan: Felice Rusconi, 1824. 35 pp.

[Not examined.]

* Escudier, Leon. *Mes souvenirs*. See item 115.

* Hiller, Ferdinand. "Plaudereien mit Rossini." See item 119.

* Michotte, Edmond. *Souvenirs: Une Soirée chez Rossini à Beau-Sejours (Passy) 1858*. See item 123.

463. Paglia, Gioachino. *Sulla musica di Rossini: pensieri*. Bologna: Nicola Zanichelli, 1875. 61 pp. ML410.R8 P2.

Addressed to Antonio Zanolini, author of the Rossini biography that features "Una passeggiata in compagnia di Rossini," Paglia's volume is more a commentary on music in general (especially of the Italian school) than on the compositions of Rossini. Of interest is the author's appreciation for Rossini's *seria* operas, works usually ranked below his comic pieces. Paglia considers Rossini's sacred music as well as individual compositions from the *Péchés de vieillesse*. See item 138 for Zanolini's biography.

* Wagner, Richard. "Eine Erinnerung an Rossini." See item 136.

* Wendt, Amadeus. *Rossinis Leben und Treiben, vornehmlich nach den Nachrichten des hrn. v. Stendhal geschildert und mit Urtheilen der Zeitgenossen über seinen musikalischen Charakter begleitet*. See item 137.

* Zanolini, Antonio. *Biografia di Gioachino Rossini*. See item 138.

464. Zerbi, Rocco de. *Rossini e la musica nuova*. Florence: Galletti e Cocci, 1892. 39 pp.

[Not examined.]

TWENTIETH- AND TWENTY-FIRST-CENTURY COMMENTARIES

465. Bonaccorsi, Alfredo. *Gioacchino Rossini*. Vol. 24 in the series *Historiae musicae cultores*. Florence: Olschki, 1968. Ml410.R8 B575.

A book of essays, more commentary than scholarly studies, by recognized Rossini authors such as Massimo Mila, Andrea Della Corte, Ada Melica,

Roman Vlad, and Riccardo Bacchelli. Topics include Rossini the musician, musical form, Rossini and modern composers, and observations on operas such as *L'italiana in Algeri*, *Il barbiere*, and *Semiramide*. Also includes Rossini's genealogical tree, a works list, discography, and suggested readings.

466. Bonafé, Félix. *Rossini et son oeuvre*. Le Puy-en-Velay: Édition La Main de Bronze, 1955. 55 pp. ML410.R8 B577.

Based on an address given at a conference organized by the Fondation Rossini in Paris in 1955 in commemoration of the centenary of the composer's residence in the French capital, the author comments on the career and selected operas of Rossini. Dedicated to a relative of singer Rosa Bonheur and of Raymond Bonheur, a friend of the composer's, Bonafé's brief commentary on Rossini's relationship to members of this family appears in the *Bollettino del Centro Rossiniano di Studi* I [no. 2] (1955): 23–25.

467. Carpitella, Diego. "Rossini tra illuminismo e populismo." In *Convegno di studi su Rossini per il Centenario della morte di Gioacchino Rossini*, pp. 76–80. See item 283.

* Caussou, Jean-Louis. *Gioachino Rossini: L'homme et son oeuvre*. See item 151.

* Curzon, Henri de. *Rossini*. See item 153.

* Dauriac, Lionel. *Rossini*. See item 154.

468. Fabbri, Paolo. "Rossini the aesthetician." *Cambridge Opera Journal* 6 [no. 1] (March 1994): 19–29.

The author cites Rossini's comments on music to Antonio Zanolini (see item 138) and Ferdinand Hiller (see items 118 and 119) and then traces his ideas to contemporary discussions and treatises with which Rossini most likely was familiar. While much of these comments center on Rossini's ideas about music as imitation, Fabbri also demonstrates the importance the composer placed on melody, rhythm, and *cantilena*. The article briefly mentions the debate between Andrea Maier and Giuseppe Carpani explained in items 492 and 498.

469. Fink, Robert Wallace. " 'Arrows of Desire': Long-Range Linear Structure and the Transformation of Musical Energy." Ph.D. dissertation, University of California, Berkeley, 1994. 556 pp.

[Not examined.] The author's aim, according to his abstract, is to employ a new analytical method in the examination and definition of "musical energy" that links to the listeners' physical responses. Fink considers the Rossini crescendo, noting that its simple repetition and release of energy results in the powerful effects of the composer's *stretta* finales.

470. Fraga, Fernando. *Rossini. Obra completa comentada. Discografía recomendada.* Barcelona: Península, 1998. 215 pp. ISBN: 8-4830-7124-X.

[Not examined.]

* Grondona, Marco. "Rossini e Wagner negli scritti: Il problema dell'-opera." See item 491.

471. Johnstone, George Harcourt [Lord Derwent]. *Rossini and Some Forgotten Nightingales.* London: Duckworth, 1934. 336 pp. ML410.R8 D32.

In his foreword, the author confesses that his book was inspired by Stendhal (indeed the book is dedicated to Beyle), whose inaccuracies, Derwent claims, are "unimportant." Derwent begins the book by looking back at Cimarosa and Paisiello, Rossini's musical ancestors. He then places the composer among his contemporaries, about whom he has little good to say. Written with the flair of a fictional narrative, the book also includes an account of the performance of the Petit messe solennelle at the Pillet-Will mansion in Paris in 1864. Contains illustrations and an appendix of musical examples from piano-vocal scores. For Stendhal's work, see item 135.

472. Kantner, Leopold Maximilian. "Rossinis Beziehung zu historischen Stilen." *Bollettino del Centro Rossiniano di Studi* 12 [no. 3] (1972): 5–11; Italian translation, pp. 49–53.

Noting that although the young Rossini may have balked at learning the "stile antico" during his earliest musical training, Kantner demonstrates instances when the composer utilized its elements, such as plagal cadenzes, polyphony, and instrumentation in his operas. The author suggests that this demonstrates the composer's use of the supernatural symbolism associated with these Baroque strategies. Kantner also briefly addresses these techniques in Rossini's sacred music. See item 791 for another opinion of Rossini's ability with counterpoint.

473. Lippmann, Friedrich. "Rossinis Gedanken über die Musik." *Die Musikforschung* 22 [no. 3] (July-September 1969): 285–98.

By extracting Rossini's comments from published accounts of the composer's conversations with Antonio Zanolini (item 138), Edmond Michotte (see items 123 and 160) and Richard Wagner (items 136 and 160) as well as from correspondence, Lippmann compiles Rossini's thoughts on colleagues such as Bellini, Donizetti, Meyerbeer, and on the music and contemporary aesthetics. Lippmann demonstrates that, even though Rossini was enticed by modern music and its affective qualities, he realized that such artistic ideas were grounded in the past.

474. ———. "Sull' estetica di Rossini." Translated by Agostino Ziino. *Bollettino del Centro Rossiniano di Studi* 8 [no. 4–6] (1968): 62–69.

Lippmann notes that, despite the effervescent character of Rossini's music, one must not mistakenly think of him as a "Figaro." He lists Rossini's musical influences, the Italian and German masters whose works he studied, and his contemporaries, whose styles he followed. Lippmann maintains that only after 1830 did Rossini formulate a coherent aesthetic; he then lists and discusses the sources in which Rossini's comments can be found. Included are Zanolini (item 138), Michotte's account of Wagner's visit to the composer (160), and letters to Lauro Rossini and Filippo Filippi (item 62). He also notes the basic differences between Rossini's thoughts on music and those of Raimondo Boucheron and Eduard Hanslick. Lippmann concludes that one must not confuse Rossini the composer with Rossini the theorist.

475. Nicastro, Aldo. *Il melodramma e gli italiani*. In the series *Musica*. Milan: Rusconi, 1982. 317 pp. ML1733.N48 1982.

In a section on Rossini (pp. 19–73), the author considers the composer's works in light of the social, political, and aesthetic environment in which they were written. Among the topics addressed are the serious and comic operas. Nicastro also notes ways in which Rossini adapted himself to the French theatrical arena. Mentions the nonoperatic works of Rossini's later years as well.

476. Rognoni, Luigi. *Gioacchino Rossini*. Turin: ERI, 1968. 509 pp. ML410.R8 R7; rev. ed. Turin: Einaudi, 1977. 559 pp. ML410.R8 R7 1977.

Rognoni's research on Rossini, begun in 1947, resulted in this volume of analyses of the composer's works and musical language. Includes chapters on the *opere buffe* and *serie*, the overtures, Parisian theatrical works, the later compositions (from the period Rognoni calls "the great vacation"), and the religious music. Appendices include a selection of letters, a reprint of Geltrude Righetti-Giorgi's *Cenni di una Donna cantante* (item 131), "Una passeggiata in compagnia di Rossini," from Antonio Zanolino's *Biografia di Gioachino Rossini* (item 138); and Edmond Michotte's account of the visit between Wagner and Rossini (item 160). A brief biography of Rossini follows. The volume ends with a bibliography compiled by Maria Ajani (with

Stefano Ajani in the 1977 edition), Philip Gossett's catalogue of Rossini's compositions (item 24), and a discography (by Edward D.R. Neill in the 1968 edition, and by Aurelio Gariazzo in the 1977 edition). Rognoni's discussions are amply supported with musical examples. The volume is illustrated with pictures and facsimiles.

* Roncaglia, Gino. *Rossini: L'Olympico.* See item 165.

477. Salvioni, Angelo, and Elisabetta Longhi. *Gioacchino Rossini.* Bergamo: Edizioni Bolis, 1991. 199 pp.

An illustrated volume with commentaries on Rossini's music and excerpts from noted writings on the composer, including Zanolini's "Una passeggiata" (item 138), Heine's "Rossini e Mendelssohn" (item 805), Michotte's account of Rossini's meeting with Wagner (item 160) and Wagner's own remembrances of Rossini (item 136). Includes a chronology of Rossini's life and a works list.

478. Senici, Emanuele, ed. *The Cambridge Companion to Rossini.* Cambridge: Cambridge University Press, forthcoming.

This significant work-in-progress will feature an introduction by its editor and essays by prominent Rossini scholars in the following areas: I. Biography and Reception: Rossini's Life: An Overview (Richard Osborne); Reception and Image (Lorenzo Bianconi); Rossini and France (Benjamin Walton); and The Rossini Renaissance (Charles Brauner); II. Words and Music: Composition, Dramaturgy, Aesthetics (Rossini's Compositional Methods (Philip Gossett); The Librettos and Their Authors (Paolo Fabbri); Musical Dramaturgy (Marco Beghelli); Melody and Ornamentation (Damien Colas); and Off the Stage (Richard Osborne); III. Representative Operas: *Tancredi* and *Semiramide* (Heather Hadlock); *Il barbiere di Siviglia* (Janet Johnson); and *Guillaume Tell* (Cormac Newark); IV. Performance: Singing Rossini (Sergio Durante and Leonella Grasso Caprioli); Staging Rossini (Mercedes Viale Ferrero); and Editing Rossini (Patricia Brauner). A works list will aid as a reference to the volume's essays.

* Toye, Francis. *Rossini: The Man and His Music.* See item 168.

479. Vitoux, Frédéric. *Gioacchino Rossini.* Paris: Mazarine, 1982. 279 pp. ML410.R8 V57. 1982; translated in Spanish by Daniel de La Iglesia and published as *Rossini.* No. 42 in the series *Alianza musica.* Spain: Alianza, 1989. 170 pp.

Vitoux begins with a fifty-eight-page chronology, which starts with the premiere of Paisiello's *Il barbiere di Siviglia* in 1782 and ends with the erection of the Rossini monument in Pesaro in 1902, thus documenting the significance that Rossini had on the musical world. The author then discusses Rossini's music by tracing and discussing his works chronologically. The work ends with an annotated catalogue of compositions. Includes a discography.

480. Zanetti, Roberto. *Gioacchino Rossini*. In the series *I grandi musicisti del passato*. Milan: Ricordi, 1971. 71 pp. ML410.R8 Z19.

Essentially an elementary study of Rossini's career and works. Zanetti begins with a biographical timeline and a works list; a brief biography follows. The author addresses the following specific issues in subsequent chapters: aspects of Rossini's music (rhythm, melody, harmony, vocal technique, recitative, *concertati* and ensemble pieces, and orchestra); the comic operas; serious operas; works for the French stage; the "silence" and the *Péchés de vieillesse*. Zanetti also includes bibliographic and discographic information.

ROSSINI'S STYLE AND CONTEMPORARY AESTHETIC DEBATE

481. Berton, Henri Montan. *De la Musique Mécanique et de la Musique Philosophique*. Paris: Alexis Eymery, 1826. vi, 48 pp. ML3845.B38.

Himself a composer, Berton criticized new styles and, indirectly, the music of Rossini. Claiming that, after Paisiello and Cimarosa, purity of style and truth of expression was lost and "the pygmies of music" chose simply to make noise. This so-called mechanical side of art was now the vogue, he maintained. He warned young composers against replacing elegant harmony with grotesque figures and ornaments such as the ever-present "roulade."

482. Brighenti, Pietro. *Della musica rossiniana e del suo autore*. Bologna: E. Dall'Olmo, 1830. vi, 33 pp. ML410.R8B6.

A lawyer, Brighenti was also a member of the Accademico Filarmonico of Bologna and of various Italian literary societies. His look at Rossini's career is chauvinistic, as he attempts at all points to underscore the composer's connections with Bologna, including his training with Mattei. Rossini was very much the returning hero in the author's eyes, since he had begun his career when the Italian musical theater was in decline and had then achieved "universal fame." In his discussion of *Semiramide*, the author traces that subject's Italian stage history back to the 1593 rendering by Muzio Man-fredi of Cesena.

483. Carpani, Giuseppe. *Le Rossiniane ossia lettere musico-teatrali.* Padua: Minerva, 1824. vi, 232 pp. ML410.R8 C28.

A collection of letters, some dating from when Carpani served as head cen-sor and inspector of theaters in Venice and others from his time in Vienna. In addition to providing significant information about Venetian theaters, the book is a defense of Rossini's music, including responses to published attacks on *Tancredi*, *Zelmira*, and *Ricciardo e Zoraide*. A chauvinist who suggested that even the best German composers were "italianized," Carpani even transformed his comments on *Der Freischütz* (which he admitted he had yet to hear) into praise for Rossini. Carpani's "rossinian" stance caused friction with Andrea Majer (see item 486). For comment on Carpani, see Gallarati (item 496).

484. Ferrer, Cavaliere di. *Rossini et Bellini. Réponse de M. le marquis de San-Jacinto à un écrit publié à Palerme. Revue, réimprimée à Bologne et traduite en français par M. le chevalier de Ferrer.* Paris: Éverat, 1836. 23 pp. Published in Italian as *Rossini e Bellini: Risposto al parallelo pubbli-cato sul merito di loro. Cronica e Critica sull'entità musicale dei Maestri Italiani.* A second title page reads: *Rossini e Bellini: Risposta ad uno scritto pubblicato a Palermo. Dissertazioni analitica e paragonata sulle opere dei due maestri. Cenno storico degli antiche compositori. Osservazioni sull'en-tità musicale dei Maestri Italiani dei nostri giorni.* Faenza: Montanari e Marabini, 1843. 52 pp. ML410.R8 F3.

The author identifies himself only as Cavaliere di Ferrer, a public instruc-tor in the City of Naples and adjunct at that city's university. Steffan (item 492) notes that Ferrer did a French translation and Parisian publication of San Jacinto's original response to Liborio Musumeci's *Parallelo dei due maestri Bellini e Rossini* (Palermo, 1832). Ferrer's text defending Rossini is based on San Jacinto's (item 489). The author suggests that Bellini aban-doned himself to the tender and sentimental, while Rossini epitomized grace, elegance, and majesty. Ferrer also comments on other contemporary composers including Michele Carafa, Gaetano Donizetti, Saverio Mer-cadante, and Giovanni Pacini. Added as appendix to *Osservazioni sul mer-ito musicale dei compositori Italiani della nostra epoca* (22 pp. ML410.B44 S19). For further comparisons of Rossini and Bellini, see items 487 and 489.

* Jouy, Victor-Joseph Étienne de. "Essai sur l'opéra français." In Volume 12 of Jouy's *Oeuvres complètes*, 226–82. Paris: Didot, 1826. See item 395.

485. Lorenzoni, Adriano. *Della necessita' d'applicare la filosofia alla musica.* Bologna: Nobili, 1817. 48 pp. ML3800. L78.

This professor at Bologna's Liceo Filarmonico claims that taste in music may be achieved by applying philosophy and reason to the creation of art. He decries contemporary theatrical music as "over-composed," for it aims to surprise and delight the ear rather than touch the heart. In addition, he says that opera is incoherent because its composers and librettists know neither music nor poetry. Praising the simplicity of Paisiello and Cimarosa, Lorenzoni nonetheless names Rossini as one who "will before long follow in the footsteps of the most renowned composers."

486. Majer, Andrea. *Discorso sulla origine, progresso e stato attuale della musica italiana.* Padua: Minerva, 1821. 177 pp. ML290.4.M15.

Published in French as *Discours sur l'origine, les progrès, les révolutions et l'état actuel de la musique italienne.* Trans. Joseph de Valeriani. Paris: Auguste, 1827.

An outspoken aesthetic critic of the *primo Ottocento* was the Venetian Andrea Majer, whose writings on art and music criticized "the outlandishness of the Italian Parnassus gone mad." This treatise, divided into four parts, deals with the history of music in Italy from antiquity to the present. As do other critics (see Lorenzoni, item 485), Majer deemed the eighteenth century as the apex of musical culture. Prior to that time, he said, art was corrupted by extravagances and abuses of taste that he felt had returned in his own day. Not mentioning Rossini by name, Majer nonetheless denounces him in a footnote by calling him "the Marini of modern Music" because of the liveliness of his imagination. Questioning motives for composing in this manner, the author condemns such an abuse of talent. Majer's views were attacked by Giuseppe Carpani (see items 483). For a commentary on Majer's *Discorso,* see Ciarlantini, item 498.

487. Mazzini, Giuseppe. *Filosofia della musica.* First published in *L'Italiano,* Paris, 1836. Later published in Volume 2 of *Scritti letterati di un Italiano vivente.* Lugano: Elvetica, 1847: 268–318. Also, ed. G.B. Penne. Rome: Bodoniana, 1936. 92 pp. ML3800.M25 1936; introduction and notes by Adriano Lualdi. *Biblioteca artistica,* no. 34. Milan: Fratelli Bocca, 1943. 189 pp. ML3800. M25 1943; 2nd ed. in *Piccola biblioteca di scienze moderne,* no. 520, *Sezione di musica,* no. 1. Rome: Fratelli Bocca, 1954. 192 pp. ML3800.M25 1954.

Mazzini briefly traced the role of music in Italy and then considered the mission of the contemporary composer. Maintaining that music was at a point of transition, he urged young composers to cease following tradition but subscribe to a philosophy that liberates art from its tyrannical past. He criticized audiences who sought nothing more than diversion and the composers who were willing to give it to them. Melody, he wrote, stands for the individual while harmony was the social. The former stood supreme in the Italian school; the latter, the German. Mazzini proposed a mixture, creating a European ideal. In comments on composers, Mazzini called Rossini the "Napoleon" of a musical epoch. Rossini, he wrote, did for music what Romanticism did for literature: liberate it with the power of genius. Rossini fulfilled his artistic mission by reconsecrating the character of the Italian school. He noted the power of such works as *Mosè, Otello,* and *Guillaume Tell*, but criticized the other libretti the composer set. Stating that Bellini did not possess a progressive intellect, Mazzini concluded that Rossini's true successor was Donizetti.

488. Pantologo, Eleuterio [pseudonym for Torriglione]. *La musica italiana del secolo XIX: Ricerche filosofico-critiche.* Florence: Coen & Comp., 1828. 80 pp. ML290.4.P19.

Another aesthetician who upholds the principles of the eighteenth century, Pantologo addresses Goodness, Beauty, and Truth. Although Rossini may be a brilliant inventor, the author contends that his music is too complicated and irregular. After discussing possible reasons for the success behind "noisy" music, he considers the difference between "l'uomo dotto," the man versed in all aspects of his profession, and "l'uomo di genio," he who demonstrates only "scientific" knowledge. The latter's music, he maintains, is artificial and trivial. Specifically, he attacks Rossini for his use of happy music at inappropriate points in the plot, as in *La gazza ladra, Otello,* and *Semiramide.* Pantologo also criticizes those who compose in Rossini's style.

489. San Jacinto, Marchese di (Stefano Mira e Sirignano). *Osservazione sul merito dei maestri Bellini e Rossini in risposta ad un parallelo tra i medesimi, pubblicato in Palermo.* Bologna: Della Volpe, 1834. 22 pp. ML410.B44 S19.

A response to Liborio Musumeci's *Parallelo dei due maestri Bellini e Rossini* (Palermo, 1832). The author, identified as Stefano Mira e Sirignano (see Steffan, item 493), founder of the Accademia Filarmonica di Palermo, maintains that Bellini's music came not from true genius but from study. In fact, he states that Rossini is "the true genius of our century." Cites operas by both composers in constructing his argument. In conclusion, he questions the "epidemic parallelomania" of his day. Translated into French by

Ferrer as *Rossini et Bellini. Rèsponse à un écrit publiè à Palerme, Revue, rèimprimée à Bologne et traduite en française par le Chevalier de Ferrer* (item 484).

490. Santucci, Marco. *Sull melodia, sull'armonia e sul metro.* Lucca: Bertini, 1828. 124 pp. ML3851.S23.

Maestro di cappella in Lucca and then at St. John Lateran in Rome (where he succeeded Pasquale Anfossi), Santucci wrote these three "dissertations" for "studious youth." In comments on meter, he echoed Andrea Majer (see item 486), agreeing that music from Scarlatti to Zingarelli reflected true perfection. Modern music, however, was in decline, he said. Although Rossini is not mentioned specifically, Santucci's comment that "a *tallalalera* accompanied by a bizarre cantilena makes a greater impression on listeners than the most touching poetry" suggests a reference to "Largo al factotum" from *Il barbiere di Siviglia.* As did Lorenzoni (see item 485), Santucci bemoaned the loss of simplicity in Italian music, claiming that it had become more "German," a criticism often leveled at Rossini.

* Wendt, Amadeus. *Rossinis Leben und Treiben.* Item 137.

Scholarly Comment on Contemporary Aesthetics

491. Grondona, Marco. "Rossini e Wagner negli scritti: Il problema dell'opera." *Nuova rivista musicale italiana* 19 [no. 4] (October-December 1985): 621–41.

The author extracts comments on musical aesthetics from the record of the meeting between Rossini and Wagner in 1860 (see Michotte 160 and Rognoni 476), examining their similarities and differences. Grondono also explores the writings of Wagner and Rossini's discussion with Zanolini (item 138) and then demonstrates his findings by applying their ideas to their music. With score excerpts.

492. Steffan, Carlida. "Presenza e persistenza di Rossini nella riflessione estetico-musicale del primo Ottocento." In *Il testo e la scena* (see item 286), 79–91.

Steffan summarizes the three periods of aesthetic writings that touch on Rossini: the pro- and con- discussions published between 1815 and 1840; the mid-century essays, which shift attention to Verdi; and the writings after 1870, which pit Rossini (the music of the present) against Wagner (the music of the future). Steffan then focuses on the first group of works by writers such as Giuseppe Carpani (see item 483), Eleuterio Pantologo (item

488), Marco Santucci (490), and the Marchese di San Jacinto (489). These authors, often writing for an elect few rather than for the multitudes, took various sides in aesthetic debates, typically focusing on the nature of ideal beauty and art as imitation. Steffan contends that the rhetoric of these writings, originally used in literary criticism, presents problems when applied to music. See also item 493.

493. ———, ed. *Rossiniana: Antologia della critica nella prima metà dell'Ottocento.* Pordenone: Edizioni Studio Tesi, 1992. xlii, 237 pp. ISBN 88-769-2343-8 ML410.R8 R82 1992.

Following the editor's introduction and a foreword by Bruno Cagli, this anthology (with brief notes and commentary) includes excerpts from the writings of leading aesthetic criticism relating to Rossini and the *primo Ottocento* musical world. Includes sections of Adriano Lorenzoni's *Della necessità d'applicare la filosofia alla musica* (item 485), Andrea Majer's *Il Discorso sulla origine, progressi e stato attuale della musica italiana* (item 486), Michele Leoni's *Opinioni intorno la Musica di Gioacchino Rossini di Pesaro*, H. Franceschini's *Osservazioni sopra la musica di Giovacchino Rossini*, Giuseppe Carpani's *Le Rossiniane* (item 483), Eleuterio Pantologo's (pseudonym of Conte Torriglione) *La musica italiana nel secolo XIX* (item 488), Ferdinando Giorgietti's response to *Signor Pantologo intorno alle sue Ricerche*, Marco Santucci's *Sulla Melodia, sull'Armonia e sul Metro* (item 490), Pietro Brighenti's *Della musica rossiniana e del suo autore* (item 482), Stefano Mira e Sirignano's (Marchese di San Jacinto) *Le Osservazioni sul merito musicale dei maestri Bellini e Rossini* (item 489), Giuseppe Mazzini's *Filosofia della musica* (item 487), Cav. di Ferrer's *Rossini e Bellini* (item 484), and Cesare Vigna's article "Sul magistero fisio-psicologico dell'armonia" (*Gazzetta musicale di Milano* 15 August 1852). Includes illustrations of Rossini and a chronology of his life. See also item 492.

494. De Angelis, Marcello, ed. *Giuseppe Mazzini Filosofia della musica e estetica musicale del primo Ottocento: testi scelti da Andrea Majer, Marco Santucci, Lorenzo Neri, Abramo Basevi, Giovanni Battista Rinuccini.* With introduction by the editor. Rimini-Florence: Guaraldi, 1977. 136 pp. ML3800 .M26.

After an introductory section that considers Mazzini's ideas on art and culture and his place in Romantic culture, De Angelis reprints the text of the *Filosofia* (item 487) and comments by other early nineteenth-century aesthetics critics.

* Lippmann, Friedrich. "Rossinis Gedanken über die Musik." See item 473.

Carpani, Giuseppe

495. Balsano, Maria Antonella. *"Le Haydine* di Carpani, ovvero lettere per la salvezza della musica." *Nuova rivista musicale italiana* 7 [no. 3] (July-September 1978): 317–41.

Balsano considers Carpani's *Le Haydine* in conjunction with *Le Majeriane* and *Le Rossiniane* (483), the three keys to Neoclassical aethestics. Balsano notes that, between editions of Carpani's biography of Haydn, first published in 1812, Carpani discovered the music of Rossini and wrote enthusiastically of him in the work's appendix. Praising both Rossini's melodies and rhythms, Carpani saw in the composer someone who had come to save music.

* Cagli, Bruno. "Da Carpani a Balzac: un itinerario estetico rossiniano." *In Raffaello, Rossini e il bello stile.* See item 99.

* Fabbri, Paolo. "Rossini the aesthetician." See item 468.

496. Gallarati, Paolo. *"Le Rossiniane* di Carpani." *La recezione di Rossini ieri e oggi* (item 288), 69–80.

With excerpts from Giuseppe Carpani's *Le Rossiniane ossia lettere musico-teatrale* (item 483), Gallarati demonstrates that, in the face of what Carpani saw as the decaying state of opera due to the decline of eighteenth-century bel canto singing and an excessive development of the orchestra's role in an opera score, Rossini's command of form and melody made him, not only the salvation of Italian melody but also the purveyor of radical innovation. Gallarati also highlights Carpani's comments about the differences between the "artificial" German style (of Beethoven and Weber), a product of intellectualism, and the *cantilena* style of the Italians, an expression of natural beauty. The essay places Carpani's comments in terms of Neoclassical aesthetics.

* Lippmann, Friedrich. "Sull'estetica di Rossini." See item 474.

* Sergardi, Margherita. *"Le Rossiniane,* lettere musico-teatrali di Giuseppe Carpani, ed altri scritti epistolari." In *Atti del convegno di studi: Rossini, edizioni critiche e prassi esecutiva,* 53–67. See item 282.

Jouy, Victor-Joseph-Étienne de

497. Gerhard, Anselm. "Incantesimo o specchio dei costumi. Un'estetica dell'-opera del librettista di *Guillaume Tell.*" Trans. Alexandra Amati. *Bollettino del Centro Rossiniani di Studi* [no. 1–3] (1997): 45–60.

A commentary to Victor-Joseph Étienne de Jouy's "Essai sur l'opéra français" (see item 395). Gerhard highlights the contradictions in Jouy's

aesthetic, which, on the one hand, lauds all that is Classical (such as the
supremacy of the poet and a preference for a happy ending), but, on the
other, acknowledges the artistic elements (such as use of local color), which
encouraged the environment in which grand opéra soon would flourish.
Gerhard tries to reconcile these contrasts, citing Jouy's theatrical contemporaries, and also suggests that, at a time when the role of the composer was
increasing in significance, Jouy's insistence on the supremacy of the poet
may have contributed to a decline in his success.

Maier, Andrea

498. Ciarlantini, Paola. "Andrea Maier e il suo *Discorso* sulla musica italiana
     (1821)." *Bollettino del Centro Rossiniano di Studi* 36 (1996): 67–129.

     Andrea Maier (also Majer) was a writer, linguist, composer, and historian of
     the beaux arts as well as an outspoken critic of the aesthetics of the early
     Ottocento. By introducing publications in which he presented his views or
     countered those of others, Ciarlantini first places Maier in his cultural envi-
     ronment and then centers on his *Discorso sulla origine, progessi e stato
     attuale della musica italiana* (see item 486). The author demonstrates that
     Maier's comments rekindled an old aesthetic battle with Giuseppe Carpani,
     who not only came to Rossini's defense but saw him as the savior of Italian
     music (see item 483). Ciarlantini traces Maier's work, noting that in its 1829
     French translation, Joseph de Valeriani included Rossini's name in the sub-
     title, realizing that this link to the composer would assure the sale of more
     copies. Ciarlantini's appendix includes excerpts from the introduction and
     Parts 3 and 4 of the *Discorso* as well as excerpts from Maier's *Appendice al
     Galateo di monsignor Della Casa, ossia Il Galateo dei teatri e delle bot-
     teghe da caffè* (Venice: Pietro Milesi, 1822).

     * Fabbri, Paolo. "Rossini the aesthetician." See item 468.

Mazzini, Giuseppe

499. De Angelis, Marcello, ed. *Mazzini, Giuseppe. Filosofia della musica e
     Estetica musicale del primo Ottocento: testi scelti da Andrea Majer, Marco
     Santucci, Lorenzo Neri, Abramo Basevi, Giovanni Battista Rinuccini*.
     Rimini-Florence: Guaraldi, 1977. 136 pp. ML3800.M26.

     After introductory sections on Mazzini's aesthetics and contemporary cul-
     ture, the text of *Filosofia* follows (item 487). Thereafter, selected comments
     by Andrea Majer (see item 486) and Marco Santucci (item 490) are included
     as juxtaposition to Mazzini's ideas.

500. Seay, Albert. "Giuseppe Mazzini's Filosofia della musica." *Notes* 30 [no. 1]
     (September 1973): 24–36.

A summary of and commentary on Mazzini's ideas on Italian opera (see item 487). Concluding with his own observations, Seay writes that Mazzini has presented a schema for an orderly, reasoned look at the progression of the development of Italian opera. He also proposes that Mazzini has aptly described what he heard, whether he approved of it or not.

501. Tomlinson, Gary. *Metaphysical Song: An Essay on Opera*. In the series *Princeton Studies in Opera*, ed. Carolyn Abbate and Roger Parker. Princeton, N.J.: Princeton University Press, 1999. x, 192 pp. ISBN 0-691-00408-0 ML3858.T66 1999.

On pp. 99–103, Tomlinson briefly considers Mazzini's *Filosofia della musica* (see item 487). Citing points of Mazzini's discussion, Tomlinson proposes that, through noumenalist interpretation, Mazzini perceived the opera of the future in certain works by Rossini.

Ritorni, Carlo
502. Fabbri, Paolo. "Le memorie teatrali di Carlo Ritorni, 'Rossiniste de 1815.' " *Bollettino del Centro Rossiniano di Studi* [no. 1–3] (1981): 85–125.

Fabbri summarizes the writings of Carlo Ritorni, who not only chronicled but also commented on theatrical productions in the Reggio during the *primo Ottocento*. After listing the Rossini productions Ritorni witnessed, Fabbri reprints extracts from Ritorni's publications that deal with these works. Ritorni's comments not only include discussion of the operas and their casts but also of aesthetics and the development of musical theater. As an appendix, Fabbri includes excerpts from *Ammaestramenti alla composizione d'ogni poema e d'ogni opera appartenente alla musica*, in which Ritorni considers the stylistic schools of Rossini and Bellini. For further application of Ritorni's *Ammaestramenti*, see items 542 and 543.

Rossini and Contemporary Philosophers
503. Lazzerini Belli, Alessandra. "Hegel e Rossini: 'Il cantar che nell'anima si sente.' " *Revue Belge de Musicologie* (1995): 211–30; also at (http://users.unimi.it/%7Egpiana/dm1rosal.htm).

The author discusses Hegel's appreciation for the music of Rossini, citing his comments on musical expression and song as symbol. Supported with quotations from Hegel's *Ästhetik* and correspondence, Belli also notes Hegel's admiration for certain Rossini interpreters such as Maria Malibran.

504. ———. "Hegel e Rossini. Intelligenza e cuore del Belcanto." *Studi musicali* 24 [no. 2] (1995): 283–306.

This essay describes both the development of Hegel's appreciation for the music of Rossini and what the author views as their shared aesthetics. After Hegel heard the works of Rossini in Vienna in 1824, he became a convert to the music of this composer whom he felt wrote "for the heart." Belli suggests that the philosopher's writings on Rossini are a dialogue between Hegel the man and Hegel the theorist; she demonstrates that both expressed similar approaches to vocal interpretation and musical expression. She cites Hegel in his belief that inexperienced listeners heard only the technical in Rossini while the able could appreciate the composer's setting of text. Belli also notes Hegel's appreciation of Maria Malibran and Benedetta Pisaroni as optimum Rossini interpreters.

505. Ruggenini, Mario. "La musica e le parole: smarrimenti filosofici in ascolto di Rossini." In *La recezione di Rossini ieri e oggi* (item 288), 55–67.

Looks at the views of Rossini's music as expressed through the "rigorous German musical intellect" of philosophers like Hegel, Schopenhauer, and Nietzsche. Also considers Rossini's own philosophy of music as expressed to Zanolini (see item 138 and Rognoni, item 476). The author concludes that these views exemplify a rapport between two types of expression: verbal and musical.

506. Zimmermann, Michael. "Rerum concordia discors. Musik und Drama bei Rossini, Schopenhauer und Richard Wagner." *Musica* 37 [no. 1] (1983): 23–28.

[Not examined.]

SPECIALIZED STUDIES

Rossini's Working Habits

507. Bonaccorsi, Alfredo. "Come componeva Rossini?" *Bollettino del Centro Rossiniano di Studi* [no. 1] (1955): 1–4.

The author considers Rossini's methods of composing, noting that, like Mozart, he worked quickly and rarely left sketches. With illustrations from an autograph sketch of a Tantum Ergo composed for performance in Bologna in 1847 and the published score, Bonaccorsi demonstrates that, in working out the musical ideas of the accompaniment and the beginning of the vocal line, Rossini had, in essence, constructed the whole piece.

508. ———. "Tre diversi modi di comporre di Rossini." In *Convegno di studi su Rossini per il Centenario della morte di Gioacchino Rossini*, pp. 70–75. Parts of this essay also appear on item 465; one section is a reprint of item 507.

509. Gossett, Philip. "Gioachino Rossini and the Conventions of Composition."
     Acta Musicologica 52 [no. 1] (1970): 48–58; also published in *Eighteenth-
     and Nineteenth-Century Source Studies*, 60–70. Ed. Ellen Rosand. Vol. 8 in
     The Garland Library of The History of Western Music. New York and Lon-
     don: Garland, 1985. 337 pp. ML193.E36 1985.

     In this consideration of Rossini's compositional practices, Gossett offers
     evidence that, because the composer worked within the conventional frame-
     works of *primo Ottocento* opera and because he was constricted by dead-
     lines, his autographs are actually his working scores. Of the few extant
     sketches (if, Gossett states, there were ever more), two date from Rossini's
     years in France, a time when he had more leisure to reflect on structure and
     drama (see item 760 for a discussion of a Rossini sketch). Gossett presents
     an interesting glimpse into Rossini's earlier methods by analyzing an un-
     finished work identified by the names of its two characters, "Teodora e
     Ricciardino," which, as Gossett demonstrates, was most likely a *buffa* or
     semiseria work predating *La Cenerentola*. Following common practices,
     Rossini notated the melody, harmonic bass, and vocal lines, with the rest to
     be filled in later. Gossett also outlines the form of the typical Rossinian
     introduzione (see items 541, 542, 543, 544, and 545 for other discussions on
     primo Ottocento operatic forms). The article includes the text of the sketch
     for "Teodora e Ricciardo," a score excerpt of its orchestral introduction,
     score excerpts from *Cenerentola*, and two comparative facsimile illustra-
     tions from the autographs of those two works.

     * ———. "Gioachino Rossini's *Moïse*." See item 716.

510. ———. "Rossini's Compositional Methods." In *The Cambridge Compan-
     ion to Rossini*. See item 478.

511. ———. "Rossini's *Ritornelli*: A Composer and His Orchestral Soloists." In
     Musique-signe-image: *Liber amicorum François Lesure*, 133–41. Ed. Joel-
     Marie Fauquet. Geneva: Minkoff, 1988. 298 pp. ISBN: 2-8266-0868-1.

     Gossett considers what he calls some of Rossini's "more splendid instru-
     mental writing": aria *ritornelli*, demonstrating that, just as the composer
     was sensitive to the abilities of his singers, he must have composed for
     musicians with specific talents. The difficulties in some of these *ritornelli*,
     Gossett proposes, may account for their disappearance from operatic
     revivals. As demonstrations, the author provides two versions of a violin
     cadenza from *Tancredi*, cello passages from *L'italiana in Algeri*, and a
     demanding horn solo from *Otello*, which Rossini simplified by editing

measures out. Gossett concludes that Rossini's decisions about his performing forces mirror those of today.

* Pirrotta, Nino. "Rossini eseguito ieri e oggi." Item 269.

Self-Borrowings

* Conati, Marcello. " ' . . . Una certa malattia, la quale può denominarsi *contagio fantastic*.' " Item 296.

* Mauceri, Marco. "*La Gazzetta* di Gioachino Rossini: fonti del libretto e autoimprestito musicale." Item 676.

512. Mauceri, Marco. " 'Voce, che tenera': Una cabaletta per tutte le stagioni." In *Il testo e la scena* (see item 286), 365–82.

Mauceri considers the specific self-borrowings associated with the cabaletta "Voce, che tenera," a substitute aria written for *Tancredi*. Supporting his discussion with score examples and analyses of the music's various guises, the author traces its use in six subsequent operas: *L'italiana in Algeri*, *Sigismondo*, *Torvaldo e Dorliska*, *La gazzetta*, *Adelaide di Borgogna*, and *Eduardo e Cristina*. Although he set new texts to it and disguised it behind new instrumentation and vocal presentation, Rossini nevertheless associated this aria with certain dramatic situations, thus demonstrating, according to Mauceri, that his self-borrowing was far from casual. Mauceri concludes that the aria was so popular that it became a "trunk aria" in productions of other composers' operas. Appendices include a listing of the aria's appearances and its different texts.

* Simionati, Giuliano. "Rossini, Canova, e Treviso: I rapporti tra il musicista e la città veneta esaminati attraverso documenti inediti ed un autografo." See item 373.

Rossini and the Orchestra

513. Diddi, Stefano. "Gli strumenti a fiato dell'orchestra rossiniana." *Bollettino del Centro Rossiniano di Studi* 8 [no. 5] (1967): 85–96 and [no. 6] (1967): 104–11.

In this two-part study, the author discusses Rossini's use of wind instruments, presenting score examples from the operas, primarily the overtures. Noting that Rossini's earliest lessons in winds would have been learned from his father, Diddi suggests that the composer's studies of Mozart might also have provided him inspiration. However, while Mozart was likely to use winds in orchestral dialogues, the author demonstrates that Rossini entrusted them with the presentation of secondary themes.

514. Koury, Daniel J. *Orchestral Performance Practices in the Nineteenth Century: Size, Proportions, and Seating.* Vol. 85 in *Studies in Musicology*, ed. George J. Buelow. Ann Arbor, Mich.: UMI Research Press, 1986. xiv, 409 pp. ISBN 0-8357-1649-X ML1200.K68 1986. Revision of the author's doctoral dissertation (Boston University, 1981).

Uses Rossini's music as examples in his discussions of new sonorities and expansion of forces in the nineteenth-century orchestra. See also item 515.

515. Meucci, Renato. "La trasformazione dell'orchestra in Italia al tempo di Rossini." In *Il testo e la scena* (see item 286), 431–64.

Meucci begins with a brief look at the eighteenth-century orchestra. Considering the duties of the first violinist as prescribed by Francesco Galeazzi, he then studies that player's transformation to the *maestro concertatore e direttore dell'opera.* In addition to noting the eventual disappearance of the keyboard (parallel to the elimination of recitative), the author notes the "invasion" of percussion and winds, linking this to the presence of members of civic and military bands in opera orchestras. Meucci suggests that it is Rossini's use of these new instruments that eventually redefined the orchestra. He concludes by proposing that only by hearing Rossini's music on period instruments will criticisms of his orchestration be understood. Includes illustrations and charts of instruments' dispositions, membership rolls, and lists of players. Also includes a facsimile of the *Semiramide* part for the *maestro concertatore.* Mentions Avventi's *Mentore teatrale* (see Antolini, item 244). For more on the nineteenth-century orchestra, see item 514.

516. Runyan, William E. "Orchestration in Five French Grand Operas." Ph.D. dissertation, University of Rochester (Eastman School of Music), 1983, 372 pp.

The author discusses the techniques of orchestrating grand opera, including *Guillaume Tell* in this study. He specifically comments on Rossini's use of instrumental color to highlight rhythm, adept scoring of solo passages, creation of local color, and able use of winds and brass.

* Torrefranca, Fausto. "Strumentalità della commedia musicale: *Buona figliuola, Barbiere,* e *Falstaff.*" See item 597.

517. Witzenmann, Wolfgang. "Grundzuge der Instrumentation in italienischen Opern von 1770 bis 1830." In *Colloquium Die Stilistische Entwicklung der italienischen Musik zwischen 1770 und 1830 und ihre beziehungen zum Norden (Rome 1978)*, edited by Friedrich Lippmann, 276–332. Vol. 21 of *Analecta Musicologica*. Arno Volk: Laaber, 1982. viii, 461 pp. ISBN 3-9215-1866-0 ML290.3.C64 1978.

Witzenmann examines changes in the orchestra's size and make-up and also the transformation of the string-dominated ensemble of the eighteenth century to the mix of strings, winds, and brass of the nineteenth century. After citing the components of several orchestras during the period under study, the author looks at various composers' instrumentation. Considered after Mayr is Rossini, whose use of brass is examined in *La cambiale di martrimonio*, *Demetrio e Polibio*, and *Tancredi*. Among other works mentioned is *Semiramide*, which Witzenmann hails as the highpoint of Rossini's dramatic instrumentation. With score excerpts.

Stage Bands

518. Creux, Fulvio. "Rossini nelle trascizioni per banda: una proposta ancora valida dopo 200 anni?" In *Rossini a Roma—Rossini e Roma*, 69–85. See item 289.

The author looks at the socio-cultural importance of band music, suggesting that it provided the general public with a repertoire to which they might not have otherwise had access. He then considers the music of Rossini as transcribed for civic bands as well as Rossini's own compositions for winds and brass. Since much of the transcription would have been made by local bandmasters, scores are often not available for study. The author notes some, however, including scores completed by Roman bandmaster Alessandro Vesella. Creux also discusses the problems involved in making transcriptions and notes that Rossini's instrumentation (e.g., ranges of instruments) and his stylistic use of ornaments and staccato notes often makes his music a challenge for band players. He concludes his essay with a look at various editions and notes that, because of the development of winds in the nineteenth century, at times this music provides a challenge for modern musicians.

* Gossett, Philip. "Musicologi e musicisti: intorno a una rappresentazione di *Semiramide*." Item 748.

519. Zoppelli, Luca. " 'Stage music' in early nineteenth-century Italian opera." *Cambridge Opera Journal*. 2 [no. 1] (March 1990): 29–39.

The author discusses various interpretations of stage music, or *musica in scena*, in *opera seria* from Rossini's day to mid-century. Listing as its uses depiction of local color, representation of dramatic emblems, transference from the narrative to a single character's perspective, preservation of dramatic continuity, and representation of "real time," Zoppelli cites Rossini's *Maometto II*, *Mosé in Egitto*, and *Otello* among the "experimental works" which utilize stage music. Specific mention is made of the gondolier's song, the "Willow Song," and the prayer in the latter work.

10

Rossini's Operas

REFERENCE WORKS

* Gossett, Philip. "Gioachino Rossini," in *The New Grove Masters of Italian Opera*: *Rossini, Donizetti, Bellini, Verdi, Puccini*. See item 458.

* Loewenberg, Alfred. *Annals of Opera, 1597–1940, Compiled from Original Sources*. See item 293.

520. Osborne, Charles. *The Bel Canto Operas of Rossini, Donizetti and Bellini*. Portland, Ore.: Amadeus Press, 1994. 378 pp. ISBN 0-931340-71-3 ML390.O82 1994.

Dedicates 130 pages (pp. 5–135) to the operas of Rossini. Presenting each work by identifying its characters and their vocal ranges, the librettist(s), the opera's setting, and facts (including the cast) about each opera's premiere, the author then summarizes its history and plot in a brief essay. Although the book purports to include musical analysis, such discussions are more descriptive than theoretical. Contains a bibliography suggesting seven biographies, a selective discography, and an appendix listing the composer's works in order of composition.

521. Osborne, Richard, and Philip Gossett. "Rossini, Gioachino (Antonio)." In *New Grove Dictionary of Opera*, edited by Stanley Sadie, 4:56–67. London: Macmillan, 1992, 4 vols. ISBN 0-333-48522-1. ML 102.O6 N5 1992.

An updated version is available to subscribers online at (http://www. grovemusic.com). An excellent source for beginning any aspect of research on Rossini's operatic career. Osborne divides the composer's career into five segments: his early successes up to 1813 (this section also includes a useful outline for the Act 1 formal structure the composer developed during these early years); the period of Italian successes, 1813–1816; the Naples years, 1816–1822; his move toward Paris in 1822; and his so-called retirement after *Guillaume Tell* (1829). In addition to commenting in the latter section on the composer's reputation, Osborne also notes the decline in popularity of Rossini's music after his death in 1868 (see Chorley, item 304) and its subsequent revival in the early decades of the twentieth century (see Prod'homme, item 325). Gossett's works list includes information on each opera's genre, number of acts, details about the libretto, premiere, manuscript sources and major revisions. (N.B.: The operas noted in connection with the *Edizione critica* were in progress in or published prior to 1992; see the listing in this book's appendix for more recent information). Osborne's bibliography includes more than two hundred sources about Rossini, his career and individual works. The *Grove Opera* volumes also contain separate entries for each of Rossini's thirty-nine operas.

* Verti, Roberto. *Un almanacco drammatico*: *L'indice de' teatrali spettacoli*: *1764–1823*. See item 23.

GENERAL STUDIES

Nineteenth-Century Works
522. Edwards, H[enry] Sutherland. *Rossini and His School*. London: Sampson, Low & Marson, 1895. In *The Great Musicians* series, ed. Francis Hueffer. 114 pp. ML410.R8 E23 1895.

Using his biography of Rossini as a basis (see item 114), Edwards consolidates the material on Rossini's life and career and adds chapters on Donizetti, Bellini, and Verdi. Although connections are made between Rossini and the first two composers, the author comments that Verdi, then 67, had "not yet surpassed *William Tell*." The works list from item 114 is duplicated, with the addition of *Sigismondo*.

* Naumann, Emil. *Italienische Tondichter von Palestrina bis auf die Gegenwart*. See item 128.

Twentieth-Century Works
523. Buenzod, Emmanuel. *Musiciens*. Vol. 6 in the series *Musiciens et leurs oeuvres*, ed. Alfred Pochon. Lausanne: Librairie F. Rouge, 1945. 235 pp. ML390.B93.

The chapter entitled "Rossini e tutti quanti" (pp. 105–16) is a critical and dismissive look at the composer and his music; also includes brief comments on Verdi, Puccini, and the operas of *verismo*. In addition to Rossini, this volume includes essays on Handel, Mozart, Schubert, Weber, Liszt, Wagner, Bizet, Ravel, and Stravinsky.

524. Colas, Damien. *Rossini: L'opéra de lumiere*. No. 149 in the series *Decouverte*. Paris: Gallimard, 1992. 160 pp.

[Not examined.] The RILM abstract notes that this study places each of Rossini's operas in its social context, considering the audience and milieu for which they were composed. Colas further dismisses criticisms of Rossini as an uninspired composer. Illustrated, the work also has a bibliography and discography.

525. ———. *Rossini, l'opera e la machera*. Turin: Electa/Gallimard, 1999. 168 pp. ISBN: 88-4450-154-6

[Not examined.]

526. Dahlhaus, Carl. *Die Musik des 19.Jahrhunderts*. Laaber: Laaber Verlag, 1980. vi, 360. ML160 .N389 Bd. 6. Published in English as *Nineteenth-Century Music*. Trans. J. Bradford Robinson. Berkeley: University of California Press, 1989. x, 417 pp. ML190 .D2513 1989.

Dahlhaus seems in his discussion on Rossini to refute August Wilhelm Ambros (see item 460); he uses much of the same language, however. Stating that the early nineteenth century was the "age of Beethoven and Rossini," he notes that prejudices depicting the former as a musical titan and the latter as a prankster are "non-historical." His conclusions, however, are chauvinistically German, for in describing Rossini's music, he uses terms such as "trivial," "banal," and "ostentatious detachment," commenting as well that the "shortcomings" of Rossini's music create its "effect." He chooses as an example of a typical Rossinian structure the terzetto "Destin terribile" from *Le siège de Corinthe*. See Philip Gossett's comments on this selection in item 530.

527. D'Amico, Fedele. [Amico, Fedele d'] *L'opera teatrale di Gioacchino Rossini con una introduzione sull'opera lirica dalle origini alla fine del Settecento*. Rome: DeSantis, 1968? 194 pp. ML410.R7A51.

Addresses a history of opera, the life of Rossini, the conditions of composing opera in France and Italy in Rossini's day, Rossini and vocal composition, *buffa* works (with sections on vocal style, orchestration, dramaturgy, and form, with specific looks at *L'italiana*, *Il barbiere* and *Cenerentola*); *seria* works (with comparative sections as in buffa) and a look at *Tancredi*, *Otello*, *La Donna del lago* and *Semiramide*. A chapter on French operas. Concludes with a works list of the operas.

528. Della Seta, Fabrizio. "Some Difficulties in the Historiography of Italian Opera." *Cambridge Opera Journal* 10 [no. 1] (March 1998): 3–13.

The author describes the problems that arise when attempting to write a history of Italian opera. Apart from the prejudices previously imposed on the study of opera by a heavily Austro-German musicological tradition, issues such as creative authorship and textual authenticity cloud a historical narrative. Della Seta proposes various approaches to opera historiography, including anthropological and ethnomusicological, consideration of the differences between the musical structure and the event of its performance, and application of the concepts of consumer and artistic expectation and experience.

529. Dent, Edward J. *The Rise of Romantic Opera*, ed. Winton Dean. Cambridge: Cambridge University Press, 1976; reprint, 1979. x, 198 pp. ISBN 0-521-21337-1 ML1704 .D46.

A collection of lectures delivered at Cornell University, this book contains a chapter on Rossini (pp. 110–24) in which Dent traces the composer's compositional heritage to fellow Italians like Simone Mayr (see Balthazar's work on this link, items 541 and 542). Dent then considers Rossini and Romanticism, hailing *Guillaume Tell* as the composer's greatest contribution to this repertoire. Dent cites all the stereotypical criticisms of Rossini's work that have since been reexamined and disproved: his sole strength in the comic genre and his inattention to the differences between comic and serious musical settings.

530. Gossett, Philip. "Carl Dahlhaus and the 'ideal type.' " *19th Century Music* 13 [no. 1] (January-February 1989): 49–56.

Gossett addresses Dahlhaus' concept of the "ideal type" in music and traces the origins of this idea to sociologist Max Weber, demonstrating the problems inherent in Dahlhaus's use of the term. Specific to Rossini are Gossett's objections to Dahlhaus's assumption that there are no "authentic" texts and that the composer's disregarded distinctions between Classical and Romantic subjects. Gossett also objects to the use of a trio from *The Siege of Corinth* as an example of the composer's formal structures. For Dahlhaus's writings on Rossini, see item 526.

531. Lippmann, Friedrich. "Mozart und die italienischen Komponisten des 19. Jahrhunderts." *Mozart-Jahrbuch* (1980–83): 104–13.

Rossini often noted his affinity for Mozart. Lippmann demonstrates two areas in which Mozart's influence can be heard in Rossini's music: the ensemble finales and, more specifically, a bass solo in *Mosè in Egitto* and its French version *Moïse et Pharaon*, which Lippmann links to the Commendator's solo in the Act II Finale of *Don Giovanni*.

* Osborne, Richard. *Rossini.* See item 181.

532. Sandelewski, Wiaorslaw. "Rossini e l'opera romantica." In *Convegno di studi su Rossini per il Centenario della morte di Gioacchino Rossini,* pp. 94–105. See item 283.

STYLE AND CHARACTERISTICS

Nineteenth-Century Views
* Chorley, Henry Fothergill. "Signor Rossini's Operas: Characteristics" in *Thirty Years' Musical Recollection.* See item 304.

533. Dauriac, Lionel. *La psychologie dans l'Opéra Français (Auber-Rossini-Meyerbeer).* Paris: Félix Alcan, 1897. xxiii, 164 pp. ML3858 .D24.

The author's premise is that music creates psychological effects on the listener through the combination of sounds. He presents a study of musical psychology—the analysis of emotions excited by music and the search for their causes. Basing much of his book on *Guillaume Tell,* Dauriac considers its tragic, pathetic, and picturesque elements and the effects these aspects have on music. The author uses specific examples from the opera (and from *Le siège de Corinthe* and *Otello*), concluding that France and Rossini had reciprocal influences on each other and that the composer gave France its first grand opera in *Tell.*

* Mount Edgcumbe, Richard. *Musical Reminiscences chiefly respecting the Italian Opera in England From the Year 1773 to the Present Time.* See item 306.

Twentieth-Century Studies
534. Betzwieser, Thomas. "A propos de l'exotisme musical de Rossini." In *Il testo e la scena* (see item 286), pp. 105–126.

Although some scholars have argued that the music of *L'italiana in Algeri* and *Il turco in Italia* lacks Turkish or exotic elements, the author suggests looking beyond obvious strategies such as instrumentation or use of a banda. Betzwieser argues, with the aid of score examples, other strategies in which Rossini sounds foreign—that is, setting apart Italian culture from others. As an example, he cites the quotation of *Don Giovanni* in *Il turco* and of *La Marseillaise* in *L'italiana* as an attempt to introduce a "foreign context." (For another interpretation of the latter quotation, see item 199). He also points to possible political connotations in the use of the *banda turca* in *Maometto II* and *Le siège de Corinthe.* Betzwieser concludes that exoticism extends beyond local color in Rossini's musical code.

535. Bisogni, Fabio. "Il melodramma rossiniano e le ideologie correnti." *Chigiana: rassegna annuale di studi musicologici* 13 (1976, publ. 1979): 211–17.

[Not examined.]

According to the RILM abstract, Bisogni compares the characteristics and innovations of Rossini's musical language. Special attention is paid to the roles of the librettist and the composer.

536. Busch, Gudrun. "Die Unwetterszene in der romantischen Oper." In *Die couleur locale in der Oper des 19. Jahrhunderts*, 161–212. Vol. 42 in the series *Studien zu Musikgeschichte des 19. Jahrhunderts*, edited by Heinz Becker. Regensberg: Bosse, 1976. 403 pp. ML1704.C68

In this study, which goes from Rameau to Tchaikovsky, Busch traces the storm scene in opera back to its Baroque roots. Not only do examples in opera literature demonstrate the development of orchestral techniques but they also suggest the growing importance of the emotional and dramatic in stage music. From Rossini's works, Busch selects the storm scenes from *Il barbiere di Siviglia* and *Otello*. She also notes the suggestion of storm music in the composer's Sonata a quattro from 1804, with its movement marked "Temporale." With musical examples. See also item 673 for another study of storm music.

537. Carvalho, Mario Vieira de. "Belcanto-Kultur und Aufklärung: Blick auf eine widersprüchliche Beziehung im Lichte der Opernrezeption." In *Zwischen Aufklärung & Kulturindustrie: Festschrift für Georg Knepler zum 85. Geburtstag II: Musik/Theater*, pp. 11–42. Hamburg: Bockel, 1993. 287 pp. ISBN: 3-928770-11-X ML3845.Z95 1993 Vol. 2.

The author proposes that the bel canto style conflicted with the audience's perception of opera as experienced during the Enlightenment, shifting the emphasis from dramatic to musical. Rossini's role in the development of this style is considered.

538. Lippmann, Friedrich. "Per un'esegesi dello stile rossiniano." Translated from German by Boris Porena. *Nuova rivista musicale italiano* 2 [no. 5] (September-October 1968): 813–56.

Lippmann discusses various aspects of Rossini's operatic music. The author first addresses types of Rossinian melodies, which he classifies as "aperta" (open), constructed of small melodic figures with considerable embellishment, and "chiusa" (closed), connected phrases that do not invite ornaments. Demonstrating both types with score examples, Lippmann then notes that even more predictable than the composer's melodic types are his uses of determined stylistic forms. Citing Rossini's comments and correspondence, Lippmann summarizes the composer's ideas on "modern" settings of dramatic music, concluding that Rossini merely explored territory which Verdi would later develop. Rossini's main concern, he contends, was the "physical joy of rhythm and sound," not the Wagnerian ideal of mixing art, philosophy, and drama. Lippmann also addresses Rossini's singers, noting the importance of the heroic tenor. Finally, the author considers Rossini as a part of the Romantic age, suggesting that he was able to retain eighteenth-century musical qualities which were in danger of being abandoned.

539. ———. "Rossini—und kein Ende." *Studi musicali* 10 [no. 2] (1981): 279–91.

In this discussion of Rossini's music, Lippmann summarizes previous studies, including those of Carl Dahlhaus (526), Fedele D'Amico (527), Stefan Kunze (592), and various works by Philip Gossett, among others. Citing comments on the *opere serie* and *buffe*, and specifically on issues of forms, rhythm, orchestration, and use of coloratura, Lippmann concludes that, while Rossini's art is many-sided, it is imbued with graceful, vital elegance.

540. Mila, Massimo. "Rossini, tutto musica (1933)." In *Cent'anni di musica moderna*, pp. 17–28. In the series *Biblioteca di cultura musicale: Documenti*. Milan: Edizione Rosa e Ballo, 1944; reprint, Turin: E.D.T., 1981. v, 212 pp. ISBN 88-7063-020-X ML196.M6 1981.

Mila describes Rossini as a classicist but notes that there are hints of Romanticism in both *La donna del lago* and *Guillaume Tell*. The author suggests that there was little about Romanticism to entice Rossini, whom he saw primarily as a buffa composer. The composer left Romantic notions to Verdi, claims Mila, who even saw Rossini's retirement as a "happy comedy." For a similar interpretation of the composer, see Della Corte, item 456.

* Roncaglia, Gino. *Rossini: L'Olympico*. Item 165.

STUDIES OF MUSICAL FORM AND STRUCTURES

* Balthazar, Scott L. "Aspects of Form in the Ottocento Libretto." See item 575.

541. ———. "Mayr, Rossini, and the Development of the Early *Concertato* Finale." *Journal of the Royal Musical Association* 116 [no. 2] (1991): 236–66.

The author examines Simon Mayr's role in the development of the *concertato* finale in *opera seria*, demonstrating that, while other composers clearly used the structure, Mayr was the first leading composer to do so consistently. Thus, Rossini's finales must be seen as an expansion of this tradition. Balthazar concludes that Rossini and his librettists established a new pattern for the finale's sections, for example, by giving more dramatic and musical weight to the *largo concertato*. Demonstrates the role librettists played in this development. Includes musical examples and tables illustrating the extended finales in Mayr's and Zingarelli's operas; tables of Milanese and Venetian operas from 1790 to 1799 with extended finales; an appendix contains an excerpt from Carlo Ritorni's description of the *concertato* finale from his *Ammaestramenti alla composizione d'ogni poema e d'ogni opera appartenente alla musica*, which Balthazar cites in his argument (on Ritorni, see also item 502).

542. ———. "Mayr, Rossini, and the Development of the Opera Seria Duet: Some Preliminary Conclusions." In *Il teatro musicale tra Sette e Ottocento*, Vol. 1 of *I vicini di Mozart*, 377–98. See item 287.

Maintains that connections exist between the eighteenth and nineteenth-century duet and examines the end stage of this development through examples in the works of Johann Simon Mayr from 1813 through Rossini's *Tancredi*. Concludes that Mayr completes the move toward what Abramo Basevi would term "la solita forma." Balthazar's appendix includes abstracts from descriptions of the *Ottocento* duet found in Carlo Gervasoni's *La scuola della musica* (1800), Alexandre Choron's *Principes de composition des écoles d'Italie* (1808), Niccola Tacchinardi's *Dell'opera in musica sul teatro italiano e de' suoi difetti* (1833), Bonifazio Asioli's *Il maestro di composizione* (1832) (item 461), Ritorni's *Ammaestramenti alla composizione d'ogni poema e d'ogni opera appartenente alla musica* (1841), [see also items 502 and 543], and Basevi's *Studio sulle opere di Giuseppe Verdi* (1859). See also item 545.

543. ———. "Ritorni's *Ammaestramenti* and the conventions of Rossinian melodramma." *Journal of Musicological Research* 8 [nos. 3–4] (1989): 281–312.

In his *Ammaestramenti alla composizione d'ogni poema e d'ogni opera appartenente all musica* (1841), Carlo Ritorni addressed *primo Ottocento* compositional practices in order to propose reform. Balthazar examines Ritorni's models of the structures in Rossini's operas, pointing out that although the models function, they often do not take into account the developments which the composer made. In addition to commenting on Ritorni's work, Balthazar describes his views on common operatic structures such as the duet, central finale, and introduzione as well as on types of recitative and the setting of Italian verse forms. Appendix A excerpts Ritorni's ideas on solo pieces such as the rondò, and Appendix B, his description of an Act I finale. See also items 502 and 542.

544. ———. "Rossini and the Development of the Mid-Century Lyric Form." *Journal of the American Musicological Society* 41 [no. 1] (Spring 1988): 102–25.

Rossini's florid treatment of melody traditionally has been contrasted to the plainer style of Bellini, Donizetti, and Verdi. The author suggests that this analysis perhaps has typecast Rossini as a conservative in other areas as well, such as in his approach to lyric form. With examples from operas including *Otello, Matilde di Shabran, L'italiana in Algeri, La donna del lago, Maometto II, Tancredi, Zelmira*, and *Ricciardo e Zoraide*, and score excerpts from *Semiramide*, the author demonstrates that Rossini's broader approach to melody includes structures that would become the mid-century lyric form (A A' B A') previously attributed to Bellini.

545. ———. "The *Primo Ottocento* Duet and the Transformation of the Rossinian Code." *The Journal of Musicology* 7 [no. 4] (Fall 1989): 471–97.

In addition to offering a careful analysis of Amenaìde and Tancredi's duet, "L'aura che intorno spiri," the author demonstrates that, during the 1830s and 1840s, Bellini, Donizetti, and Verdi made substantial and progressive changes to the musico-dramatic duet design used by Rossini. This research counters scholars who had claimed that such innovations were the work of Verdi in the 1850s. See also item 542.

546. Beghelli, Marco. "La retorica del melodramma: Rossini, chiave di volta." In *Il testo e la scena* (see item 286), 49–77.

Beghelli reviews opera's structural forms and dramaturgical conventions, such as the four-movement finale, *scena ed aria*, largo concertato, off-stage *banda*, accompanied recitative, and letter scenes (see item 278), explaining that although Rossini did not invent these, he developed them. Along with these comes a consistent use of a musical rhetoric including such devices as employing dactylic rhythms in a *stretta* and iambic figures to introduce characters or solemn moments; reiteration of musical phrases to build tension; and the "triple colpo," or three-chord figure, to announce the arrival of an important character. These devices were used by Rossini's successors, including Verdi, whom Beghelli includes in his discussion. describing the differences between Rossini's and Verdi's characterizations and their conception of musical "speech."

547. ————. "Musical Dramaturgy." In *The Cambridge Companion to Rossini*. See item 478.

548. ————. "Tre slittamenti semantici: cavatina, romanza, rondò." In *Le parole della musica*, Vol. 3 of *Studi di lessicologia musicale*, edited by Fiamma Nicolodi and Paolo Trovato, 185–217. No. 27 of *Studi di musica veneta*. Florence: Leo S. Olschki, 2000. xi, pp. 317 pp. ISBN 88-222-4906 2 ML63 .P26 1994 Vol. 3.

Beghelli looks at the meanings of the terms *cavatina*, rondò, and romanza in nineteenth-century scores. Using various Rossini operas from which to draw examples, he constructs a pattern of arias given to the principal singers in *opere serie* of the *primo Ottocento*, describing their position in the act, dramatic function, formal structure, musical characteristics, and preferred terminology. Cites Carlo Ritorni's *Ammaestramenti* (see items 502 and 543).

549. Bianconi, Lorenzo. " 'Confusi e stupidi': di uno stupefacente (e bana-lissimo) dispositivo metrico." In *Il testo e la scena* (see item 286), 129–161.

The author considers how the *largo concertato* can halt dramatic action but create musically dynamic moments. In his discussion of both the textual and musical phrasing in such scenes, he looks specifically at the harmonic and poetic flow in the *largo* from *L'italiana in Algeri* (although examples are cited from *Donna del lago*, *Tancredi* and *Guillaume Tell* as well). Rossini's strategies for musically structuring such scenes include harmonic changes and building chains of interlocking groups of beats. Bianconi cites Bonifacio Asioli's 1836 treatise *Maestro di composizione* on phrasing (item 461).

550. Colas, Damien. "Melody and Ornamentation." In *The Cambridge Companion to Rossini*. See item 478.

551. Dahlhaus, Carl. "Zür Methode der Opern-Analyse." *Musik und Bildung* 7 [no. 9] (September 1980): 518–23.

Dahlhaus suggests that because opera is not abstract, its analysis must focus on the relationship between music and drama. Examining the finale of Act I of *Otello*, Dahlhaus demonstrates how its contents build the dramatic conflict critical at that juncture in theatrical music.

* Emanuele, Marco. *L'Ultimo stagione italiana: Le forme dell'opera seria di Rossini da Napoli a Venezia*. See item 585.

552. Liebscher, Julia. "Introduktion und Exposition in der Oper: Eine musikdramatugische Untersuchung am Beispiel des *Otello* (1816) von Gioacchino Rossini." *Die Musikforschung* 44 [no. 2] (1991): 105–29.

The author examines the role of the *introduzione*, briefly touching upon those in the operas of Donizetti and Verdi. The thrust of her investigation concerns the work of Rossini, in particular his use of *introduzioni* with chorus. Examining *Otello* in detail, she discusses the musical characteristics of its *introduzione*, demonstrating how its numbers suggest both Otello's past and his visions for the future, thus establishing the opera's main dramatic conflicts. Includes diagrams of scene complexes, musical examples, and excerpts from the libretto.

553. Lippmann, Friedrich. " 'Casta diva': la preghiera dell'opera italiana della prima metà dell'Ottocento." Trans. from German into Italian by Renato Bossa. *Recercare* 2 (1990): 173–209.

Lippmann notes that, ironically, the frequency of the *preghiera*, or prayers, as part of nineteenth-century opera scores stemmed from the general religious indifference of the audience, serving only to excite sentiment. Lippmann examines various types of prayers: the intimate, static *preghiera* with limited melodic range, such as Amenaide's "Giusto Dio" from *Tancredi*; the antiphonal solo-choral prayer, such as "Dal tuo stellato soglio" in *Mosè*; the dramatic prayer with intense orchestral accompaniment, as is "Deh! pietoso" in *Mosè*; and the last, a combination of the first three which synthesizes action and stasis, such as Hedwig's "Toi qui du faible" from *Guillaume Tell*.

554. ———. "Vincenzo Bellini e l'opera seria del suo tempo: Studi sul libretto, la forma delle arie e la melodia." In *Vincenzo Bellini*, by Maria Rosaria Adamo and Friedrich Lippmann. Turin: ERI, 1981. 576 pp. ML410.B44 A43 1981.

New edition of the author's *Vincenzo Bellini und die italienische Opera seria seiner Zeit. Studien über Libretto, Arienform und Melodik*. Vol 6. of *Analecta Musicologica*. Cologne-Vienna: Böhlau, 1969. xii, 402 pp. ML410.B44 L57.

In addition to referring to Rossini in various sections of this book dedicated to Bellini, Lippmann includes a section on Rossini in the chapter on arias. General considerations include aria type, coloratura, rhythm, and the role of the orchestra as accompaniment. Lippmann suggests the unifying element in Rossini's art is graceful elegance and liveliness. (N.B.: The section on Rossini in the 1969 edition is not as full a discussion; this chapter in the

1981 edition, as Lippmann notes, has been almost completely rewritten.) In the general discussion of Italian libretto conventions, Lippmann mentions prison scenes in Rossini operas (see item 589).

555. Lühning, Helga. "Die Cavatina in der italienischen Oper um 1800." In *Colloquium Die Stilistische Entwicklung der italienischen Musik zwischen 1770 und 1830 und ihre beziehungen zum Norden (Rome 1978)*, edited by Friedrich Lippmann, 333–69. Vol. 21 of *Analecta Musicologica*. Arno Volk: Laaber, 1982. viii, 461 pp. ISBN 3-9215-1866-0 ML290.3.C64 1978.

The author traces the change in meaning of the term "cavatina" from the late eighteenth century when, as an operatic solo song, it was not considered an aria per se. Later, however, the cavatina became the entrance aria and the one-section aria that often concluded a work. Examples from cavatinas from *Tancredi* are cited. With score excerpts.

Overtures
Studies concerning the overtures of specific operas may be found in Chapter 11.

* Asioli, Bonifazio. *Il maestro di composizione ossia séguito del Trattato di armonia*. Item 461.

556. Gossett, Philip. "Le sinfonie di Rossini." *Bollettino del Centro Rossiniano di Studi* (1979): 5–123.

In the first of three sections in this study, the author arrives at a definition of the archetypical Rossinian overture by identifying melodic, harmonic, and instrumental characteristics. Next, dividing the composer's career into five periods and identifying the overtures in each, Gossett traces the structural and dramatic developments in these *sinfonie*, and by implication, in the operas. The composer's thematic self-borrowings are identified in both the text and accompanying tables. Lastly, applying the findings from the first two sections, the author addresses the question of overtures of dubious authenticity, such as the one in the archives of the orchestra at Odense, Denmark (item 558). Includes musical examples.

557. ———. "The Overtures of Rossini." *19th Century Music*, 3 [no. 1] (1979–80): 3–31.

An abridged version of item 556, this article contains the section defining the overture archetype and then limits further discussion to the overtures from Rossini's first period (1808–1813), including those of uncertain authenticity. Contains tables and musical examples.

558. Ingerslev-Jensen, Povl. "An Unknown Rossini Overture: Report of a Discovery in Odense," *Music Review* 11 (1950): 19–22; also published as "Una sinfonia sconosciuta," *Bollettino del Centro Rossiniano di Studi* [no. 5] (1956): 81–83.

The author, conductor of the city orchestra in Odense, Denmark, heralds his discovery of twenty-four parts for an overture found in a portfolio of Rossini scores. Because the music had been signed with the letter "R" and based on an analysis of its musical characteristics, he attributes the work to Rossini. (See items 556 and 557 in which Philip Gossett rejects this theory of authorship.)

VOCAL CHARACTERISTICS AND INTERPRETATION

General Studies

559. Celletti, Rodolfo. *Storia del belcanto*. Vol. 15 in the series *Contrappunti*. Fiesole: Discanto Edizioni, 1983. 221 pp. ML1460.C4 1983. Translated by Helene Pasquier and Roland Mancini and published in French as *Histoire du bel canto*. Paris: Fayard, 1987. 280 pp. Translated by Frederick Fuller and published as *A History of Bel Canto*. Oxford: Clarendon Press, 1991. 218 pp. ISBN 0-19-313209-5 ML1460.C413 1991; reprint: Oxford: Clarendon Press and New York: Oxford University Press, 1996 ML1460.C413 1996.

After an account of the history of bel canto in the Baroque, Celletti includes a chapter on Rossini, examining the composer's views on melody and singing, the characteristics of his vocal writing, types of voices in his operas, and vocalism in Rossini's day. Much of Celletti's information is drawn from important vocal treatises by the likes of Manual García, Gilbert Duprez, and Luigi Lablache, making this work useful for those interested in performance practice. Celletti also includes relevant comments from Stendhal's *Vie de Rossini* (item 135), citing them as "documents" on the vocal arts in the *primo Ottocento*. Includes musical examples.

Rossini's Vocal Writing

560. Brandenburg, Daniel. "Francesco Florimo, la vocalità a la didattica vocale dell'Ottocento." In *Atti Francesco Florimo e l'Ottocento musicale del convegno: Morcone, 19–21 aprile 1990*, Vol. 1, edited by Rosa Cafiero and Marina Marino, 163–73. Reggio Calabria: Jason Editrice, 1999. ISBN: 88-8157-069-0 ML423.F63 F73 Vol. 1.

The author discusses Florimo's *Breve metodo di canto*, comparing it with a similar work by Heinrich Panofka. Brandenburg discusses Rossini's role in the development of the new *Ottocento* vocal style and Panofka's criticism of

Rossini roles such as Aroldo in *Guillaume Tell*. He notes that unprepared singers attempting to imitate the role's creator, Gilbert Louis Duprez (see item 273), had often destroyed their voices.

561. Capri, Antonio. "Rossini e l'estetica teatrale della vocalità." *Rivista musicale italiana* 46 (1942): 353–73.

The author begins with comments by Stendhal, which suggest that Rossini was the quintessential symbol of "italianità." Capri then examines the conditions under which he believes Rossini composed operas, concluding that the composer was driven by the voices of his singers rather than by the drama of his libretto. This aesthetic helps to explain the incongruities in the relationships between Rossini's music and the plots of his operas, Capri claims. This study is an example of vintage Rossini scholarship prior to the "Rossini Renaissance." For example, conclusions about Rossini's ideas about ornamentation have since been reexamined (see Caswell, items 271 and 569). Capri briefly addresses several of the more "memorable" operas, concluding that Rossini's individuality is tied to nationality.

562. Celletti, Rodolfo. "Il vocalismo italiano da Rossini a Donizetti. Parte I: Rossini." In *Studien zur italienische-deutschen Musikgeschichte*, Vol. 5 of *Analecta Musicologica*, edited by Friedrich Lippmann, 267–94. Cologne: Graz, 1968.

Celletti notes that the thirty-year period of 1810–1840 was important for the development of vocal styles and to music of the Romantic/bel canto era. Part of this significance was due to the rise of *melodramma* and the "color" ascribed to its roles. Celletti considers the "Rossini revolution": the composer's writing of coloratura, his methods of treating the solo voice, and his vision of the rapport between vocal ranges and roles. With excerpts from melodic lines taken from Rossini roles for the various ranges (including contralto), Celletti notes Rossini's roles in the vocal developments of this era. Also considers the composer's writing for Isabella Colbran. See also item 701.

* ———. "La vocalità rossiniana e *La gazza ladra*." See item 701.

563. ———. "Origine e sviluppi della coloratura rossiniana." *Nuova rivista musicale italiana* 2 [no. 5] (1968): 872–919.

After a brief discussion of preexistent models of virtuosic ornamentation in Italian opera, the author considers Rossini's role in developing a style of coloratura writing. Citing the well-worn tale that the composer chose to write embellishments himself because singers no longer knew how to improvise such lines, Celletti then examines coloratura examples from operas ranging from *Demetrio e Polibio* to *Semiramide*, demonstrating that Rossini developed this style not in the role of reformer but rather to complement his text or the vocality of specific singers, including his first wife, Isabella Colbran. Celletti cites examples of both *seria* and *buffa* style ornaments as well as embellishments that would have suited certain vocal ranges, such as the "Rossini tenori di grazia." He concludes that, as Rossini matured and grew content in his profession, his vocal lines became more embellished. Rather than restraining singers, Rossini wrote to exhibit their talents, even approving of the numerous variants on certain popular numbers.

564. Colas, Damien. "Anamorphoses et metamorphoses dans l'arabesque rossinienne: Étude stylistique des varientes ornamentales." *Analyse musicale* 17 (October 1989): 38–45.

As do other scholars (see items 271 and 569), Colas notes the fallacy in stating that Rossini tried to suppress improvised ornamentation. By giving examples from various operas, the author demonstrates certain embellishment characteristics and figures as they appear in Rossini's concept of ornamentation. Colas proposes that in isolating these figures, one can analyze Rossini's melodic style, demonstrating as well how the composer transformed the ideas of his immediate predecessors.

* ———. "Melody and Ornamentation." See item 550.

565. DeMarco, Laura E. *Rossini and the Emergence of Dramatic Male Roles in Italian and French Opera*. Ph.D. dissertation, Columbia University, 1998. 501 pp.

Not examined. The author's abstract notes that the dissertation examines Rossini's role in developing vocal categories for male heroes and lovers in serious works. Beginning with the castrato and the disappearance of this range in Italian opera, she follows Rossini's experimentation with travesty roles and then, during his Neapolitan years, his pairing of high and low tenors and use of basses. With his move to France, she writes, Rossini needed to appeal to French tastes and appropriate vocal ranges. Finally, with *Guillaume Tell*, Rossini created the dramatic tenor and baritone roles, at that point a novelty in both the Italian and French traditions. DeMarco concludes with an analysis of the impact of Rossini's operas on subsequent works for the Italian and French stages.

* Landini, Giancarlo. "Riflessioni su alcuni aspetti della vocalità francese di Rossini." In *Atti del convegno di studi: Rossini, edizioni critiche e prassi esecutiva*, 153–72. See item 282.

566. Pagannone, Giorgio. "Tra 'cadenza felicità felicità felicità' e 'melodie lunghe lunghe lunghe': Di una tecnica cadenziale nel melodramma del primo Ottocento." *Il saggiatore musicale* 4 [no. 1] (1997): 53–86.

In his discussion of *primo Ottocento* cadential technique, Pagannone considers Rossini's participation in the composition of so-called *Bettel cadenzen*, or cadenzas that "beg for applause." The goal of such long phrases is to postpone a resolution to the tonic in order to sustain dramatic tension, according to the author. To demonstrate, he gives examples from *Ciro in Babilonia, Maometto II*, and *Il barbiere di Siviglia*.

The Composer's Comments
* Michotte, Edmond. *Souvenirs: Une Soirée chez Rossini à Beau-Sejours (Passy) 1858.* See item 123.

Modern Studies
567. Aspinall, Michael. "Il cantante nelle interpretazioni delle opere rossiniane." *Bollettino del Centro Rossiniano di Studi* 10 [no. 1] (1970): 11–21.

The author considers issues involved in modern interpretations of Rossini roles. Working with specific singers, Rossini was able to introduce their individual vocal characteristics into their roles. Aspinall demonstrates this concept with musical examples and then discusses the performance of ornaments, cadenzas, and the embellishment of recitatives and repeated melodies. He also considers changes Rossini authorized for subsequent performances, noting that knowledge of these can help the modern interpreter who performs for an audience of different tastes and needs.

568. Caswell, Austin B., ed. *Embellished Opera Arias.* Vols. 7 and 8 in *Recent Researches in the Music of the Nineteenth- and Early Twentieth-Centuries.* Rufus Hallmark and D. Kern Holoman, general editors. Madison, Wisc.: A-R Editions, 1989. xxxii, 219 pp. ISBN 0-89579-240-0 M2.R23834 Vol. 7 and 8.

Among the arias from the nineteenth-century repertoire covered in this study of embellishments are selections from *Il barbiere di Siviglia, Cenerentola, La gazza ladra, Guillaume Tell, L'italiana in Algeri, Mosè in Egitto, Otello, Semiramide, Le siège de Corinth*, and *Tancredi*. Embellished passages included were written by Rossini for specific singers or, in many cases, were written by the singers themselves. Among the singers cited are Manuel García, Laure Cinti-Damoreau, Jenny Lind, Giuditta Pasta, G.B. Rubino, Antonio Tamburini, and a certain Mme. Gregoire for whom Rossini embellished "Di tanti palpiti" from *Tancredi*, presented herein in facsimile. Caswell not only discusses Rossini's style in embellishing arias and recitative but also demonstrates that, rather than opposing such virtuosic displays, the composer actually encouraged them by opening a broad range of vocal possibilities that challenged the singers' own inventiveness. Prefatory materials include the texts of the arias in the collection.

569. ———. "Vocal Embellishment in Rossini's Paris Operas: French Style or Italian?" *Bollettino del Centro Rossiniano di Studi* 15 [no. 1–2] (1975): 5–21; Italian translation, 82–97.

Caswell traces the history of French prejudices against the Italian vocal style, noting that, even though critics disapproved of the ornamentation of melodies, the popularity of Italian works demonstrates that the audiences appreciated them. Caswell then considers Laure Cinti-Damoreau, Rossini's favorite French soprano. After discussing the Rossini roles she premiered, Caswell considers her *Méthode de Chant*, a treatise of vocal exercises written for her students at the Paris Conservatoire, in which she explained and gave examples of the coloratura style. With excerpts from Caswell's edition of Cinti-Damoreau's book. See also 568.

* Celletti, Rodolfo. "Origine e sviluppi della coloratura rossiniana." See item 563.

570. Durante, Sergio, and Leonella Grasso Caprioli. "Singing Rossini." In *The Cambridge Companion to Rossini*. See item 478.

571. Faller, Hedwig. *Die Gesangskoloratur in Rossinis Opern und ihre Ausführung*. Berlin: Triltsch & Huther, 1935. 127 pp. ML410.R8 F17.

In this publication of her doctoral dissertation, the author traces the history of coloratura singing and its application in Rossini's operas. Citing period vocal treatises, such as those of Manual García and Gilbert Duprez, and information on singers in various histories of Rossini's music, Faller considers the various forms of ornaments in coloratura passages as well as the application of arbitrary embellishments. The volume also includes chapters on orchestral coloratura passages and declamation in French and Italian music. With ample musical examples and score excerpts, a Rossini works list, and bibliography.

572. Steane, John. "Semiramide." *Musical Times* 127 [no. 1718] (April 1986): 204–5. The author considers the technical aspects of singing the roles in this work, connecting the music with its main interpreters in performances at Covent Garden from the nineteenth and twentieth centuries.

LIBRETTO STUDIES

Studies specific to individual works may be found in Chapter 11.

573. Alberici, Stefano. "Appunti sulla librettistica rossiniana." *Bollettino del Centro Rossiniano di Studi* [no. 1–3] (1978): 45–60.

   Noting that operas are usually studied in terms of their music rather than their libretti, Alberici examines the special case of Rossini, whose texts have traditionally been dismissed as disastrous and whose attitude toward text-setting has been stereotyped as careless. Citing previous studies on Rossini's libretti, the author clarifies Rossini's relationships with his librettists, who, notwithstanding commonly held prejudices, were first-class poets. Alberici then notes that libretti may be studied as literary, theatrical, or musical products, and he comments on the major studies of Rossini libretti to date, among them Tartak (items 674 and 744), Cagli (item 609), Carli Ballola (items 654 and 722), Isotta (item 717), Tozzi (item 721), Casini (item 656), Cacai (item 622) and Gossett (item 581). Albertici then mentions recent editions of libretti, including Viviani's (items 855 and 856) and Isotta's (item 854). [For more recent editions of libretti, see the volumes in *I libretti di Rossini*, publications of the Fondazione Rossini, in the section on editions and facsimiles at the end of this volume.]

574. Angemüller, Rudolph. "Grundzuge des nachmetastasianischen Librettos." In *Colloquium Die Stilistische Entwicklung der italienischen Musik zwischen 1770 und 1830 und ihre beziehungen zum Norden (Rome 1978)*, edited by Friedrich Lippmann, 192–235. Vol. 21 of *Analecta Musicologica*. Arno Volk: Laaber, 1982. viii, 461 pp. ISBN 3-9215-1866-0 ML290.3 .C64 1978.

   Citing examples, the author looks at Italian libretti after Metastasio, considering the new designations for serious and comic operas. In addition, Angemüller also examines the librettists' role in connection with singers and theater administrations. He uses Rossini libretti to demonstrate the introduction of biblical topics (*Mosè in Egitto*), commedia dell'arte (*Il barbiere di Siviglia* and *La scala di seta*), and the growing use of chorus (*Il turco in Italia*). The author demonstrates that the development of the post-Metastasian libretto was not clear cut; both the older and newer structures were present until the emergence of Romanticism.

575. Balthazar, Scott L. "Aspects of Form in the Ottocento Libretto." *Cambridge Opera Journal* 7 [no. 1] (1995): 23–35.

The author considers the transformation of the eighteenth-century, intrigue-laden Metastasian libretto to the *Ottocento*'s more linear, interlocking dramas, based on unity of action. Citing examples from the works of Rossini, Bellini, Donizetti, and Verdi, Balthazar discusses elements of this dramatic shift, such as the adoption of the tragic ending, rejection of trivial plots, and minimizing of moral dilemmas. Noting the growing dramatic import of lyrical numbers, he also indicates that these changes engendered the large-scale musical structures such as the *introduzione* and first act finales.

576. Fabbri, Paolo. "The Librettos and Their Authors." In *The Cambridge Companion to Rossini*. See item 478.

577. Goldin, Daniela. *La vera Fenice: Librettisti e libretti tra Sette e Ottocento*. Vol. 454 in the series *Piccola biblioteca Einaudi*. Turin: Einaudi, 1985. 386 pp. ML2110.G64 1985.

Includes three sections dealing with Rossini. One considers Gaetano Rossi (*La cambiale di matrimonio*, *Tancredi*, and *Semiramide*) as poet (pp. 56–63). The second examines Giuseppe Petrosellini's libretto for Paisiello's *Il barbiere di Siviglia*, noting that Rossini's librettist, Cesare Sterbini, wrote with more comic energy (pp. 164–89). A third section traces prior settings of *Semiramide* and then discusses Rossi's setting (pp. 190–229).

* Gossett, Philip. "The Operas of Rossini: Problems of Textual Criticism in Nineteenth-Century Opera." See item 582.

578. Huebner, Steven. "Lyric Form in *Ottocento* Opera." *Journal of the Royal Musical Association* 117 [part 1] (1992): 122–47.

The author gives a precis of the scholarship on Italian lyric forms, including Friedrich Lippmann (item 554) and Scott Balthazar (item 544), which depend on alpha-numeric analyses of poetic phrase structure. Huebner proposes an alternative method that considers the inclusion of tonality and cadential articulation as analytical criteria. This functional analysis, he claims, permits a unified view of how melodic phrases interact with each other rather than treating them as segments of music and verse. He demonstrates how this is better from a historical perspective as well. As an example, he offers an alternative solution to Balthazar's analysis of melodies from *Semiramide* (see above-cited item).

579. Lippmann, Friedrich. "Zur italianità der italienischen Oper im 19. Jahrhundert." In *Die couleur locale in der Oper des 19. Jahrhunderts*, 229–56. See item 536.

Lippmann diagrams various rhythmic patterns and links them to Italian versification, noting that several rhythms could be employed for each verse-type. This isorhythm, as he calls it, was one of Rossini's great successes. He gives musical examples from Rossini operas, demonstrating that they commonly appear in arias, ensembles, and choruses, particularly in works from the second decade of the *primo Ottocento.*

STUDIES OF VERSIONS

580. Gossett, Philip. "Gli autografi rossiniani al Museo Teatrale alla Scala di Milano." *Bollettino del Centro Rossiniani di Studi* 8 [no. 3] (1967): 48–54 and [no. 4] (1967): 65–68.

In this article, written at the beginning of his scholarly career, Gossett discusses several of the Rossini autographs in the Museo Teatrale of the Teatro alla Scala: the complete score of *Tancredi*, the duet "Ai capricci della sorte" from *L'Italiana di Algeri*, the bass aria "Alla voce della gloria," and the cantata "Dalle quete e pallid'ombre." In the first part of the article, Gossett explains the various substitutions in *Tancredi*'s autograph indicated by his research into libretti from various productions of the work (see item 582 for more of Gossett's doctoral research). Among his conclusions is that the original *aria di sortita* in *Tancredi* was "Dolci d'amor parole," which later was substituted by "Di tanti palpiti." In the second part of this article, Gossett notes the importance of the discovery of the duet from *L'italiana*, since the rest of the autograph is located in the Ricordi archives. He also discusses the cantata, including a musical example from the bass aria. He adds that one of the other manuscripts at La Scala is Gaetano Braga's transcription from memory of Rossini's setting of "Mi lagnerò tacendo" "sopra una nota sola." (See item 256).

* ———. "Le fonti autografe delle opere teatrale di Rossini." See item 18.

581. ———. "Rossini and Authenticity." *The Musical Times* 109 (1968): 1006–10.

Gossett defines authenticity in terms of all versions of an opera with which Rossini was in some way personally connected. Examples of substitutions and revivals of which Rossini was cognizant are drawn from *L'italiana in Algeri, Otello, Tancredi, Cenerentola, Matilde di Shabran,* and *Adina.* For a more extensive discussion of substitutions in *Tancredi,* see item 632.

582. ———. "The Operas of Rossini: Problems of Textual Criticism in Nineteenth-Century Opera." Ph.D. dissertation, Princeton University, 1970. 629 pp.

In this text-critical analysis, which has inspired and served as a foundation for subsequent Rossini research, Gossett considers all possible sources for "authentic" versions of Rossini's works—productions in which the composer was directly connected. Returning to sources such as printed libretti, autograph scores, manuscript copies, and printed editions, Gossett demonstrates how operatic texts can be reconstructed in order to reflect authentic material. Fourteen operas are examined; for each, the author provides a list of musical sources, a list of printed libretti for the premiere and revivals, commentary on textual problems, discussion of authenticity of revivals, and a list of new music provided by Rossini for these later productions. Appendices include information about nineteenth-century Italian publishers of librettos, *copisterie*, and publishers of printed editions. Gossett also gives details on dated plate numbers for Italian and French music publishers.

THE *SERIA* WORKS

583. Balthazar, Scott L. "Evolving Conventions in Italian Serious Opera: Scene Structure in the Works of Rossini, Bellini, Donizetti, and Verdi, 1810–1850." Ph.D. dissertation, University of Pennsylvania, 1985. xvii, 614 pp.

Balthazar studies arias, duets, and central finales from the works of these four composers, suggesting that the traditional notion of conventional scene structures is erroneous. Instead, he writes, many of Rossini's structural outlines were altered to allow for stronger musico-dramatic connections. Balthazar devotes chapters to Rossini's arias, duets, and central finales and ensembles, considering such aspects as individual movements, dramatic process, and melodic structure. He suggests that by the end of his career, Rossini and his librettists made changes that anticipated the development credited to later composers. Examples are drawn from *Tancredi, Aureliano in Palmira, Elisabetta, regina d'Inghilterra, Otello, Armida, Mosè in Egitto, Ricciardo e Zoraide, Ermione, Maometto II, Zelmira,* and *Semiramide.* Includes score examples and tables. Studies drawn from this dissertation include items 420, 541, 542, 543, 544, 545 and 575.

584. Baricco, Alessandro. *Il genio in fuga: Due saggi sul teatro musicale di Gioachino Rossini.* Genoa: Il melangolo, 1988. 132 pp. ML410.R8 B32 1988 ISBN 88-701-8082-4.

These two essays consider Rossini's music in philosophical terms. The first presents a look at what Baricco sees as transcendental characteristics in Rossini's comic operas; the second deals with the drammaturical constructs of the *opere serie* from *Tancredi* to *Semiramide* and also includes the author's schematic of the archetypical drama and a diagram of its realization in *Bianca e Falliero.*

585. Emanuele, Marco. *L'Ultimo stagione italiana*: *Le forme dell'opera seria di Rossini da Napoli a Venezia.* Florence: Passagli, 1997 315 pp. ISBN 88-368-0339-3 ML410.R8 E43 1997.

Emanuele begins with a discussion of Rossini's musical language. After examining the forms of the Neapolitan works, he studies the composer's revision of *Maometto II* and *Semiramide*, both done for Venice. Although these two works are often seen as breaking away from the operas for Naples, Emanuele suggests rather that the operas of Rossini's last Italian season should be viewed as the culmination of what had come before. The author analyzes the connections between these two compositional periods with the use of musical examples.

* Fabbri, Paolo. "Gioachino Rossini uno e due." Item 629.

586. Isotta, Paolo. "I diamante della corona. Grammatica del Rossini napole-tano." In *Gioacchino Rossini. Mosè in Egitto, Moïse et Pharaon, Mosè*, 145–346. See item 854.

Isotta's editions of the three operas and his subsequent discussion of these works includes an examination of Rossini's serious operas, which the author deems undervalued. At a time when consideration to the *seria* works was rarely given, Isotta's commentary added validity to their study. Includes musical analysis with score examples. Illustrated with portraits of inter-preters of *Mosè* (Isabella Colbran and Giuseppe Ciccimarra) and of *Moïse* (Laure Cinti-Damoreau and Adolphe Nourrit), as well as of Domenico Bar-baja, under whose Neapolitan *imprese* the great *seria* works were composed.

* Nicastro, Aldo. *Il melodramma e gli italiani.* See item 475.

587. Tomlinson, Gary. "Italian Romanticism and Italian Opera: An Essay In Their Affinities." *19th-Century Music* 10 [no. 1] (Summer 1986): 43–60.

Citing criticism of Italians and their theater in the age of burgeoning Romanticism, Tomlinson proposes that, while Rossini may not have been aware of these polemical writings, he did have his own notion of Romantic melodrama. The author continues that, in the Italian *seria* works, Rossini explored new dramatic ground, and by mixing *seria* and *buffa* elements, he helped to create a new genre: the sentimental drama. He also notes how Rossini manipulated musical structures in order to create dramatic flexibil-ity. Yet, he argues, there still remain elements of the Classical in these works; thus, Rossini created a balance between the old and new. Tomlinson also comments on the writings of Mazzini (item 487) and that author's favorable views of the works of Rossini. See also Tomlinson, item 501.

588. Tortora, Daniela. *Drammaturgia del Rossini serio: Le opere della maturità da "Tancredi" a "Semiramide."* Biblioteca musicologica, 3. Rome: Torre d'Orfeo, 1996. 315 pp. ISBN: 88-851-4746-1 ML410.R8 T67 1996.

An abundant study, which offers formal and dramaturgical analyses of Rossini's serious operas from 1813 to 1823. Supported by ample score and text examples, Tortora, who based the study on her Laurea thesis (*Morfologia drammatica e musicale nel Rossini serio: Le opere della maturità da Tancredi a Semiramide* [University of Bologna, 1993]), examines major structural elements such as the *introduzione*, first-act finales, and the internal acts of three-act works. Through these examples, the author demonstrates the structure of opera in the *primo Ottocento*. Offers a musical and poetic breakdown of each work, identifying individual numbers by tempo, time signature, and key as well as poetic verse type. Material from this book was also published as item 589.

589. ———. "Il personaggio recluso: Un *topos* drammaturgico dello scioglimento." In *Il testo e la scena* (item 286), 273–95. An excerpt from the author's *Tesi di Laurea, Morfologia drammatica e musicale nel Rossini serio. Le opere della maturità da "Tancredi" a "Semiramide* ([University of Bologna, 1993])." (See also item 588.)

The author examines parallel instances of imprisonment scenes in the second acts of Rossini's serious operas from 1813–1823 (with the exception of *Aureliano in Palmira* and *Sigismondo*). These "scene carcerarie" (see also Lippmann, item 554) serve to unravel the dramatic knot leading to the climax. Tortora's conclusions compare these scenes by commenting on their "modularity," which permits both certain constants in structure but also the possibility of varying the sequence of events. She also addresses the important musicodramatic potential of these scenes. See also item 588.

THE *SEMISERIA* AND *BUFFA* WORKS

* Baricco, Alessandro. *Il genio in fuga: Due saggi sul teatro musicale di Gioachino Rossini*. Item 584.

590. Gallarati, Paolo. "Per un interpretazione del comico rossiniano." *Il testo e la scena* (item 286), 3–12.

The author suggests that comedy, as it developed from the eighteenth century, reflects two threads: everyday realism and farce. According to Gallarati, the latter, stemming from popular comedy such as the *commedia dell'arte*, is where Rossini's genius lies. Gallarati looks at what he calls the trilogy *carnevalesco*: *L'italiana in Algeri*, *Il barbiere di Siviglia*, and *La*

Cenerentola, all novel comedic settings in which life is treated as a game of constant turns of events. Of interest is the author's conception that this type of comedy is reflected in the alternating expressions of voice and orchestra. (see Gallarati, item 591 for further discussion of this idea). Also considers Rossini's musical pacing and the psychological and musical energy unleashed by the static *concertato* sections.

591. ———. "Dramma e *ludus* dall'*Italiana al Barbiere*." In *Il melodramma italiano dell'Ottocento: Studi e ricerche per Massimo Mila*, No. 575 in the series *Saggi*, edited by Giorgio Pestelli, 237–80. Turin: Einaudi, 1977. xv, 653 pp. ML 1733.4.M5.

Examines the stylistic elements, in particular, the relationship between voice and orchestra in *L'italiana in Algeri* and *Il barbiere di Siviglia*, concentrating on arias, duets, trios and *concertati* sections (except for the static *larghi concertati*). Gallarati suggests that, while the collaboration between voice and instruments in *L'Italiana* is flexible, their relationship in *Barbiere* is more complex; he describes these as I (orchestra leads voice), II (voice leads orchestra, usually during periods of suspended action), and III (declamatory sections or *parole sceniche*). *L'Italiana*, he says, is in the tradition of Mozartian *opera buffa*, but *Barbiere*, which features a perfect structuring of the three relationships, is a conscious mixture of "dramma" and "ludus." The alternation of three collaborations is tied strictly to the work's psychological and comedic significance. (See also Gallarati, 590.) The creative change opened by Rossini in *L'Italiana* culminates in *Barbiere*, concludes the author.

592. Kunze, Stefan. "Ironie des Klassizismus: Aspekte des Umbruchs in der musikalischen Komödie um 1800." In *Analecta Musicologica* No. 21, 72–98. See item 606.

Kunze suggests that by the time Rossini began his career in *opera buffa* with *La cambiale di matrimonio*, the aim of comic opera had turned toward irony and parody, and had even become political, as in Isabella's "Pensa alla patria" in *L'italiana in Algeri*. The author demonstrates this development by comparing Basilio's "La calunnia" as set by both Paisiello and Rossini, and comments on the latter's comedies by their new rhythmic quality. Includes Heine's comments on Rossini's music as support for the argument (see item 805). With score excerpts.

* Nicastro, Aldo. *Il melodramma e gli italiani*. See item 475.

593. Osthoff, Wolfgang. "Die Opera buffa." In *Gattungen der Musik in Einzelderstellungen. Gedenkschrift Leo Schrade*. Ed. Wult Arlt, Ernest

Lichtenhahn, Hans Oesch and Max Haas. Bern: Francke, 1973. 895 pp. ML55.S375.

This Festschrift essay suggests that an overall view of society is a determinant in the differentiation of serious and comic opera. After examining the history of *buffa* opera, Osthoff notes that, contrary to Mozart's creative milieu, the view of an aristocracy no longer existed in Rossini's world. He demonstrates his point by comparing aspects of *Le nozze di Figaro* and *Il barbiere di Siviglia*. This stress on society rather than on individual heroes underscores the importance of finale ensembles in these comic masterpieces. Osthoff also proposes that Rossini's humor, constructed of rhythm and dynamics, is often more musical than text-based. Also includes examples from *L'italiana in Algeri*.

594. Ruffin, Gianni. "Drammaturgia come auto-confutazione teatrale: Aspetti metalinguistici alle origini della comicità nelle opere comiche di Rossini." *Recercare* 4 (1992): 125–63.

The author discusses various theories of temporal qualities in music, or the sense of time as perceived by the listener. Using techniques that can also be found in Mozart, according to the author, Rossini manipulated time musically by repeating syllables and text. Ruffin concludes that the humor is not in the situation but rather in its linguistic-musical representation. As an example, he examines the sneezing scene in *L'italiana in Algeri*, showing how music serves to interrupt action with comic results. Also considers *Il barbiere* and *Cenerentola*.

595. Senici, Emanuele. "Verdi's *Luisa*, a semiserious Alpine Virgin." *19th Century Music* [Fall 1988]: 144–68.

Before offering an analysis of *Luisa Miller* and the pastoral and sentimental in this Verdi work, Senici discusses it forerunners, among them *La gazza ladra*, which he notes was a considered the "standard-setter" in the "mezzo carattere" or *semiseria* genre. With their picturesque locales, works such as this one transported their audiences to an idealized pastoral environment. By the 1830s, Rossini's *Guillaume Tell*, although not a *semiseria* work, still reflected the Alpine idyll through Rossini's use of musical echo, open fifths, and the oft-noted local color effect, the *ranz des vaches*.

596. Tartak, Marvin H. *The Italian Comic Operas of Rossini*. Ph.D. dissertation, University of California at Berkeley, 1968. 234 pp.

The author gives an introduction to Italian opera for those who have not studied it (a useful section, given the date of the dissertation) and calls for further research. One focus is the libretti of the works considered, which Tartak notes, come from French sources. In addition to relating the backgrounds of the librettists, Tartak addresses the musical structure and forms found in Rossini's operas and goes on to discuss various versions of works. Considered specifically are *Il barbiere*, *La Cenerentola* and *Matilde di Shabran*. In essence, Tartak notes, although laced with levity, Rossini's comic operas have their serious points as well. With musical examples.

597. Torrefranca, Fausto. "Strumentalità della commedia musicale: *Buona figliuola*, *Barbiere*, e *Falstaff*." *Nuova rivista musicale italiana* 18 [no. 1] (January-March 1984): 1–9; originally published in the *Rivista italiana del teatro* 2 (15 March 1942).

Torrefranca contends that in order to understand *opera buffa*, one must see its connections to instrumental music. Using the works of Antonio Vivaldi as a basis of his argument, the author proposes that the sense of orchestra of composers such as Rossini was key to Italian musical theater. Torrefranca cites the second act of *Il barbiere* as one of his examples, demonstrating the comic effects of Rossini's rhythms and melodic fluidity. With musical examples.

The Farse

598. Bini, Annalisa. "Esiti ottocenteschi della farsa in Rossini e Donizetti." In *Il testo e la scena* (see item 286), 565–85.

Summarizing current research on and history of the *farsa* as a genre, Bini attempts to see to what extent—if any—Donizetti's *farse* were influenced by those of Rossini. Cites Bruno Cagli's architypical design of Rossini's *farse* (see item 601). Concludes that Rossini brought the *farsa* to perfection in Venice; on the other hand, Donizetti, working in a completely different manner, reframed the genre, reviving it through Neapolitan and French influences.

599. Bryant, David. "La farsa musicale: coordinate per la storia di un genere non-genere." In *La farsa musicale veneziana (1750–1810)*, 431–55. Vol. 2 of *I vicini di Mozart*. See item 287.

Traces the genre of *farsa*, demonstrating its occasional links to the French *comédie mêlée d'ariettes* and, especially in the case of *farse veneziane*, to the *intermezzo comico*, or *farsetta*. From contemporary sources, Bryant defines *farsa* as a "short comedy" the "sole object of which is to please." In addition to describing a typical evening's performance of farses and the genre's characteristics, Bryant examines the history of the *farsa* in Venetian theaters. Includes a table of Venice's theaters and *farsa* productions by season and year from 1792 to 1818, which includes Rossini's five *farse* at the Teatro San Moisè.

600. ———, and Maria Giovanna Miggiani. "Organizzazione impresariale e struttura socio-economica nel teatro della farsa." In *La farsa musicale veneziana*, 457–66. Vol. 2 of *I vicini di Mozart*. See item 287.

Examines the production of *farse* in Venice from the angles of business and production. Also considers the development of the "new bourgeois" audience and how their taste for the sentimental affected programming. Focuses on the history of the Teatro San Moisé where Rossini's five *farse* premiered. See also Miggiano, item 375.

601. Cagli, Bruno. "Le farse di Rossini." In *La farsa musicale veneziana*, 633–40. Vol. 2 of *I vicini di Mozart*. See item 287.

Cagli offers a construct of the archetypical structure of Rossini's one-act *farse*, which he describes as the kernel of the musical schema to be found in the composer's future two-act comic operas. In addition to plotting out the eight-numbered structure, Cagli discusses how it functions in each of the five *farse* written for Venice's Teatro San Moisè (see item 375). He concludes with comments on Rossini's use of the *farsa*, pointing out that these works served him later as a rich reserve for self-borrowings.

602. Castelvecchi, Stefano. "Alcune considerazioni sulla struttura drammaturgico-musicale della farsa." In *La farsa musicale veneziana*, 625–31. Vol. 2 of *I vicini di Mozart*. See item 287.

The author suggests that, rather than comparing the *farsa* to the first act of a two-act *dramma giocoso*, it is more logical to see it as a condensation of the *dramma*'s two acts, with a *concertato* movement which serves as "pseudo First Finale" (No. 4 of Bruno Cagli's model of the *farsa*—see item 601). In addition to considering the position and role of this *concertato* piece, Castelvecchi also demonstrates how some *dramma giocosi* were transformed into *farse*. Also mentions the "sentimental" subjects favored by the Venetian audiences (see also Bryant and Miggiani, item 600, and Paissa, item 278). Rossini's activity in *farsa* came at the mature phase of the genre's development (see also Bini, item 598).

* Paissa, Roberto. "La carriera di un cantante di *farsa*: Luigi Raffanelli." See item 278.

603. Surian, Elvidio. "La farsa della carriera dell'operista italiano degli anni 1795–1820." In *La farsa musicale veneziana*, 467–77. Vol. 2 of *I vicini di Mozart*. See item 287.

Surian considers the composers of *farsa* and its role in their careers. Some, for example, were at the end of their compositional lives; others used it to launch their careers in other genres, such as *opera seria*. In most cases, Surian suggests, the *farse* came at critical points in their careers, and, for this reason, they were composed with great care. Included as an appendix is a list of *farsa* composers (beginning with Marcello Bernardini da Capua and ending with Gaetano Donizetti) in which they are identified by geographic "school," debut opera, and genre.

SCENOGRAPHY

604. Biggi, Maria Ida. "Scenografie rossiniane di Giuseppe Borsato." *Bollettino del Centro Rossiniano di Studi* 35 (1995): 61–83.

Considers the sets designs of Giuseppe Borsato for Rossini productions at Venice's Teatro La Fenice. Basing her discussion on sketches found at the Bibliothéque-Musée de L'Opéra in Paris (Rés 2247), the author describes the dramatic-scenographic connections for *Tancredi* and its Act I interval ballet, *Arsinoe e Telemaco* (1813); *Sigismondo* and the ballet *Gli Arabi* (1814); *Maometto II* (1822); and *Semiramide* and the ballet *La morte di Ettore* (1823). Illustrated with thirty-one plates of Borsato's sketches. Also includes inventories of scenographic supplies and materials available at La Fenice during the years encompassing Rossini's productions there.

605. Henze-Döhring, Sabine. "La 'natura' nelle opere di Rossini." Translated from German into Italian by Lorenzo Bianconi. *Bollettino del Centro Rossiniano di Studi* [no. 1–3] (1983): 113–23.

Citing nature imagery in *Aureliano in Palmira*, *Sigismondo*, *La donna del lago*, and *Guillaume Tell*, the author suggests that its use underscores the shift from Classical *opera seria* to Romantic opera in Italy and France, particularly in grand opera. In addition to onstage tableaus, musical elements, such as the famous "ranz des vaches" in *Tell*, stress local color. Henze-Döhring proposes that these Rossini operas demonstrate the profound change from the static pastoral scenes of the eighteenth century to those that depict nature as an integral part of new dramatic subjects.

606. Leopold, Silke. "Zur Szenographie der Türkenoper." In *Colloquium Die Stilistische Entwicklung der italiensichen Musik zwischen 1770 und 1830 und ihre beziehungen zum Norden (Rome 1978)*, edited by Friedrich Lippmann, 370–79. Vol. 21 of *Analecta Musicologica*. Arno Volk: Laaber, 1982. viii, 461 pp. ISBN 3-9215-1866-0 ML290.3.C64 1978.

The author begins by citing some aesthetic opinions on scenography from nineteenth-century writings and then notes the interest in works based on Turkish, Arabic, and Moorish settings, providing a list of operas (noting composer, librettist, and scenographer) and ballets (choreographer, composer, and scenographer) from the late eighteenth century through the 1820s. Leopold discusses elements of Moorish architecture and decor such as the depiction of mosques, minarets, arches, and mosaics. Among the Rossini works included in the essay are *L'italiana in Algeri, Ricciardo e Zoraide,* and *Maometto II* at La Scala, where Alessandro Sanquirico was scenographer. Includes illustrative plates of set designs.

607. Polovedo, Elena. "Le prime esecuzioni delle opere di Rossini e la tradizione scenografica italiana del suo tempo." In *Rossini 1792–1992* (item 95), 285–313.

With excerpts from contemporary commentary, Povoledo examines scenography in Rossini's theatrical arena. With color illustrations of designs from productions of his works.

* Viale Ferrero, Mercedes. "*Guglielmo Tell* a Torino (1839–1840), ovvero una 'procella' scenografica." Item 780.

* ———. "Staging Rossini." See item 294.

"ROSSINI RENAISSANCE": MODERN INTERPRETERS AND PRODUCTIONS

608. Brauner, Charles. "The Rossini Renaissance." In *The Cambridge Companion to Rossini.* See item 478.

609. Cagli, Bruno. "Momento di Rossini." *Bollettino del Centro Rossiniano di Studi* 11 [no. 1–3] (1971): 5–10.

Starting with the "Rossini Renaissance" in the 1950s, Cagli looks both backwards at the period of ignorance and myth that surrounded Rossini and forward to the new era of research spearheaded by Philip Gossett and Alberto Zedda. The author considers early studies such as that of Radiciotti (see item 164), which, he notes, *should* have been a point of departure, but instead became the most consulted source on Rossini. Cagli also considers Rossini's historic position, noting that few composers enjoyed the success he did during his lifetime. Yet in later criticism, he writes, Rossini came to be surrounded by anecdotes and errors. Briefly addressing some of these issues, Cagli concludes that, with new research and revivals of his works, Rossini's moment had come.

* Gualerzi, Giorgio. "Vicende novecentesche del teatro rossiniano." In *Atti del convegno di studi*: *Rossini, edizioni critiche e prassi esecutiva*, 173–81. See item 282.

610. Quattrocchi, Arrigo. "La Rossini Renaissance." (www.mclink.it/mclink/classica/ROSSINI/rossini.ren.htm); also published in *Musica & Dossier* (July-August 1989).

[Print source not examined.]

The author discusses how Rossini's works fell out of fashion from late nineteenth to the early twentieth centuries and how Rossini biographers and proponents such as Vittorio Gui helped to reinstate him in the international repertoire. See items 616 and 695 by Gui and items 618 and 619 about him.

Performing Rossini

Horne, Marilyn
611. Williams, Jeannie. "La Rossiniana: A Conversation with Marilyn Horne." *The Opera Quarterly* 9 (Summer 1993): 64–91.

Marilyn Horne distinguished herself as not only one of the top interpreters of Rossini's music but as one of the leading figures in Rossini revival. Much of the interview centers around performance practice, but Horne also comments on the use of the contralto in "breeches roles" in nineteenth-century Italian opera through Verdi. Her reminiscences are laced with comments on twentieth-century audiences' reactions to Rossini music, which they did not yet know. Musical examples include Rossini's embellishments to Bellini's "La tremenda ultrice" from *I Capuleti e i Montecchi* and Andromaca's vocal line from an Act 2 duet from *Ermione*. Illustrated with photos of Horne in various Rossini roles.

Ramey, Samuel
612. Kors, Stacey. "Assur Ascendant: A Conversation With Samuel Ramey." *The Opera Quarterly* 9 [no. 4]: (Summer 1993): 90–112.

This interview with Ramey demonstrates his part in championing the works of Rossini. Includes illustrations of the singer in various roles.

Schneiderman, Helene
613. Seil, Michael. "Michael Seil im Gespräch mit Helene Schneiderman." *La Gazzetta* 4 [no. 1] (1994): 17–18.

In this interview, mezzo-soprano Helene Schneiderman discusses performing Rossini roles, in particular Rosina in *Il barbiere di Siviglia*. Interviewer

Seil and she address issues such as Alberto Zedda's edition of the work (used for the 1993 Stuttgart production in which she sang), which returned the vocal line of Rosina to its original lower range; vocal embellishments; and dramatic coloratura roles in Rossini's serious works.

Producing Rossini

614. Barbero, Luca B. " 'Ho sbagliato: La testa va chinata dall'altra parte': Savinio regista dell'*Armida* all'origine della Rossini-Renaissance." *Rivista italiana di musicologia* 26 [no. 1] (1991): 79–94.

Considers the last work of scenic director Alberto Savinio and his work on *Armida* for the 1951 Maggio Musicale season. Includes a sketch demonstrating Savinio's vision of the stage design.

* Cagli, Bruno, and Franco Mariotti. *Il teatro Rossini: Le nuove edizioni e la messinscena contemporanea*. See item 91.

615. Gossett, Philip. *Divas and Scholars: Performing Italian Opera*. Chicago: The University of Chicago Press, 2002.

Forthcoming.

616. Gui, Vittorio. "Ricordi rossiniani." In *Convegno di studi su Rossini per il Centenario della morte di Gioacchino Rossini*, 81–93. See item 283.

617. Serafin, Tullio, and Alceo Toni. *Stile, tradizioni e convenzioni del melodramma italiano del Settecento e dell'Ottocento*. Milan: Ricordi, 1958.

The authors offer advice on how to perform works from the eighteenth- and nineteenth-century opera repertoire. In this manual of traditional performances, they consider commonly prescribed cuts, for example, offering no consideration of scholarly editions or issues. The following Rossini works are included: *Il barbiere di Siviglia* (49–89), *L'italiana in Algeri* (91–110), *La Cenerentola* (111–42), and *Guglielmo Tell* (143–64).

Gui, Vittorio

618. Gualerzi, Giorgio. "Il 'Rossiniano' Gui a Torino." *Bollettino del Centro Rossiniano di Studi* 17 [no. 3] (1977): 7–15.

In explaining the role Vittorio Gui played, beginning in 1925, in reintroducing Rossini's operas, the author first traces production history of the composer's works in the nineteenth century, noting that apart from *Il barbiere di Siviglia* and *Guillaume Tell*, programming of the other operas was infrequent. Gualerzi notes Gui's productions of Rossini in Turin, citing reviews that demonstrate how well they and the interpreters (such as Conchita

Supervia) were accepted by audiences. Gualerzi calls Gui "a faithful interpreter" of the Rossinian spirit.

619. Spada, Marco. *Numero speciale dedicato a Vittorio Gui nel centenario della
     nascita (Roma, 14 settembre 1885) e nel decennale della morte (Fiesole, 16
     ottobre 1975). Bollettino del Centro Rossiniano di studi*, [no. 1–3] (1985).
     83 pp.

Following an introduction by Fondazione president Bruno Cagli, which
describes the efforts of Gui in conducting and programming the works of
Rossini, Spada briefly introduces this compilation of Gui's writings. A sampling of these appear as individual items (616 and 695). Giorgio Gualerzi
and Carlo Marinelli Roscioni offer lists of Rossini operas directed by Gui;
first is a chronological presentation of musical productions with which he
was involved, and, second, a list by years (1911–1972). Finally, Maurizio
Modugno compiles a discography of Gui's recordings of Rossini works.
Includes illustrations of Gui and his colleagues as well as of scenes from
productions he conducted.

11

Studies about Individual Operas

Demetrio e Polibio

> * Gallino, Nicola. "Lo 'scuolaro' Rossini e la musica strumentale al Liceo di Bologna." See item 340.

620. Russo, Francesco Paolo. "Alcune osservazioni sul *Demetrio e Polibio* di Rossini." *Studi musicali* 23 [no. 1] (1994): 175–99.

> Russo elaborates on many of the same issues found in the author's contribution to *Rossini a Roma* (see item 621). He discusses the work's history, including the actual year Domenico Mombelli commissioned the opera; Vincenzina Viganò Mombelli's libretto and Rossini's setting of the text (with score excerpts); attributions of Mombelli's compositional contributions to the score; and the eighteenth-century roots of both the libretto and the opera's structure.

621. ———. "La prima 'differita' (maggio 1812) di *Demetrio e Polibio*." *Rossini a Roma—Rossini e Roma* (item 289), 35–51.

> According to Russo, *Demetrio e Polibio* poses difficulties, due, in part, to the lack of the autograph and to the dearth of studies on operas that bridge the late Classical era and the *primo Ottocento*. In order to resolve several of those issues, the author examines the creative roles of singer/composer/impresario Domenico Mombelli, who commissioned the work, and his wife Vincenzina Viganò Mombelli, who wrote its libretto. After demonstrating that, years later, Rossini had dated the work some two years too early, Russo argues that Mombelli actually composed the overture in addition to two of

the numbers in Act II. Despite previous scholarly criticism of the libretto, Russo proposes that Viganò Mombelli's text is an example of a work that contains traces of the Metastasian ideal as well as forward-looking structural elements. Although Russo mentions only one instance of Rossini's subsequent self-borrowings, a table outlining the opera identifies numbers that later appeared in *Tancredi*, *Ciro in Babilonia*, *Il signor Bruschino*, *La pietra del paragone*, *Sigismondo*, and *L'equivoco stravagante*. See also item 620.

La cambiale di matrimonio

622. Cacai, Francesco. "*La Cambiale di matrimonio* da Federici a Rossi." *Bollettino del Centro Rossiniano di Studi* 15 [no. 1–2] (1975): 22–64.

The author traces the sources of Gaetano Rossi's libretto for *La cambiale di matrimonio* to a libretto entitled *Il Matrimonio per lettera di cambio* by Giuseppe Checcherini (set by Carlo Coccia in 1807) and to a five-act comedy *La Cambiale di matrimonio* by Camillo Federici (1791). Cacai first offers a scene-by-scene comparison of the two libretti, demonstrating their relationship to their common source. He then gives a complete outline of Federici's play. Cacai notes that it is impossible to select the best of the three but praises Rossi's ability to successfully reduce the five-act play and the two-act opera to a one-act *farsa*. Also includes biographical information on Checcherini and Federici. An appendix contains a list of extant works by Federici.

L'equivoco stravagante

* Beghelli, Marco, and Stefano Piana. "Anmerkungen zur Neuausgabe von *L'equivoco stravagante*." See item 862.

623. Damerini, Adelmo. "La prima ripresa moderna di un' opera giovanile di Rossini: 'L'equivoco stravagante' (1811)." *Chigiana* 22 [no. 2] (1965): 229–36.

Damerini's comments come after a 1965 production of this opera in Siena, the first performance of the work in 154 years. The author cites reviews of the premiere that condemned the work's "indecent" libretto, explaining its almost immediate withdrawal. Damerini counters the idea that this is the worst of the five *farse*, proposing that in its score is the embryo of the genius in the later comic masterpieces.

624. Deutsche Rossini Gesellschaft, Homepage link. "*L'equivoco stravagante*." (www.rossinigesellschaft.de/data/werke/equivoco/equivocoi.html)

In conjunction with the Gesellschaft's edition of this opera (see item 862), this page offers information on the work, including roles and ranges, orchestral ensemble, length, sources, editions, premiere and modern performances, and bibliography, all compiled by Thomas Lindner (see also item 625). Audio examples are available via midi files, arranged by Stefano Piana, one of the editors of the DRG's edition. Accessed 31 December 2001.

625. Lindner, Thomas. "Analytischer Überblick über *L'equivoco stravagante.*" *La Gazzette* 10 (2000): 17–20.

After presenting details about the opera's genre, debut, characters, instrumentation, sources, and editions, Lindner outlines the musical numbers and then presents a diagram of the work's tonal scheme. Also includes a brief bibliography.

L'inganno felice

626. Gossett, Philip. "L'Inganno felice." In "The Operas of Rossini: Problems of Textual Criticism in Nineteenth-Century Opera," 164–94. See item 582.

627. Melica, Ada. "Due opere giovani di Rossini." *Bollettino del Centro Rossiniano di Studi* 9 [no. 1] (1969): 12–16.

Melica discusses *L'inganno felice* and *L'occasione fa il ladro*, offering a brief history of each work, excerpts from contemporary criticism, a schema of the musical numbers, and commentary on notable elements in each work.

Ciro in Babilonia, ossia La caduta di Baldassare

* Fabbri, Paolo. "Il Conte Aventi, Rossini e Ferrara." See item 245.

* Russo, Francesco Paolo. "La prima 'differita' (maggio 1812) di *Demetrio e Polibio.*" See item 621.

La pietra del paragone

* Grondona, Marco. *"La perfetta illusione"*: *Ermione e l'opera seria rossiniana*. Item 725.

L'occasione fa il ladro

* Bini, Annalisa. " 'Accidente curioso a proposito di *Un curioso accidente*': Un contestato pasticcio rossiniano (Parigi, 1859)." Item 783.

* Melica, Ada. "Due opere giovani di Rossini." Item 627.

Il signor Bruschino, ossia Il figlio per azzardo

628. Orselli, Cesare. "Il futuro e il passato del Signor Bruschino." In *Convegno di studi su Rossini per il Centenario della morte di Gioacchino Rossini*, 130–36. See item 283.

Calling for a reevaluation of Rossini's early comedies, Orselli discusses Rossini's *Il signor Bruschino*. The author claims that in this work Rossini demonstrates techniques he learned as a student as well as the innovations of his own developing style. To fully comprehend this work and its characters, Orselli suggests a broader study placing it in the *Ottocento* tradition as well as an exploration of *Bruschino's* criticisms. The author suggests that what has been noted as "Bellinian" in this work stems from the composers' common "Neapolitan" culture.

* Radiciotti, Giuseppe. "Il 'Sig. Bruschino' ed il 'Tancredi' di G. Rossini: leggenda e storia." See item 636.

Tancredi

* Balthazar, Scott L. "Evolving Conventions in Italian Serious Opera: Scene Structure in the Works of Rossini, Bellini, Donizetti, and Verdi, 1810–1850." See item 583.

* ———. "The *Primo Ottocento* Duet and the Transformation of the Rossinian Code." See item 545.

* Biggi, Maria Ida. "Scenografie rossiniane di Giuseppe Borsato." See item 604.

629. Fabbri, Paolo. "Gioachino Rossini uno e due." *Musica/Realtà* 36 (December 1991): 33–54.

Fabbri lauds the enriched Rossini scholarship from 1968 to 1991, mentioning in particular the work of the Fondazione Rossini. He indicates that principal areas of study include biographical documentation, libretto sources (the topic of this article), and Rossini's years in Naples and in Paris after his "retirement." Fabbri looks at the importance of the arrival of the French in Italy during the composer's childhood and the impact this had on his life. He then considers the new dramatic conventions of *Tancredi*, a work that for contemporary critics like Stendhal (item 135) and Carpani (item 483) signaled a new brand of *opera seria*. Fabbri then compares various versions of *Tancredi*, including those of Voltaire, Silvio Balbis, Alessandro Pepoli, Luigi Romanelli, and Gaetano Rossi. After comparing scenes, Fabbri describes their musico-dramatic constructions. (Versions of this work are now available in the edition of the libretto edited by Fabbri [1994] in the Fondazione Rossini's series *I libretti di Rossini*).

* Fauré, Michel. "Opéra historique et problematique sociale en France, du premier au second Empire." See item 313.

* Gossett, Philip. "Gli autografi rossiniani al Museo Teatrale alla Scala di Milano." See item 580.

* ———. "Rossini's *Ritornelli*: A Composer and His Orchestral Soloists." See item 511.

630. ———. "*Tancredi*." In "The Operas of Rossini: Problems of Textual Criticism in Nineteenth-Century Opera." See item 582.

631. ———. "The 'candeur virginale' of *Tancredi*." *The Musical Times* 112 (April 1971): 326–29.

Forming his argument from a quotation from Stendhal extolling the purity and simplicity of *Tancredi*, Gossett demonstrates how, in that work, Rossini introduced the formal conventions and compositional model that would go on to dominate the *primo Ottocento* stage. After briefly considering musical revisions of the opera for various Italian theaters, the author contends that *Tancredi*'s first-act finale, with its alternating kinetic (active or emotional) and static (contemplative) sections, became the archetype for the "mature Rossini finale."

632. ———. "The Tragic Finale of *Tancredi*." *Bollettino del Centro Rossiniano di Studi* [no.1–3] (1976): 5–88; Italian translation follows, 89–164.

Shortly after its premiere in Venice in February of 1813, *Tancredi* was produced in Ferrara with one important revision: the substitution of a tragic ending. Gossett has edited the score of this important find, hitherto known only through its libretto, and presents it in its social and political context. After contrasting Gaetano Rossi's libretto for the original *Tancredi* with its source, Voltaire's *Tancrède*, Gossett demonstrates that the tragic ending written by Luigi Lechi is closer to its French model. The author then traces an intricate web of relationships between the Lechi and the Rossini families, both of whom were involved with liberal efforts during the Napoleonic era. In addition to providing examples from his edition of the score (with abundant critical notes), Gossett also addresses the issues of Rossini's self-borrowings both in the composition of the revision and from the new finale to later works. Includes information on a song composed for the first Tancredi, Adelaide Malanotte-Montrésor, on Rossini's patriotism, and the relationship of the Mozart family to the Lechis. Illustrated with engravings, portraits and score facsimiles.

633. Hadlock, Heather. "*Tancredi* and *Semiramide*." In *The Cambridge Companion to Rossini*, see item 478.

    * Lippmann, Friedrich. " 'Casta diva': la preghiera dell' opera italiana della prima metà dell' Ottocento." Item 553.

634. ———. "Il 'grande finale' nell'opera buffa e nell'opera seria: Paisiello e Rossini." Translated into Italian by Renato Bossa. *Rivista italiana di musicologia* 27 [no. 1–2] (1992): 225–55.

    Examines the first-act finales of *Tancredi* and *L'italiana in Algeri*, signaling the similarities and differences between this dramatic climax as it appears in the *buffa* and *seria* genres. Next, Lippmann traces the development of these musical structures from their eighteenth-century origins. As examples, he analyzes the first-act finales of Giovanni Paisiello's comedy *Frascatana* (1774) and his *seria* works *Sismano nel Mogol* (1773) and *Pirro* (1787).

    * Lühning, Helga. "Die Cavatina in der italienischen Oper um 1800." Item 555.

635. Maeder, Constantino C.M. "Politique et opéra: Représentation de l'étranger dans *Totila* et *Tancredi*." In *L'Europe et son combat pour la liberté a travers le théâtre et l'opéra*, 91–105. Vol. 6 in the series *Théâtre européen, opéra, ballet*, edited by Irene Mamczarc and Algirdas Jonas Ambrazas. Paris: Klincksiek, 1996. 234 pp. ISBN: 2-252-03068-2

    [Not examined.]

636. Radiciotti, Giuseppe. "Il 'Sig. Bruschino' ed il 'Tancredi' di G. Rossini: leggenda e storia." *Rivista musicale italiana* 27 (1920): 231–66.

    This Rossini biographer (see items 163 and 164) demonstrates the anecdotal nature of many early accounts of the composer's life, citing as examples passages from Zanolini (item 138), Azevedo (item 105), and others about *Il signor Bruschino* and *Tancredi*. By citing reviews (and, in his more extensive discussion of *Tancredi*, using musical examples), Radiciotti corrects some of the popular misconceptions. In his appendix, he demonstrates the popularity of *Tancredi* by listing performances from its premiere in 1813 to a production in Paris in 1862. Illustrated with an engraving of Giuditta Pasta as Tancredi.

637. Tortora, Daniela. "Fortuna dei 'Palpiti' rossiniani nella musica strumentale a stampa dell' Ottocento." *Bollettino del Centro Rossiniano di Studi* 28 (1988): 5–25.

Tortora suggests that the widespread fame of *Tancredi* was helped in part by the publication of instrumental versions of its most popular aria, the cabaletta "Di tanti palpiti." Transcibed for a variety of solo instruments and small and large ensembles, these compositions, featuring faithful arrangements and variations, were designed for levels of performers ranging from amateur to virtuoso. After analyzing the original aria and its preceding sections, the author demonstrates how several of the arrangements modified or embellished it. In addition to musical examples, contains a catalog of arrangements, which include those by composers such as Carl Czerny, Ignace Moscheles, and Niccolò Paganini.

L'italiana in Algeri

638. Fabbri, Paolo. "Due Italiane in Algeri: Da Mosca a Rossini." In *Convegno italo-tedesco "Mozart, Paisiello, Rossini e l'opera buffa (Rom 1993),"* 349–86. See item 284.

    Fabbri does a textual and musical comparison of parallel sections in Angelo Anelli's libretto for *L'italiana in Algeri* as set by Luigi Mosca (Milan 1808) and Rossini (Venice 1813). Noting that major changes stem from either the elimination, substitution, or addition of various musical elements, the author analyses several major numbers, constructing tables that demonstrate the two composers' different approaches to or rearrangement of the metrical structure of the text. Also presented in table form is a brief musical analysis of the number's tempi, tonalities, modulations, and movements. Fabbri concludes that even though Mosca's opera is well-designed, Rossini's exhibits characters with greater musical formation, more elaborate harmonic designs, and structures of larger scale designed with an acute sense of form. A transcript of the conference discussion follows the text. With score examples.

    * Gallarati, Paolo. "Dramma e *ludus* dall' *Italiana* al *Barbiere*." See item 591.

    * ———. "Per un interpretazione del comico rossiniano." See item 590.

639. Gossett, Philip. "L'Italiana in Algeri." In "The Operas of Rossini: Problems of Textual Criticism in Nineteenth-Century Opera." See item 582.

    * ———. "Rossini's *Ritornelli*: A Composer and His Orchestral Soloists." See item 511.

    * Grembler, Martina. *Rossini e la patria: Studien zu Leben und Werk Gioachino Rossinis vor dem Hintergrund des Risorgimento*. See item 200.

    * Kunze, Stefan. "Ironie des Klassizismus: Aspekte des Umbruchs in der musikalischen Komodie um 1800." Item 592.

* Lippmann, Friedrich. "Il 'grande finale' nell'opera buffa e nell'opera seria: Paisiello e Rossini." See item 634.

640. Locke, Ralph P. "Cutthroats and Casbah Dancers, Muezzins and Timeless Strands: Musical Images of the Middle East." *19th-Century Music* 22 (Summer 1998): 20–53; also in *The Exotic in Western Music*, edited by Jonathan Bellman, 104–36. Boston: Northeastern University Press, 1998. xiii, 370 pp. ISBN: 1-555-5332-05 ML55.E9 1998.

In his study of musical depictions of Middle East Orientalism, Locke briefly considers *L'italiana in Algeri* in a section entitled "*Alla Turca and Alternatives*: *1800–35*," concluding that while the libretto attempts to represent Muslims, albeit in a stereotypical way, Rossini's score not only avoids exotic local color, but rather underscores the nationality of its Italian characters. (See also Gossett, item 199. For a discussion of exotic elements in this opera, see Thomas Betzwieser, item 534.)

* Mauceri, Marco. " 'Voce, che tenera': Una cabaletta per tutte le stagioni." See item 512.

* Osthoff, Wolfgang. "Die Opera buffa." See item 593.

641. Questa, Cesare. *Il ratto del serraglio*: *Euripide, Plauto, Mozart, Rossini*. Vol. 1 of *Semiologia della narrazione*. Bologna: Pàtron Editore, 1979. 176 pp. ML2100.Q47; new edition with appendix on Iphigenia (with Renato Raffaelli). Vol. 6 in *Letterature e antropologia*. Urbino: Quattro Venti, 1997. 211 pp. ISBN 88-392-0441-5 ML2100.Q47 1997.

Questa first identifies fables from classical literature with themes dealing with a woman, held captive in a foreign land through the power of a dominant male, who longs to rejoin a lover she believes to be dead or missing. Her love, however, appears, and, with the help of others, they escape. Questa suggests that the same fable is the basis of Euripides' *Elena* and *Iphigenia in Taurus*, Plautus' *Miles gloriosus et rudens*, Mozart's *Abduction from the Seraglio* and Rossini's *L'italiana in Algeri*. In his discussion of Rossini's music and Anelli's text, he cites Gossett's mention of the quotation of the Marseillaise in "Pensa alla patria" (see item 199). With musical examples and libretto excerpts.

642. *Rossini, L'italienne a Alger. Avant-scène opéra* 157 (January-February 1994) Paris: Avant-scène, 1994. 143 pp.

Not examined. According to the RILM abstract, this opera guide includes an essay on Rossini biographer Stendhal, on the work's history, on orientalism in the opera, and profiles of the characters. With illustrations, musical examples, a bibliography, and discography and videography.

643. Yeazell, Ruth Bernard. "Harems for Mozart and Rossini." *Raritan* 16 [no. 4] (Spring 1997): 86–105.

The author considers how the libretto of *L'italiana* fits in with Western portrayals of harems and the notion of love.

Aureliano in Palmira

* Balthazar, Scott L. "Evolving Conventions in Italian Serious Opera: Scene Structure in the Works of Rossini, Bellini, Donizetti, and Verdi, 1810–1850." See item 583.

* Henze-Döhring, Sabine. "La 'natura' nelle opere di Rossini." Item 605.

644. Kaufman, Tom. "A Performance History of *Aureliano in Palmira*." *Opera Quarterly* 15 [no. 1] (Winter 1999): 33–37.

A table of performances of *Aureliano* listed by date, venue, and cast. The data extends from the work's premiere at LaScala in 1813 to a production in 1999 at Bad Wildbad.

645. Kern, Bernd-Rüdiger. " 'Hort der Freiheit': *Aureliano in Palmira*—Rossinis Festlabor." *Neue Zeitschrift für Musik* 153 [no. 3] (March 1992): 18–19.

The author contends that the reputation of this early work has suffered because scholars have ignored it. After discussing the genesis of both libretto and score, Kern traces its performance history (see also item 644). He concludes that Rossini deemed the work significant enough to borrow from it; thus, the opera deserves reevaluation. With musical examples. See item 646.

646. Lindner, Thomas. "Rossini's 'Aureliano in Palmira': A Descriptive Analysis." *Opera Quarterly* 15 [no. 1] (Winter 1999): 18–32.

After touching upon the history of Rossini's commission for this work, Lindner reevaluates it and offers an analytic description. Presenting a solution to the enigmatic "G.F.R." as its librettist, Lindner suggests that the initials are a blend of the names Luigi Romanelli and Felice Romani. He also discusses the dramatic impact of Rossini's use of mixed chorus and the development of characters predating those found in operas from the Naples years. Includes a table identifying self-borrowings and another of the opera's musical schema.

* Roccatagliati, Alessandro. "Derivazioni e prescrizioni librettistischi: come Rossini intonò Romani." See item 249.

Il turco in Italia

647. Isotta, Paolo. "Per una lettura di '*Il turco in Italia*.'" *Nuova rivista musicale italiana* 19 [no. 2] (April-June 1985): 227–53.

In contrast to *L'italiana in Algeri*, *Il barbiere*, and *La Cenerentola*, in which the aria is more important, in *Il turco*, the emphasis is on ensembles. Characterization in these structures is achieved by assigning specific musical motives and then allowing the orchestra to take the lead. Isotta discusses ensembles in *Turco*, mentioning Rossini's musical quotation from Haydn's *Seven Last Words of Christ*. Stating that Rossini's ensembles in this opera mix comic with dramatic, Isotta suggests that *Turco* stands apart from the above-mentioned works because it is not all by Rossini (parts have been attributed to Vincenzo Lavigna) and that it is less *farsa* than bourgeois parody. With musical examples.

648. Mila, Massimo. " 'Il Turco in Italia': Manifesto di dolce vita." *Nuova rivista musicale italiana* 2 [no. 5] (Sept.-Oct. 1968): 857–71.

For nearly a century, *Il turco in Italia* was not performed until its triumphant return to the stage in 1950 during the post-war period of "la dolce vita" in Italy. Mila, tracing the history of its criticism as a poor copy of the more popular *L'italiana in Algeri*, demonstrates that twentieth-century commentators, who had often echoed earlier writers such as Stendhal (see item 135), changed their views once they had heard the work. Mila suggests that *Il turco*, while it will never be as popular as *L'italiana* or *Il barbiere di Siviglia*, nevertheless is one of Rossini's most original works, going beyond opera buffa. He discusses in particular the ensembles in the work, praising them for their dramatic development. Finally, Mila proposes links between *Il turco* and the music of Mozart. Includes score examples.

* Roccatagliati, Alessandro. "Derivazioni e prescrizioni librettistischi: come Rossini intonò Romani." See item 249.

649. *Rossini, Le Turc en Italia/Il turco in Italia, dramma buffa per musica. Avant-scène opéra* 169 (January-February 1996) Paris: Premieres Loges, 1996. 143 pp.

[Not examined.] According to the RILM abstract, this opera guide includes information on the work's history, vocal profiles of the roles, a look at Filippo Galli who premiered the role of Selim, and consideration of the work as produced in Brussels and Paris. Illustrated, the guide also includes a discography and videography.

Sigismondo

* Biggi, Maria Ida. "Scenografie rossiniane di Giuseppe Borsato." See item 604.

* Henze-Döhring, Sabine. "La 'natura' nelle opere di Rossini." Item 605.

* Mauceri, Marco. " 'Voce, che tenera': Una cabaletta per tutte le stagioni." See item 512.

Elisabetta, regina d'Inghilterra

* Balthazar, Scott L. "Evolving Conventions in Italian Serious Opera: Scene Structure in the Works of Rossini, Bellini, Donizetti, and Verdi, 1810–1850." See item 583.

* Fauré, Michel. "Opéra historique et problematique sociale en France, du premier au second Empire." See item 313.

650. Lippmann, Friedrich. "Rossini 1815: *Elisabetta, regina d'Inghilterra*." In *Studien zur italienischen Musikgeschichte XV*, Vol. 2. Vol. 30 in *Analecta musicologica*, edited by Friedrich Lippmann. Regensburg: Laaber-Verlag, 1998. ISBN: 3-8900-7398-0.

[Not examined.]

651. Spada, Marco. "*Elisabetta, regina d'Inghilterra* di Gioachino Rossini: fonte letterarie e autoimprestito musicale." *Nuova rivista musicale italiana* 24 [no. 2] (April-June 1990): 147–82.

Spada offers a brief history of *Elisabetta*'s composition history. He then identifies its literary source as Carlo Federici's play *Il paggio di Leicester*, performed in Naples as early as 1813 and gaining widespread popularity after the premiere of Rossini's opera in 1815. The author discusses librettist Giovanni Schmidt's faithful transformation of the dramatic source and includes a comparison of the play's third act with the opera's corresponding point, the first-act finale. Spada then considers Rossini's self-borrowings by including a chart of the pieces in *Elisabetta*, identifying their sources and original tonalities. Self-borrowings include reuse of thematic and rhythmic formulas and cadential phrases, full themes, sections of music with different texts, and music with identical texts. With score examples and facsimiles of title pages of programs and published scores. See also item 652.

652. Spina, Giuseppe. "Stendhal aveva ragione?" *Nuova rivista musicale italiana* 24 [no. 3–4] (July-December 1990): 487–90.

In his biography of Rossini (item 135), Stendhal claimed that the source of *Elisabetta, regina d'Inghilterra* was a French drama. Although many had assumed that the idea came from Walter Scott's novel *Kenilworth*, Marco Spada (item 651) demonstrated that Schmidt took the idea from Federici's play *Il paggio di Leicester*. Spina proposes that Stendhal may have been correct, for the source of Federici's play most likely was the French drama *Les deux pages*.

653. Tortora, Daniela. "La ceremonia interrota: sul Finale del primo dell' *Elisabetta* rossiniana." In *Studien zur italienischen Musikgeschichte XV* (see item 650).

[Not examined.]

Torvaldo e Dorliska

* Bini, Annalisa. " 'Insomma, mio signore, che è lei, si può sapere?': Note biografiche su Cesare Sterbini, poeta romana." See item 255.

654. Carli Ballola, Giovanni. "Una *pièce à sauvetage* da salvare." *Bollettino del Centro Rossiniano di Studi* 11 [no. 1–3] (1971): 11–27.

Torvaldo e Dorliska has been condemned in Rossini literature. Carli Ballola places it in the French tradition from which similar *semiseria* works descended, suggesting that, in that light, Sterbini's libretto does not merit the criticism it has received. Citing traditional Rossini sources such as Rognoni (476) and Roncaglia (165), the author addresses issues such as the use of *recitativo secco* and Rossini's instrumentation, all points of prior criticism. He concludes that it is important to consider this opera in the traditional of contemporary *semiseria* works rather than simply in comparison with other Rossini operas.

* Mauceri, Marco. " 'Voce, che tenera': Una cabaletta per tutte le stagioni." See item 512.

Il barbiere di Siviglia

* Aversano, Luca. "Eine Paërische Quelle für di *Cavatina di Rosina*." See item 227.

* Bini, Annalisa. " 'Insomma, mio signore, che è lei, si può sapere?': Note biografiche su Cesare Sterbini, poeta romana." See item 255.

* Busch, Gudrun. "Die Unwetterszene in der romantischen Oper." See item 536.

* Cametti, Alberto. "*La musica teatrale a Roma cento anni fa.*" In *Annuario della R. Accademia di Santa Cecilia 1915–1916*, 44–97. See item 367.

655. Carnevale, Nadia. " ' . . . that's the barber!': Henry Rowley Bishop e l'adattamento del *Barbiere* rossiniano." In *Ottocento e oltre: scritti in onore di Raoul Meloncelli*, 99–113. Eds. Francesco Izzo and Johannes Streicher. Rome: Pantheon, 1993. ix, 608 pp. ISBN 88-78-001-203-4.

Carnevale addresses Henry Bishop's adaptation, *The Barber of Seville*, presented at London's Covent Garden in 1818, seven months after the premiere of Rossini's original at King's Theatre. The author notes that Bishop's version was more popular than its Italian source, even entertaining New Yorkers in 1819, some six years before they would see the work in Italian. After introducing Bishop and placing him in the theatrical arena of early nineteenth-century London, Carnevale discusses the musical adaptation and its text, a pastiche of Beaumarchais's play and Paisiello's and Rossini's librettos. Of significance is Bishop's development of the role of Fiorello due to the inability of Almaviva's interpreter to sing. Carnevale considers these plot changes and the introduction of other characters they necessitated.

656. Casini, Claudio. "Iterazione, circolarità e metacronica del Barbiere di Siviglia." *Bollettino del Centro Rossiniano di Studi* 14 [no. 2–3] (1974): 37–100.

Casini considers the three *Barbers* in this article: Beaumarchais's original and the operas of Paisiello and Rossini. In tracing the origins of Beaumarchais's comedy, he demonstrates that character types found in the play were derived from those in the French *parades*. Casini then addresses Paisiello's and Rossini's operatic treatments of the original subject. After comparing the numbers in the two musical versions, he considers their tonal, metric, and rhythmic plans. He concludes his study with an analytical examination of the two works. An appendix diagrams the three *Barbers* by act and scene. With ample score excerpts in the analysis section.

657. Christen, Giovanni. "Cicala als Pate von Figaro (und Malatesta)? Über ein kompliziertes librettistisches Beziehungsgeflecht." Translated from Italian into German by Reto Müller. *La Gazzetta* 8 (1998): 16–18.

Antonio Salieri's opera *Angiolina, ossia Il matrimonio sussurro* (1800), based on Jean-Baptiste Rousseau's comedy *L'Hypocondre, ou La Femme qui ne parle point*, borrowed the character of the barber Cigale for the role of Cicala. By presenting the text of Cicala's aria "Più bel mestiere," Christen suggests that Sterbini probably modeled Figaro's "Largo al factotum" on this number.

658. Everist, Mark. "Lindoro in Lyon: Rossini's *Le Barbier de Séville.*" *Acta Musicologica* 64 [no. 1] (Jan.-June 1992): 50–85.

Everist considers François-Henri-Joseph Blaze's (Castil-Blaze) transformation of *Il barbiere di Siviglia* into *Le Barbier de Séville* (1821), a true opéra comique. Everist demonstrates that by opting to use dialogue from Beaumarchais' play rather than translating Cesare Sterbini's libretto, Castil-Blaze was considering not only the reception of the work but also its impact on a French provincial audience in Lyon. In addition to listing the differences between *Il barbiere* and *Le Barbier*, Everist also describes the latter with the aid of score examples. A part of this discussion also deals with the substitution of "Di tanti palpiti" from *Tancredi* for the original "Contro il cor" and Castil-Blaze's setting part of it with text from Étienne Méhul's opéra comique *Bion*. For more on Castil-Blaze, see item 330.

* Franchi, Saverio. "*Il barbiere di Siviglia*: Confronti, suggestioni, linguaggio." See item 222.

* Gallarati, Paolo. "Dramma e *ludus* dall'*Italiana* al *Barbiere.*" See item 591.

* ———. "Per un interpretazione del comico rossiniano." See item 590.

659. Gatti, Guido M. *Le Barbier de Séville de Rossini: Étude historique et critique-Analyse Musicale.* In the series *Les Chefs-D'Oeuvres de la Musique Expliqués*, edited by Paul Landormy. Paris: Mellottée, 1925. 194 pp. MT100 .R6 B22.

This guide to understanding Rossini's *Barbiere* includes a biography of the composer; a history of the opera, an incomplete production history, and a list of operas on the same theme by other composers; the history of the libretto, including information on Petrosellini's libretto for the *Barbiere* by Paisiello and a plot summary of Sterbini's text; and a musical analysis of the opera, illustrated with musical examples.

660. Gautier, Théophile. *Les Souvenirs de Théâtre, d'Art et de Critique.* Paris: G. Charpentier, 1883. 332 pp. PQ2258. S6 1883.

In the section entitled, "Les Beautés de l'Opéra," Gautier includes a brief history of *Le Barbiere de Seville* (pp. 111–28). Noting the popularity of the characters as drawn from Beaumarchais, the author summarizes the action of the opera in dialogue and brief descriptions of the musical numbers. Gautier mentions Paisiello's *Le barbiere* and then concludes that, although

Rossini's work was considered sacrilege at its premiere, it has eclipsed the earlier setting.

* Goldin, Daniela. *La vera Fenice: Librettisti e libretti tra Sette e Ottocento*. See item 577.

661. Gossett, Philip. "Il barbiere di Siviglia." In "The Operas of Rossini: Problems of Textual Criticism in Nineteenth-Century Opera." See item 582.

662. Grier, Albert. "quando . . . cantava Caffariello . . ." Bartolos musikalische Bildung (*Barbiere di Siviglia*, II, 3)." *La Gazzetta* 11 (2001): 22–26.

When Bartolo praises the singing of Caffariello (or Caffarello) during Rosina's voice lesson, he refers to the castrato Gaetano Majorano (1710–1783). Grier calculates that if Bartolo had heard this singer, he would be between seventy-five and eighty, rather old to desire to wed his sixteen-year-old ward. Reference to this singer also appeared in the libretto of the 1791 version of the DaPonte pasticche *L'ape musicale*. Grier also cites a letter from Metastasio to his friend castrato Farinelli in which Caffarello's singing is criticized. The author concludes that the use of Caffarello's name signaled a reference to an older, outmoded style. He also notes, as Philip Gossett has pointed out, that the castrato's name was written into the score in a hand other than Rossini's, which suggests that the composer's intent was to allow singers to substitute whatever name would draw the audience's laughter.

663. John, Nicolas, series ed. *The Barber of Seville–Il Barbiere di Siviglia/Moses–Moïse et Pharaon*. Vol. 36 of *English National Opera Guide* series. London: John Calder and New York: Riverrun Press, 1985. vi, 160 pp. ISBN: 0-7145-4080-3 ML50 .R835.

In addition to an edition of the libretto and a parallel English version of *Il barbiere* by Edward J. Dent, this guide includes essays by Philip Gossett on Rossini's comic and serious works; Rossini's working habits and his theatrical world by John Rosselli (see also items 240, 270, and 337); a musical analysis of the opera by Marco Spada; and a discussion about performing Rossini's music by Ubaldo Gardini. Also contains a guide to musical themes (with musical examples), a bibliography, and a discography. Illustrated.

664. Johnson, Janet. "*Il barbiere di Siviglia*." In *The Cambridge Companion to Rossini*. See item 478.

665. Krones, Hartmut. "1805–1823: Vier Opern—ein Vokabular. Musiksprachliche Bedeutungskonstanten in *Fidelio*, *Il Barbiere di Siviglia*, *Der Freischütz*, und *Fierrabras*." *Österreichische Musikzeitschrift* 44 [no. 7–8] (July-August 1989): 338–45.

The author demonstrates the rhetoric and symbolic links among these four works by calling attention to their composers' similar uses of tonality, harmony, melodic motives, and declamatory text-setting. With musical examples.

* Kunze, Stefan. "Ironie des Klassizismus: Aspekte des Umbruchs in der musikalischen Komodie um 1800." Item 592.

666. Limoncelli, Mattia. *Il barbiere di Siviglia*. Naples: Edizioni Dell'Arte Pianistic, 1937. 50 pp. ML410.R8 L5.

The author comments on the excellence of *Il barbiere*, briefly looking at the subject's development from Beaumarchais' play to Rossini's score. Based on opinion, not scholarship, this brief volume suggests that *Il barbiere* is the greatest of Rossini's works and that not only his career but subsequent opera history would be vastly different had the work not been composed.

* Marinelli, Carlo, gen. ed. *Progetto Rossini*, Vol. 3—*Almaviva, o sia, L'inutile precauzione: Il barbiere di Siviglia*. See item 851.

667. Ormay, Imre. *Skandal in der Oper: Vier denkwürdige Premieren: "Fidelio"*, *"Der Barbier von Sevilla," "Tannhäuser", und "Tosca."* Originally published as *Botrány az operában*, by István Frommer and Imre Ormay, Budapest: Zrínyi, 1967. Leipzig: Veb Deutscher Verlag für Musik, 1967. 190 pp.

An account, narrated with dialogue, of the calamitous opening night of Rossini's *Il barbiere* in Rome, 1816. Illustrated.

* Osthoff, Wolfgang. "Die Opera buffa." See item 593.

668. Pahlen, Kurt, ed. *Gioacchino Rossini: Der Barber von Sevilla*. In series *Opern der Welt*. Munich: Wilhelm Goldmann, 1985. 303 pp. ISBN 3-442-33113-7 ML50 .R835 B24 1985.

The Italian libretto with a parallel German translation. Also includes biographical information on Rossini, a history of the opera, an essay on Manuel García, an essay on Beaumarchais and Cesare Sterbini (by Rosemarie König) and a discography through 1982 (by Albert Thalmann).

669. Piontek, Steffan. " 'Strahlt auf mich der Glanz des Goldes'—oder: Der glückliche Ausgang einer missglückten Entführung. Gedanken zu Rossinis *Barbier von Sevilla*." In *Opern und Opernfiguren: Festschrift für Joachim Herz*, edited by Ursula and Ulrich Müller. Vol. 2 in the series *Wort und Musik*, 427–32. Salzburg: Müller-Speiser, 1989. xi, 450 pp.

The author examines the development of comic characters in Rossini and Sterbini's *Il barbiere*, suggesting that it is closer to Beaumarchais' original idea than is Paisiello and Petrosellini's opera. Piontek also proposes that Rossini and Sterbini created characters which were representative of contemporary society.

670. Poriss, Hilary. "Bartolo's Naps and Rosina's Reactions: The Lesson Scene of *Il barbiere di Siviglia*." In "Artistic License: Aria Interpolation and the Italian Opera World, 1815–1850," 46–95. Ph.D. dissertation, University of Chicago, 2000. xvii, 324 pp.

Poriss explores the practice of aria interpolation in operatic productions of the *primo Ottocento*. In this chapter, she considers the Singing Lesson scene, long famous for its aria substitution, as both the exception and the rule of this common performance custom.

671. Radiciotti, Giuseppe. *G. Rossini: Il barbiere di Siviglia; guida attraverso la commedia e la musica*. Milan: Bottega di poesia, 1923. 170 pp. MT100.R6 B2.

Before his musical analysis of the score, Radiciotti offers a brief biography of the composer, some notes on Rossini's *buffa* works, the history of the opera's premiere, and a look at its reception in Italy and France. He concludes this guide with comments on the work's continued appeal.

* Rinaldi, Mario. "Una ouverture per *Il barbiere di Siviglia*." In *Atti del convegno di studi: Rossini, edizioni critiche e prassi esecutiva*, 85–104. See item 282. See also items 556 and 557.

672. Robinson, Paul A. *Opera & Ideas From Mozart to Strauss*. Ithaca, N.Y.: Cornell University Press, 1985. 279 pp. ISBN 0-8014-9428-1 ML1720 .R6 1986.

Robinson compares and contrasts Mozart and Rossini and their treatments of Figaro in "Enlightenment and Reaction: Wolfgang Amadeus Mozart's *The Marriage of Figaro* and Gioachino Rossini's *The Barber of Seville*" (pp. 8–57). After pointing out that both works share a literary heritage and certain musical characteristics, the author contends that Mozart's music is more round and complex while Rossini's is angular and mechanical. To demonstrate, Robinson contrasts scenes and character representations. Based on his thesis that operas reflect the intellectual climate of their times, he concludes that Mozart's work, a product of the Enlightenment, is intellectually and compositionally richer; Rossini's opera, relentlessly comic, he says, represents a narrower segment of culture.

673. Rosing, Helmut. "Fast wie ein Unwetter: Zur Rezeption von Pastoral–und Alpensinfonie-Gewitter. Über verschiedene Darstellunsebenen der musikalischen Informationsübermittlung." *In Über Symphonien: Beit. zu e. musikal. Gattung: Festschrift Walter Wiora zum 70. Geburtstag,* edited by Christoph-Hellmut Mahling, 65–89. Tutzing: Schneider, 1979. ix, 198 pp. ML1255.U3.

The author polled seventy-four listeners' reactions to musical compositions depicting storm music, among them Rossini's *Il barbiere.* Gauging results by using a list of twenty-nine adjectival antonyms, Rosing charted the responses in terms of musical form, tone color, and rhythmic energy. See also item 536 for another study of storm music.

* Scherliess, Volker. "*Il Barbiere di Siviglia:* Paisiello und Rossini." Item 231.

* Tartak, Marvin H. *The Italian Comic Operas of Rossini.* See item 596.

674. Tartak, Marvin. "The Two 'Barbieri.' " *Music and Letters* (October 1969): 453–69.

Beginning with a brief review of the background of Beaumarchais' *Le Barbier de Séville* (including a discussion of the interpolation of incidental music into its plot), Tartak goes on to an act-by-act comparison and contrast of Paisiello's *Il barbiere di Siviglia* (1782) with Rossini's 1816 setting. Finding frequent comedic weaknesses in Paisiello's libretto (attributed without question to Giuseppe Petrosellini), the author demonstrates how Rossini's librettist, Cesare Sterbini, was often more in harmony with Beaumarchais's original. However, although Paisiello's version has fared poorly against Rossini's, the author defends it as a perfect musical product of its time and illustrates how Rossini and Sterbini relied on it, even borrowing textual and musical elements. For other comparisons between Paisiello and Rossini, see item 231.

* Thompson, Donald. "Nineteenth-Century Musical Life in Puerto Rico." See item 378.

* Torrefranca, Fausto. "Strumentalità della commedia musicale: *Buona figliuola, Barbiere,* e *Falstaff.*" See item 597.

675. Zeman, Herbert. "Treue Liebe wahrt die Seele sorgend in verschwig'ner Brust: Zur Libretto-Gestaltung der deutschen Oper im frühen 19. Jahrhundert (Beethoven, Rossini, Weber und Schubert)." *Österreichische Musikzeitschrift* 44 [no. 7–8] (July-August 1989): 357–67.

Although one must question why the author lists *Il barbiere* as a "German" opera, he suggests that it shares the theme of true love with works of the contemporary German stage. In addition, all feature characters are intriguing young people who challenge more powerful elders.

La gazzetta

676. Mauceri, Marco. "*La Gazzetta* di Gioachino Rossini: fonti del libretto e autoimprestito musicale." In *Ottocento e oltre: Scritti in onore di Raoul Meloncelli*, 115–49. See item 655.

The author begins by placing Rossini in the Neapolitan theatrical arena and describing the role of the Teatro dei Fiorentini in the city's musical life. Mauceri then considers the libretto's source, demonstrating, with parallel passages, that its author, Giuseppe Palomba, borrowed characters and text from Gaetano Rossi's *Avviso al pubblico*. Rossini's musical self-borrowings are also addressed with score examples. The essay concludes with a table listing the position and tonality of each number in the opera, identifying it either as original to *La gazzetta* or by its source work, original tonality, and type of self-borrowing (repetition of an entire number, of a section, or of a theme). Illustrated with a caricature of the composer.

* ———. " 'Voce, che tenera': Una cabaletta per tutte le stagioni." See item 512.

Otello ossia Il moro di Venezia

677. Aldrich-Moodie, James. "False Fidelity: *Othello*, *Otello*, And Their Critics." *Comparative Drama* 28 [no. 3] (Fall 1994): 324–47.

The author proposes that criticism of Rossini's *Otello* and praise for Verdi's stem from the acceptance of the post-Enlightenment concept of a Shakespearean "work" and the crusade for textual authenticity. The veneration of Shakespeare, commonplace by the time of Verdi's composition, was just emerging when Rossini set his opera. In addition, citing recent scholarship on Elizabethan dramatic processes, Aldrich-Moodie suggests that Verdi's insistence on fidelity to the dramatic personae in *Othello* in no way follows the playwright's approach to characterization, in essence making Rossini's more practical creative process truer to the original. Also includes a discussion of parallels between Othello's concerns about Desdemona's fidelity and the critics' obsession with the composers' fidelity to a Shakespearean "text" as well as the gendered language used in critical rhetoric. See items 684 and 687 for commentary on Shakespeare's *Othello* and Rossini's opera.

678. ———. "Toward a Society of Opera and Literature: Three cases." Ph.D. dissertation, Stanford University, 1998. 198 pp.

[Not examined.] According to the author's abstract, the second chapter in this study deals with difference between Rossini's and Verdi's *Otello* settings. See also Aldrich-Moodie, item 677.

* Balthazar, Scott L. "Evolving Conventions in Italian Serious Opera: Scene Structure in the Works of Rossini, Bellini, Donizetti, and Verdi, 1810–1850." See item 583.

* Busch, Gudrun. "Die Unwetterszene in der romantischen Oper." See item 536.

679. Cametti, Alberto. *"La musica teatrale a Roma cento anni fa*: "Otello." In *Annuario della R. Accademia di Santa Cecilia 1919–1920*, 46–67. Rome: Tipografica A. Manuzio, 1920. MT5 .R6 A35 1920. See item 367 for a description of the series.

* Dahlhaus, Carl. "Zür Methode der Opern-Analyse." See item 551.

680. Gossett, Philip. "Otello." Chapter in "The Operas of Rossini: Problems of Textual Criticism in Nineteenth-Century Opera." See item 582.

* ———. "Rossini's *Ritornelli*: A Composer and His Orchestral Soloists." See item 511.

681. Grondona, Marco. *Otello, una tragedia napoletana*: *Commento a Rossini*. Vol. 1 of *Musica rappresentata*. Lucca: Libreria Musicale Italiana, 1997. 146 pp. ISBN 88-7096-203-2 ML410R8. G75 1997.

A guide to the opera, Grondona's chapters deal with its history and sources, musical analysis by act, and the opera's revised "happy" ending. Grondona's work includes all recent literature on *Otello* (see Marvin, item 684, and Questa and Raffaelli, 687). With musical excerpts.

682. ———, and Guido Paduano, eds. *I quattro volti di Otello*: *William Shakespeare, Arrigo Boito, Francesco Berio di Salsa, Jean-François Ducis*. Milan: Biblioteca Universale Rizzoli, 1996. 397 pp. ISBN 88-1717-058-5. PR 2829.

In addition to Paduano's new comparative translation of Shakespeare's *Othello*, the volume includes the French text of Ducis' adaptation from which Rossini's opera was drawn (see Marvin, item 684, and Questa and Raffaelli, item 687), Berio's libretto, and Boito's libretto for Verdi. With the editors' commentary.

683. Klein, John W. "Verdi's *Otello* and Rossini's." *Music and Letters* 45 (1964): 130–40.

In a comparison of each composer's *Otello*, Klein tips the scales heavily in favor of Verdi's work, accusing Rossini and his librettist, Francesco Berio di Salsa, of "completely ignoring Shakespeare" and indeed treating the subject with "bored nonchalance." As support, he cites the criticisms of Stendhal and Verdi's librettist, Arrigo Boito, both of whom demeaned Rossini's work. More recent research, however, has identified the real sources of Rossini's libretto as the treatments of *Othello* by dramatists Jean-François Ducis and Giovanni Carlo Cosenza (see items 684 and 687).

* Liebscher, Julia. "Introduktion und Exposition in der Oper: Eine musik-dramatugische Untersuchung am Beispiel des *Otello* (1816) von Gioacchino Rossini." See item 552.

684. Marvin, Roberta Montemorra. "Il libretto di Berio per l'*Otello* di Rossini. *Bollettino del Centro Rossiniano di Studi* 31 (1991): 53–76. Published in English under the title "Shakespeare and *Primo Ottocento* Italian Opera: The Case of Rossini's *Otello*" in *The Opera and Shakespeare*, 71–95. Eds. Holger Klein and Christopher Smith. *The Shakespeare Yearbook*, Vol. 4. Lewiston, N.Y.: The Edwin Mellon Press, 1994. 378 pp. ISBN 0-7734-9016-7 PR2885. S647 Vol. 4.

Rossini's librettist Francesco Berio di Salsa has long been criticized for his rendering of Shakespeare's *Othello* (see Stendhal, item 135, and item 683, for example). Marvin demonstrates, however, that Berio based his work not on Shakespeare but on two particular contemporary adaptations, those of Jean-François Ducis and Giovanni Carlo Cosenza and demonstrates specific points of these borrowings. Includes tables listing the French and Italian translations of *Othello* available before 1816 and compares the dramatic personae and the finale structures in the *Othello*s of Shakespeare, Berio, Ducis, and Cosenza. See also 687.

685. Müller, Reto. "Glückliche Desdemona. Zu Rossinis Lieto-fine-Fassung von *Otello*." *La Gazzetta* 8 (1998): 4–8.

Citing prior research on this work, (see items 684 and 687), the author considers the happy ending Rossini added to *Otello* for the Roman production. Müller discusses several of the musical numbers, suggesting that Rossini's choice of music actually is consistent with the overall integrity of the original score.

686. Petrobelli, Pierluigi. "On Dante and Italian music: Three moments." *Cambridge Opera Journal* 2 [no. 3] (November 1990): 219–49.

In the second of three slightly altered versions of lectures delivered in 1988 at the University of California, Berkeley, Petrobelli cites Rossini's *Otello* as a nineteenth-century example of quotation from the Divine Comedy. Just before Desdemona's "Willow Song," the gondolier off-stage sings lines from the fifth canto of the *Inferno*. The author demonstrates that this style of gondolier song was a Venetian tradition; however, the usual text came from Tasso rather than Dante ("Tasso cantà alla barbariola"). Librettist Francesco Berio di Salsa quoted Dante, however, since the lines best reflected Desdemona's sorrow. Petrobelli concludes that since Verdi knew Rossini's *Otello*, it can hardly be coincidence that, in his own setting, the former alludes to Dante as well, making his *Ave Maria volgarizzata da Dante* in Desdemona's *Ave Maria* and placing it after the "Willow Song."

687. Questa, Cesare, and Renato Raffaelli. "I due finali di *Otello*." *Il testo e la scena* (item 286), 183–203.

Francesco Berio di Salsa's sources for the libretto for *Otello* have been identified as adaptations of Shakespeare by playwrights Jean-François Ducis and Giovanni Carlo Cosenza (see item 684). After discussing the contemporary cultural aesthetics, Questa and Raffaelli explain the tradition behind giving *Othello* a happy ending, such as the *lieto fine* substituted by Rossini for the 1820 revival of his opera in Rome. In addition, the authors also attempt to clarify issues about the independence and borrowings among Berio, Ducis, and Cosenza.

688. Rozett, Martha Tuck. "*Othello, Otello*, and the Comic Tradition." *Bulletin of Research in the Humanities* 85 [no. 4] (1982): 386–411.

The author demonstrates that Shakespeare used comic elements in *Othello* to anticipate and heighten its tragedy. She traces Jago's origins to the "trickster" of Roman comedy and Vice in Morality plays and links aspects of Othello's character to the braggart soldier and the comic dupe; the line between comedy and tragedy, she explains, is that in the former, order is restored while in the latter, evil (as personified in a Jago-like character) is allowed to run wild. Before a discussion of Verdi's opera, Rozett comments on Rossini's, suggesting that the earlier *Otello* is less a tragedy of character than a plot dependent on timing, one of the elements of comedy. Unaware of Rossini's true source play and his opera's tragic and comic endings (see items 684 and 687), her comment that the Rossini/Berio *Otello* could easily have had a happy ending unwittingly provides a defense for their much-maligned version (see, for example, Klein, item 683).

689. Schmidgall, Gary. "The Other *Otello*." In *Shakespeare and Opera*, 306–12. New York: Oxford University Press, 1990. xxii, 394 pp. ISBN: 0-19-506450-X ML3858.S373 1990.

Schmidgall discusses the plot and character development in Rossini's opera, with the assumption that Berio's libretto was based on Shakespeare's play (for information on the real source, see items 684 and 687). To that end, he cites contemporary and scholarly criticism of the work. Also includes descriptions of various numbers in relationship to dramatic elements in the plot.

690. Tammaro, Ferruccio. "Ambivalenza dell'*Otello* rossiniano." In *Il melo-dramma italiano dell'Ottocento: Studi e ricerche per Massimo Mila*, 187–235. No. 575 in the series *Saggi*. ed. Giorgio Pestelli. Turin: Einaudi, 1977. xv, 653 pp. ML 1733.4.M5.

Suggests that *Otello* is a work of Italian *Sturm und Drang*, which served to prepare Rossini for French opera. Although the author suggests that Francesco Berio di Salsa knew of Jean-François Ducis's French adaption of Shakespeare (see items 684 and 687), Tammaro, as he examines the opera's action, still faults Berio for weaknesses in the libretto. Briefly mentions some of the interpolations made for various productions. Tammaro states that while Rossini and Donizetti brought an end to the *buffa* tradition, they also opened the era of Romantic drama on the Italian stage.

La Cenerentola, ossia La bontà in trionfo

691. Alier, Roger. *La Cenerentola*. No. 4 in the series *Introducción a la Ópera*. Barcelona: Ma Non Troppo, 2001. 158 pp. ISBN 8-4956-0227-6 ML50.R835 C32 2001 Case.

A basic guide to the opera, containing commentary on Rossini's life and career, a history of the work, and the author's Spanish translation of the libretto. Illustrated.

* Bini, Annalisa. " 'Altro è l'Arcadia, altro è poi Valle': *Jacopo*, un *diver-tissement* letterario di Jacopo Ferretti a proposito di *Cenerentola*." See item 246.

692. Cametti, Alberto. "*La musica teatrale a Roma cento anni fa*: 'La Ceneren-tola.' " In *Annuario della R. Accademia di Santa Cecilia* 1916–1917, 43–67. Rome: Tipografica A. Manuzio, 1917 MT5.R6 A35 1917. See item 367 for a description of the series.

* Ferretti, Jacopo. "Alcune pagine della mia vita: Delle vicende della poesia melodrammatica in Roma. Memoria seconda." See item 248.

* Gallarati, Paolo. "Per un interpretazione del comico rossiniano." See item 590.

693. Gossett, Philip. "*La Cenerentola*." In "The Operas of Rossini: Problems of Textual Criticism in Nineteenth-Century Opera." See item 582.

694. Graziano, John, ed. *Italian Opera in English: Cinderella (1831)*. Vol. 3 in the series *Nineteenth-Century American Musical Theater*. New York: Garland Publishing, 1994. xlvii, 330 pp. ISBN 0-8153-1327-1 M1503.R835 C5 1994.

An edition of and commentary on Michael Rophino Lacy's adaptation of *Cenerentola*, which premiered in London in 1830 and then at New York's Park Theatre the following year. In his introduction, Graziano gives a history of the work, demonstrating with score examples that it is a pastiche of numbers from *Cenerentola*, *Armida*, *Guillaume Tell* and *Maometto II*. Includes the libretto from Lacy's Covent Garden production and the score from the first New York edition of the music, as well as the scores of several cotillion dances based on *Cinderella* music.

695. Gui, Vittorio. "[Su *La Cenerentola*]. *Bollettino del Centro Rossiniano di Studi* [no. 1–3] (1985): 26–28. Title by editor Marco Spada (see item 619).

In 1964, Gui, a conductor active during the "Rossini Renaissance," expressed his opinions on the supremacy of *Cenerentola* among the composer's comic masterpieces. An interesting look at the muses of a man who helped to reintroduce Rossini to modern audiences. See also items 616 and 618.

696. Henze-Döhring, Sabine. "*La Cenerentola*: Rossini und das phantastische Genre." In *Convegno italo-tedesco "Mozart, Paisiello, Rossini e l'opera buffa (Rom 1993)*," 319–47. See item 284.

The author begins by citing librettist Jacopo Ferretti's comment that, because of the sensibilities of the Roman audience, the fairy tale elements of other versions of the story were not included. Henze-Döhring, however, suggests that such elements did influence both the poet and the composer, concluding that, in *Cenerentola*, Rossini's ingenious treatment created a character unlike any other known in *buffa* works. By musically transforming the melancholy of "Una volta c'era un Re" into the joyous coloratura of Cenerentola's final rondo, Rossini demonstrates the utopian moral of fairy tales, which states that love and virtue can be victorious. With score examples. The essay is followed by a transcription of the conference discussion. See also Philip Gossett's essay in item 697.

697. John, Nicolas, series ed. *La Cenerentola (Cinderella)*. Vol. 1 of *English National Opera Guide* series. London: John Calder and New York: Riverrun Press, 1980. vi, 96 pp. ISBN: 0-7145-3818-1 ML50 .R835.

In addition to an edition of the libretto and a parallel English translation by Arthur Jacobs, this guide includes essays on the opera's fairy-tale origin and *buffa* genre by Philip Gossett, a musical commentary by Jacobs, and transcriptions of conversations with Mark Elder (ENO Music Director) and Colin Graham (ENO Director of Productions) on "Cinderella" in performance. The guide also contains a guide to musical themes (with score examples), a bibliography, and a discography. Illustrated.

698. Mauceri, Marco. "F.F. Padre ignoto dell'*Agatina* di Pavesi." *Bollettino del Centro Rossiniano di Studi* [no. 1–3] (1980): 65–76.

Mauceri suggests that the libretto for Pavesi's opera *Agatina o la virtù premiata*, a source for *Cenerentola*, thought to be the product of Felice Romani, was actually written by tenor Francesco Fiorini, whose theatrical activities include libretto writing. The author cites relevant correspondence as evidence.

699. Rogers, Stuart W. "*Cenerentola* a Londra." *Bollettino del Centro Rossiniano di Studi* 37 (1997): 51–67.

Rogers traces the history of *Cinderella, or The Fairy Queen and the Glass Slipper*, an 1830 London adaption of *Cenerentola*, presented first at Covent Garden and later in America. The author demonstrators how the adapter, Michael Rophino Lacy, revamped Rossini's opera for British audiences by returning it to the fairy tale version with which they were familiar (for example, the fairy godmother and the glass slipper are restored to the plot); in addition, because of British tastes, the original opera was shortened and much of its musical material was replaced by spoken dialogue. Finally, to better utilize the theatrical resources at his disposal, Lacy also inserted into *Cinderella* music adapted from *Armida, Guillaume Tell*, and *Maometto II*. Rogers's study offers a look at British stage practices in the 1830s. Includes a table that not only lists the musical numbers in *Cinderella* but also locates their position in the source operas. See also item 694 on Lacy.

700. *Rossini, La Cenerentola. Avant-scène opéra* 85 (March 1986) Paris: Avant-scène, 1986. 129 pp.

[Not examined.] Based on the RILM abstract, this opera guide contains the libretto with French translation and musical and literary commentary by Alberto Zedda. It also includes articles on the history of the opera and a performance chronology. With musical examples, bibliography and discography.

* Tartak, Marvin H. *The Italian Comic Operas of Rossini*. See item 596.

* Zedda, Alberto. "Problemi testuali della *Cenerentola*." See item 872.

La gazza ladra

* Brauner, Charles S. " 'No, No, Ninetta': Observations on Rossini and the Eighteenth-Century Vocabulary of Opera Buffa." See item 331.

701. Celletti, Rodolfo. "La vocalità rossiniana e *La Gazza ladra*." *Bollettino del Centro Rossiniano di Studi* 13 [no. 2] (1973): 5–21.

Celletti begins by presenting the terminology needed to discuss Rossini's writing style; the syllabic style, which is normally set in the middle of the vocal range, and the vocalized style, embellished lines that take the voice to the extremes of its range. The author demonstrates that composers had already begun to write ornamented vocal lines by the time Rossini began his operatic career. Celletti then describes the development of Rossini's vocal writing in the operas through *Semiramide*, mentioning specific roles and the singers for which they were composed. The author also describes the problems in *La gazza ladra* for modern singers, more familiar with performing Verdi and Puccini. See also item 562.

702. Gossett, Philip. "*La Gazza ladra*." In "The Operas of Rossini: Problems of Textual Criticism in Nineteenth-Century Opera." See item 582.

703. ———. "*La Gazza ladra*: Notes towards a Critical Edition." *Bollettino del Centro Rossiniano di Studi* 12 [no. 1] (1972): 12–29; Italian translation by Raffaello Delfino, 31–44.

Gossett first discusses the complexities involved in preparing a critical edition. He then meticulously describes the autograph, manuscript, and printed sources of *La gazza ladra* he has studied. Areas addressed include textual problems pertaining to the original versions and revisions for Pesaro in 1818 and Naples in 1819. Noting that Rossini's changes mainly affected the role of Ferdinando, Gossett underscores the importance of considering these source materials and suggests that they be made available for modern performance in a critical edition. (See items 857 and 859, the editorial norms for the Rossini Critical Edition).

704. *Rossini, La pie voleuse. Avant-scène opéra* 110 (June 1988) Paris: Avant-scène, 1988. 115 pp.

Not examined. Based on RILM abstract, this opera guide, edited by Alain Duault, contains the original libretto with French translation and articles dealing with the work's genesis and production history. With illustrations, music examples, a bibliography, and discography.

705. Sala, Emilio. "Alla ricerca della *Pie voleuse*." In *Il testo e la scena* (see item 286), 205–53. An English translation of this article by William Ashbrook appears under the title "On the Track of 'La pie voleuse' " in *The Opera Quarterly* 13 [no. 3] (Spring 1997): 19–40.

Sala studies the source of *La gazza ladra*, a Parisian *mélodrame historique* entitled *La pie voleuse ou La servante de Palaiseau* (1815). The author concentrates on the importance of the incidental music, likening its dramatic role to that of film music. In fact, he argues, the *mélos* were operas without singing; their musical insertions were so important a component of the drama that such plays were easily adaptable into Italian melodramas. Sala relates the music of *La pie voleuse* to the musical structure of Rossini's opera. Includes excerpts from the script that demonstrate musical rubrics. Illustrated with facsimiles of the "libretto" of *La pie voleuse*, a cover of its score (music by Alexandre Piccini), the cover of its piano reduction, and part of the orchestral score.

Armida

* Balthazar, Scott L. "Evolving Conventions in Italian Serious Opera: Scene Structure in the Works of Rossini, Bellini, Donizetti, and Verdi, 1810–1850." See item 583.

706. Gier, Albert. " 'Ecco l'ancilla tua . . . ' Armida in der Oper zwischen Gluck und Rossini (mit einem Seitenblick auf Antonin Dvorak." In *Torquato Tasso in Deutschland: Seine Wirkung in Literatur, Kunst und Musik seit der Mitte des 18 Jahrhunderts*, edited by Achim Aurnhammer, 643–60. Vol. 3 in the series *Quellen und Forschungen zur Literaturund Kulturgeschichte*. Berlin and New York: Walter de Gruyter, 1995. ix, 742 pp. ISBN: 3-1101-4546-4.

[Not examined.]

707. Gossett, Philip. "Armida." In "The Operas of Rossini: Problems of Textual Criticism in Nineteenth-Century Opera." See item 582.

708. Henze-Döhring, Sabine. "Che ci dice la 'solita forma'?: Un'analisi drammaturgicomusicale dell'aria finale di *Armida*." In *Il testo e la scena* (item 286), 297–306. Translated from German to Italian by Nicoletta Negri.

The author challenges Harold S. Powers's attempt (item 425) to apply fixed ideas, such as the "solita forma," to all works equally, rather than examining each composition in its own right. Using the aria finale of *Armida*, Henze-Döhring suggests that it is an irregular form that Rossini had used previously in *Otello* and *La Cenerentola*. The analysis demonstrates that *Armida*'s final aria cannot be divided into two closed numbers. The author suggests that such pieces belie the notion that composers simply inserted ready forms and that individual analyses offer better perspectives on the history and aesthetics of Rossini's works. Illustrated with two pages of facsimile.

709. Lentzen, Manfred. "Tassos Armida-Stoff im italienischen Opernlibretto des 18. Jahrhunderts." In *Opernheld und Opernheldin im 18. Jahrhundert: Aspekte der Librettoforschung—Ein Tagungsbericht*, 21–33. Hamburg: Wagner, 1991. 264 pp. ISBN: 3-8897-9052-4 ML3858.O6 1991.

Traces various settings of the Armida story, demonstrating hints of early Romanticism in the Rossini/Schmidt version.

710. Tozzi, Lorenzo. "*Armida* ou la couleur fantastique." *Bollettino del Centro Rossiniano di Studi* [no. 3] (1975): 27–56.

After briefly addressing the reception history of *Armida* in Europe, Tozzi considers the Metastasian literary tradition to which the story belonged and the fantastic element therein. Calling this work the most "French" of Rossini's Italian operas, Tozzi offers a musical analysis of the work and concludes that in this score, the composer achieved a balance between the lyrical and the fantastic. Furthermore, he writes, the work must be examined as an important step in Rossini's theatrical development. Tozzi's analysis features ample score examples. For other discussions on Rossini and the "fantastic," see items 696 and 697.

Adelaide di Borgogna

711. Cametti, Alberto. "*La musica teatrale a Roma cento anni fa*: "Adelaide di Borgogna." In *Annuario della R. Accademia di Santa Cecilia 1917–1918*, 59–89. Rome: n.p., 1918 MT5.R6A35 1918. See item 367 for a description of the series.

* Mauceri, Marco. " 'Voce, che tenera': Una cabaletta per tutte le stagioni." See item 512.

Mosè in Egitto

* Balthazar, Scott L. "Evolving Conventions in Italian Serious Opera: Scene Structure in the Works of Rossini, Bellini, Donizetti, and Verdi, 1810–1850." See item 583.

712. Bonaccorsi, Alfredo. "Una 'Via Crucis' e una 'Bonamorte' rossiniane." *La rassegna musicale* 24 [no. 3] (July-September 1954): 270–72; also in the *Bollettino del Centro Rossiniano di Studi* 8 [no. 4–6] (1968): 74–75.

The author demonstrates, with musical examples, the similarities between two melodies used in religious rites, a "Via Crucis" from the province of Lucca and the so-called Bonamorte from Florence, with the Preghiera from *Mosè*. He concludes that while Rossini may well have heard either or both of these, the melody may just as well have been borrowed from the opera based on its popularity.

713. Brzoska, Matthias. "Mosè und Massimilla: Rossinis *Mosè in Egitto* und Balzacs politische Deutung." In *Oper als Text: Romanistische Beitrage zur Libretto-Forschung*, edited by Albert Gier, 125–45. Heidelberg: Carl Winter, 1986. 318 pp. ISBN 3-53-303729-0 ML2110.O64 1986.

In the work *Massimilla Doni*, Honoré Balzac incorporates Rossini's *Mosè* rather than its French version *Moïse et Pharaon*, which could not be interpreted as politically. Balzac's view of the work corresponded to that of Giuseppe Mazzini (item 487). Brzoska examines the philosophy behind the interpretations of both writers. For further discussion of Balzac's use of *Mosè*, see Glascow, item 715.

* Cheskin, Jonathan L. "Catholic-Liberal Opera: Outline of a Hidden Italian Musical Romanticism." See item 197.

714. Conati, Marcello. "Between Past and Future: The Dramatic World of Rossini in *Mosè in Egitto* and *Moïse et Pharaon*." *19th Century Music*, 4 [no. 1] (Summer 1980): 32–47.

Conati contrasts the dramatic conceptions between *Mosè* (Naples, 1818) and its vaster French revision, *Moïse* (Paris, 1827), defending the former against the traditionally held view that the latter version is superior. In fact, he maintains, changes in plot and structure made for Paris not only weakened its characters (save for Moses and Anaï) but, more important, destroyed what he views as the perfect musico-dramatic balance between *opera seria* and oratorio in the original. The author concludes that *Mosè* is not only a milestone in Rossini's dramatic career but in the history of musical drama; it is a transition between eighteenth-century *opera seria* and nineteenth-century *melodramma*. Contains musical examples, a facsimile of the opening of the *Scena delle Tenebre* from *Mosè*, and a quotation about dramatic music by Rossini (cited from Zanolini; see item 138).

715. Glascow, E. Thomas. "Rossini's *Mosè* According to Balzac: Excerpts from *Massimilla Doni*." *The Opera Quarterly* 9 [no. 4] (Summer 1993): 23–41.

The author briefly discusses Honoré de Balzac's novella and presents in translation the passage in which the character of the duchess painstakingly

describes *Mosè* to a visiting French physician during a fictional performance at La Fenice. Since Balzac's character describes the original three-
act score from Naples (1819), Glascow provides a table comparing this
version with the more commonly known four-act one generally performed
today. Glascow's notes clarify historical inaccuracies in Balzac's text. Illustrations include photos of Rossini from c. 1850 and c. 1860. See also
Brzoska, item 713.

716. Gossett, Philip. "*Mosè*; *Moïse*." In "The Operas of Rossini: Problems of
     Textual Criticism in Nineteenth-Century Opera." See item 582.

717. Isotta, Paolo. "Da *Mosè* a *Moïse*." *Bollettino del Centro Rossiniano di Studi*
     11 [no. 1–3] (1971): 87–117.

     Traditionally, *Mosè in Egitto* has received less consideration than *Moïse et
     Pharaon*. Isotta proposes a study of both works (or, as he prefers, two ver-
     sions of the same opera) beyond a simple comparison of numbers. Briefly
     tracing the history of *Mosè* from its oratorio origins in Naples to its trans-
     formation into melodrama in France and *melodramma sacro* in its final Ital-
     ian version, Isotta considers librettist Andrea Leone Tottola's literary
     source, *L'Osiride*, from which the plot's love interest derives. After placing
     Mosè among Rossini's dramatic works, Isotta states that it is critical in the
     genesis of the composer's psychological problems. In changing the work,
     Rossini tipped the scales away from a musical to a dramatic structure; with
     examples, Isotta proposes a reevaluation of the judgment that *Mosè* is less
     significant than *Moïse*.

     * ———, ed. *Gioacchino Rossini. Mosè in Egitto, Moïse et Pharaon, Mosè*.
     Item 854.

     * Lippmann, Friedrich. " 'Casta diva': la preghiera dell'opera italiana della
     prima metà dell'Ottocento." Item 553.

     * ———. "Mozart und die italienischen Komponisten des 19. Jahrhun-
     derts." See item 531.

718. Piperno, Franco. " 'Effetto Mosè': Fortuna e recezione dell *Mosè in Egitto* a
     Napoli e in Italia (1818–1830). In *La recezione di Rossini ieri e oggi* (item
     288), 165–94.

     Mosè was one of the most significant productions of the Barbaja-Rossini
     years in Naples. It reestablished the tradition of Lenten operas with Biblical
     themes popular during the *ancien regime* of the Bourbons. The author
     examines the effect that *Mosè* had on subsequent seasons in Naples, noting

that no other work achieved its success. Piperno also looks at other productions, determining that since this sacro-dramatic tradition was peculiar to Naples, *Mosè* attracted a mixed reception elsewhere in Italy. Includes musical examples and tables of productions from the San Carlo Lenten seasons and of productions of *Mosè* throughout Italy from 1817 to 1830. See also items 359 and 719.

719. ———. "Il *Mosè in Egitto* e la tradizione napoletana di opere bibliche." In *Il testo e la scena* (item 286), 255–71.

The author proposes that, rather than regarding *Mosè* as a product of the Romantic era, the work should be viewed in light of an eighteenth-century Neapolitan practice, fostered by the Bourbons, of presenting biblical works during Lent. Rossini, librettist Andrea Leone Tottola, and impresario Domenico Barbaja, sensitive to this custom, planned *Mosè* as the first such work staged after the Bourbons reassumed power after the Parthenopean republic. Tables document other Lenten biblical dramas in this tradition. See also item 359 and 718.

* ———. " 'Stellati sogli' e 'immagini portentose': Opere bibliche e stagioni quaresimali a Napoli prima del *Mosè*." Item 359. See also items 718 and 719.

720. Smither, Howard E. *A History of the Oratorio* Vol. 4: *The Oratorio in the Nineteenth and Twentieth Centuries*. Chapel Hill, N.C.: The University of North Carolina Press, 2000. 829 pp. ISBN: 0-8078-2511-5 ML3201.56.

Smither approaches both *Mosè in Egitto* and *Moïse et Pharaon* as staged oratorios rather than operas. Noting that French journalists referred to any work featuring chorus and soloists as an oratorio, Smither discusses the changes Rossini made to the Italian version of this work in order to appeal to the tastes of French audiences.

Ricciardo e Zoraide

* Balthazar, Scott L. "Evolving Conventions in Italian Serious Opera: Scene Structure in the Works of Rossini, Bellini, Donizetti, and Verdi, 1810–1850." See item 583.

721. Tozzi, Lorenzo. "Sulle trace di un péché de jeunesse: *Ricciardo e Zoraide*." *Bollettino del Centro Rossiniano di Studi* 14 [no. 2–3] (1974): 9–36.

Tozzi lists the musical sources of *Ricciardo*, including the autograph, editions of the score, and reductions for piano and voice, and solo piano. He then presents the history of its premiere, noting that critics applauded this work as Rossini's rejection of foreign (French and German) styles in a return to traditional Italian techniques. He discusses the source of Francesco Berio di Salsa's libretto, the thirty-canto poem *Ricciardetto* by Niccolò Forteguerri, noting areas of strict adherence to the original and points of the librettist's invention. He outlines and describes the musical numbers of the opera, concluding that it is imperative to place this among Rossini's better-known *seria* works in order to understand his development in that genre. With musical examples.

Ermione

* Balthazar, Scott L. "Evolving Conventions in Italian Serious Opera: Scene Structure in the Works of Rossini, Bellini, Donizetti, and Verdi, 1810–1850." See item 583.

722. Carli Ballola, Giovanni. "Lettura dell'Ermione." *Bollettino del Centro Rossiniano di Studi* 12 [no. 3] (1972): 12–39.

The author considers the text and music of *Ermione*. In addition, he demonstrates the self-borrowings from this work used for other Rossini works, including the lost opera *Ugo, re d'Italia*, comparing passages from both librettos. Carli Ballola offers a musical description of *Ermione* as well, supporting his discussion with score excerpts. He comments on the ill fortune of this work in comparison to other Rossini *seria* compositions. For more on *Ugo*, see item 784.

723. ———. "Ritorno di *Ermione*." *Chigiana, rassegna annuale di studi musicologici* 14 (1977, publ. 1981): 291–99.

[Not examined.] RILM abstract notes that this is an examination of Tottola's libretto in comparison to Racine's *Andromaque*, as well as a description of the score. See also item 722.

724. Farcy, Gerard-Denis. "Andromaque a l'épreuve de l'opéra." *Revue d'histoire du théâtre* 181 (January-March 1994): 73–86.

The author considers the issues of transforming a literary work into an opera, in this case Racine's *Andromaque* into Gretry's *Andromaque* into Rossini's *Ermione*. Farcy suggests that the adaptations are not always true in spirit to their source. For more of *Ermione*'s connection to *Andromaque*, see also item 723.

725. Grondona, Marco. *"La perfetta illusione"*: *Ermione e l'opera seria rossini-ana*. Lucca: Akademos & Lim, 1996. 356 pp. ISBN 88-7096-167-2 ML410.R8 G76 1996.

Using *Ermione* as a point of departure, the author looks at the rapport between music and text in Rossini's operas. In addition to tracing *Ermione*'s roots in Racine, Grondona examines musical and dramatic structures in Rossini's work. The author also applies his ideas to comic works, particularly *La pietra del paragone*. See also item 724.

Eduardo e Cristina

726. Beghelli, Marco. "Die (scheinbare) Unlogik des Eigenplagiats." In *Rossinis Eduardo e Cristina*, Item 731, 101–22. Translated into German by Angelo Raciti.

Taking his title from Arrigo Quattrocchi's essay (item 732), Beghelli examines Rossini's self-borrowings for *Eduardo e Cristina* from a different angle, proposing that the rationale beyond Rossini's substitutions may not be quite as obvious as Quattrocchi suggests. Nonetheless, he agrees that Rossini's self-borrowings work in their new positions.

727. Cametti, Alberto. *"La musica teatrale a Roma cento anni fa*: "Eduardo e Cristina." In *Annuario della R. Accademia di Santa Cecilia 1927–1928*, 79–111. Rome: Tipografica R. Mezzetti, 1928 MT5.R6 A35 1928; reprinted and issued as a separate publication. 32 pp. ML1733.8 .R6 C2 1928.

See item 367 for a description of the series.

728. Gier, Albert. "Im Wechselbad der Gefühle." In *Rossinis Eduardo e Cristina*, Item 731, 137–50.

Gier begins by tracing the tradition of melodrama into which Rossini's opera falls. He then discusses the production history of Pavesi's *Odoardo e Cristina* and its libretto by Giovanni Schmidt, which served as a source for Rossini's. The author continues his examination of Rossini's work, considering the father-daughter conflict as well as emotionally charged passages borrowed from *Ermione*. (See items 726 and 732 for more on Rossini's self-borrowings in this work.) Illustrated with a theater poster from the Viennese debut of *Eduardo* in May of 1824.

729. Kern, Bernd-Rüdiger. "Aspekte der Vertrages." In *Rossinis Eduardo e Cristina*, Item 731, 159–64.

The author discusses the negotiations between Rossini and Giuseppe Cortesi, impresario at Venice's San Benedetto Theater, for the composition of *Eduardo*. The appendix contains a transcription of Cortesi's letter offering Rossini the commission and of the actual contract. See also Ragni, item 733.

730. Marino, Marina. "Rossini e Pavesi: A proposito di un'aria dell'*Eduardo e Cristina.*" *Bollettino del Centro Rossiniano di Studi* [no. 1–3] (1986): 5–14.

Examining the bass aria "Questa man la toglie a morte," Marino demonstrates that, in addition to self-borrowings, Rossini relied on Stefano Pavesi's setting of *Eduardo e Cristina* for his own score. Tracing the opera's early history, the author shows that although the aria appears in published scores, it is frequently cut or replaced in performance. Finally, she briefly addresses the other subjects which both Rossini and Pavesi set (*Matilde di Shabran*, *Elisabetta d'Inghilterra*, *Tancredi* and *Cenerentola*), suggesting that perhaps Pavesi served as source of inspiration for Rossini. Illustrated with a facsimile of Pavesi's setting of "Questa man," facsimiles of the libretto page on which the aria is found in both the 1810 premiere of Pavesi's *Odoardo* and Rossini's 1819 premiere of *Eduardo*, and a portrait of Pavesi.

* Mauceri, Marco. " 'Voce, che tenera': Una cabaletta per tutte le stagioni." See item 512.

731. Müller, Reto, and Bernd-Rüdiger Kern, eds. *Rossinis Eduardo e Cristina*: *Beiträge zur Jahrhundert-Erstaufführung*. German translations by Angelo Raciti. Vol. 2 in *Schriftreihe der Deutschen Rossini Gesellschaft*. Leipzig: Universitätsverlag, 1997. 253 pp. ISBN 3-931922-71-5 ML410.R8 R84 1997.

A book dedicated to this opera, prepared in conjunction with its performance at the Rossini in Wildbad Festival. The first section is dedicated to the work and includes a summary of musical numbers and plot (Reto Müller), a facsimile of the libretto published for the 1819 premiere in Venice, a parallel German translation (Angelo Raciti), and a musical analysis (Thomas Lindner). The second section deals with performance history, with a table listing productions and casts throughout the nineteenth century (Tom Kaufman), a list of libretti from subsequent productions with notations about productions variants (Müller), and a summary of musical transcriptions and a list of copyists' scores and published music (Stefano Piana); the third section considers issues concerning the Wildbad performances (Müller), the edition of the score in the absence of an autograph (Anders Wiklund and Patricia B. Brauner), and reflections on the production

(Annette Hornbacher and Jochen Schönleber). With illustrations and musical examples. Individual essays appear as items 726, 728, 729, 732, 733, 863, and 869.

732. Quattrocchi, Arrigo. "La logica degli autoimprestiti: *Eduardo e Cristina.*" In *Il testo e la scena* (item 286), 333–63; German translation by Angelo Raciti, published in *Rossinis Eduardo e Cristina* (item 731), 71–99.

The author examines the issue of Rossini's self-borrowings, in particular those involved in the composition of *Eduardo e Cristina.* After discussing specific details of the work's commission, Quattrocchi addresses first the libretto, comparing Rossini's text with its source, Giovanni Schmitt's *Odoardo e Cristina* (set by Stefano Pavesi), and the roles of Rossini's librettists, Andrea Leone Tottola, Gherardo Bevilacqua Aldobrandini, and Francesco Berio di Salsa. The author then considers the music in terms of various types of transplants from other scores as well as newly-composed numbers (which themselves later found their way into other Rossini scores). He concludes that Rossini borrowed music which would not be known in Venice, but states that the composer, wanting to impress the Venetian public, was far from indifferent in his choices of self-borrowings. The logic behind his selection, however, was not driven by the drama but solely by musical considerations. Includes a table which lists all of the numbers in the opera by key, tempo, and meter, and then identifies their sources and, where applicable, their subsequent reuse in other scores.

733. Ragni, Sergio. "Eine Tochter namens Eduardo." In *Rossinis Eduardo e Cristina*, item 731, 151–58. Translated into German by Angelo Raciti.

Ragni offers a history of the commissioning of *Eduardo* by tracing Rossini's dealings with impresario Giuseppe Cortesi (see Kern's article "Aspekte der Vertrages," also in 731). Cortesi stipulated that the role of Eduardo was to be written for his daughter, Carolina. Ragni also discussing details of the premiere, citing Rossini biographers Azevedo (item 105), Weinstock (item 188) and Zanolini (item 138) as well as reviews from contemporary periodicals. Ragni notes that although Cortesi's contract with Rossini stipulated that the commissioned work should be "completely new," the work in a sense is pastiche, its libretto borrowed from one by Giovanni Schmidt (see item 728 and 732) and its score, a tapestry of self-borrowings (see items 726, 730, and 732). Illustrated with an engraving of Carolina Cortesi.

La donna del lago

734. Cametti, Alberto. "*La musica teatrale a Roma cento anni fa*: "La donna del lago." In *Annuario della R. Accademia di Santa Cecilia 1922–1923*, 47–67. Rome: Tipografica A. Manuzio, 1923 MT5.R6 A35 1923.

     See item 367 for a description of the series.

735. Castelvecchi, Stefano. "Walter Scott, Rossini e la *couleur ossianique*: il contesto culturale della *Donna del lago*." *Bollettino del Centro Rossiniano di Studi* 33 (1993): 57–71.

     Although Rossini's *Donna del lago* was thought responsible for introducing Walter Scott and the Romantic local color of Scotland into Italian culture, the author demonstrates that, via a French translation of Scott's poem (the source used by librettist Andrea Leone Tottola), and, more important, an Italian translation of the Ossian poems, that tradition was already well established. Castelvecchi also demonstrates with examples that, aside from Melchio Cesarotti's translations of Ossian, the opera *Aganadeca* (Naples, 1817) not only provided inspiration but apparently some of Tottola's verse.

736. Forbes, Elizabeth. "Sir Walter Scott and Opera." *Opera* 19 (1968): 872–78.

     Discusses Scott's overall literary output and its numerous transformations into operas; included is a brief mention of Rossini's *La donna del lago*, which was based on the poem "The Lady of the Lake." Illustrated with set designs from some Scott-based operas.

737. Gossett, Philip. "*La Donna del lago*." In "The Operas of Rossini: Problems of Textual Criticism in Nineteenth-Century Opera." See item 582.

     * Henze-Döhring, Sabine. "La 'natura' nelle opere di Rossini." Item 605.

738. Isotta, Paolo. " 'La donna del lago' e la drammatugia di Rossini." *Bollettino del Centro Rossiniano di Studi* 10 [no. 2] (1970): 45–61.

     The author considers Rossini's dramatic works before *Guillaume Tell*, applying linguistic terminology. For example, he explains, while music's denotative significance would always remain the same, its connotative meaning would change, in this case, from one century to the next. Rossini's music, though, is often perceived in terms of his more familiar comic works, and other problems arise when one is faced with self-borrowings in which one piece of music works equally well with different texts. Using examples from the opera, Isotta discusses how Rossini's music communicates the dramatic elements in *La donna del lago*.

739. Mitchell, Jerome. *The Walter Scott Operas: An Analysis of Operas Based on the Works of Sir Walter Scott.* University, Ala.: University of Alabama Press, 1977. xiii, 402 pp. ISBN 0-8173-6401-3 ML2100 .M59 1977.

Mitchell considers various operatic versions of Scott's literature, giving a brief performance history and discussion of action and musical setting (with score examples) for each work. He includes sections on *La donna del lago*, the first opera to be derived from a Scott work, and on the pastiches *Ivanhoé* and *Robert Bruce* (based on a version of the story in chapters 6 through 9 of *Tales of a Grandfather*, the first series). Illustrated.

Bianca e Falliero, ossia Il consiglio dei tre

* Baricco, Alessandro. *Il genio in fuga: Due saggi sul teatro musicale di Gioachino Rossini.* See item 584.

740. Cagli, Bruno. "Le fonti letterarie delle opere di Rossini: *Bianca e Falliero, ossia Il Consiglio dei tre.*" *Bollettino del Centro Rossiniano di Studi* [no. 1] (1973): 8–22.

By examining correspondence of Stendhal, Cagli discounts earlier theories suggesting that the source of Felice Romani's libretto was *Il Conte di Carmagnola* by Alessandro Manzoni. The author then compares the libretto with the work Romani cited as his source: the five-act tragedy *Blanche et Montcassin* (1798) by Antoine-Vincent Arnault. By examining the plots and parallel passages of text, Cagli suggests that in some cases the librettist amplified the original drama, but his addition of the requisite happy ending weakens the original tale. Cagli demonstrates that Rossini's return to recitative, which he had abandoned with *Elisabetta*, suggests that perhaps the composer felt that theaters and audiences outside of Naples were less progressive. Cagli urges a study of Rossini and his connections to the cities and theaters for which he composed.

* G.[iazotto], R.[emo]. "Due lettere di Rossini." See item 45.

Maometto II

* Balthazar, Scott L. "Evolving Conventions in Italian Serious Opera: Scene Structure in the Works of Rossini, Bellini, Donizetti, and Verdi, 1810–1850." See item 583.

* Biggi, Maria Ida. "Scenografie rossiniane di Giuseppe Borsato." See item 604.

741. Cagli, Bruno. "Le fonti letterarie dei libretti di Rossini: Maometto II." *Bollettino del Centro Rossiniano di Studi* 12 [no. 2] (1972): 10–32.

     Cagli begins by stating the literary and sociological importance of tracing the sources of libretti. He then corrects inexactitudes regardings the sources of *Demetrio e Polibio*, *Tancredi*, *Mosè in Egitto*, *Ricciardo e Zoraide*, and *Bianca e Falliero*. The remainder of his discourse is dedicated to identifying the source of *Maometto II*, which he argues did not come from Voltaire but from librettist Cesare Della Valle's own tragedy *Anna Erizio* (1824). In addition to comparing the script of *Anna* with the libretto, Cagli demonstrates the inclusion of a scene found similarly in *Tancredi*, *Otello*, and *La donna del lago*: that of a father forcing an undesired marriage on his daughter. Cagli concludes that the opera's misfortune on the stage had nothing to do with its libretto and surmises that Rossini himself most likely worked with the librettist on transforming the play for the operatic stage. Contains comparative passages of both texts.

     * Cheskin, Jonathan L. "Catholic-Liberal Opera: Outline of a Hidden Italian Musical Romanticism." See item 197.

742. Gossett, Philip. "*Maometto II*; *Le Siège de Corinthe*." In "The Operas of Rossini: Problems of Textual Criticism in Nineteenth-Century Opera." See item 582.

     * Simionati, Giuliano. "Rossini, Canova, e Treviso: I rapporti tra il musicista e la città veneta esaminati attraverso documenti inediti ed un autografo." See item 373.

Matilde di Shabran, ossia Bellezza, e cuor di ferro

743. Cametti, Alberto. "*La musica teatrale a Roma cento anni fa*: "*Matilde di Shabran*." In *Annuario della R. Accademia di Santa Cecilia 1920–1921*, 57–82. Rome: Tipografica A. Manuzio, 1921 MT5.R6 A35 1921; reprinted and issued as a separate publication. 28 pp. ML1733.8 .R6C2 1921.

     See item 367 for a description of the series.

     * Marino, Marina. "Morlacchi e Pavesi: Due occasioni di confronto." See item 223.

     * Spada, Marco. "Giovanni Schmidt librettista: biografia di un fantasma." See item 254.

744. Tartak, Marvin. "Matilde and Her Cousins: A Study of the Libretto Sources for Rossini's *Matilde di Shabran*." *Bollettino del Centro Rossiniano di Studi*

[no. 3] (1973): 13–23; Italian translation by Raffaello Delfino appears in the Appendix, 36–44.

Tartak briefly traces the history of this unsuccessful work and then explores the likely sources Jacopo Ferretti used for its libretto. Although Étienne Méhul's opera *Euphrosine* (1790) has been considered the work upon which *Matilde* was based, Tartak demonstrates connections between Ferretti's libretto and those of Francesco Morlacchi's and Stefano Pavesi's musical settings of *Corradino*. All trace back to a medieval French source. Tartak then discusses how Ferretti amplified the mood of the original tale, making this opera "one of the most serious 'comedies' Rossini ever wrote." He also suggests that, perhaps, the name of Matilde came from the story of Matilde di Morwel, set by Carlo Coccia in 1811. Tartak concludes that, in addition to *Il barbiere* and *La Cenerentola*, this work is most likely Rossini's third adaptation of a French source and that this combination of moralistic French drama and Italian farce contributed to the development of Italian Romantic opera.

* ————. *The Italian Comic Operas of Rossini*. See item 596.

Zelmira

* Balthazar, Scott L. "Evolving Conventions in Italian Serious Opera: Scene Structure in the Works of Rossini, Bellini, Donizetti, and Verdi, 1810–1850." See item 583.

745. Lanfranchi, Ariella. "Alcune note su *Zelmira*." *Bollettino del Centro Rossiniano di Studi* [nos. 1–3] (1981): 55–84.

The author considers aspects of the compositional and production history of the opera, including conflicting criticisms by Viennese and Italian reviewers. The bulk of the article deals with librettist Andrea Leone Tottola's adaptation of his source, Belloy's *Zelmire*; included is a comparison of the scenes from the five-act drama and those of the two-act libretto. "Official" productions (those with Rossini's intervention) of *Zelmira* were Naples and Vienna (both 1822), London (1824) and Paris (1826); the published versions of the libretto most faithful to the original are those from Naples, Vienna, and Paris, according to Lanfranchi.

746. Raffaelli, Renato. "Tracce di allattamento filiale nella *Zelmira* di Tottola per Rossini." *Bollettino del Centro Rossiniano di Studi* 36 (1996): 45–66.

After demonstrating how the perception of the character of Zelmira changes as it is revealed that she is her father Polidoro's savior rather than his murderer, Raffaelli concentrates on passages in which Polidoro states that he has been "nourished" by Zelmira's visits to the crypt where she has hidden him. The author then examines Classical prototypes of this tale in which a daughter prevents the starvation death of an imprisoned parent by offering her breast milk. Citing Andrea Leone Tottola's source, the eighteenth-century French play *Zelmire*, in which the main character saves her father in this way, Raffaelli suggests that Rossini's librettist used mere allusion to filial nourishment because the original concept would have been suppressed by contemporary censors. Includes illustrations of two sixteenth-century representations of "La carità romana," a daughter offering the breast to her aged father.

Semiramide

* Balthazar, Scott L. "Evolving Conventions in Italian Serious Opera: Scene Structure in the Works of Rossini, Bellini, Donizetti, and Verdi, 1810–1850." See item 583.

* Biggi, Maria Ida. "Scenografie rossiniane di Giuseppe Borsato." See item 604.

747. Cametti, Alberto. *"La musica teatrale a Roma cento anni fa*: "Semiramide." In *Annuario della R. Accademia di Santa Cecilia 1925–1926*, 49–77. Rome: Tipografica A. Manuzio, 1926. MT5.R6 A35 1926.

See item 367 for a description of the series.

* Giazotti, Remo. "Alcune ignote vicende riguardanti la stampa e la diffusione della 'Semiramide.'" See item 262.

* Goldin, Daniela. *La vera Fenice: Librettisti e libretti tra Sette e Ottocento*. See item 577.

748. Gossett, Philip. "Musicologi e musicisti: intorno a una rappresentazione di *Semiramide*." Translated into Italian by Paolo Fabbri. *Bollettino del Centro Rossiniano di Studi* 32 (1992): 17–31.

Based on significant practical experience, Gossett discusses the challenging relationship between musicologists and musicians and the problems inherent in producing a so-called authentic interpretation of a work. As an example, he proposes the 1990 Metropolitan Opera production of *Semiramide*, which used the critical edition of the work that he and Alberto Zedda had edited. Gossett explains the benefits of having a critical edition: it is complete, contains material from all autograph sources, and offers accurate dynamics, articulations and phrasing. In the case of *Semiramide*, the edition made available the scoring for the stage band. The author then candidly discusses the pros and cons of performing from a critical edition. Gossett concludes that musicologists need to understand practical issues of production as well as the research methods of scholarship. See also item 615.

749. ———. "Rossini, Seriously." *Opera News* 55 (Dec. 22, 1990): 20–23.

Written primarily as an introduction to *Semiramide* in connection with its first production at the Metropolitan Opera since the 1890s, this article considers the return of Rossini's serious operas to the international repertory. Gossett observes that, although Rossini's fame has rested upon the comedies, he was above all a *seria* composer. After destroying the myth that Rossini approached his serious libretti hastily and unenthusiastically, the author proposes that it is the *opere serie* that delineate the composer's path to artistic maturity. In a brief sidebar, Gossett discusses the critical edition of *Semiramide* and the discoveries that led to a reconstruction of the complete score. Illustrations include a costume sketch for Assur and Sanquirico's set design for the 1853 premiere of *Semiramide* at La Scala.

750. ———. "*Semiramide*." In "The Operas of Rossini: Problems of Textual Criticism in Nineteenth-Century Opera." See item 582.

* Hadlock, Heather. "*Tancredi* and *Semiramide*." See item 633.

751. Joerg, Guido Johannes. "Zur Verwendung des Volkslied "Freut euch des Lebens" in den Werken Gioachino Rossini." *La Gazzetta* 1 (1992): 3–5.

When Rossini visited Vienna in 1822, he met Metternich. Joerg relates that the statesman may have introduced the composer to the folksong "Freut euch des Lebens," the theme of which Rossini subsequently incorporated into a solfeggio exercise as well as the overture, Act I Finale quintet, and Act II Finale Chorus of *Semiramide*. Joerg demonstrates these citations with music examples. See Bonaccorsi, item 830, for another instance of quoting popular song.

* Pirrotta, Nino. "Semiramis e Amneris, un anagramma o quasi." Item 424.

752. Questa, Cesare. *Semiramide redenta: archetipi, fonti classiche, censure antropologiche nel melodramma*. Vol. 2 of *Letteratura e antropologia*, ed. Renato Raffaelli. Urbino: Edizioni Quattro Venti, 1989. 403 pp. ISBN 88-392-0103-3 ML1700.Q47 1989.

Questa compares Rossi's libretto for Rossini's setting of *Semiramide* with previous approaches to the tale. Questa concludes that, although similar in plot to earlier versions, this libretto, no longer Metastasian, reflects a work constructed in terms of a dramatic chain of events and hence a different musico-dramatic logic. Includes a detailed examination of the libretto and the music. Includes musical examples.

* Steane, John. "Semiramide." See item 572.

Il viaggio a Reims, ossia L'albergo del giglio d'oro

753. Claudon, Francis, and Jean-Robert Mongrédien. "Rhétorique convenue et developpements: Rossini's *Viaggio a Reims* en 1825 au Théâtre Italien de Paris." In *Le parole della musica II: Studi sul lessico della letteratura critica del teatro musicale in onore di Gianfranco Folena*, Vol. 22 in *Studi di Musica Veneta*, edited by Maria Teresa Muraro, 183–93. Florence: Leo S. Olschki, 1995. 334 pp. ISBN 88-222-4340-4 ML63.P26 1994 Vol. 2.

The authors extracted comments from about twenty-five articles about *Il Viaggio a Reims*, among them, two by Stendhal. They analyze these reviews, noting the uniformity of opinion. Most of the writers remained anonymous, they found, and, despite flowery rhetoric, offered no real judgment of the work, even avoiding use of first person. Even Stendhal distanced himself by using "we." The authors conclude that these banal examples of writing demonstrate that true criticism had yet to appear.

* Gossett, Philip. "Le Comte Ory (Il Viaggio a Reims)." See item 582.

754. Johnson, Janet. "A Lost Rossini Opera Recovered: *Il viaggio a Reims.*" *Bollettino del Centro Rossiniano di Studi* [no. 1–3] (1983): 5–57; Italian translation, "Un'opera rossiniana recuperata." follows in the same issue, 59–112.

From five extant sources for *Il viaggio a Reims* (including an 1828 edition of *Le comte Ory*, a work for which Rossini borrowed much of *Viaggio*'s music), Johnson was able to reconstruct the nine numbers of the score of *Viaggio*. Her study also confirms that a hymn and an overture (see Gossett, items 556 and 557) were not a part of the score, and that an *Air de danse* from the finale was later reworked for *Le siège de Corinthe*. In addition to providing a performance history of *Viaggio*, Johnson mentions its two subsequent pasticcios, *Andremo a Parigi?* and *Il viaggio a Vienna*. After describing the original 1825 production, Johnson identifies aspects of the work, particularly in the character of Corinne, as metaphor for specific contemporary works of literature and art, positing as well that Rossini might have contemplated a second opera, *La figlia dell'Aria*, which would have built upon this theme. Includes score excerpts, tables, and illustrations.

* Müller, Reto. "Rossinis 'Reise nach Reims.' " In *Rossini in Paris: Eine Veranstaltung des Frankreichzentrums der Universität Leipzig, in Zusammenarbeit mit der Deutschen Rossini Gesellschaft e.V.* See item 290.

755. *Rossini, Le voyage a Reims*; *Le comte Ory. Avant-scène opéra* 140 (July-August 1991) Paris: Avant-scène, 1991. 149 pp.

[Not examined.] The opera guide includes the original libretti of both works as well as plot summaries, articles on their genesis, and musical commentaries. Illustrated, with a bibliography and discography.

* Walton, Benjamin. *Romanticisms and Nationalisms in Restoration France.*

Le siège de Corinthe (L'assedio di Corinto)

* Bartlet, M. Elizabeth C. "Rossini e l'Académie Royale de Musique a Parigi." Item 316.

756. Cametti, Alberto. *"La musica teatrale a Roma cento anni fa*: "L'assedio di Corinto" e "Il Conte Ory" di Rossini." In *Annuario della R. Accademia di Santa Cecilia 1929–1930*, 377–418. Rome: Tipografica Mezzetti, 1930. MT5.R6 A35 1930.

See item 367 for a description of the series.

* Gossett, Philip. "Maometto II (Le Siège de Corinthe)." See item 582.

* Johnson, Janet. "A Lost Rossini Opera Recovered: *Il viaggio a Reims*." See item 754.

* Kallberg, Jeffrey. "Marketing Rossini: Sei lettere di Troupenas ad Artaria." Item 47.

757. *Rossini, Le Siège de Corinthe. Avant-scène opéra* 81 (November 1985) Paris: Avant-scène, 1985. 129 pp.

[Not examined.] Based on the RILM abstract, this guide to understanding the opera contains articles on the work, including information on the transformation from *Maometto II* to *Le siège* for the French stage. With illustrations, bibliography, and a discography.

* Walton, Benjamin. *Romanticisms and Nationalisms in Restoration France.*

Moïse et Pharaon (Mosè)

758. Bailbè, Joseph-Marc. "Le sacre dans l'art lyrique: Autour de l'opéra
français de XIXe siècle." In *Littérature et opéra: Colloque de Cerisy 1985*,
edited by Philippe Berthier and Kurt Ringger, 117–27. Grenoble: Presses
Université de Grenoble, 1987. 183 pp. ISBN: 2-7061-0277-2 ML1700.L58
1987.

Considers works for the French stage with biblical themes, among them
Moïse et Pharaon, called in the French press an "oratorio in quatre parties."
Bailbè views the work's "austere and religious" character, briefly mentioning the differences between the Italian original and the French version,
which, he claims, Rossini brought in line with the tradition of tragédie
lyrique and the tastes of the Parisian audiences. Mentions as well the references to the work in *Massimila Doni*, which Bailbè suggests, helps to
underscore the religious nature of the work. See also item 438.

759. Gautier, Théophile. *La Musique*. Paris: Bibliothèque-Charpentier, 1911.
310 pp.

Originally published in *La Presse*, 8 November 1852, the author's article
(pp. 124–32) applauds the Paris Opéra and Nestor Roqueplan's projected
reproduction of *Moïse*. Gautier discusses Balzac's use of description of the
work in *Massimilla Doni*, unaware, however, that Balzac's description was
of the original Neapolitan version of the work (see Glascow, item 715 and
Brzoska, item 713). Gautier also reprints a letter from Joseph Méry to
Rossini, which, Gautier claims, expresses his own thoughts about the composer's genius. See item 442 on Gautier.

760. Gossett, Philip. "Gioachino Rossini's *Moïse*." In *The Rosaleen Moldenhauer Memorial: Music History from Primary Sources: A Guide to the
Moldenhauer Archives*, 369–74. See item 9.

After briefly explaining Rossini's plan to adapt serious operas from his
Neapolitan years for production at the Opéra, Gossett addresses the autograph of recitative for *Moïse*, housed in the Moldenhauer Archives at the
Library of Congress. The manuscript points to the editorial practices of
Rossini's French publisher Troupenas, who closely followed Rossini's original, save for a change in the tempo marking. A rare Rossini sketch, found
on the verso of folio 2, suggests that the composer resorted to this practice
when faced with problematic passages. See also Gossett, item 509, on
Rossini's compositional practices.

* Isotta, Paolo. "Da *Mosè* a *Moïse*." See item 717.

* Isotta, Paolo, ed. *Gioacchino Rossini. Mosè in Egitto, Moïse et Pharaon, Mosè.* Item 854.

761. John, Nicolas, series editor. *The Barber of Seville-Il Barbiere di Siviglia/Moses-Moïse et Pharaon.* See also item 663 for full contents.

In addition to an edition of the libretto and a parallel English translation of *Moïse et Pharaon* by John and Nell Moody, the guide includes information on Stendhal's judgment of *Móse* and Balzac's use of it in *Massimilla Doni* (see also items 438, 441, 713, and 715); on the performance of Rossini's music, by Ubaldo Gardini; and a musical analysis, by Richard Bernas. Also contains a guide to musical themes (with musical examples), a bibliography, and a discography. Illustrated.

762. Lacombe, Hervé. "Contributo allo studio delle fonti del 'Moïse' di Rossini." *Bollettino del Centro Rossiniano di Studi* 19 (1989): 47–62. Translated from French into Italian by Paola Chiarini.

The author examines a group of scores of *Moïse et Pharaon* in Paris that sheds new light on the work's transformation from *Mosè in Egitto*. Lacombe discusses how these scores contribute to a new understanding of the opera's finale, raise questions about the Act IV reprise of the Act I Marche, and help reconstruct the dance in Act III. With an explanatory table. Includes musical incipits.

* Lippmann, Friedrich. "Mozart und die italienischen Komponisten des 19. Jahrhunderts." See item 531.

* Smither, Howard E. *A History of the Oratorio Vol. 4: The Oratorio in the Nineteenth and Twentieth Centuries.* See item 720.

Le comte Ory

* *Rossini, Le voyage a Reims; Le comte Ory.* See item 755.

* Cametti, Alberto. "*La musica teatrale a Roma cento anni fa:* 'L'assedio di Corinto' e 'Il Conte Ory' di Rossini." See item 756.

763. Delgado, Arturo. "La leyenda del Conde Ory: El problem de los origenes y las fuentas literarias." *Revista de filologia* 7 (1991): 409–22.

[Not examined.]

764. Gossett, Philip. "*Le Comte Ory (Il Viaggio a Reims).*" In "The Operas of Rossini: Problems of Textual Criticism in Nineteenth-Century Opera." See item 582.

* Johnson, Janet. "A Lost Rossini Opera Recovered: *Il viaggio a Reims*." See item 754.

* Landini, Giancarlo. "Riflessioni su alcuni aspetti della vocalità francese di Rossini." In *Atti del convegno di studi: Rossini, edizioni critiche e prassi esecutiva*, 153–72. See item 282.

765. Turchi, Guido. "Un sottile riflesso narcissico." *Chigana. Rassegna annuale di studi musicologici* 14 (1977, publ. 1981) 255–58.

   [Not examined.]

Guillaume Tell

* Aversano, Luca. "Brief des Musikverlages C.F. Peters an Rossini." See item 59.

766. Baggioli, Andrea. "Le fonti letterarie di *Guillaume Tell*." *Bollettino del Centro Rossiniano di Studi* 37 (1997): 5–50.

   Examines the stage and literary versions of the Tell story, which preceded Rossini's *Guillaume Tell* in France. Comparing various episodes and characterizations, Baggioli demonstrates that many aspects of the opera's narrative derive from earlier French texts rather than from Friedrich Schiller's (1804; French trans., 1818). Pointing to social and political elements in the various versions, the author concludes that the Rossini libretto, penned initially by Victor-Joseph-Etienne Jouy and reworked by Hippolyte-Louis-Florent Bis (with Adolphe Nouritt), was stripped of its liberal tendencies in order to reflect the reactionary reign of Charles I. Other *Tell*s explored include those by Antoine-Marin Lemierre (1766, publ. 1767); Michel-Jean Sedaine (1790; set by André-Ernest-Modeste Grétry in 1791 and revised by M. Pelissier in 1828); Jean-Pierre Claris de Florian (1805); Guilbert de Pixérécourt (1828); and Michel Pichet (1828).

767. Bartlet, M. Elizabeth C. "Staging French *Grand Opera*: Rossini's *Guillaume Tell* (1829)." *Il testo e la scena* (item 286), 623–48.

   After having examined descriptions and diagrams of stage blocking found in the *mise en scène* of *Guillaume Tell*, Bartlet demonstrates the extent to which the Opéra's *metteur en scène* helped to shape the production and indeed revolutionize grand opera. Among the staging techniques (already standard at other Parisian theatres, including the Opéra-Comique) were facial expressions and natural gestures by both principals and choristers; character interaction; placement of main action upstage as well as down;

asymmetrical blocking patterns, which often positioned characters with their backs to the audience; use of illusion in scenery; and, for dramatic reinforcement, movement involving simultaneous acting and singing. In addition to a reproduction of the title page of the libretto's first edition (1829), which demonstrates the innovative placement of characters, the article also includes diagrams that contrast traditional French stage blockings with several diagrams from *Tell*'s *mise en scène*. An appendix includes two letters (untranslated), the first suggesting that Solomé be named "Régisseur de la Scène" at the Opéra and the second confirming his appointment. See also item 318.

* ————. "Rossini e l'Académie Royale de Musique a Parigi." See item 316.

* ————, with Mauro Bucarelli. *Guillaume Tell di Gioachino Rossini: fonti iconografiche*. See item 89.

768. Bellaigue, Camille. *"Guillaume Tell."* In *Promenades lyriques*, 79–96. Paris: Nouvelle Libraire Nationale, 1924. 250 pp. ML1700 .B32.

Bellaigue devotes this book to individual discussions of popular nineteenth-century operas. In a chapter on *Tell*, the author considers musical issues but does little more than praise Rossini's genius.

769. ————. "Un chef d'oeuvre patriotique; le second acte de *Guillaume Tell*." Chapter in *Propos de musique et de guerre*, 179–98. Paris: Nouvelle Libraire Nationale, 1917. 317 pp. ML60 .B44.

Guillaume Tell, a work on a Swiss subject written for the French stage by an Italian composer, reflects an alliance. Writing in March of 1916, Bellaigue points to the relevant nature of the patriotism in the second act of the opera, concluding that while it relates intimate and private tragedy, it also represents popular, national drama.

770. Cametti, Alberto. "Il 'Guglielmo Tell' e le sue prime rappresentazioni in Italia." *Rivista musicale italiana* 6 (1899): 580–92.

Cametti documents the history of Rossini's *Tell* in Italy, noting the roles of impresario Alessandro Lanari and tenor Gilbert Duprez in its initial success in Lucca and subsequent productions in Florence, Naples, Milan, Turin, and Rome. Cametti discusses the various casting changes as well as issues of censorship that resulted in changing the title of the work to *Guglielmo Vallace* and *Rodolfo di Sterlinga*.

* Dauriac, Lionel. *La psychologie dans l'Opéra Français (Auber-Rossini-Meyerbeer)*. See item 533.

* DeMarco, Laura E. *Rossini and the Emergence of Dramatic Male Roles in Italian and French Opera.* See item 565.

771. Edler, Arnfried. " 'Glanzspiel und Seelenlandschaft': Naturdarstellung in der Oper bei Weber und Rossini." In *Weber—jenseits des Freischütz: Referate des Eutiner Symposions 1986 anlasslich des 200. Geburtstag von Carl Maria von Weber,* No. 32 in the series *Kieler Schriften zur Musikwissenschaft,* edited by Friedhelm Krummacher and Heinrich W. Schwab, 71–83. Kassel: Bärenreiter, 1989. ix, 234 pp. ML410.W3 W47 1989.

     Nature appears in both Weber's *Der Freischütz* and Rossini's *Guillaume Tell.* Edler describes the different presentation, noting that Weber's depiction of nature stems from German Romanticism while Rossini's nature doubles as a symbol for freedom. Edler addresses how both composers musically achieve their objectives. Briefly mentions Weber's perception of Rossini as a rival.

772. Gerhard, Anselm. "L'eroe titubante e il finale aperto: Un dilemma insolubile nel *Guillaume Tell* di Rossini." Trans. Marco Bolzani. *Rivista italiana di musicologia* 19 [no. 1] (1984): 113–30.

     The author considers the role of Arnold as an early example of the indecisive hero, an emotionally fragile character with a certain egocentrocism that hinders him from rational behavior. In addition to his discussion of this part, Gerhard also looks at the finales of *Tell, Tancredi, Otello,* and *Maometto II* in their various versions. With musical examples.

773. ———. " 'Sortire dalle vie comuni'? Wie Rossini einem Akademiker den *Guillaume Tell* verdarb." In *Oper als Text: Romanistische Beitrage zur Libretto-Forschung,* 185–219. Ed. Albert Gier. Heidelberg: Carl Winter, 1986. 318 pp. ISBN 3-53-303729-0 ML2110 .O64 1986.

     The early version of the libretto of *Guillaume Tell* has traditionally been criticized for its weaknesses. The author presents information from a handwritten version of the text that suggests that perhaps the notion of politicizing the work may have created these faults. By comparing the 1829 version with the final text, Gerhard not only demonstrates the compositional history of various significant scenes but also portrays how the roles of characters were changed. Nonetheless, with *Tell,* Rossini made a radical departure from traditional dramatic opera.

* G.[iazotto], R.[emo]. "Due lettere di Rossini." See item 45.

774. Gossett, Philip. "*Guillaume Tell.*" In "The Operas of Rossini: Problems of Textual Criticism in Nineteenth-Century Opera." See item 582.

775. Hensel, Christoph. "Tell in Tirol: Zu einer antirevolutionaren Rossini-Bearbeitung." In *Music befragt—Musik vermittelt: Peter Rummenholler zum 60, Geburtstag*, edited by Thomas Ort and Heinz von Loesch, 405–20. Augsburg: Wissner, 1996. 451 p. ISBN: 3-89639-016-3 ML55.R76 1996.

Rossini's *Guillaume Tell* was performed in various revisions under different titles, such as *Karl der Kühne* (St. Petersburg), *Vallace* (Milan), and *Rodolfo di Sterlinga* (Rome and Bologna). Hensel considers *Andrea Hofer*, the revision of *Guillaume Tell* done in Berlin by Karl August von Lichenstein and its London version, *Hofer, the Tell of Tirol*. The author notes that the Berlin production reflected the conservative political elements and religious overtones representative of the Prussian court. He adds, however, that by 1842, the political arena had changed enough for the work to be offered under its original title. Hensel includes a chart which gives an act and scene breakdown of the Berlin and London versions.

* Henze-Döhring, Sabine. "La 'natura' nelle opere di Rossini." Item 605.

* Kallberg, Jeffrey. "Marketing Rossini: Sei lettere di Troupenas ad Artaria." Item 47.

776. Kirby, Percival R. "Rossini's Overture to 'William Tell,' " *Music and Letters* 33 (1952): 132–40.

After comparing Rossini's autograph to five printed editions of the overture, the author cites errors, omissions, and inconsistencies, concluding that what is frequently played "is not Rossini at all."

* Landini, Giancarlo. "Riflessioni su alcuni aspetti della vocalità francese di Rossini." In *Atti del convegno di studi: Rossini, edizioni critiche e prassi esecutiva*, 153–72. See item 282.

* Lippmann, Friedrich. " 'Casta diva': la preghiera dell'opera italiana della prima metà dell'Ottocento." See item 553.

777. Newark, Cormac. "*Guillaume Tell.*" In *The Cambridge Companion to Rossini*. See item 478.

778. O'Grady, Deirdre. "La fonction du choeur dans l'opéra patriotique du XIXe siècle." In *L'Europe et son combat pour la liberté a travers le théâtre et l'opéra*, 107–22. See item 635.

[Not examined.]

* Quattrocchi, Arrigo. "Le accademie romane e Rossini." Item 372.

* Rienäcker, Gerhard. " 'Wilhelm Tell'–Eine Werkanalyse." In *Rossini in Paris: Eine Veranstaltung des Frankreichzentrums der Universität Leipzig, in Zusammenarbeit mit der Deutschen Rossini Gesellschaft e.V.* See item 290.

779. *Rossini, Guillaume Tell. Avant-scène opéra* 118 (March 1989) Paris: Avant-scène, 1989. 133 pp.

[Not examined.] Based on the RILM abstract, this opera guide contains articles on the libretto and librettists of *Tell*, a look at the sources of the story, information on the original interpreters, and various aspects of the plot. Includes illustrations, musical excerpts, a bibliography, and discography.

780. Viale Ferrero, Mercedes. "*Guglielmo Tell* a Torino (1839–1840), ovvero una 'procella' scenografica." *Rivista italiana musicale* 14 [no. 2] (1979): 378–94.

When Rossini's *Guillaume Tell* was produced in Italy, major changes were often made to its title and text (see item 770). Such was the case in Turin in 1839–1840 where, even though the story was known through a ballet set on the Tell story, censors rewrote sections of the libretto and revamped the plot to make the enemy a government functionary rather than the government itself. The author traces these changes and demonstrates that the critics' poor opinions came more from charges that *Tell* was not "Italian" than from questions about its musical character. Also under fire was the scenography, which proved too innovative for the audiences. Illustrated with set designs. An appendix gives examples of the changes made to the libretto used in Florence in 1831 for the Turin production.

* Walton, Benjamin. *Romanticisms and Nationalisms in Restoration France.*

781. Weisstein, Ulrich. "Der Apfel fiel recht weit vom Stamme: Rossinis *Guillaume Tell*, eine musikalische Schweizerreise." In *Oper als Text: Romanistische Beitrage zur Libretto-Forschung*, edited by Albert Gier, 147–84. Heidelberg: Carl Winter, 1986. 318 pp. ISBN 3-53-303729-0 ML2110 .O64 1986.

In discussing the analysis of opera through study of a libretto, in this case, that of Rossini's *Guillaume Tell*, the author borrows criteria from Aristotle's *Poetics*, which permit an examination of the rhythmic, melodic, and dramatic elements of the text. Also looks at literary forerunners for *Tell*, including Florian's *Guillaume Tell ou la Suisse libre* (1800).

PASTICHES

Cinderella

* Graziano, John, ed. *Italian Opera in English: Cinderella (1831)*. See item 694.

Ivanhoé

* Turner, J. Rigbie. "Nineteenth-Century Autograph Music Manuscripts in The Pierpont Morgan Library: A Check List (II). See item 15.

Robert Bruce

782. Desnoyers, Louis. *De l'Opéra en 1847 a propos de Robert Bruce; des directions passées, de la direction présente et de quelques-unes des cinq cent Directions futures; par M. Louis Desnoyers: Dissertation accompagnée des proclamations de M. Duponchel a ses concitoyens sur cette même question, et des répliques de M. Léon Pillet à icelles.* Paris: E.-B. Delanchy, 1847. 129 pp. ML410.R8 D39.

While Rossini was in Bologna in 1846, he was visited by representatives from the Opéra who sought permission for a French version of *La donna del lago*; instead, with Rossini's agreement, the pastiche *Robert Bruce* was produced. It unleashed a battle in the press led by Desnoyer, who bitterly criticized Rossini, resorting even to *ad hominem* attacks, and Charles Duponchel and Léon Pillet, who later wound up in joint directorship of the Opéra. Desnoyer reprinted six of his feuilletons along with responses by Duponchel and Pillet. Also attacked in the articles were Rossini's friend, banker Alejandro María Aguado, and the singer Rosine Stoltz, whose relationship with Pillet was common knowledge.

Un curioso accidente

783. Bini, Annalisa. " 'Accidente curioso a proposito di *Un curioso accidente*': Un contestato pasticcio rossiniano (Parigi, 1859)." In *Ottocento e oltre: scritti in onore di Raoul Meloncelli*, 339–53. See item 655.

The author traces the history of *Un curioso accidente*, the publicity for which Rossini protested. Touted by the Théâtre Italien to be a newly composed work, Rossini demanded that advertisements state that the opera was a compilation of formerly composed music. After presenting a brief biographical sketch, Bini considers the role of librettist Arcangelo Berretoni, demonstrating that this two-act pastiche, presented 26 November 1859, was an expansion of *L'occasione fa il ladro* with additional borrowings from several other Rossini operas. Contains an outline of the opera with identification of the sources of its numbers; an illustration of Berretoni concludes the essay.

UNFULFILLED OPERATIC PLANS

La figlia dell'aria

* Cagli, Bruno. "Rossini a Londra e al Théâtre Italian di Parigi: Documenti inediti dell'impresario G. B. Benelli." See item 57.

* Joerg, Guido Johannes. "Rossini a Londra e la cantata *Il pianto delle Muse in morte di Lord Byron*." See item 818.

* Johnson, Janet. "A Lost Rossini Opera Recovered: *Il viaggio a Reims*." See item 754.

Teodora e Ricciardino

* Gosset, Philip. "Gioachino Rossini and the Conventions of Composition." See item 509.

Ugo, re d'italia

* Cagli, Bruno. "Rossini a Londra e al Théâtre Italian di Parigi: Documenti inediti dell'impresario G. B. Benelli." See item 57.

* Carli Ballola, Giovanni. "Lettura dell'Ermione." See item 722.

* Joerg, Guido Johannes. "Rossini a Londra e la cantata *Il pianto delle Muse in morte di Lord Byron*." See item 818.

784. Porter, Andrew. "A Lost Opera by Rossini." *Music and Letters* 45 (1964): 39–44.

The author traces the history of the opera, which Rossini was commissioned to compose for King's Theatre, London, in 1823. Citing documents found in the archives of Barclays Bank, Porter reports that the opera, entitled *Ugo, ré d'Italia*, was actually completed. The impresario's bankruptcy, however, created a legal quagmire, and the issue remained unresolved even after Rossini had moved on to Paris. The last known reference to the manuscript, according to Porter's research, appeared in a letter written in April of 1831 by James Kemp of the law firm Fyson & Beck, in which he claimed to be in possession of "two Packets of Music purporting to be the Opera of Ugo, Ré d'Italia."

12

Nonoperatic Works

GENERAL STUDIES

* Gossett, Philip. "Gioachino Rossini," in *The New Grove Masters of Italian Opera*: *Rossini, Donizetti, Bellini, Verdi, Puccini*. See item 458.

785. Osborne, Richard. "Off the Stage." In *The Cambridge Companion to Rossini*. See item 478.

SACRED MUSIC

786. Basso, Alberto. "Rossini e la musica sacra." *Bollettino del Centro Rossini-ano di Studi* [no. 1–3] (1984): 5–20.

Basso first establishes the Romantic belief that any work of art was "sacred." Using this argument, he then suggests that, even though the Stabat Mater and the Petite messe solennelle have been criticized for their theatricality, Rossini was writing works his listeners would have understood as authentic expressions of sacred music. The author, in affirming Rossini's training in counterpoint, traces the line of his Bolognese teachers from Padre Stanislao Mattei back to the sixteenth-century composers Marco Antonio Ingegneri and Vincenzo Ruffo. Also includes a discussion of the history of the Stabat mater (see also Adam, item 803) and the Petite messe solennelle. In reference to the latter, Basso discusses Rossini's request to Pius IX for permission for women to sing in church. (See also item 41).

* Fabbri, Paolo. "Alla scuola dei Malerbi: altri autografi rossiniani." Item 346.

787. ———. "Die Sakralmusik aus Lugo und die Jugendwerke Rossinis." *La Gazzetta* 11 (2001): 5–13. German translation by Roberto Gelsomino and Reto Müller.

Fabbri continues his examination of works from Rossini's youth, during which time the composer studied with Giuseppe and Luigi Malerbi in Lugo. The author lists the works in question, all from around 1808–1810; some, however, can not be given precise dates. Fabbri again links Rossini with Lugo and the Malerbis (see also items 159, 179, 346, 347, 348, and 349), but also comments on what the orchestration of the early works demonstrates in Rossini's compositional development. More than just exercises in counterpoint, he argues, these point to the beginnings of an operatic style.

* Gossett, Philip. "Rossini in Naples: Some Major Works Recovered." Item 814.

788. Joerg, Guido Johannes. "Zur Wiederentdeckung von Gioachino Rossinis einziger geistlicher Kantate, dem *Miserere* für Solostimmen, Männerchor und Orchester." *La Gazzetta* 7 (1997): 4–7.

The author discusses the *Miserere*, published in Leipzig in 1831 as *Trost und Erhebung*. Joerg states that this work is the "Misererino" Rossini wrote of in a letter to Giovanni Ricordi (see item 75), the autograph of which had been given to the Venetian nobleman Filippo Grimani. In addition to listing the numbers of the cantata and identifying vocal and instrumental performing forces, tempi, and tonalities of each, Joerg mentions Rossini's self-borrowings from the *Miserere* for sections of *Otello* and *Semiramide*. He comments that because of Grimani, the setting of Otello, and the Fenice premiere of *Semiramide*, the three works are linked to Venice. Also mentions the 1996 performance of the work in Stuttgart.

789. Kantner. Leopold. "Stilistische Stromungen in der italienischen Kirchenmusik 1770–1830." In *Colloquium Die Stilistische Entwicklung der italienischen Musik zwischen 1770 und 1830 und ihre beziehungen zum Norden (Rome 1978)*, edited by Friedrich Lippmann, 380–92. Vol. 21 of *Analecta Musicologica*. Arno Volk: Laaber, 1982. viii, 461 pp. ISBN 3-9215-1866-0 ML290.3.C64 1978.

The author notes that, during the period covered in his study, many of the reigning opera composers in Italy were also *maestri di cappella* for ecclesiastical musical establishments. Adding to this group other theatrical composers who wrote church music, including Rossini, he questions the line of demarcation between sacred music and opera, both *seria* and *buffa*. Citing Rossini's Messa di Gloria as well as noting that Rossini's style of coloratura writing could also be heard in Italian church music, Kantner considers the cross-fertilization between sacred and theatrical music.

* M[ila], M[assimo]. "Un 'Miserere' sconosciuto di Rossini." See item 75.

790. Rimoli, Francesco. "Del sacro in Rossini: divagazioni soggettive sull'oggettività in musica." *Bollettino del Centro Rossiniano di Studi* [no. 1–3] (1987): 25–43.

The author theorizes about Rossini as a composer of sacred music, considering in particular the Stabat mater and the Petite messe solennelle. Discussing the balance of objectivity and subjectivity in Rossini's compositional character, Rimoli examines the place of sacred music in the composer's oeuvre, beginning with the earliest masses written during his student years. Rimoli also considers the composer's use of a cappella chorus in the quartet of the Stabat mater and the Sanctus of the Petite messe, demonstrating that instances of unaccompanied singing in the operas suggest religious significance. Rimoli also addresses the issues of self-borrowings and of Rossini's attempts to include female voices in his religious works (see also item 41).

791. Rosenberg, Jesse. "Rossini, Raimondi e la *Messa di Gloria* del 1820." *Bollettino del Centro Rossiniano di Studi* 35 (1995): 85–102.

Despite contemporary reports that composer Pietro Raimondi had assisted Rossini in the composition of the 1820 Messa di Gloria, Philip Gossett suggested that this was not the case (see item 814). Basing his arguments on Rossini's own comments about the work as well as illustrations from similar contrapuntal passages by Raimondi, Rosenberg proposes that there is sufficient proof that Rossini had Raimondi's help for the work's "Cum Sancto Spiritu" fugue. See also Rosenberg, item 232.

Petite messe solennelle

Contemporary Accounts

792. Ambros, A[ugust] W[ilhelm]. "Die 'Messe Solennelle' von Rossini." Chapter 6 (pp. 81–92) in Vol. 1 of *Bunte Blätter: Skizzen und Studien für Freunde der Musik und der bildenden Kunst*. Leipzig: F.E.C. Leuckart, 1872. xiv, 336 pp. ML60.A523.

Because of his negative opinion of the Stabat mater, Ambros says he initially perceived the "solemn Mass" as rather a "salon Mass," but after studying the recently published score, he now believes that the work was inspired by the spirits of Beethoven and Bach. The author applauds the individual movements of the mass but makes disparaging statements about the state of sacred music in Italy.

* Castil-Blaze [François Henri Joseph Blaze]. *L'Opéra-Italien de 1548 à 1856*. See item 319.

793. Giacomelli, A. *Messe Solennelle de G. Rossini, composée en 1863, orchestrée en 1864: Introduction, Opinions des journaux*. Paris: M. Lévy frères, 1869. 30 pp.

[Not examined.]

Modern Studies

* Cagli, Bruno. "Rossini tra Illuminismo e Romanticismo." See item 174.

794. Capitanio, Fabrizio. "L'esecuzione della Stabat Mater di Rossini diretta da Donizetti (Bologna, 1842) in una recensione dell'epoca." *Studi su Gaetano Donizetti nel bicentenario della nascita (1797–1997)* in *Bergomum: Bollettino della Civica Biblioteca Angelo Mai di Bergamo* 92 [no. 1] (January-March 1997): 137–80.

The article discusses a review of the Italian premiere of the Stabat mater, conducted in Bologna by Donizetti. The author notes the presence of a piano-vocal score of the work in the archive of the Museo Donizettiano in Bergamo that contains Donizetti's notes for the Viennese premiere, which he also conducted.

795. Carli Ballola, Giovanni. "Modulazioni stilistiche nelle polifonia della *Petite messe Solennelle*." In *Il testo e la scena* (see item 286), 669–79.

The aesthetics of the Cecilian movement guided popular judgments of nineteenth-century sacred music, approving of pieces only if they were written in this "Christian" style. Briefly commenting on the difference between Rossini's earlier sacred settings of polyphony in the Messa di Gloria (see also item 814) and the Stabat mater, Carli Ballola suggests that the composer often trades traditional fugal modulations for modern harmonies in a spirit of "adventurous freedom." Includes an analytic comparison of Rossini's treatment of fugal themes (with examples).

* Collisani, Amalia. "Umorismo di Rossini." See item 808.

796. Donella, Valentino. "Musica d'organo e organisti in Italia dalla decadenza all riforma (secolo XIX e prima meta del secolo XX)." *Rivista internazionale di musica sacra* 3 [no. 1] (January-March 1982): 27–88.

In this study of Italian organists, Donella justifies the tradition of performing the harmonium part in the Petite messe on an organ.

797. Fleming, Nancy Pope. *Rossini's "Petite Messe Solennelle."* D.M.A. Dissertation, University of Illinois at Champaign-Urbana, 1986 xii, 217 pp.

The author introduces Rossini's mass in its historical context and offers an
analysis of the work, a history of its various editions, and a critical evalua-
tion. Fleming demonstrates the care Rossini put into this work and suggests
that it is the ultimate statement of his style. In addition, she considers earlier
mass settings by Rossini, including the Ravenna Mass (1808), the Rimini
Mass (1809) and the Naples Messa di Gloria (1820) and how far stylistically the composer had come between those works and the Petite messe of
1864. Fleming points out errors in the early editions of the mass, none of
which reflects Rossini's score. With structural tables and musical examples,
including excerpts from the Rimini and Ravenna masses. See also item 798.

798. ————. "Rossini's Petite Messe Solennelle." *The Choral Journal* 30 [no. 7]
(February 1990): 15–21.

In addition to setting the five usual prayers of the mass's Ordinary, in the
Petite messe, Rossini added two movements, the "Prelude religieux" and
the hymn "O salutaris hostia." These additions demonstrate that Rossini was
well aware of the Eucharistic devotion in France. Fleming also suggests that
the harmonic richness of the work proves that Rossini was also aware of
contemporary compositional innovations. Examines the history of the
work's performance and publication. See also item 797.

799. Handt, Herbert. "A proposito del Sanctus della Petite Messe." *Bollettino del
Centro Rossiniano di Studi* 12 [no. 2] (1972): 5–9.

While preparing a performance of Rossini's Petite messe solennelle (1968),
Handt noted that none of the scores available at that time reflected Rossini's
original. His concern in this article is the Sanctus. Offering a description of
the score, he concludes that at the original performance, with Rossini present, the audience most likely heard the following: Credo, Ritournelle,
Prélude, Ritournelle, Sanctus. He also suggests that a more careful examination of the score will lead performers to an understanding of the mystical
element Rossini intended to portray with this composition.

* Johnstone, George Harcourt [Lord Derwent]. *Rossini and some Forgotten
Nightingales.* See item 471.

* Pritsch, Norbert. "Gedanken zu den drei Fassungen der 'Petite Messe Solennelle.' " In *Rossini in Paris: Eine Veranstaltung des Frankreichzentrums der Universität Leipzig, in Zusammenarbeit mit der Deutschen Rossini Gesellschaft e.V.* See item 290.

800. ———. " 'Melodia semplice—Ritmo chiaro': Anmerkungen zum Ineinandergreifen von Melodik, Rhythmik, und Harmonik bei G. Rossini anhand dreier Ausschnitte aus der Petite messe Solennelle." *La Gazzetta* 11 (2001): 14–18.

In discussions, Rossini seems to have highlighted the importance of melody and rhythm over harmony. His often ironic and playful use of harmony in some works further clouds the issue. Examining three excerpts from the Petite messe (the alto solo and chorus section of the Agnus Dei, "Et vitam venturi saeculi" from the Credo, and the Kyrie), Pritsch proposes that harmony is the musical element which dominates the composition.

* Rattalino, Piero. "Problemi de esecuzione della Petite messe Solennelle." In *Atti del convegno di studi: Rossini, edizioni critiche e prassi esecutiva*, 209–15. See item 282.

801. ———. " 'Torniamo all'antico e sarà un progresso': Temo di Giuseppe Verdi svolto da Gioachino Rossini." *Bollettino del Centro Rossiniano di Studi* [no. 1–3] (1976): 165–77.

As the author states, this article, rather than being a scholarly investigation, is based on liner notes for a recording of Rossini's Petite messe solennelle. In addition to a description of the movements, Rattalino offers a brief compositional and performance history, and speculates on the influence the Cecilian movement and the French piano school may have had on this work.

802. Stefani, Gino. "Le Messe Solennelle di Rossini nella critica dell'epoca." In *Convegno di studi su Rossini per il Centenario della morte di Gioacchino Rossini*, pp. 137–48. See item 283.

Stefani proposes a study of Rossini's mass, which he feels moderns scholars have neglected. He cites contemporary reviews of the work's earliest performances, noting that the religious elements of the music interested the writers least; they were, however, taken with Rossini's ability to compose in a serious style, using such traditional techniques as theme and variations. It was the composer's intent to use the mass in liturgy, Stefani notes, for he requested Pius IX to lift the ban on women's voices in church (see item 41). The author notes, however, that although critics thought it sounded best performed in a church, it was generally rejected for ecclesiastical use.

Stabat mater

Contemporary Accounts

803. Adam, Adolphe. "Rossini: Le Stabat Mater." In *Derniers souvenirs d'un musicien*, 249–75. Paris: Michel Lévy Freres, 1859. 319 pp. ML390 .A19.

Fellow composer Adam lauds Rossini in this posthumously published memoir describing a performance of selections of the Stabat mater. In addition to discussing the movements performed (and, later in the essay, four that were not), Adam praises the variety that Rossini could achieve as a composer, proclaiming him "the greatest composer of our century," greater than Weber and even Beethoven. Includes a diversion on the qualities of church music.

* Ambros, A[ugust] W[ilhelm]. "Die 'Messe Solennelle' von Rossini." See item 792.

804. Blaze de Bury, Henri. *Musiciens Contemporains*. Paris: Michel Lévy, 1856. xvi, 289 pp. ML385 .B64; reprint, Paris: Editions D'Aujourd'hui, 1982. xvi, 289 pp. ISBN 2-7307-0279-2 ML385.B64 1982.

In a brief commentary (pp. 198–204), the author discusses Rossini's Stabat mater as an ingenious and necessary attempt at reforming the traditional ideals of religious music. Claiming that the Church and its art is in the process of change, Blaze de Bury then demonstrates why critics would be disturbed by the theatrical nature of Rossini's composition. He concludes that, whatever its nature, it is a work of great interest.

805. Heine, Heinrich. "Rossini und Mendelssohn: Kirchenmusik." First published 9 May 1842 in the *Allgemeine Zeitung*; translated into Italian in Vol. 2 of Radiciotti (see item 164); reprint in *Zeitungsberichte über Musik und Malerie*, edited by Michael Mann, 136–41. Frankfurt: Insel Verlag, 1964. 225 pp. ML60.H45.

Heine discusses the German opinion of Rossini's Stabat mater: the piece is considered "too happy for a sacred subject," demonstrating an "exaggerated religiosity." Heine, however, defends the work, claiming it to be more religious than Mendelssohn's *Paulus*. Rossini, according to Heine, had more religious experience, and the work suggests that he was harkening back to his days as a child singing in the churches of Pesaro. See also Collisani, item 808.

806. Ortique, Joseph d'. *Le Stabat Mater di Rossini*. Paris, n.p., 1841

[Not examined.]

Modern Studies
    * Angelis, Marcello de. "La prima italiano dello Stabat Mater: Precisazioni
    e documenti." In *Atti del convegno di studi: Rossini, edizioni critiche e
    prassi esecutiva*, 105–51. See item 282.

807. Burchi, Guido. "Una cadenza inedita per il soprano nello Stabat Mater di
     Rossini." *Nuova rivista musicale italiana* 17 [no. 1] (January-March 1983):
     36–42.

     The author presents, with musical examples, an unpublished cadenza for the
     "Sancta Mater istud agas" composed by Rossini for soprano Clara Novello
     for the 1842 Italian premiere of the Stabat mater in Bologna. The cadenza is
     housed, along with her part book, at the Accademia musicale Chigiana in
     Siena.

     * Capitanio, Fabrizio. "L'esecuzione della Stabat Mater di Rossini diretta da
     Donizetti (Bologna, 1842) in una recensione dell'epoca. See item 794.

808. Collisani, Amalia. "Umorismo di Rossini." *Rivista italiana di musicologia*
     33 [no. 2] (1998): 301–49.

     Writing to God on the autograph of the Petite messe solennelle, Rossini
     noted that he was, above all, a composer of *opere buffe*. Through essays by
     Heine (item 805), Luigi Pirandello *(L'umorismo)* and Sigmund Freud ("Der
     Humor"), Collisani considers humor in the Stabat mater and the Petite
     messe, looking as well at the irony found in the *Péchés*. The author suggests
     that, through humor, the composer was free to explore a new musical lan-
     guage, which he found liberating, although his listeners thought these ele-
     ments disconcerting. With musical examples and a structural table of three
     movements from the messe's Credo.

809. Collita, Carlo. *Il Palazzo dell'Archiginnasio e l'antico studio bolognese:
     con il Teatro Anatomico, le Funzioni dell'Anatomia; prima esecuzione dello
     Stabat Mater di Rossini*. Bologna: Stampa Officina Grafica Bolognese,
     1975. 101 pp. Illustrated.

     [Not examined.]

810. Faravelli, Danilo. "Stabat Mater: poesia e musica." *Rivista internazionale di
     musica sacra* 4 [no. 1] (January-March 1983): 9–43.

     The author discusses various settings of this sequence, attributed to Jaco-
     pone da Todi, proposing that Rossini's version revitalizes the text, taking it
     beyond church Latin and exploiting all its poetic possibilities.

811. Kirsch, Winfried. "Gioacchino Rossinis *Stabat Mater*: Versuch einer Exegese." *Kirchenmusikalisches Jahrbuch* 73 (1990): 71–96.

The author interprets Rossini's work in terms of "naturalistic Christian piety," relating it to contemporary devotional practices, particularly in Catholic Italy. The particular appeal of the work came from its ability to draw the listener into identifying with the work's characters.

* Rienäcker, Gerhard. " 'Stabat Mater'—Eine Werkanalyse." In *Rossini in Paris: Eine Veranstaltung des Frankreichzentrums der Universität Leipzig, in Zusammenarbeit mit der Deutschen Rossini Gesellschaft e.V.* See item 290.

812. Spada, Marco. "Francesco Rangone e la *Narrazione* sullo Stabat Mater a Bologna con altri documenti." *Bollettino del Centro Rossiniano di Studi* 19 (1989): 5–46.

The author extracts comments on Rossini and his connections to Bologna from the volumes kept by Count Francesco Rangone. Spada then discusses Rangone's little-known, first-person account of performances of Rossini's Stabat mater in Bologna in 1842: the *Narrazione di quando riguarda la musica dello Stabat Mater*. Includes the author's edition of the *Narrazione* as well as texts of other documents, letters, and notes about the performances and production costs. Following is a partial bibliography of press notices about the Stabat Mater published in Italy from 1823 to 1824.

* Sprang, Christian. "Reichtliche Auseinandersetzungen um das 'Stabat Mater.' " In *Rossini in Paris: Eine Veranstaltung des Frankreichzentrums der Universität Leipzig, in Zusammenarbeit mit der Deutschen Rossini Gesellschaft e.V.* See item 290.

* Wehrmann, Harald. "Heines Musikanschauung." See item 440.

CANTATAS, INCIDENTAL MUSIC, HYMNS, CHORUSES

Il pianto d'Armonia sulla morte di Orfeo (1808)
* Tozzi, Lorenzo. "Rossini con le dande." In *Atti del convegno di studi: Rossini, edizioni critiche e prassi esecutiva*, 69–84. See item 282.

Contains an analysis of Rossini's first cantata, a prize-winning student work at the Liceo in Bologna.

L'Aurora (1815)
813. Rudakova, E. "Una Cantata scoperta in Russia." Trans. Garaldo Fanti. *Bollettino del Centro Rossiniano di Studi* 2 [no. 3] (1956): 51–52.

The author notes the discovery in Russia of the autograph of *L'Aurora*

(1815), composed for the nameday of Caterina Kutuzov. The author notes
that in the scene in which Aurora appears, Rossini made use of a Russian
folk tune, identified in this article with the Italian title "Ah! perché mai tutto
questo daffare"; Rudakova maintains that Rossini reused this song in the
finale of *Il barbiere di Siviglia*.

Le nozze di Teti, e di Peleo (1816)

814. Gossett, Philip. "Rossini in Naples: Some Major Works Recovered." *Musical Quarterly* 54 (1968): 316–40; also published as "Rossini a Napoli" in the *Bollettino del Centro Rossiniano di Studi* 11 [no. 1–3] (1971): 53–71.

The author dispels the belief that the nonoperatic compositions from
Rossini's Neapolitan tenure were lost. Having located the autograph of the
cantata *Le Nozze di Teti, e di Peleo* (1816) in the Naples Conservatory, Gossett is able to reconstruct the work, identifying the self-borrowings therein
(of the eleven numbers, eight include multiple borrowings of music from
eight previous compositions, including *Il barbiere di Siviglia* and *Il turco in
Italia*). Gossett next considers the cantata for solo voice and chorus performed in 1819 in celebration of the first appearance of the monarch after an
illness and the cantata for three voices and chorus sung in honor of Francis
I of Austria's visit that same year. The author demonstrates not only that
these works were more than likely composed in 1818, but that they share
musical material (the score of which seems to be missing). He then suggests
the possibility of yet another cantata entitled *Igea* (1819 or 1820), which
introduces material. Finally, although performance descriptions exist for a
complete mass performed in 1820, Gossett proves that the work was rather
a *messa di gloria*, a setting of only the Kyrie and Gloria. Of particular significance is Gossett's introduction of a discussion about the various ways
Rossini used self-borrowings. Includes musical examples, an illustration of
a page from *Le Nozze di Teti* demonstrating use of music from *Il barbiere*,
and one of the verso of the sole-surviving autograph page from the mass.

Edipo a Colono (Edipo Coloneo) (before 1817)

815. Tozzi, Lorenzo. "Edipo a Colono di Rossini." *Chigiana: rassegna annuale di studi musicologici*, 13 (1976, publ. 1979): 361–67.

[Not examined.] According to the RILM abstract, Tozzi traces the history of
Rossini's incidental music to Sophocles' *Edipo a Colono* from its rediscovery in 1933 to its recording twenty years later. The author also provides a
critical commentary.

La riconoscenza (1821)

816. Turchi, Guido. "La cantata 'Argene e Melania.'" *Bollettino del Centro Rossiniano di Studi* 8 [no. 1] (1968): 11–18.

Turchi, preparing an edition of "Argena e Melania" for the Quaderno Rossiniano series, offers a history of this work, which appeared first under the title of "La riconoscenza" at the San Carlo in Naples in 1821. Other versions of the work, which included numerous variants, were later performed at Naples' Teatro del Fondo (1822) and in Bologna (1829). Other titles associated with the work are "Notturno" and "I pastori." After tracing the performance history, Turchi discusses specific problems associated with considering all versions for an edition of the work.

La santa alleanza (1822)

817. Cavazzocca Mazzatinti, Vittorio. "Rossini a Verona durante il Congresso del 1822." In *Atti e memorie dell'Accademia di agricoltura, scienze, e lettere di Verona*. 4th series, 24 (1922): 53–112; also reprinted by Verona: Tipografica Veronese, 1922. 112 pp.

The author discusses Metternich's request for Rossini to compose the cantata *La santa alleanza*. Noting the errors in Escudier's record of the first performance, the author gives details of the performance (24 November 1822), including its cost. Documents include the three versions of the libretto as written by Gaetano Rossi. Also cites excerpts from correspondence between Rossini and Rossi relative to the work.

* Kern, Bernd-Rüdiger. "Rossini e Metternich." See item 281.

Omaggio pastorale (1823)

* Simonato, Giuliano. "Rossini, Canova, e Treviso: I rapporti tra il musicista e la città veneta esaminati attraverso documenti inediti ed un autografo." See item 373.

Il pianto delle muse in morte di Lord Byron (1824)

818. Joerg, Guido Johannes. "Rossini a Londra e la cantata *Il pianto delle Muse in morte di Lord Byron*." *Bollettino del Centro Rossiniano di Studi* 28 (1988): 47–76.

Discusses the composition, performance, and edition of this work. The author briefly examines Rossini's role in the concert life of London during his visit there in 1823–1824 (see also item 307). Supplementing his discussion with contemporary reviews, he centers on this composition, questioning its generic designation as a cantata. He demonstrates that it was reviewed as an "Ottavino" (perhaps for the "ottavario" or two-month commemoration of the poet's death) and published as a "Canzone con coro." Also notes Rossini's self-borrowings from *Maometto II* and briefly mentions *Ugo, re d'Italia* and *La figlia dell'aria* (see items 57, 754, and 784).

Illustrated with a facsimile of the King's Theatre poster announcing Rossini's arrival, the program of a public concert, and the title page of the 1824 piano reduction of *Il pianto*.

Cantata per il battesimo del figlio del banchiere Aguado (1827)

819. Joerg, Guido Johannes. "La cantata per il battesimo del figlio del banchiere Aguado." *Bollettino del Centro Rossiniano di Studi* 31 (1991): 21–54. Translated from the German to Italian by Paolo Fabbri.

Joerg proposes that, based on Rossini's works in the genre, one may conclude that by the early nineteenth century, the cantata had lost its traditional form and had become a chamber work with many structural possibilities. He considers the various problems in cataloging the cantatas. As an example, he examines (and later describes) the cantata composed for the baptism of the son of banker Alejandro María Aguado, demonstrating with facsimiles of the initial section of both that it was also published as a vocal chamber quartet. The article addresses the difficulties of identifying works published in various editions; also considers Rossini's self-borrowings, calling the cantatas "an experimental field" for the operas.

L'armonica cetra del nume (1830)

820. Joerg, Guido Johannes, " '. . . o Francesco in questo giorno . . .' Ein Namenstagsgeschenk von Gioachino Rossini." *La Gazzetta* 1 (1994): 3–9; a shorter version without score examples appeared in *Die Musikforschung* 46 [no. 2] (1993): 181–83.

After listing works he claims can bear the designation "cantata," the author divides Rossini's composition in this genre into three periods. The first (1808–1815) and third (1824–1847) saw compositions that often were destined for private individuals; the second (1816–1822) inspired more public compositions, usually intended for members of the Bourbon monarchy in Naples, which Rossini served. The author then describes the discovery of the manuscript of the cantata for the name day of Francesco Sampieri (1830) in Staatsbibliothek in Berlin in 1991 (although this score is marked "cantata," some works lists identify it as the Coro "L'armonica cetra del nume"). Through use of musical examples, Joerg demonstrates self-borrowings from the 1821 cantata *La riconoscenza* and the operas *Aureliano in Palmira* (1813) and *Le comte Ory* (1828). He also stresses that this cantata is the first of the many compositions that post-date *Guillaume Tell*.

Giovanna d'Arco (1832)

821. Bolzani, Marco. "Un intervento di Rossini nella cantata *Giovanno d'Arco* di Luigi Campiani (1845)." *Bollettino del Centro Rossiniano di Studi* 34 (1994): 69–89.

In his work on composer Luigi Campiani, Bolzani discovered that two recitatives by Rossini, previously thought to belong to that composer's cantata *Giovanna d'Arco*, actually were Rossini's contribution to a cantata of the same name composed by Campiani, a student (and son of friend of Rossini) at the Conservatorio in Bologna where Rossini served as an honorary advisor. Includes the author's edition of the recitatives with critical notes.

822. Valente, Erasmo. "La cantata 'Giovanna d'Arco.' " *Bollettino del Centro Rossiniano di Studi* 10 [no. 1] (1970): 22–24.

The author describes the movements of this cantata, suggesting that it shares certain characteristics with the Stabat mater and even foreshadows the mood of the Petite messe solennelle.

Cantata in onore del Sommo Pontefice Pio Nono (1847)
823. Bucarelli, Mauro. "L'inedita cantata per Pio IX." *Rossini a Roma—Rossini e Roma* (item 289), 53–68.

Considers the history of two compositions, or rather refashioned self-borrowings, in honor of Pope Pius IX. Briefly mentioning "Grido di esultazione riconoscente alla paterna clemenza di Pio" (Bologna 1846), Bucarelli then centers on the cantata in honor of the new pontiff (libretto by Giuseppe Marchetti), which was commissioned for performance in Rome in 1847. Like the hymn, a musical resetting of the Coro dei Bardi from *La donna del lago*, the cantata is composed of self-borrowings, the numbers having been drawn from *Ricciardo e Zoraide*, *Ermione*, *Armida*, and *L'assedio di Corinto*. The author reconstructs the cantata's five numbers, concluding that Rossini's corrections of the original settings, as well as his reorchestration and reharmonizing, demonstrate the composer's careful attempt to create from old music a new, unified musical structure. Contains transcriptions of correspondence to and from Rossini about the commission of both compositions and the text of the cantata's libretto.

CHORAL MUSIC

824. Braun, William R. "From Youth to the 'Sins of Old Age': The Choral Music of Rossini." *The Choral Journal*, 32 [no. 7] (February 1992): 7–14.

The author examines the nonoperatic choral compositions of Rossini.

MISCELLANEOUS VOCAL MUSIC

825. Joerg, Guido Johannes. " 'Paroles et musique du singe': Animalisches in den Kanons von Gioachino Rossini." *La Gazzetta* [no. 1] (1993): 3–7.

Joerg discusses the autographs of two Rossini canons. One, found under various names including "Canone Scherzoso a Quattro Soprani Democratici," later appears with its text changed from "il canti strano udiam de castrati" to "il canto strano udiam d'animali." The latter canon contains a personal joke in which Rossini refers to himself not as the "cynge" or "swan" of Pesaro but as the "singe" or monkey. With facsimiles of the canon autographs.

* Pritsch, Norbert. "Die musikalischen Quellen des Balletts 'La boutique fantasque'—ein Beitrag zur Rossini-Rezeption durch Ottorino Respighi." See item 430.

INSTRUMENTAL MUSIC

826. Atwell, Bruce W. "History of the Natural Horn Quartet in Selected Works from the Symphonic Literature, Chamber Music, and Opera: From the Baroque to the Romantic Period." D.M.A dissertation, University of Cincinnati, 1999. 321 pp.

The author traces the history of horn orchestration from the Baroque era through the nineteenth century, by which time the horn quartet had become standard in the orchestra and as a chamber ensemble. Included is a consideration of Rossini's role in the horn quartet tradition.

* Busch, Gudrun. "Die Unwetterszene in der romantischen Oper." See item 536.

827. Diddi, Stefano. "La Corono d'Italia." *Bollettino del Centro Rossiniano di Studi* 4 [no. 4] (1960): 71–73.

Diddi discusses this late Rossini composition, a military fanfare composed for Vittorio Emanuele II in 1868. The author stresses the importance of this piece in that, like many of the composer's late works, it demonstrates a certain liberation from his older style. Contains a description of the work and a brief history of its significance.

* Fabbri, Mario. "Ignoti momenti rossiniani: Contributo all'indagine sul 'lungo silenzio' di Rossini e alla conoscenza dell'attività creativa minore del maestro—Le segrete confessioni a Ferdinando Giorgetti e le sconosciute 'Variazioni' per Alessandro Abate (1817)." See item 64.

* Fabbri, Paolo. "Luoghi rossiniani: Villa Triossi al Conventello." See item 364.

828. Gallino, Nicola. *"Di sei sonate orrende"*: *Alcuni aspetti stilistici e strutturali delle sonate a quattro di Gioacchino Rossini.* Turin: Artale, 1990. 30 pp.

This monograph considers the similarities between these early chamber pieces (1804) and Rossini's subsequent operatic style. Gallino compares the melodic construction of themes, examining the chamber pieces' metric structures with poetic texts from librettos. Other points of comparison are the use of the crescendo and employment of slow introductions. Gallino demonstrates that these youthful compositions foreshadow Rossini's theatrical works. For more on these connections, see also item 340.

* ——— "Lo 'scuolaro' Rossini e la musica strumentale al Liceo di Bologna." See item 340. See also item 828.

829. Martinotti, Sergio. "I 'peccati' del giovane e del vecchio Rossini." *Quadrivium* 14 [no. 2] (1973): 249–71.

The author considers the chamber and instrumental works of Rossini, dividing them into his earliest compositions, followed by works composed along with his operas, and then those written during the so-called period of silence. The earliest works are likened to apprentice compositions, developing the instrumental techniques that would later appear in his overtures. The final works, although often ironic, reflect what Martinotti feels is the degeneration of the humor that appeared in Rossini's great *buffa* operas. These later chamber pieces, however, presage the works of Satie and Busoni. (See also items 432 and 433.)

* Simionato, Giuliano. "Rossini, Canova, e Treviso: I rapporti tra il musicista e la città veneta esaminati attraverso documenti inediti ed un autografo." See item 373.

PÉCHÉS DE VIEILLESSE

General Studies

830. Bonaccorsi, Alfredo. "Spunti popolari." *Bollettino del Centro Rossiniano di Studi* 2 [no. 1] (1956): 1–3.

After considering definitions of "popular" music, the author cites examples of Rossini's use of folk melodies in selections from *Les Péchés*. Two popular songs from the Marche region appear in the Chansonette de cabaret ("La lazzarone") in the *Album Français*. A popular lullaby inspired the theme of "Ouf! les petits pois!" in the *Album pour les enfants adolescents* and a comic tune from Pesaro is the theme of "La pesarese" in the *Album des enfants dégourdis*. Bonaccorsi concludes that, although it can not be determined whether these were conscious quotations, they demonstrate that an older Rossini in Paris still had ties to his homeland. With musical excerpts. For another instance of a quotation of folk music, see item 751.

* Bruson, Jean-Marie. "Olympe, Pacini, Michotte e altri: la vendita dei *Péchés de vieillesse* e le sue vicende." See item 208.

831. Gossett, Philip. "Rossini e i suoi *Péchés de vieillesse*." *Nuova rivista musicale italiana.* 14 [no. 1] (Jan.-Mar. 1980): 7–26. Translated into Italian by Laura Meconcelli.

Although all autographs of Rossini's *Péchés* were composed on paper purchased after 1855, it has come to light that some were written prior to that. Examining the issue of dating these works, Gossett presents a table of pieces for which dating is possible; he also considers Rossini's compositional process for these pieces (see also item 509). Gossett suggests a thorough study of the history of these compositions, which will flesh out that period in the composer's life often referred to as the "years of silence."

832. Lanza Tomasi, Giovacchino. "Gusto del silenzio rossiniano." *Bollettino del Centro Rossiniano di Studi* 11 [no. 1–3] (1971): 73–85.

Lanza Tomasi corrects misconceptions about Rossini's so-called period of silence, demonstrating that the composer actively wrote music but simply did not publish it. The author divides the last thirty-nine years of Rossini's life into two phase: 1829–1857 (during which he composed and, indeed, published works such as *Les Soirées musicales* and the Stabat mater) and 1857–1868 (which begins with the *Musique anodine* of the *Péchés de vieillesse*). Lanza Tomasi suggests that, by not publishing these late works, Rossini avoided critical debate; the opinions of his audiences at the Saturday *soirées* were sufficient. He also notes a widespread critical incomprehension of the musical elements of the *Péchés*, and, in the remainder of the article, addresses the pianistic style and analytical elements in these salon pieces.

* Martinotti, Sergio. "I 'peccati' del giovane e del vecchio Rossini." See item 829.

* ————. "Rossini's *Péchés*: 'blague sous l'aisselle.' " In *Atti del convegno di studi: Rossini, edizioni critiche e prassi esecutiva*, 183–208. See item 282.

833. Petazzi, Paolo. "Aspetti dell'ultima produzione di Rossini." *Bollettino del Centro Rossiniano di Studi* 10 [no. 1] (1970): 27–44; [no. 2] (1970): 74–90; [no. 3] (1970): 91–112.

In this series, the author discusses Rossini's late works, primarily the *Péchés de vieillesse*, suggesting that they are compositions driven by the composer's isolation from the contemporary musical world. Parts I and II consider the piano albums, exploring issues such as Rossini's pianism. Part III deals with the vocal albums. With ample score excerpts.

* Pritsch, Norbert. "Die musikalischen Quellen des Balletts 'La boutique fantasque'—ein Beitrag zur Rossini-Rezeption durch Ottorino Respighi." See item 430.

* Rohmann, Ralf. " 'Péchés de vieillesse.' " In *Rossini in Paris: Eine Veranstaltung des Frankreichzentrums der Universität Leipzig, in Zusammenarbeit mit der Deutschen Rossini Gesellschaft e.V.* See item 290.

Ensemble Albums

* Redditi, Aldo. "Un mot a' Paganini." See item 229.

Piano Albums

834. Fiuzzi, Stefano. "Osservazioni sui '24 Petit Riens' di G. Rossini." *Bollettino del Centro Rossiniano di Studi* [no. 3] (1973): 8–12.

Fiuzzi states that these twenty-four piano works are, from a psychological standpoint, the most emblematic of Rossini's late works. Not typical "album" pieces, these works characterize Rossini's ironic sense of humor. Although they were published between 1880–1885, their eventual assembly as a collection was most likely not Rossini's original intent. Fiuzzi considers the titles of the pieces and their modifications by publishers who perhaps felt that the composer's wit would not be understood. The genius in these pieces, the author maintains, stems from the newness of their musical ideas. Fiuzzi ends by questioning whether these works represent a demystification of Romanticism, an expression of Rossini's psychological disorders, or an example of the musical tastes of the Parisian class interested in *salon* compositions.

835. Guillot, Pierre. "La Pacific 231 sur les rails de la locomotion musicale." In *Honegger et Milhaud: Musique et esthetique*, edited by Manfred Kelkel, 64–83. Paris: Vrin, 1994. 397 pp. ISBN: 2-7116-4279-8.

This look at music inspired by modes of transportation includes Rossini's "Un petit train de plaisir comico-imitatif," in the *Album pour les enfants dégourdis*.

836. Momany, Sharon Miller. *Form and Genre in Selected Keyboard Works from Rossini's "Péchés de vieillesse."* D.M.A. dissertation, Memphis State University, 1990. 137 pp.

The author analyzes the following albums from Rossini's late piano works: *Album pour les enfants adolescents*, *Album pour les enfants dégourdis*, *Album de chaumière*, *Album de château*, and "Quatre hor d'oeuvres" from

Quatre mendiants et quatre hor d'oeuvres. In her study, she notes the recurrence of four basic forms, three types of introductions, two groups of codas (which reiterate the tonic) and, above all, Rossini's penchant for repetition of musical elements. With musical examples.

837. Park, Chunson. "Rossini's Late Piano Pieces: An Analysis and Revalution." D.M.A. dissertation, Boston University, 1997. 111 pp.

As the author notes, piano works make up some two-thirds of Rossini's *Péchés de vieillesse*. Examining the place of piano compositions in Rossini's ouevre, Park notes that these special compositions were private fare, meant for audiences at Rossini's famous salons. Encouraging performance of these pieces, Park offers a stylistic analysis and suggests how these pieces are not representative of contemporary piano literature, but foreshadow future types of compositions. See also items 432 and 433.

* Teske-Spellerberg, Ulrike. "Die Klavieralben Rossinis." In *Rossini in Paris: Eine Veranstaltung des Frankreichzentrums der Universität Leipzig, in Zusammenarbeit mit der Deutschen Rossini Gesellschaft e.V.* See item 290.

838. ———. *Die Klaviermusik von Gioacchino Rossini*. Vol. 27 of *Frankfurter Beiträge zur Musikwissenschaft*, ed. Musikwissenschaftlichen Institut der Johann Wolfgang Goethe-Universität. Tutzing: Hans Schneider, 1998. 283 pp. ISBN 3-7952-0905-6 ML410.R8 T47 1998.

Based on the author's dissertation. In addition to examining Rossini's piano compositions in terms of form, harmony, rhythm, and pianistic technique, the author considers these pieces in their overall nineteenth-century social and cultural context. Includes an examination of the musical life in Frankfurt between 1830 and 1870. Several works are analyzed; score examples are included. An appendix contains a catalog of the piano works.

Vocal Albums
839. Cagli, Bruno. "Un'anacreontica per Olimpia." *Bollettino del Centro Rossiniano di Studi* 14 [no. 2–3] (1974): 5–8.

Cagli identifies the author of the poetic text of Rossini's "L'ultimo ricordo" (no. 4 in the *Album italiano* of the *Péchés de vieillesse*) as Giovanni Radaelli (1785–1815). In Rossini's version of the poem, he substituted the name of his wife, Olympe, for the original name, Elvira, identified variously as Radaelli's wife, daughter, or lover. Also linking the work to Rossini, notes Cagli, is that Stendhal seems to have used the dying poet Radaelli as the model for the character of Salviati in *De l'Amour*.

* Huber, Hans Rudolf. "Rossini zitiert Offenbach." See item 226.

SPURIOUS WORKS

840. Crafts, Edward J. "A Tale of Two Cats." *Bollettino del Centro Rossiniano di Studi* [no. 3] (1975): 5–12; Italian translation, 61–68.

   The author demonstrates, with score examples, that the popular "Duetto buffo di due gatti" attributed to Rossini, is actually based on Danish composer C.E.F. Weyse's "Katte-Cavatine." G. Berthod's oft-performed "potpourri" arrangements of Weyse's work, combined with quotations from "Ah! come mai non senti" from *Otello*, parodies Rossini's *seria* style.

   * Gossett, Philip. "Le sinfonie di Rossini." See item 556.

   * Ingerslev-Jensen, Povl. "An Unknown Rossini Overture: Report of a Discovery in Odense." See item 558.

13

Discographies and Videographies

This chapter lists major audiovisual references. Some biographies and studies of specific works include lists of recordings and videos (often outdated and incomplete); notation of these is made under individual citations.

841. Celletti, Rodolfo. *Il teatro d'opera in disco: Il primo catalogo di tutte le edizioni complete di opere liriche con commenti sulle esecuzioni e le interpretazioni.* Milan: Rizzoli, 1976. 614 pp. ML156.4 O46 C4.

   The author lists and comments on recordings of operas through 1975, including a section on Rossini's works (pp. 382–408). In addition to providing discographic information, Celletti critiques the quality of the recordings and performances and comments on the score editions upon which the performances are based.

842. Heierling, Alfred. *Rossini auf CD, Katalog Nr. 18 Ausgabe Juli 2000 mit über 2500 Einspielungen.* Leipzig: Deutsche Rossini Gesellschaft, 2000. 80 pp.

   Updated yearly, this publication lists, in alphabetical order, recordings of Rossini's music available on compact disc.

843. Marinelli, Carlo. "Discografia rossiniana." *La rassegna musicale* 24 [no. 3] (July-September 1954): 273–89.

   The author provides a chronological works list of Rossini's compositions, annotating under each work information about the composition and whether it has been recorded. In cases where a recording exists, critical comments are given along with data identifying the recordings.

844. ———. "La discografia rossiniana." In *Convegno di studi su Rossini per il Centenario della morte di Gioacchino Rossini*, 164–77. See item 283.

Marinelli explains the issues and methodology involved in compiling the discography of an opera composer. Even after eliminating recordings of selections of works, the discographer must be aware that the musical text of a recorded version may not reflect the actual composition and that the recording itself is only a "reading" of a selected text. These issues were particularly problematic when this article was written. During the late 1960s, notes the author, most recordings lacked the vitality present in the composer's music. An interesting look at the beginnings of Rossini discographic projects (see items 849, 850, and 851). Following Marinelli's discussion is a discography of Rossini operas as of 1968.

845. Modugno, Maurizio. "Discografia rossiniana 1.A—Le opere serie e le musiche di scena." With the collaboration of Alberto Bottazzi. *Bollettino del Centro Rossiniano di Studi* [no. 1–3] (1982): 55–100.

In this publication, Modugno begins what he calls a "work in progress": a discography of Rossini's operas through which one may study the history of vocal interpretation as well as the development of the "Rossini interpreter." He begins this project with the *opere serie* because of their importance in the 1950s "Rossini Renaissance." The discography includes complete recordings of operas as well as those containing acts, scenes, and selections from them; it omits instrumental transcription, arrangements, and overtures. (N.B.: Because of the date of the project, most of these recordings are LPs). Sections dedicated to each opera begin with the title, structure, librettist, and information on its premiere venue and interpreters. Following this is information on the language of the performance (if not Italian), the production's cast or, in the case of selections, individual performers; the conductor, orchestra, and chorus; venue or occasion of the performance (if live); date of the recording; speed (33 rpm, for example) and type of recording (cylinder, acoustic, electric, LP or EP); company and catalogue information. Part 1.B, is a critical commentary on the *serie* recordings (item 846); Part 2 is discography and critical commentary of the *opere semiserie* (see item 847); Part 3, A and B, was to be respectively the discography and critical commentary of the *buffe* works.

846. ———. "Discografia rossiniana 1.B—Le opere serie e le musiche di scena: Commento critico." *Bollettino del Centro Rossiniano di Studi* [no. 1–3] (1984): 53–126.

Modugno states in Part 1.A of this series that his study is dedicated to the history of vocal interpretation and the development of the Rossini interpreter (see item 845). His critical comments on the recordings are guided by the following criteria: consideration of the score used in performance, with the Rossini Critical Edition as a point of departure; the completeness of the score relative to material cut; the stylistic integrity—both vocal and instrumental—of the performance. Includes a brief discussion on bel canto style and on the *primo Ottocento* orchestra. See item 847 for a parallel discussion of *semiserie* works. Illustrated with photographs of singers pictured in Rossini roles.

847. ———. "Discografia rossiniana 2. Le opere semiserie: Discografia e commento critico." *Bollettino del Centro Rossiniano di Studi* [no. 1–3] (1986): 73–85.

Considers recordings of the four semiserious works (*L'inganno felice, Torvaldo e Dorliska, La gazza ladra*, and *Matilde di Shabran*). See items 845 and 846 for an explanation of Modugno's methodology and critical criteria.

848. Occelli, Celso. "Discoteca." *Bollettino del Centro Rossiniano di Studi* 3 [no. 3] (1957): 54–57; 3 [no. 4] (1957): 74–77; 3 [no. 5] (1957): 93–96; 3 [no. 6] (1957): 113–17.

This series presented a current discography of phonograph recordings of Rossini's compositions, now useful for historic purposes. The three installments listed recordings of theatrical works and the last concluded with sacred music, vocal and instrumental chamber pieces, and orchestral transcriptions of Rossini works. Occelli notes that there were, at this time, no recordings of cantatas, hymns, or choruses. A supplement updating this discography appears in Vol. 5 [no. 6] (1959): 112–15.

849. *Repertorio delle fonti sonore e audiovisive rossiniane esistenti in Italia*. A publication of the Progietto Rossini of the Ministero del Turismo e dello Spettacolo and the Istituto di Ricerca per il Teatro Musicale (I.R.TE.M.). 5 vols. Rome: I.R.TE.M.: 1991–93. ML156.5 .R6 R4 Vols. 1–5.

Lists all records, tape recordings, compact discs, films, and videos of Rossini operas in theater archives in Rome, Florence, Cremona, Reggio Emilio, and Milan. The following volumes have been published: Vol. 1: *Ente Autonomo Teatro dell'Opera Roma* (ed. Umberto Nicoletti Altimari. xi, 43 pp. 1991 ML156.5.R6 1); Vol. 2: *Teatro Comunale Firenze* (ed. Silvano Pieri. xi, 47 pp, 1992 ML156.5.R6 2); Vol. 3: *Scuola di Paleografia, Università degli Studi di Pavia*, Valeria Carlotti and Renato Borghi, eds. xi,

63 pp. 1993 ML156.5.R6 3); Vol. 4: *Teatro Municipale "Romolo Valli," Reggio Emilio* (ed. Annarita Ferri, revised for publication by Claudia Polo and Carlo Marinelli. xi, 218 pp., 1992 ML156.5.R6 4); and Vol. 5: *Teatro alla Scala, Milan* (ed. Laura Serra. xi, 176 pp., 1993 ML156.5.R6 5 ISBN 88-86704-12-7). Basing the organization and identification of works on Philip Gossett's catalog of Rossini's works (item 24), recordings are further identified by title of work, Gossett's numerical listing, genre and librettist/translator, and language of recording; archival catalog number; interpreters, orchestral and choral directors, production information (for films and videos), date and venue of recording, and publication data; recording company and catalog information; type of recording, duration, and information about any program notes. Each volume has an index. Further information about this and other I.R.TE.M. projects can be accessed at (www.irtem.it.)

850. Giuliani, Roberto. *Le fonte audiovisive e gli archivi die teatri italiani: I repertori mozartiani e rossiniani dell'I.R.TE.M.* Vol. 7 in *Le fonti musicali in Italia: Studi e ricerche*, Rome: CIDIM, 1993.

The author reports on the Istituto di Ricerca per il Teatro Musicale's ongoing project of cataloging audiovisual sources in Italian theater archives (see item 849).

Discographies of Individual Works

851. Marinelli, Carlo, gen. ed. *Progetto Rossini of the Dipartimento dello Spettacolo del Consiglio dei Ministri and the Istituto di Ricerca per il Teatro Musicale (I.R.TE.M)*. Vol 3: *Almaviva, o sia, L'inutile precauzione: Il barbiere di Siviglia*. Rome: I.R.TE.M., 1991. xviii, 132 pp. 88-867042-24-0.

In a special part of this discographic project, Marinelli lists recordings of *Il barbiere di Siviglia*. Other individual projects are in the planning stages. For further information, check the I.R.TE.M. website at (www.irtem.it) (see item 876).

14

Libretto Collections and Editions

The most significant additions to libretto studies are the volumes in the Fondazione Rossini's series *I libretti di Rossini*. These studies include all "authentic" versions of the libretti (those from productions involving Rossini) as well as their poetic sources. The available volumes as of the publication of this book are listed with the volumes of the Rossini Critical Edition. See the section on editions and facsimiles.

GENERAL COLLECTIONS

852. Beghelli, Marco, and Nicola Gallino, eds. *Tutti i libretti di Rossini*. Milan: Garzanti, 1991. xxxvii, 1015 pp. ISBN 88-11-41059-2 ML49.R85 B4 1991.

   The editors include all of Rossini's opera libretti, including parallel French-Italian texts for *Le siège de Corinthe*, *Moïse et Pharaon*, *Le comte Ory* and *Guillaume Tell*, as well as of the pastiches *Ivanhoé* and *Robert Bruce*. Each libretto is preceded by a list of the opera's characters and vocal range, a brief commentary, and information on the premiere and cast. Beghelli's introduction discusses Rossini's place in Italian opera history as well as the twentieth-century "Rossini Renaissance." Other topics covered include the subjects of the operas and their musico-dramatic schema, sources and published versions of the libretti, and the editorial apparatus used for the catalog. Galliano, the editor of the libretti, comments on the texts. An appendix identifies the sources of the libretto. Illustrated.

SELECTED EDITIONS AND TRANSLATIONS

* Alier, Roger. *La Cenerentola*. Contains the author's Spanish translation of this work's libretto. See item 691.

853. Dapino, Cesare. *Il libretto del melodramma dell'Ottocento*. Vol. 5 in the series *Il teatro italiano*. Turin: Einaudi, 1983. lxx, 346 pp. ISBN: 88-0605-636-0 PQ4231.A8.

    Includes the libretti of *L'italiana in Algeri* and *Il barbiere di Siviglia*.

854. Isotta, Paolo, ed. *Gioacchino Rossini. Mosè in Egitto, Moïse et Pharaon, Mosè*. Vol. 4 in *Opera: Musical Guides,* series ed. Alberto Basso. Turin: Unione, 1974. viii, 350 pp. ML50 .R835 M7 1974.

    An edition of the libretti of the original Italian *azione tragico-sacra*, the French opera and its translation into an Italian *melodramma sacro*. Includes Isotta's "I diamante della corona. Grammatica del Rossini napoletano" (pp. 145–346), an oft-cited discussion of these operas and the overall significance of Rossini's *seria* works (see item 586).

    * Pahlen, Kurt, ed. *Gioacchino Rossini: Der Barber von Sevilla*. See item 668.

855. Viviani, Vittorio, ed. *I libretti di Rossini: Il barbiere di Siviglia, di Cesare Sterbini. La Cenerentola, di Jacopo Ferretti*. Milan: Rizzoli, 1965. 328 pp. ML50 .R835 B2 Vol. 1.

    Viviani's editions take into account both the original poem and the text that was set; omissions are included in the appendix. Throughout the edition, Viviani identifies various sections as recitative, arias, duets, etc., also listing each number's instrumentation and tempo. Includes notes on the autograph and editions of each work as well as the commentary "La librettistica italiana di Gioacchino Rossini" and "Del popolare nella musica e Rossini" from *Zibaldone* (Leopardi).

856. ———, ed. *I libretti di Rossini: Mosè, di Andrea Leone Tottola. Guglielmo Tell, di V.G. de Jouy, I. Bis, A. Marrast*. Milan: Rizzoli, 1965. 365 pp. ML50 .R835 B2 Vol. 2.

    Follows the format of Vol. 1 (item 855). Contains Italian translations by Calisto Bassi of *Moïse et Pharaon* and *Guillaume Tell* as well as their original texts; also includes the essay "La librettistica francese di Gioacchino Rossini."

15

Editions and Editing Practices

THE ROSSINI CRITICAL EDITION

857. Brauner, Patricia B. "Opera Omnia di Gioachino Rossini: norme editoriali integrative per i curatori." *Bollettino del Centro Rossiniano di Studi* 32 (1992): 157–69.

Brauner explains the methods for editors of volumes of the Rossini Critical Edition. The essay deals more explicitly with issues facing editors than did the essay by the editorial committee published in 1974 (see item 859). In addition, it discusses more updated criteria, such as the use of notation software.

858. ———. "The Opera Omnia of Gioachino Rossini." *Journal of the Conductors' Guild* 14 [no. 2] (Summer-Fall 1993): 2–7.

Brauner discusses the problems of creating a critical edition, explaining the necessity for going beyond the autograph to all possible sources in order to reconstruct a work. See also item 865.

859. Cagli, Bruno, Philip Gossett, and Alberto Zedda. "Criteri per l'edizione critica delle opere di Gioacchino Rossini." *Bollettino del Centro Rossiniano di Studi* 1 (1974): 5–34; English translation by Elvidio Surian and Gossett follows, 37–61.

In this special edition of the Rossini *Bollettino*, three members of the editorial committee introduce the aims and methodology of the critical edition of Rossini's works. Presented first is the publication plan (approximately seventy-five volumes divided in series reflecting the operas, *musica di scena* and cantatas, sacred music, hymns and choruses, vocal chamber music, instrumental music, *Péchés de Vieillesse*, and miscellaneous works). The following sections delineate general editorial procedures, organization of individual volumes, sources, and the preparation of each volume (with precise examples of common editorial questions found in nineteenth-century scores). Finally, the authors consider the accompanying critical commentaries for each score and the piano-vocal reduction. With musical examples elucidating editing problems.

860. Gossett, Philip. "The Rossini Thematic Catalog: When Does Bibliographical Access Become Bibliographical Excess?" *Music Reference Services Quarterly* 2 [no. 3/4] (1993): 271–80. Part II of *Foundations in Music Bibliography*, ed. Richard D. Green.

Gossett outlines the problems associated with compiling a thematic catalogue and presents the specific aims of the Rossini edition. By examining every publication either in full score or piano-vocal reduction, scholars editing the works will attempt to provide information on authentic versions and sources as well as on reception history, he writes.

861. Zedda, Alberto. "Rossini: neu entdeckt." In *Über Musiktheater: eine Festschrift gewidmet Arthur Scherle anlasslich seines 65. Geburtstages*, 191–93. Trans. Karin Andrae. Eds. Stefan G. Harpner and Birgit Gotzes. Munich: Ricordi, 1992. 207 pp. ISBN: 3-980-3090-0-2 ML1700.U24 1992.

Zedda notes that the new Rossini Critical Edition not only offers an expanded knowledge of the music and its production history but also portrays the composer himself as more than just a happy epicurean.

OTHER EDITIONS

862. Beghelli, Marco, and Stefano Piana. "Anmerkungen zur Neuausgabe von *L'equivoco stravagante*." *La Gazzetta* 9 (1999): 4–10.

The authors discuss the background of this early work and the issues involved in editing a work for which there is no known autograph score. They explain their use of other sources to reconstruct this edition, published by the Deutsche Rossini Gesellschaft.

ISSUES IN EDITING ROSSINI'S MUSIC

863. Brauner, Patricia. "Die Oper ohne Partitur." In *Rossinis Eduardo e Cristina*, 237–40. See item 731.

Brauner considers the problems involved in editing an opera in the absence of an autograph, relying on all possible secondary sources such as manuscript copies, printed vocal scores and, in the case of *Eduardo e Cristina*, autographs of the earlier works from which Rossini borrowed numbers. For the newly composed pieces in the opera, the author notes that an editor must rely on a knowledge of Rossini's style and of the way copyists transformed their original scores.

864. ———. "Editing Rossini." In *The Cambridge Companion to Rossini*. See item 478.

865. ———. "La primario importanza delle fonti secondarie." Trans. from English into Italian by Paolo Fabbri. In *Il testo e la scena* (item 286), 315–24.

Discusses the importance of using secondary sources (copyists' manuscripts and published scores) to "reintegrate" an opera by pointing to pieces Rossini removed for use elsewhere. These sources, according to Brauner, can also help to identify lost parts or suggest how other instruments were added to an original score. Stage band scores, in particular, are useful since they define practices at individual theaters. Using as examples the *Cantata in onore di Pio IX* and the *Choeurs de chasseurs démocrates*, No. 12 of the *Album français*, Brauner demonstrates how secondary sources elucidate Rossini's constant process of composition. Discusses the difficulties in determining a "definitive version" of an opera. See also item 867.

866. Castelvecchi, Stefano. "Sullo statuto del testo verbale nell'opera." In *Il testo e la scena* (item 286), 309–14.

An answer to Paolo Trovato's criticisms of the editorial practices used in both the Rossini and Verdi editions (see item 868). Restating Trovato's arguments against the principle that the main musical source (often the autograph) always is considered the principal source for the text, the author explains the musicological flaws in Trovato's objections. Two texts exist, Castelvecchi demonstrates: the first is the poem with its metrical structure (the *poesia*) while the second is the text as it is sung with musical phrasing (the *poesia per musica*). These two can—and should—be united only to a certain degree. Castelvecchi would extend the meaning of "text" to include many factors about which the composer is not the sole arbitrator.

* Fabbri, Paolo. "Gioachino Rossini uno e due." Item 629.

867. Gossett, Philip. "I manoscritti di Rossini." In *Rossini 1792–1992* (item 95), 345–52.

Gossett presents an essay on the autograph manuscripts, discussing Rossini's compositional process (for another discussion of this topic, see item 509). Mentions the specific problems associated with the autographs of the *Péchés de vieillesse*, and, in some cases, their reworking, as is the case with the "Choeur de chasseurs démocrates." (See also item 865).

* ———. *"La Gazza ladra*: Notes towards a Critical Edition." See item 703.

* ———. "Musicologi e musicisti: intorno a una rappresentazione di *Semiramide*." Item 748.

* ———. "Rossini and Authenticity." See item 581.

868. Trovato, Paolo. "Nota sulla fissazione dei testi poetici nelle edizioni critiche dei melodrammi." *Rivista italiana di musicologia* 25 [no. 2] (1990): 333–52.

This language scholar comments on the editorial practice for both the Rossini and the Verdi critical editions that, to determine the poetic text, the main musical source (generally the autograph) is given preference when it differs from the printed libretto unless there are obvious errors. While, in principle, the author agrees with this policy, he states that such decisions are not always "clean" and objective, and that the practice is not good philology. See item 866, for a response to Trovato.

* Turchi, Guido. "La cantata 'Argene e Melania.' " See item 816.

869. Wiklund, Anders. "Zur Herausgabe des Aufführungsmaterials." In *Rossinis Eduardo e Cristina*, 235–36. See item 731.

In this brief essay, the author addresses concerns when editing scores for performance. For the specific issues involved in the editing process of an opera without an autograph, see Brauner, item 863.

870. Zedda, Alberto. "In margine all'edizione critica del '*Barbiere di Siviglia*.' " *Bollettino del Centro Rossiniano di Studi* 10 [no. 1] (1970): 3–10.

After noting that Ricordi had just announced a two-volume critical edition of *Il barbiere*, Zedda discusses the task, noting that this opera lends itself particularly well to such a project: it has a clear autograph, the libretto corresponds faithfully with the text in the manuscript, substitute arias are thought not to exist, and contemporary manuscripts and scores were well copied and easy to consult. Mentioning the issues involved in editing the works of other composers such as Verdi, Puccini, and Bruckner, Zedda notes the challenges editors face and the importance of considering sources as precious documents.

871. ———. "L'edizione critica del *Barbiere di Siviglia*." In *Convegno di studi su Rossini per il Centenario della morte di Gioacchino Rossini*, 149–55. See item 283.

872. ———. "Problemi testuali della Cenerentola." *Bollettino del Centro Rossiniano di Studi* 11 [no. 1–3] (1971): 29–51.

Zedda's article demonstrates the differences between operatic source materials and modern performance editions. The author first identifies the historical materials used in his study: the first edition of the libretto; a manuscript, the majority of which is an autograph; manuscript scores and piano-vocal reductions; the memoirs of librettist Jacopo Ferretti; and contemporary newspaper sources. Zedda then compares what he has gleaned from these sources with the commonly used Ricordi score. Differences include changes in instrumentation, voicing, rhythms, phrasing, and vocal lines. Zedda uses this study to call for critical editions that would not only explain many of these changes but provide greater knowledge of the history of the production of nineteenth-century Italian operas.

16

Rossini Resources on the Internet

HOMEPAGES DEDICATED TO ROSSINI

873. Center for Italian Opera Studies (CIAO) at the University of Chicago (http://humanities.uchicago.edu/orgs/ciao/).

The homepage of the American seat of the critical editions of both Rossini's and Verdi's works. Information on the Rossini edition includes a general description of the project, the publication plan, and list of titles currently in print and of the editors of these volumes. A list of Rossini operas offers information on title, number of acts, premiere data, librettist, and libretto source (when known). Provides a link to the homepage of the Fondazione Rossini in Pesaro, Italy (item 875). The page is updated to reflect the latest publications in the Critical Edition. Accessed on 31 December 2001.

874. Deutsche Rossini Gesellschaft (http://rossinigesellschaft.de).

Homepage of the German Rossini Society. Constantly adding new features and links, this page (when accessed on 22 December 2001) offered information on the Society, including its structure and future activities (as well as an archive of past conferences and meetings); pages on Rossini's works; an alphabetical listing of premiere interpreters of Rossini roles (with search features), online libretti and MIDI excerpts of Rossini's music; iconographic pages of Rossini, his theaters, scenography and costume design; information on the Gesellschaft's various publications such as its journal *La Gazzetta* (see item 20 for an online index); and links to various other Rossini sites. Text in German and Italian.

875. Fondazione Rossini, Pesaro (www.fondazionerossini.org).

An introduction to the Fondazione and lists of its various publications such as the Rossini Critical Edition, the *Bollettino del Centro Rossiniano di Studi, Quaderni Rossiniani, Libretti di Rossini, Gioachino Rossini: Lettere e documenti, Iconografia Rossiniana,* and volumes of acts from Rossini conferences. Also notes upcoming Rossini study sessions and special programs. Text in Italian and English. Accessed on 31 December 2001.

876. Istituto di Ricerca per il Teatro Musicale, Progetto Rossini page (www.irtem.it/ITA/attivita/discografie.htm#PROGETTO ROSSINI), under the direction of Carlo Marinelli.

Among the audiovisual cataloging initiatives of I.R.TE.M. is the Progetto Rossini. Information on the Rossini page includes the current list of volumes published in the series *Repertorio delle fonti sonore e audiovisive rossiniane esistenti in Italia* (see items 849 and 850) and volumes in the series *Discografia rossiniana.*

Published so far is Volume 3, *Almaviva o sia L'inutile precauzione. Il barbiere di Siviglia* (item 851). Future volumes include Vol. 1—Opere teatrali 1806–1812 (*Demetrio e Polibio, La cambiale di matrimonio, L'equivoco stravagante, L'inganno felice, Ciro in Babilonia, La scala di seta, La pietra del paragone, L'occasione fa il ladro*); Vol. 2—Opere teatrali 1813–1815 (*Il signor Bruschino, Tancredi, L'italiana in Algeri, Aureliano in Palmira, Il turco in Italia, Sigismondo, Elisabetta regina d'Inghilterra, Torvaldo e Dorliska*); Vol. 4—Opere teatrali 1816–1819 (*La gazzetta, Otello, La Cenerentola, La gazza ladra, Armida, Adelaide di Borgogna, Mosè in Egitto, Adina, Ricciardo e Zoraide, Ermione, Eduardo e Cristina, La donna del lago, Bianca e Falliero*); and Vol. 5—Opere teatrali 1820–1829 (*Maometto II, Matilde di Shabran, Zelmira, Semiramide, Il viaggio a Reims, Le siège de Corinthe, Moïse et Pharaon, Le comte Ory, Guillaume Tell*).

Reprints are planned for the following out-of-print discographies: Vol. 6—Musica sacra (Messa di Gloria, Stabat Mater, and the Petite Messe solennelle); Vol. 7—Musiche di scena, Cantate, Inni e Cori, musica vocale (*Edipo Coloneo, Il pianto di Armonia, La morte di Didone, La riconoscenza, Il pianto delle muse, Giovanna d'Arco, Soirées musicales*; Vol. 8—Musica strumentale; and Vol. 9—*Péchés de vieillesse.* I.R.TE.M.'s Homepage, which lists the institute's other activities, can be accessed at (www.irtem.it). Accessed on 4 November 2001.

SELECTED LINKS

* Deutsche Rossini Gesellschaft. "La bibliografia rossiniana di P. Fabbri." See item 19.

* Deutsche Rossini Gesellschaft. *"La Gazzetta*—Zeitschrift der Deutschen Rossini Gesellshaft." See item 20.

* Deutsche Rossini Gesellschaft. *"L'equivoco stravagante."* See item 624.

* Lazzerini Belli, Alessandra. "Hegel e Rossini: 'Il cantar che nell'anima si sente.' " Web version of item 503.

* Museo di Casa Rossini (www.fondazione.scavolini.com/iniziativo/casa_rossini/). See item 361.

* Quattrocchi, Arrigo. "La Rossini Renaissance." See item 610.

* Rossini a Lugo. (www.teatrorossini.it/rossini_HTML/storia/Rossini.html). See item 349.

OPERA FESTIVAL HOMEPAGES

877. Rossini Opera Festival, Pesaro (www.rossinioperafestival.it). Accessed on 31 December 2001.

The Rossini Festival in Pesaro is held annually from late August into early September and features performances based on the Rossini scores in the Fondazione's Critical Edition. This site gives a history of the festival and announces the program for the current season. Also includes a list of available recordings from festival productions. Text in Italian and English. Accessed on 15 December 2001.

878. Rossini in Wildbad, Germany (www.rossini-in-wildbad.de). Accessed on 31 December 2001.

In 1856, Rossini traveled to Wildbad to take a spa cure. The importance of this place in Rossini history is commemorated with this annual opera festival, which celebrates its fourteenth season in 2002. The homepage of this Belcanto Opera Festival lists past seasons and currently planned productions. Text in German and English.

Appendix

CATALOG OF ROSSINI'S COMPOSITIONS[1]

Operas[2]

1. *Demetrio e Polibio*. Dramma serio (two acts): 18 May 1812, comp. c.1810.

2. *La cambiale di matrimonio*. Farsa comica (one act): 3 November 1810.

3. *L'equivoco stravagante*. Dramma giocoso (two acts): 26 October 1811.

4. *L'inganno felice*. Farsa (one act): 8 January 1812.

5. *Ciro in Babilonia, ossia La caduta di Baldassare*. Dramma con cori (two acts): 14 March 1812.

6. *La scala di seta*. Farsa comica (one act): 9 May 1812.

7. *La pietra del paragone*. Melodramma giocoso (two acts): 26 September 1812.

8. *L'occasione fa il ladro*. Burletta per musica (one act): 24 November 1812.

9. *Il signor Bruschino, ossia Il figlio per azzardo*. Farsa giocosa (one act): 27 January 1813.

10. *Tancredi*. Melodramma eroico (two acts): 6 February 1813.

11. *L'italiana in Algeri*. Dramma giocoso (two acts): 22 May 1813.

12. *Aureliano in Palmira*. Dramma serio (two acts): 26 December 1813.

[1]Information in this chapter is taken from the most recent works list compiled by Philip Gossett for the Rossini entry in *The Revised New Grove* (2001).

[2]Rossini usually composed his operas shortly before their premieres. Exceptions are noted.

13. *Il turco in Italia*. Dramma buffo (two acts): 14 August 1814.

14. *Sigismondo*. Dramma (two acts): 26 December 1814.

15. *Elisabetta, regina d'Inghilterra*. Dramma (two acts): 4 October 1815.

16. *Torvaldo e Dorliska*. Dramma semiserio (two acts): 26 December 1815.

17. *Il barbiere di Siviglia* (originally entitled *Almaviva, ossia L'inutile precauzione*). Commedia (two acts): 20 February 1816.

18. *La gazzetta*. Dramma [opera buffa] (two acts): 26 September 1816.

19. *Otello, ossia Il moro di Venezia*. Dramma (three acts): 4 December 1816.

20. *La Cenerentola, ossia La bontà in trionfo*. Dramma giocoso (two acts): 25 January 1817.

21. *La gazza ladra*. Melodramma (two acts): 31 May 1817.

22. *Armida*. Dramma (three acts): 9 November 1817.

23. *Adelaide di Borgogna*. Dramma (two acts): 27 December 1817.

24. *Mosè in Egitto*. Azione tragico-sacra (three acts): 5 March 1818; with revised Act III, 7 March 1819.

25. *Adina, o Il califfo di Bagdad*. Farsa (one act): 12 June 1826; comp. 1818.

26. *Ricciardo e Zoraide*. Dramma (two acts): 3 December 1818.

27. *Ermione*. Azione tragica (two acts): 27 March 1819.

28. *Eduardo e Cristina*. Dramma (two acts): 24 April 1819.

29. *La donna del lago*. Melodramma (two acts): 24 October 1819.

30. *Bianca e Falliero, ossia Il consiglio dei tre*. Melodramma (two acts): 26 December 1819.

31. *Maometto II*. Dramma (two acts): 3 December 1820.

32. *Matilde (di) Shabran, ossia Bellezza, e cuor di ferro*. Melodramma giocoso (two acts): 24 February 1821.

33. *Zelmira*. Dramma (two acts): 16 February 1822.

34. *Semiramide*. Melodramma tragico (two acts): 3 February 1823.

35. *Il viaggio a Reims, ossia L'albergo del giglio d'oro*. Dramma giocoso (one act): 19 June 1825.

36. *Le siège de Corinthe*. Tragédie lyrique (three acts): 9 October 1826.

37. *Moïse et Pharaon, ou Le passage de la Mer Rouge.* Opéra (four acts): 26 March 1827.

38. *Le comte Ory.* Opéra [opéra comique] (two acts): 20 August 1828.

39. *Guillaume Tell.* Opéra (four acts): 3 August 1829.

Operatic Adaptations with Rossini's Acknowledgment and Participation

1. *Ivanhoé* (adaptation by A. Pacini of pieces from Rossini's operas): 15 September 1826 [E. Deschamps and G.-G. de Wailly].

2. *Robert Bruce* (adaptation by A.-L. Niedermeyer from several of Rossini's operas, especially *La donna del lago*): 30 December 1846 [A. Reyer and G. Vaëz].

Cantatas, Incidental Music, Hymns, and Choruses[3]

1. *Il pianto d'Armonia sulla morte di Orfeo*, tenor, male chorus, orchestra: 11 August 1808 [Cantata, G. Ruggia].

2. *La morte di Didone*, soprano, chorus, orchestra: 1811; 2 May 1818 [Cantata].

3. *Dalle quete e pallid'ombre*, soprano, bass, pianoforte: 1812 [Cantata, P. Venanzio].

4. *Apprendete, o cari amanti*, soprano, two violins, cello: c.1812 [Cantata].

5. *Egle ed Irene*, soprano, alto, pianoforte: 1814 [Cantata].

6. Inno dell'Indipendenza ("Sorgi, Italia, venuta è già l'ora"): 15 April 1815 [Hymn, G. Giusti].

7. *La gratitudine*: 1815 [Cantata].

8. *L'Aurora*, alto, tenor, bass, pianoforte: November 1815 [Cantata].

9. *Giunone*, composed for the birthday of Ferdinando IV, soprano, chorus, orchestra: 12 January 1816 [Cantata].

10. *Le nozze di Teti, e di Peleo*, three sopranos, two tenors, chorus, orchestra: 24 April 1816 [Cantata, A.M. Ricci].

---

[3]As with the operas, in most cases the date of composition is close to that of the work's premiere. Exceptions are noted.

11. *Edipo a Colono*⁴, incidental music, bass, male chorus, orchestra (orchestration completed anon.): before 1817 [Giusti, after Sophocles].

12. *Omaggio umiliato a Sua Maestà*, soprano, chorus, orchestra: 20 February 1819 [Cantata, A. Niccolini].

13. Cantata for Francis I's visit, soprano, two tenors, chorus, orchestra: 9 May 1819 [G. Genoino].

14. *Il voto filiale*, soprano, pianoforte: 1820 [Cantata].

15. *La riconoscenza*, soprano, alto, tenor, bass, chorus, orchestra: 27 December 1821 [Cantata, G. Genoino].

16. *La santa alleanza*, two basses, chorus, orchestra: 24 November 1822 [Cantata, G. Rossi].

17. *Il vero omaggio*, sopranista, soprano, two tenors, bass, chorus, orchestra: 3 December 1822 [Cantata, G. Rossi].

18. *Omaggio pastorale*: three female voices, orchestra: ?1 April 1823 (ms. dated 17 May 1823 [Cantata].

19. *Il pianto delle muse in morte di Lord Byron*, canzone, tenor, chorus, orchestra: 11 June 1824.

20. *De l'Italie et de la France*, ?hymn for Charles X's nameday, soprano, bass, chorus, orchestra: ?3 November 1825.

21. Cantata per il battesimo del figlio del banchiere Aguado, six solo voices, pianoforte: 16 July 1827.

22. *L'armonica cetra del nume*, in honor of Marchese Sampieri, soprano, alto, tenor, bass, male chorus, flute, 2 oboes, 2 clarinets, bassoon, two horns, harp: 2 April 1830.

23. *Giovanna d'Arco*, soprano, pianoforte: 1832 [Cantata].

24. *Santo Genio dell'Italia terra*, for tercentenary of Tasso's birth, chorus, orchestra: 11 March 1844 [G. Marchetti].

25. Recitatives for cantata *Giovanni d' Arco* by Lucio Campiani: 10 July 1845.

26. *Su fratelli, letizia si canti*, for Pope Pius IX, chorus, orchestra: 23 July 1846 [Canonico Golfieri].

---

⁴The work is also known as *Edipo Coloneo*; see the Rossini Critical Edition: Series II, Volume 1.

27. Cantata in onore del Somma Pontefice Pio Nono, four solo voices, chorus, orchestra: 1 January 1847 [Marchetti].

28. *Segna Iddio ne' suoi confini*, chorus of the Guardia Civica of Bologna, accompaniment arranged for band by D. Liverani, 21 June 1848 [F. Martinelli].

29. *È foriera la Pace ai mortale*, hymn, baritone, male voices, pianoforte: 26 June 1850 [G. Arcangeli, after Bacchilde].

30. Hymne à Napoléon III e à son vaillant peuple ("Dieu tout puissant"), baritone, chorus, orchestra, military band: 1 July 1867 [E. Pacini].

Sacred Works

Early works listed without dates were student compositions written between 1802 and 1809:

1. Kyrie a tre voci, two tenors, bass, orchestra.

2. Gloria, alto, tenor, bass, male chorus, orchestra.

3. Laudamus, alto, bassoon, orchestra.

4. Gratias, tenor, male chorus, orchestra.

5. Domine Deus, two basses, orchestra.

6. Qui tollis, tenor, orchestra.

7. Laudamus, Qui tollis: tenor, violin, orchestra.

8. Quoniam, bass, orchestra.

9. Crucifixus, soprano, alto, orchestra.

10. Dixit, two tenors, bass, orchestra.

11. De torrente, bass, orchestra.

12. Gloria patri, tenor, orchestra.

13. Sicut erat, two tenors, bass, orchestra.

14. Magnificat, two tenors, bass, orchestra.

15. Messa [Bologna] (three sections of a work by students at the Liceo Musicale), performed 2 June 1808.

16. Christe eleison, two tenors, bass, orchestra.

17. Benedicta et venerabilis (grad), two tenors, bass, orchestra.

18. Qui tollis; Qui sedes, soprano, horn, orchestra.

19. Messa[5] [Ravenna], solo male voices, male chorus, orchestra; another version. for soprano, alto, tenor, bass, male chorus, orchestra: 1808.

20. Messa[6], solo male voices, male chorus, orchestra: ?1802–1809.

21. Messa [Rimini], soprano, alto, tenor, bass, orchestra: 1809.

22. Quoniam, bass, orchestra: September 1813.

23. Messa di gloria, solo voices, chorus, orchestra: 24 March 1820.

24. Preghiera "Deh tu pietoso cielo," soprano, pianoforte: c.1820.

25. Tantum ergo, soprano, tenor, bass, orchestra: 1824.

26. Stabat mater, two sopranos, tenor, bass, orchestra: first version[7], comp. 1832, perf. Good Friday 1833; second version[8], comp. 1841, perf. 7 January 1842.

27. Three choeurs religieux female voices, pianoforte: 20 November 1844.

   27a. "La foi" [Text: P. Goubaux]

   27b. "L'espérance" [Text: H. Lucas]

   27c. "La charité" [Text: L. Colet]

28. Tantum ergo, two tenors, bass, orchestra: 28 November 1847.

29. O salutaris hostia, soprano, alto, tenor, bass: 29 November 1857.

30. Laus Deo, mezzosoprano, pianoforte: 1861.

31. Petite Messe solennelle: first version, 12 solo voices, two pianofortes, harmonium, comp. 1863, perf. 14 March 1864; second version, soprano, alto, tenor, bass, chorus, orchestra, comp. 1867, perf. 24 February 1869.

Miscellaneous Vocal Works

1. Se il vuol la molinara, soprano, pianoforte: ?1801.

2. Cara, voi siete quella, tenor, orchestra: 1806, perf. autumn 1806.

3. Dolce aurette che spirate, tenor, orchestra: 1809; perf. carnevale 1809–1810.

---

[5]Only Kyrie, Gloria, and Credo.
[6]Only Kyrie, Gloria, and Credo.
[7]Six of the 12 numbers by Rossini; others by G. Tadolini.
[8]All numbers by Rossini.

4. Coro e cavatina "Viva Roma e Quinto viva," "Cara Patria, invitta Roma," soprano, chorus, orchestra: 1811; perf. autumn 1811.

5. Alla gloria un genio eletto, tenor, orchestra: 1812; perf. spring 1812.

6. La mia pace io già perdei, tenor, orchestra: 1812.

7. Qual voce, quai note, soprano, pianoforte: 1813.

8. Alle voc della gloria, bass, orchestra: 1813.

9. Amore mi assisti, soprano, tenor, pianoforte: c.1814.

10. Aria "Guidò Marte i nostri passi," tenor, chorus, orchestra, and Duet "Ah! per pietà t'arresta," two sopranos, orchestra: 1817; perf. carnevale 1817.[9]

11. Il trovatore ("Chi m'ascolta il canto usato"), tenor, pianoforte: 1818.

12. Il Carnevale di Venezia ("Siamo ciechi, siamo nati"), two tenors, two basses, pianoforte: carnevale, 1821.[10]

13. Beltà crudele ("Amori scendete") [N. di Santo-Magno], soprano, pianoforte: 1821.

14. La pastorella ("Odia la pastorella") [Santo-Magno], soprano, pianoforte: c.1821.

15. Canzonetta spagnuola "En medio a mis colores" ("Piangea un dì pensando"), soprano, pianoforte: 1821.

16. Infelice ch'io son, soprano, pianoforte: 1821.

17. Addio ai viennesi ("Da voi parto, amate sponde"), tenor, pianoforte: 1822.

18. Dall'Oriente l'astro del giorno, soprano, two tenors, bass, pianoforte: 1824.

19. Ridiamo, cantiamo, che tutto sen va, soprano, two tenors, bass, pianoforte: 1824.

20. In giorno sì bello, two sopranos, tenor, pianoforte: 1824.

21. 3 quartetti da camera (publ. 1827):

    1. unidentified.

    2. In giorno sì bello, two sopranos, tenor, bass, pianoforte: 1827.

    3. Oh giorno sereno, soprano, alto, tenor, bass, pianoforte: 1827.

[9]For G. Nicolini's *Quinto Fabio*; Duet is possibly not by Rossini.
[10]For Rossini, Paganini, M. d'Azeglio, and Lipparini.

22. Les adieux à Rome ("Rome pour la dernière fois") [C. Delavigne], tenor, pianoforte/harp: 1827.

23. Orage et beau temps ("Sur les flots inconstants") [A. Betourne], tenor, bass, pianoforte: c.1830.

24. La passeggiata ("Or che di fiori adorno"), soprano, pianoforte: 1831.

25. La dichiarazione ("Ch'io mai vi possa lasciar d'amare") [Metastasio], soprano, pianoforte: c.1834.

26. Les soirées musicales: c.1830–1835.

    1. La promessa ("Ch'io mai vi possa lasciar amare") [Metastasio], soprano, pianoforte.

    2. Il rimprovero ("Mi lagnerò tacendo") [Metastasio], soprano, pianoforte

    3. La partenza ("Ecco quel fiero istante") [Metastasio], soprano, pianoforte.

    4. L'orgia ("Amiamo, cantiamo") [C. Pepoli], soprano, pianoforte.

    5. L'invito ("Vieni o Ruggiero") [Pepoli], soprano, pianoforte.

    6. La pastorella dell'Alpi ("Son bella pastorella") [Pepoli], soprano, pianoforte.

    7. La gita in gondola ("Voli l'agile barchetta") [Pepoli], soprano, pianoforte.

    8. La danza ("Già la luna è in mezzo al mare") [Pepoli], tenor, pianoforte.

    9. La regata veneziana ("Voga o Tonio benedetto") [Pepoli], two sopranos, pianoforte.

    10. La pesca ("Già la notte s'avvicina") [Metastasio], two sopranos, pianoforte.

    11. La serenata ("Mira, la bianca luna") [Pepoli], soprano, tenor, pianoforte.

    12. Li marinari ("Marinaro in guardia stà") [Pepoli], tenor, bass, pianoforte.

27. Two nocturnes [Crével de Charlemagne], soprano, tenor, pianoforte: c.1836.

    1. Adieu à l'Italie ("Je te quitte, belle Italie").

    2. Le départ ("Il faut partir").

28. Nizza ("Nizza, je puis sans peine") [E. Deschamps], soprano, pianoforte: c.1836.

29. L'âme délaissée ("Mon bien aimé") [Delavigne], soprano, pianoforte: c.1844.

30. Recitativo ritmato ("Farò come colui che piange e dice") [Dante], soprano, pianoforte: 1848.

31. La separazione ("Muto rimase il labbro") [F. Uccelli], soprano, pianoforte: c.1858.

32. Two nouvelles compositions [Pacini], soprano, pianoforte: c.1860.

    1. A Grenade ("La nuit règne à Grenade").

    2. Le veuve andalouse ("Toi pour jamais").

33. Mi lagnerò tacendo [Metastasio], numerous settings[11]

    1. L'amante discreto, soprano, pianoforte: 1835.

    2. Mi lagnerò tacendo, soprano, pianoforte: ?1833–1839.

    3. Mi lagnerò tacendo, soprano, pianoforte: before 1847.

    4. Mi lagnerò tacendo, soprano, pianoforte: 1850.

Instrumental Works

1. Six sonate a quattro, G, A, C, B-flat, E-flat, D, two violins, cello, double bass: c.1804.

2. Sinfonia "al Conventello", D, orchestra: c.1806.

3. Five duets, E-flat, E-flat, B-flat, E-flat, E-flat, two horns: c.1806.

4. Sinfonia, D, orchestra: 1808.

5. Sinfonia, E-flat, orchestra: 1809.

6. Grand'overtura obbligata a contrabasso, D, orchestra: c.1809.

7. Variazioni a più istrumenti obbligati, F, two violins, viola, cello, clarinet, orchestra: c.1809.

8. Variazioni a clarinetto, C, clarinet, orchestra: c.1809.

9. Andante e Tema con variazioni, F, flute, clarinet, horn, bassoon: 1812.

10. Terzetto, horn, bassoon, pianoforte: 1812.

---

[11]Gossett lists the following settings as representative.

11. La notte, la pregheria, la caccia, two flutes, two violins, viola, cello: c.1813.

12. Andante con variazioni, F, harp, violin: c.1820.

13. Passo doppio, military band: 1822.

14. Waltz, E-flat, pianoforte: ?1823.

15. Serenata, E-flat, two violins, viola, cello, flute, oboe, English horn: 1823.

16. Duetto, D, cello, double bass: 1824.

17. Rendez-vous de chasse, D, four corni di caccia, orchestra: 1828.

18. Fantasie, E-flat, clarinet, pianoforte: 1829.

19. Three marches, military band: 1834.

    1. Passage du Balcan, grande marche, E-flat.

    2. Prise d'Ervian, pas redoublé, E-flat.

    3. Assaut de Varsovie, pas redoublé, E-flat.

20. Scherzo, A minor, pianoforte: 1843, rev. 1850.

21. Tema originale di Rossini variato per violino da Giovacchino Giovacchini, A, violin, pianoforte: 1845.

22. March ("Pas-redoublé"), C, military band: 1852.

23. Thème de Rossini suivi de deux variations et coda par Moscheles Père, E, horn, pianoforte: 1860.

24. La corona d'Italia, E-flat, military band: 1868.

Péchés de vieillesse (1857–1868)[12]

Vol. I - Album italiano

1. Quartettino "I gondolieri" [?G. Torre], soprano, alto, tenor, bass, pianoforte [?orig. written to the text Mi lagnerò tacendo].

2. Arietta "La lontananza" [Torre], tenor, pianoforte.

3. Bolero "Tirana alla spagnola (rossinizzata)" [Metastasio], soprano, pianoforte.[13]

---

[12]The ordering of these works reflects that presented in *The New Grove* works list.
[13]The music to this piece is identical to that of Vol. XI, no. 3.

4. Elegia "L'ultimo ricordo" [G. Redaelli], baritone, pianoforte.

5. Arietta "La fioraja fiorentina" [?Torre], soprano, pianoforte [?orig. written to the text Mi lagnerò tacendo].

6. Duetto "Le gittane" [Torre], soprano, alto, pianoforte [orig. written to the text Mi lagnerò tacento].

7. Ave Maria su due sole note [Torre], alto, pianoforte [?orig. written to the text Mi lagnerò tacendo].

8–10. La regata veneziana, 3 canzonettas [F.M.Piave], mezzosoprano, pianoforte.

   8. Anzoleta avanti la regata (Barcarolle "Plus de vent perfide").

   9. Anzoleta co passa la regata.

   10. Anzoleta dopo la regata.

11. Arietta (Sonetto) "Il fanciullo smarrito" [A. Castellani], tenor, pianoforte.

12. Quartettino "La passeggiata," soprano, alto, tenor, bass, pianoforte.

Vol. II - Album français [E. Pacini]

1. Ottettino "Toast pour le nouvel an," two sopranos, two altos, two tenors, two basses.

2. Roméo, tenor, pianoforte.

3. Arietta, "Pompadour, la grande coquette," soprano, pianoforte [orig, written to the text Mi lagnerò tacendo].

4. Complainte à deux voix ("Un sou"), tenor, baritone, pianoforte.

5. Chanson de Zora ("La petite bohémienne"), [E. Deschamps], mezzosoprano, pianoforte.

6. La nuit de Noël, baritone solo, two sopranos, two altos, two tenors, two baritones, pianoforte, harmonium.

7. Ariette "Le dodo des enfants," mezzosoprano, pianoforte [orig. written to the text Mi lagnerò tacendo"].

8. Chansonette de cabaret ("Le lazzarone"), baritone, pianoforte.

9. Elégie ("Adieux à la vie"), sur une seule note, mezzosoprano, pianoforte [orig. written to the text Mi lagnerò tacento].

10. Nocturne ("Soupirs et sourire"), soprano, tenor, pianoforte; also with Italian text as Il cipresso, e la rosa [Torre].

11. Ballade élégie ("L'orphéline du Tyrol"), mezzosoprano, pianoforte.

12. Choeur de chasseurs démocrates, male voices, tam-tam, two tamburi.

Vol. III - Morceaux réservés

1. Quelques mesures de chant funèbre: à mon pauvre ami Meyerbeer [Pacini], male voices, tamburo.

2. Arietta "L'esule" [Torre], tenor, pianoforte.

3. Tirana pour deux voix ("Les amants de Séville") [Pacini], alto, tenor, pianoforte.

4. Ave Maria, soprano, alto, tenor, bass, organ.

5. L'amour à Pékin: petite mélodie sur la gamma chinoise [Pacini], alto, pianoforte.

6. Le chant des Titans [Pacini], four basses, pianoforte, harmonium; arranged for four basses, orchestra, vs [orig. written to text of Mi lagnerò tacendo].

7. Preghiera [Torre], four tenors, two baritones, two basses [also French text "Dieu créateur du monde" by Pacini].

8. Elégie ("Au chevet d'un mourant") [Pacini], soprano, pianoforte.

9. Romance "Le sylvain" [Pacini], tenor, pianoforte.

10. Cantemus: imitazione ad otto voci reali, two sopranos, two altos, two tenors, two basses.

11. Ariette à l'ancienne [J.-J. Rousseau], mezzosoprano, pianoforte.

12. Tyrolienne sentimentale ("Le départ des promis") [Pacini], two sopranos, two altos, pianoforte.

[Vols. IV - VIII: Un peu de tout: recueil de 56 morceaux semi-comiques pour le piano]

Vol. IV - Quatre mendiants et quatre hors d'oeuvres

Quatre mendiants

1. Le figues sèches, D.

2. Les amandes, G.

3. Les raisins, C.

4. Les noisettes, b minor-B.

Quatre hors d'oeuvres

1. Les radis, A minor.

2. Les anchois, D.

3. Les cornichons, E.

4. Le beurre, B-flat.

Vol. V - Album pour les enfants adolescents

1. Première Communion, E-flat.

2. Thème naïf et variations idem, G.

3. Saltarello à l'italienne, A-flat.

4. Prélude moresque, E minor.

5. Valse lugubre, C.

6. Impromptu anodin, E-flat.

7. L'innocence italienne; La candeur française, A minor, A.

8. Prélude convulsif, C.

9. La lagune de Venise à l'expiration de l'année 1861!!!, G-flat.

10. Ouf! les petits pois, B.

11. Un sauté, D.

12. Hachis romantique, A minor.

Vol. VI - Album pour les enfants dégourdis

1. Mon prélude hygiénique du matin, C.

2. Prélude baroque, A minor.

3. Memento homo, C minor.

4. Assez de memento: dansons, F.

5. La pesarese, B-flat.

6. Valse torturée, D.

7. Une caresse à ma femme, G.

8. Barcarole, E-flat.

9. Un petit train de plaisir comico-imitatif, C.

10. Fausse couche de polka mazurka, A-flat.

11. Etude asthmatique, E.

12. Un enterrement en Carnaval, D.

Vol. VII - Album de chaumière

1. Gymnastique d'écartement, A-flat.

2. Prélude fugassé, E.

3. Petite polka chinoise, B minor.

4. Petite valse de boudoir, A-flat.

5. Prélude inoffensif, C.

6. Petite valse ("L'huile de Ricin"), E.

7. Un profond sommeil; Un reveil en sursaut, B minor, D.

8. Plein-chant chinois, scherzo, A minor.

9. Un cauchemar, E.

10. Valse boiteuse, D-flat.

11. Une pensée à Florence, A minor.

12. Marche, C.

Vol. VIII - Album de château

1. Spécimen de l'ancien régime, E-flat.

2. Prélude pétulant-roccoco, G.

3. Un regret; Un espoir, E.

4. Boléro tartare, A minor.

5. Prélude prétentieux, C minor-C.

6. Spécimen de mon temps, A-flat.

7. Valse anti-dansante, F.

8. Prélude semipastorale, A.

9. Tarantelle pur sang (avec Traversée de la procession), B minor, chorus, harmonium and clochette ad lib, with full scoring or as pianoforte solo.

10. Un rêve, B minor.

11. Prélude soi-distant dramatique, F-sharp.

12. Spécimen de l'avenir, E-flat.

Vol. IX - (Album pour piano, violon, violoncelle, harmonium et cor)

1. Mélodie candide, A, pianoforte.

2. Chansonette, E-flat, pianoforte.

3. La savoie aimante, A minor, pianoforte.

4. Un mot à Paganini, élégie, D, violin.

5. Impromptu tarantellisé, F, pianoforte.

6. Echantillon du chant de Noël à l'italienne, E-flat, pianoforte.

7. Marche et reminiscences pour mon dernier voyage, A-flat, pianoforte.

8. Prélude, thème et variations, E, horn, pianoforte.

9. Prélude italien, A-flat, pianoforte.

10. Une larme: thème et variations, A minor, cello, pianoforte.

11. Echantillon de blague mélodique sur les noires de la main droite, G-flat, pianoforte.

12. Petite fanfare à quatre mains, E-flat, pianoforte, pianoforte four hands.

Vol. X - Miscellanée pour piano

1. Prélude blaguer, A minor.

2. Des tritons s'il vous plaît (montée-descente), C.

3. Petite pensée, E-flat.

4. Une bagatelle, E-flat.

5. Mélodie italienne: une bagatelle ("In nomine Patris"), A-flat.

6. Petite caprice (style Offenbach), C.

Vol. XI - Miscellanée de musique vocale

1. Ariette villageoise [J.-J. Rousseau], soprano, pianoforte.

2. La chanson de bébé [Pacini], mezzosoprano, pianoforte.

3. Amour sans espoit ("Tirana all'espagnole rossinizé") [Pacini], soprano, pianoforte.[14]

4. A ma belle mère ("Requiem eternam"), alto, pianoforte.

5. O salutaris, de campagne, alto, pianoforte.

6. Aragonese [Metastasio], soprano, pianoforte.

7. Arietta all'antica, dedotta dal O salutaris ostia [Metastasio], soprano, pianoforte.[15]

8. Il candore in fuga, two sopranos, alto, tenor, bass.

9. Salve amabilis Maria ("Hymne à la musique"), motet for soprano, alto, tenor, bass.

10. Giovanna d'Arco (cantata), soprano, pianoforte.

Vol. XII - Quelques riens pour album, 24 pieces, pianoforte

Vol. XIII - Musique anodine [Metastasio], 15 April 1857

1. Prélude, pianoforte.

2. Six petites mélodies:

    1. alto, pianoforte.

    2. and 6. baritone, pianoforte.

    3. and 4. soprano, pianoforte.

    5. mezzosoprano, pianoforte.

Other Late Works

1. Canone scherzosa a quattro soprani democratici, four sopranos, pianoforte.

2. Canone antisavant [Rossini], three voices.

3. Canzonetta "La vénitienne," C, pianoforte.

4. Petite promenade de Passy à Courbevoie, C, pianoforte.

5. Une réjouissance, A minor, pianoforte.

---

[14]Music identical with that of Vol. 1, no. 3.
[15]Based on the O salutaris hostia (29 November 1857).

6. Encore un peu de blague, C, pianoforte.

7. Tourniquet sur la gamme chromatique, ascendante et déscendante, C, pianoforte.

8. Ritournelle gothique, C, pianoforte.

9. Un rien (pour album): Ave Maria, soprano, pianoforte.

10. Pour album: Sogna il guerrier [Metastasio], baritone, pianoforte.

11. Brindisi "Dei fanciullo il primo canto," bass, chorus.

12. Solo per violoncello, A minor.

13. L'ultimo pensiero ("Patria, consorti, figli") [L.F. Cerutti], baritone, ?pianoforte.

Miscellaneous

1. *Teodoro e Ricciardino*, introduction to opera: sketched c.1815.

2. *Gorgheggi e solfeggi*, studies, voice, pianoforte: c.1827.

3. 15 petits exercises, voice: 1858.

4. Petit gargouillement, exercise, voice, 1867.

5. *Giovinetta pellegrina*, variations on a romance by Vaccai.

6. Vocal variants, cadenzas, etc., for Rossini's operas.

Lost or Spurious Works

Vocal—Sacred and secular

1. Miserere, solo voices, chorus, orchestra; published in 1831 as *Trost und Erhebung*.

2. Dixit Domino, solo voices, chorus, orchestra.

3. Duetto buffo dei due gatti, 2 solo voices, pianoforte (spurious).

4. Aria di Filippuccio ("Il secreto se si perde") buffo voice, orchestra.

5. La calabrese ("Colla lanterna magica"), soprano, alto, pianoforte.

6. Ariette de Perruchini ("Gondolier la mer t'appelle"), "arrangée en barcarolle par son ami R[ossini]" and sung in C. Delavigne's play *Marino Falliero* (Paris, c.1829).

7. Quando giunse que Belfior, soprano, orchestra: ?1824–1835.

8. Il rimprovero ("Se fra le trecce d'Ebano"), soprano, pianoforte.

9. Vieni sull'onde, soprano, tenor, pianoforte.

10. L'absence (?Paris): not traced.

11. Il baco da seta ?1862 (?Paris, 1862): not traced.

Instrumental

1. Sinfonia di Odense, A, orchestra (spurious).

EDITIONS AND FACSIMILES

***Contents of* The Works of Gioachino Rossini/Le Opere di Gioachino Rossini**
The Critical Edition is published by The University of Chicago Press and Casa Ricordi, Milan. Updated publication information may be accessed at the University of Chicago's Center for Center for Italian Opera Studies (CIAO) homepage at (http://humanities.uchicago.edu/orgs/ciao/) (see item 873).

Series I - Operas (42 volumes)

Volumes with editorial information have yet to be assigned.

1. *Demetrio e Polibio.*

2. *La cambiale di matrimonio*, ed. Alexandra Amati-Campari (in preparation).

3. *L'equivoco stravagante*, ed. Marco Beghelli (2002).

4. *L'inganno felice.*

5. *Ciro in Babilonia.*

6. *La scala di seta*, ed.Anders Wiklund, 1991.

7. *La pietra del paragone*, ed. Patricia Brauner and Anders Wiklund (in preparation).

8. *L'occasione da il ladro*, ed. Giovanni Carli Ballola, Patricia Brauner, and Philip Gossett, 1994.

9. *Il signor Bruschino*, ed. Arrigo Gazzaniga, 1986.

10. *Tancredi*, ed. Philip Gossett, 1984.

11. *L'Italiana in Algeri*, ed. Azio Corghi, 1981.

12. *Aureliano in Palmira.*

13. *Il Turco in Italia*, ed. Margaret Bent, 1988.

14. *Sigismondo*.

15. *Elisabetta, regina d'Inghilterra* (in preparation).

16. *Torvaldo e Dorliska*.

17. *Il barbiere di Siviglia*.

18. *La gazzetta*, ed. Fabrizio Scipioni (in course of publication).

19. *Otello*, ed, Michael Collins, 1994.

20. *La Cenerentola*, ed. Alberto Zedda, 1998.

21. *La gazza ladra*, ed. Alberto Zedda, 1979.

22. *Armida*, ed. Charles S. Brauner and Patricia B. Brauner, 1997.

23. *Adelaide di Borgogna*.

24. *Mosè in Egitto*, ed. Charles S. Brauner (in preparation).

25. *Adina*, ed. Fabrizio Della Seta, 2000.

26. *Ricciardo e Zoraide*, ed. Federico Agostinelli and Gabriele Gravagna (in preparation).

27. *Ermione*, ed. Patricia B. Brauner and Philip Gossett, 1995.

28. *Eduardo e Cristina*.

29. *La donna del lago*, ed. H. Colin Slim. 1990.

30. *Bianca e Falliero*, ed. Gabriele Dotto, 1996.

31. *Maometto II*, ed. Patricia B. Brauner, Claudio Scimone, and Philip Gossett (in preparation).

32. *Matilde di Shabran*, ed. Jürgen Selk (in preparation).

33. *Zelmira*, ed. Kathleen K. Hansell, 1989.

34. *Semiramide*, ed. Philip Gossett and Alberto Zedda, 2002.

35. *Il viaggio a Reims*, ed. Janet L. Johnson, 2000.

36. *Le Siège de Corinthe*.

37. *Moïse et Pharaon*.

38. *Le Comte Ory*, ed. Damien Colas (in preparation).

39. *Guillaume Tell*, ed. M. Elizabeth C. Bartlet, 1992.

40. Music written by Rossini for operas of other composers.

41. *Ivanhoé* (pastiche).

42. *Robert Bruce* (pastiche).

Series II - Incidental Music and Cantatas

1. *Edipo Coloneo*, ed. Lorenzo Tozze and Piero Weiss, 1995.

2. Youthful cantatas with orchestra.

3. *Le nozze di Teti, e di Peleo*, ed. Guido Johannes Joerg, 1993.

4. Tre cantate napoletane

   Cantata in omaggio di Ferdinando IV detta "Giunone," ed. Ilaria Narici.

   Omaggio umiliato a Sua Maestà, ed. Marco Beghelli.

   Cantata in onore di Francesco I d'Austria, ed. Stefano Castelvecchi.

5. *La riconoscenza - Il vero omaggio*, ed. Patricia B. Brauner (with its several revisions) (in preparation).

6. Cantata in onore del Sommo Pontefice Pio Nono, ed. Mauro Bucarelli, 1996.

Series III - Sacred Music

1. Youthful Masses (in preparation).

2. Messa di gloria, ed. Claudio Aciai (in preparation).

3. Stabat Mater.

4. Petite messe solennelle (original version with pianoforte and harmonium), ed. Pierluigi Petrobelli (in preparation).

5. Petite messe solennelle (version with orchestra), ed. Fabrizio Scipione (in preparation).

6. Other sacred music.

Series IV - Hymns and Choruses

Series V - Vocal Music

1. Songs for voice and piano.

2. Songs for voice and piano.

3. Songs for several voices and piano.

4. *Soirées musicales.*

Series VI - *Instrumental Music*

1. Sinfonie giovanili, ed. Paolo Fabbri, 1998.

2. Other music for orchestra.

3. Music for band.

4. Six sonatas a quattro.

5. Chamber music without piano.

6. Music for piano of for instruments and piano.

Series VII - Péchés de vieillesse

1. Album italiano/ Musique anodine, ed. Marvin Tartak, 1995.

2. Album français/ Morceaux réservés, ed. Rossana Dalmonte, 1985.

3. Other vocal pieces.

4. Quatre mendiantes—Quatre hors d'oeuvres—Album de Chaumière.

5. Album pour les enfants dégourdis.

6. Album de Château - Miscellanée pour piano.

7. Quelques riens pour album, ed. Marvin Tartak, 1982.

8. Other piano pieces (in preparation).

9. Chamber music.

Series VIII - *Other Works*

1. Theoretical works (Gorgheggi e solfeggi, etc.).

2. Miscellaneous.

Appendixes will be added to published volumes should relevant sources be discovered.

CRITICAL EDITIONS OF LIBRETTOS

I libretti di Rossini

These volumes, published by the Fondazine Rossini, include all source libretti as well as all versions in productions associated with Rossini.

Tancredi - edited by Paolo Fabbri (1994).

La gazza ladro - edited by Emilio Sala (1995).

Otello - edited by Renato Raffaelli (1996).

L'italiana in Algeri - edited by Paolo Fabbri and M.C. Bertieri (1997).

La scala di seta, L'occasione fa ladro, Il signor Bruschino, ossia Il figlio per azzardo - edited by Maria Giovanna Miggiani (1998).

Quaderni Rossiniani

These early publications can not be considered critical editions; all have prefaces by Alfredo Bonaccorsi.

1. Sei Sonate a quattro—Lino Liviabella.

2. Prima Scelta di Pezzi per Pianoforte—G. Macarini-Carmignani.

3. Prelude Theme et Variations pour cor—Domenico Ceccarossi.

4. Melodie Italiane per canto e pianoforte—Piero Giorgi.

5. Melodie francesi per canto e pianoforte—Alberto Gallina.

6. Musiche da camera—Amedeo Cerasa.

7. Cori a voci pari o dispari—Ada Melica.

8. Sinfonia (di Bologna); Sinfonia (di Odense)[16]; Le Chant des Titans—Lino Liviabella.

9. Variationi a piú strumenti obbligati—Amedeo Cerasa.

10. Seconda scelte di pezzi per pianoforte—Luisa de Sabbata.

11. *Giovanna d'Arco*, cantata a voce solo, e altre musiche religiose—Piero Giorgi.

12. *Inno alla Pace* per baritono, coro e pianoforte; *Inno a Napoleone III* per baritono (un pontife), coro e grande orchestra—Piero Giorgi.

13. "Argene e Melania," Cantata profana per soli, coro e orchestra—Guido Turchi.

14. 11 pezzi per pianoforte da *L'Album de Chaumiére*—Sergio Cafaro.

15. 10 pezzi per pianoforte da *L'Album pour les enfants adolescents*—Sergio Cafaro.

16. 10 pezzi per pianoforte da *L'Album pour les enfants dégourdis*—Sergio Cafaro.

---

[16]Spurious.

17. 6 pezzi per pianoforte da *L'Album de Château*—Sergio Cafaro.

18. 10 pezzi per pianoforte da *I miscellanée* e altri autografi—Sergio Cafaro.

19. Quatre mendiantes et quatre hor d'oeuvres per pianoforte—Marcello Abbado.

Editions published by the Deutsche Rossini Gesellschaft
These editions are independent of the Critical Edition listed above; they are, however, also based on historical sources.

Operas
  1. *L'equivoco stravagante*, ed. Marco Beghelli and Stefano Piana, 1999.

  2. *Eduardo e Cristina*, ed. Anders Wiklund, 1997.

Sacred Works
  1. Stabat Mater 1831–32, reconstructed by Reto Müller, 1997.

  2. Early Mass pieces, ed. Paolo Fabbri and Maria Chiara Bertieri, 2001.

Vocal selections
1. Two arias for tenor, ed. Stefano Piana, 1999.

    Cavatina "Dolci aurette che spirate" [1810].

    Scena and aria "La mia pace io già perdei" [1812].

2. Aria for Madame La Rose from *La gazzetta*, ed. Anders Wiklund, 1997.

    "Sempre in amore" (for mezzosoprano and orchestra).

Selected Facsimile Editions
La Cenerentola. Edited with introduction by Philip Gossett. Vol. 4/92 in the series. *Biblioteca musica bononiensis*. Bologna: Forni Editore, 1969. 2 vols.

Elisabetta, regina d'Inghilterra: dramma per musica in two acts/music by Gioachino Rossini; libretto by Giovanni Schmidt. Edited with introduction by Philip Gossett. Vol. 7 in *Early Romantic Opera*. New York: Garland Publishing, 1979. 2 vols. Photoreprint of the original in the Fondazione Rossini, Pesaro.

Guillaume Tell; opéra in four acts/libretto by Étienne de Jouy and Hippolyte-Louis-Florent Bis; music by Gioachino Rossini. Introduction by Philip Gossett. Vol. 17 in *Early Romantic Opera*. New York: Garland, 1980. 2 vols. A facsimile of the original printed orchestral score.

Il barbiere di Siviglia: commedia in due atti/Gioacchino Rossini; [libretto] di Cesare Sterbini. With critical commentary by Philip Gossett. Lucca: Libreria Musicale Italiana, 1993. 2 vols. Facsimile of the autograph in the Civico Museo Bibliografico Musicale, Bologna (shelf number UU 1/1–2).

Le siège de Corinthe: tragédie-lyrique in three acts/libretto by Luigi Balocchi and Alexandre Soumet; music by Gioachino Rossini. Introduction by Philip Gossett. Vol. 14 in *Early Romantic Opera.* New York: Garland Publishing. Photoprint of the 1826–1827 edition published by E. Troupenas, Paris.

Maometto II: dramma in two acts/music by Gioachino Rossini; libretto by Cesare della Valle. Edited with an introduction by Philip Gossett. Vol. 11 of *Early Romantic Opera.* New York: Garland Publishing, 1981. 2 vols. Photoreprint of the manuscript in the Sezione Musicale of the Biblioteca Palatina, Parma.

Otello: dramma in three acts/music by Gioachino Rossini; libretto by Francesco Berio di Salsa. Edited with an introduction by Philip Gossett. Vol. 8 of *Early Romantic Opera.* New York: Garland Publishing, 1979. 2 vols. Facsimile of the holograph at the Fondazione Rossini, Pesaro.

Semiramide: melodramma tragico in two acts/music by Gioacchino Rossini; libretto by Gaetano Rossi. Edited with introduction by Philip Gossett. Vol. 13 of *Early Romantic Opera.* New York: Garland Publishing, 1978. 2 vols. Facsimile of the autograph in the Archives at the Teatro La Fenice, Venice.

LOCATIONS OF PREMIERES OF ROSSINI'S OPERAS

Bologna
Teatro del Corso   *L'equivoco stravagante* (1811)

Ferrara
Teatro Comunale   *Ciro in Babilonia*, ossia *La Caduta di Baldassare* (1812)

Lisbon
Teatro de S Carlos   *Adina, o Il califfo di Bagdad* (1826)

Milan
Teatro alla Scala   *La pietra del paragone* (1812)

                                                                   Aureliano in Palmira (1813)

                                                                      Il turco in Italia (1814)

                                                                       La gazza ladra (1817)

                              Bianca e Falliero, ossia *Il consiglio dei tre* (1819)

Naples

Teatro dei Fiorentini

La gazzetta (1816)

Teatro del Fondo

Otello, ossia *Il moro di Venezia* (1816)

Teatro S Carlo

Elisabetta, regina d'Inghilterra (1815)

Armida (1817)

Mosè in Egitto (1818)

Ricciardo e Zoraide (1818)

Ermione (1819)

La donna del lago (1819)

Maometto II (1820)

Zelmira (1822)

Paris

Opéra

Le siège de Corinthe (1826)

Moïse et Pharaon, ou *Le passage de la Mer Rouge* (1827)

Le comte Ory (1828)

Guillaume Tell (1829)

Théâtre Italien

Il viaggio a Reims, ossia *L'albergo del giglio d'oro* (1825)

Rome

Teatro Argentina

Almaviva, ossia *L'inutile precauzione* [later *Il barbiere di Siviglia*] (1816)

Adelaide di Borgogna (1817)

Teatro Apollo

Matilde di Shabran, ossia *Bellezza, e cuor di ferro* (1821)

Teatro Valle

Demetrio e Polibio (1812)

Torvaldo e Dorliska (1815)

La Cenerentola ossia *La bontà in trionfo* (1817)

Venice

Teatro La Fenice	*Tancredi* (1813)
	Sigismondo (1814)
	Semiramide (1823)
Teatro S Benedetto	*L'italiana in Algeri* (1813)
	Eduardo e Cristina (1819)
Teatro S Moisè	*La cambiale di matrimonio* (1810)
	L'inganno felice (1812)
	La scala di seta (1812)
	L'occasione fa il ladro (1812)
	Il signor Bruschino ossia *Il figlio per azzardo* (1813)

ROSSINI'S LIBRETTISTS

Anelli, Angelo (1761–1820)

    L'italiana in Algeri

Aventi [Avventi], Francesco (1779–1858)

    Ciro in Babilonia, ossia *La caduta di Baldassare*

Balocchi, Luigi [Louis Balochy] (1766–1832)

    Il viaggio a Reims, ossia *L'albergo del giglio d'oro*

    Le siège de Corinthe (with Soumet)

    Moïse et Pharaon, ou *Le passage de la Mer Rouge* (with Jouy)

Berio di Salsa, Francesco (1765–1820)

    Otello, ossia *Il moro di Venezia*

    Ricciardo e Zoraide

Bevilacqua-Aldobrandini, Gherardo (dates unknown)

    Adina, o Il califfo di Bagdad

    Eduardo e Cristina (revision, with Tottola)

Bis, Hippolyte-Louis-Florent (1789–1855)

    Guillaume Tell (with Jouy)

Delestre-Poirson, Charles-Gaspard (1790–1859)

   Le comte Ory (with Scribe)

Della Valle, Cesare (1776–1860)[17]

   Maometto II

Ferretti, Jacopo (1784–1852)

   La Cenerentola, ossia *La bontà in trionfo*

   Matilde (di) Shabran, ossia *Bellezza, e cuor di ferro*

Foppa, Giuseppe Maria (1760–1845)

   L'inganno felice

   La scala di seta

   Il signor Bruschino, ossia *Il figlio per azzardo*

   Sigismondo

Gasparri [Gasbarri], Gaetano (dates unknown)

   L'equivoco stravagante

Gherardini, Giovanni (1778–1861)

   La gazza ladra

Jouy, Victor-Joseph-Etienne de (1764–1846)

   Moïse et Pharaon, ou *Le passage de la Mer Rouge* (with Balocchi)

   Guillaume Tell (with Bis)

Lechi, Luigi (1786–1867)

   Tancredi (provided the tragic ending)

Palomba, Giuseppe (fl. 1765–1825)

   La gazzetta

Prividali, Luigi (1771–1844)

   L'occasione fa il ladro

Romanelli, Luigi (1751–1839)

   La pietra del paragone

[17]According to dates in the Library of Congress catalog.

Romani, Felice (1788–1865)

 Aureliano in Palmira

 Il turco in Italia

 Bianca e Falliero, ossia *Il consiglio dei tre*

Rossi, Gaetano (1774–1855)

 La cambiale di matrimonio

 Tancredi (original version)

 Semiramide

Schmidt, Giovanni (c. 1775–1839)

 Elisabetta, regina d'Inghilterra

 Armida

 Adelaide di Borgogna

 Eduardo e Cristina

Scribe, Eugène (1791–1861)

 Le comte Ory (with Delestre-Poirson)

Soumet, Alexandre (1788–1845)

 Le siège de Corinthe (with Balocchi)

Sterbini, Cesare (1784–1831)

 Torvaldo e Dorliska

 Almaviva, ossia *L'inutile precauzione* [later *Il barbiere di Siviglia*]

Tottola, Andrea Leone (d. 1831)

 Mosè in Egitto

 Ermione

 Eduardo e Cristina (revision, with Bevilacqua-Aldobrandini)

 La donna del lago

 Zelmira

Viganò-Mombelli, Vincenzina (dates unknown)

 Demetrio e Polibio

Index of Authors, Editors, and Translators

Numbers refer to bibliography items rather than page numbers.

Index of Works

For foreign titles beginning with an article, that article has been omitted.

OPERAS

Adelaide di Borgogna 254, 512, 711, 876
Adina, o Il califfo di Bagdad 581, 876
Almaviva, ossia L'inutile precauzione see
    Barbiere di Siviglia
Armida 254, 405, 583, 614, 694, 699, 706,
    707, 708, 709, 710, 823, 876
Aureliano in Palmira 249, 268, 270, 350,
    583, 589, 605, 644, 645, 646, 820, 876

Barbiere di Siviglia (originally *Almaviva,*
    ossia L'inutile precauzione) 39, 114,
    115, 123, 128, 131, 142, 188, 222,
    227, 230, 231, 240, 255, 282, 335,
    367, 368, 370, 378, 386, 402, 404,
    443, 448, 465, 478, 479, 490, 527,
    536, 566, 568, 574, 577, 590, 591,
    592, 593, 594, 596, 597, 613, 617,
    618, 647, 648, 656, 657, 659, 661,
    662, 663, 664, 665, 666, 667, 669,
    670, 671, 672, 673, 674, 675, 744,
    761, 813, 814, 851, 853, 855, 870,
    871, 876
  as *Barbier de Séville* 4, 217, 658, 660

  as *Barber of Seville* 152, 383, 385, 389,
    655
  as *Barber von Sevilla* 668, 669
Bianca e Falliero, ossia Il consiglio dei tre
    45, 249, 350, 584, 740, 741, 876

Cambiale di matrimonio 278, 375, 517,
    577, 592, 622, 876
Cenerentola, ossia La bontà in trionfo 2,
    131, 240, 246, 247, 248, 370, 371,
    384, 461, 509, 527, 568, 581, 590,
    594, 596, 617, 647, 691, 692, 693,
    694, 695, 696, 697, 698, 700, 708,
    730, 744, 855, 872, 876
  as *Cinderella* 394, 694, 699
Ciro in Babilonia, ossia La caduta di Bal-
    dassare 39, 244, 245, 566, 621, 876
Comte Ory 4, 47, 217, 271, 455, 754, 755,
    756, 763, 764, 765, 820, 852, 876

Demetrio e Polibio 340, 517, 563, 620,
    621, 741, 876
Donna del lago 199, 240, 527, 540, 544,
    549, 605, 734, 735, 736, 737, 738,
    739, 741, 782, 823, 876

OTHER LATE WORKS

LOST OR SPURIOUS WORKS